INDIAN ORPHANAGES

INDIAN ORPHANAGES

MARILYN IRVIN HOLT

UNIVERSITY PRESS OF KANSAS

For my parents, Joe and Vera Irvin, who taught me to read,
and for my husband, Daniel Holt, who encouraged me to write

Published by the University Press of Kansas (Lawrence, Kansas 66049), which was
organized by the Kansas Board of Regents and is operated and funded by Emporia
State University, Fort Hays State University, Kansas State University, Pittsburg State
University, the University of Kansas, and Wichita State University

Library of Congress Cataloging-in-Publication Data

Holt, Marilyn Irvin, 1949–
Indian orphanages / Marilyn Irvin Holt.
p. cm.
Includes bibliographical references and index.
ISBN 0-7006-1119-3 (cloth : alk. paper)
1. Indian orphanages—United States—History. 2. Indian
children—Government policy—United States. 3. Indian
children—Institutional care—United States. 4. Indians, Treatment
of—United States—History. 5. United States. Indian Child Welfare
Act of 1978. I. Title.
E98.O76 H65 2001
362.7'089'97—dc 21   2001000809

British Library Cataloguing in Publication Data is available.

Printed in the United States of America

10 9 8 7 6 5 4 3 2 1

The paper used in this publication meets the minimum requirements of the American
National Standard for Permanence of Paper for Printed Library Materials Z39.48-1984.

CONTENTS

PREFACE

In 1998 I attended a special reception for the opening of the Tamustalik Cultural Institute on the Umatilla Reservation in Oregon. The
building was impressive; the exhibits even more so. Our hosts for the
evening were rightfully proud of the institute. From one room to
another we moved in small groups. Coming to the area that featured
the reservation school—with the recorded sounds of children singing
and a full-size photographic image of students standing outside the
school—I turned to a member of the tribal delegation. Were there
orphans in the school? His look was one of surprise and then of confusion. How to politely answer this misinformed question? The
response was short and to the point: "We had no orphans."

The answer was not unexpected. It went to the heart of my
research. By tradition, an extended network of relatives made it virtu-
ally impossible for an Indian child to be an orphan, as white culture
defined that term. How, then, to explain the appearance of orphanages
for Indian children? How to explain any need for these institutions?

At the time of the visit to the Tamustalik Cultural Institute, my
research on Indian orphanages was well under way. It began when R.
Reed Whitaker, executive director of the National Archives and
Records Administration—Central Plains Region, suggested that I
might be interested in some Indian orphanage records at the Kansas
City repository. That began the search. From earlier work on the
orphan trains I was familiar with references to institutions that took
in Indian children, but there were real doubts as to the possibility that
a number of orphanages existed just for Indian children. Still, it was
fascinating that they existed at all, and their possible correlations to
both Indian boarding schools and non-Indian orphanages were intrigu-
ing. The Indian orphanage suggested a juxtaposition of two cultures

whose conflicting values met when orphanages became an option for child care. In the searches that followed, I found more Indian orphanages than I hoped or bargained for, but the records were not necessarily large or complete. Secondary sources, including those by well-respected historians, barely suggested the presence of orphanages. And, when institutional records were found, they, as with most institutional resources, told the story through the words of officials and directors. The voices of those inside the institution were not captured through a recorded song and seldom preserved through a reminiscence.

This book is an attempt to tell the story of Indian orphanages. It has three primary purposes. First, it examines traditional Indian culture and the transitional moments that brought a group to the point of accepting the alien idea of an orphanage for their children. Certain transitional events in Indian-white contact were uniform. Responses, however, varied greatly, and for a number of reasons. Specific regional and tribal experiences meant that not every native group had an orphanage—in fact, few did. The Umatilla response, "We had no orphans," spoke to more than traditional custom. It spoke to a specific experience. Second, the orphanages are examined as individual institutions because they have not been addressed as such in any other publication. In that examination, orphanages are discussed within the broader context of Indian boarding schools and non-Indian orphanages; this addresses policies for Americanization and assimilationist education, since the dominant culture's agenda applied to all. Finally, the book examines child dependency in Indian society and the ways in which this issue has been addressed. For that reason, it begins with recent history and the Indian Child Welfare Act.

I did not begin with the intention of focusing on the Indian groups in Oklahoma, but of all the states and/or territories, Oklahoma emerged as the area having the largest number of Indian orphanages. Other states with Indian-only orphanages were New York, Minnesota, and South Dakota. In other areas, including New Mexico, orphanages served Indian children—but not in a segregated setting. The locations in which Indian orphanages were found, although geographically separated, suggest two fundamental similarities that fostered creation of these institutions. First, in each area there was a long history of Indian-European contact that both passively and aggressively influenced traditional culture. Second, a missionary presence at an early stage influenced tribal groups in these areas to abandon traditions in favor of Christian teachings and white education. At early pivotal stages, these factors introduced Euro-American values for addressing the needs of children.

The reader will be presented with a number of voices and viewpoints. There are the words of missionaries and government representatives, of reformers and tribal leaders, of orphanage officials and, when possible, the children and teenagers who lived inside the orphanages—a kaleidoscope of words. The language is that used by those who left the records. For that reason, "civilization" and "savage" appear. "Orphan," "half-orphan," and "destitute" become almost synonymous. I would argue that the only way to understand the tenor of a time is to use the language with which people communicated their beliefs and perceptions of the world around them. When referring to orphans, the language can be sentimentally saccharine or morally puritanical. When describing native peoples, it can be ethnocentric and racist or concerned and sympathetic. Only by including all the possibilities can one approach a realistic re-creation of the forces at work. Most often, I have used the term "Indian" because that is the preferable word; tribal groups sometimes are referred to by more than one name because they applied several names to themselves and because federal terminology was not always the same as that used by a tribal group to describe itself.

For this discussion, Indian culture is a broad generality. It does not suggest that nations, confederacies, tribes, clans, and bands were carbon copies of one another. Here "culture" means the characteristic features and typical behavior patterns of a large group. The same applies in references to white culture, since it, too, was diverse in its makeup of ethnic backgrounds and internal prejudices, such as Catholic versus Protestant or English versus Irish.

A word on the organizational plan is needed. Although this is not intended to be a chronology of each institution, a large measure of institutional history is presented. If for no other reason, this is necessary because other works have not outlined or provided details about these orphanages. They were, and have remained, like other orphanages, at the margin of public consciousness.

There are innumerable individuals and institutions to thank for their advice and help. Foremost among them is "my" archivist, Barbara Constable, at the Dwight D. Eisenhower Presidential Library. Not only do the library's holdings of presidential records have some bearing on the subject, but Barbara—along with archivist Dwight Strandberg—assisted in arranging interlibrary loans and locating records at other repositories within the National Archives and Records Administration (NARA) system. Regional NARA repositories that must be thanked are Rocky Mountain, Central Plains, and Fort Worth—to Meg Hacker, I offer sincere gratitude. I owe considerable thanks to staff at the National Archives, Archives I, Washington, D.C.; Oklahoma Historical Society; Oklahoma State Archives; Kansas State Historical Society; New York State Archives; New Mexico State Library; New Mexico State Records Center and Archives; Museum of the Cherokee Indian; Seneca-Iroquois National Museum; Washburn University School of Law Library; and Special Collections and University Archives at Marquette University, particularly archivist Mark G. Thiel. Thanks also must go to the archives of the Menninger Foundation; Catholic Diocese of Sioux Falls; St. Paul's Indian Mission, Marty, South Dakota; Sacred Heart Monastery, Richardson, North Dakota; Catholic Community Center, Sisseton, South Dakota; and Sisters of the Divine Savior, Milwaukee, Wisconsin.

For their advice, and for letting me bend their ears, a special thanks goes to Patt and Lynn Murphy, who suggested reading materials and made loans from their personal library; to William Unrau; and to Jack Ericson. During the search, I encountered enrolled tribal members who willingly shared their experiences and thoughts. I particularly wish to thank Gayle Edmunds, Wichita, Kansas, and the elders at the Mid-America All-Indian Center, Wichita, who offered their opinions and stories.

INTRODUCTION: ROOTS OF PROTEST

> The mother is a Pueblo Indian who had been living in California. She and her husband are separated. . . . She got tired of wrestling these two little children around, and last week she came and dropped them right at the village, and took off.[1]

This was just one of many worries addressed at a meeting of the All-Pueblo Council of New Mexico in 1959. Since the grandparents were too old and too poor to look after these two little boys, the responsibility rested on the shoulders of the Pueblo leaders. Looking at the situation from the mother's side, it was clear that the emotional distress of a broken marriage and financial upheaval had sapped her abilities to cope with caring for the children. If she was unable to provide for them, she faced the prospect of being labeled unfit by a state social service agency and of forfeiting her children to strangers. She did the only thing that could possibly ensure that her children would not become wards of the state, perhaps separated from her forever. By leaving her children "right at the village," she put them into the hands of tribal care—not the white-controlled social service system.

It was a fine but definite point. In too many cases, professional social workers off-reservation were quick to end parental custody and slow to provide the sort of family support that kept parents and children together during a time of crisis. In whose best interests state social services acted was a question argued and reargued during most of the twentieth century. It was this debate that, for Native Americans, wove itself around the fundamental question of a culture's right to its own children and the ways in which the dominant culture enforced its child welfare and parental custodial statutes. It was within this context that the federal government for the first time, in 1978, acted through law to directly confront the issues of tribal rights in regard to children and the practices of state social service systems and private child welfare agencies. The result was the Indian Child Welfare Act.

The act did not appear magically out of a void. It was preceded by lengthy, and sometimes turbulent, discourse. Some discussions stemmed directly from the civil rights movement of the 1950s and 1960s, which was not just about voting rights or school integration. The movement also focused attention on preserving, recognizing, and reinvigorating racial and ethnic cultures. In that context, as well as others, many took a closer look at what had become, over the years, a significant factor in the lives of many—social services.

Although numerous commentators looked to the immediate past to explain the increasing role of social service agencies and intervention, the precedents for child removal were rooted in the nineteenth century. Perhaps the first recorded instances of children taken from their people occurred during the Creek Wars of 1813–15. At the time, Andrew Jackson retrieved a toddler whose parents were killed by Jackson's troops. The boy was sent to the general's home, where he served as a playmate to Jackson's son. The Creek child received an education and was apprenticed to learn a trade, but at the age of sixteen the boy died of tuberculosis. On the heels of Jackson's "adoption" of a Creek child, Peggy Eaton, wife of Jackson's secretary of war, followed suit. She "adopted" a youngster who survived the Creek Wars. After three years in the Eaton household, "Johnny" had not taken to white ways, and he found a way to escape. Wrote Eaton, "I never saw him afterwards; but we heard of him. . . . John had found his own people."[2]

Precedents for intrusion into domestic life grew out of a number of social and political events, but one of the most significant was the American Civil War. The whole spectrum of ethnic and national groups, including Indian familial networks, felt the ramifications of that war. Away from the battleground, the Civil War created an environment of rising urban crime, dependent and destitute children and families, and a marked increase in charities and institutions that served war widows and orphans. Euro-American culture looked for ways to stem criminal activity, particularly that of poor women and children, who desperately tried to survive by any means possible. Charities, state and local governments, and private organizations came to the aid of the impoverished and abandoned.

The long-term result was an escalation in rules and regulations for family and personal behavior. During the last decades of the nineteenth century, white, middle-class values and standards were increasingly enforced through civil courts, laws defining juvenile delinquency, and rules established for child protection agencies. Supported by local expectations and state laws, these agencies began to interpret how parents were supposed to fulfill their responsibilities and to define delinquency, neglect, and maltreatment. Through legislation and newly established boards of charities and corrections, states widened their powers to intercede into the privacy of domestic life.

In the last decades of the 1800s and into the early twentieth century, the fields of sociology and social work became recognized areas of study. In 1865 the American Social Science Association, which later became the National Conference of Social Work, was the first organization to deal with questions relating to charity and institutionalized populations. It was followed by other associations for social work professionals. Social work gained high visibility in 1909 after James E. West, an orphan raised in an institution, persuaded President Theodore Roosevelt to hold the first White House Conference on social issues related to children. College training replaced individualistic approaches and overshadowed the religious calling that many felt to work among the poor and disadvantaged. Sociology was a social science. As such, there was no room for those who believed that charity was intrinsically coupled with religious teachings. Professional social work attempted to distance itself from religion. This did not mean that church-supported charities disappeared, but they were faced with secular appropriation of their good works. Some joined the social science movement; others rejected it outright. Meanwhile, the academically trained social worker and sociologist emerged, bringing along a myriad of systematic surveys and analyzed data that labeled and sought to explain specific populations, behavior patterns, and psychological tendencies for groups defined by race, ethnicity, or economic status. It was the duty of social workers, said one writer, "to supply that diagnosis and initiative which would lead to the solution of social problems."[3]

In the first half of the twentieth century, social workers, with support from state and local governments, felt obligated to take charge. Indeed, it was a "sacred obligation to intercede" when families failed to function within the parameters of white, middle-class expectations. States passed child protection statutes. Those without boards of charities established them. At the local level, protective leagues and regulatory commissions proliferated. Despite vocal commitment to preserve the family, increased state and local action did not necessarily aid families or promote child care within the home. Rather, more children, across racial and ethnic lines, were removed from relatives and placed in institutions or in the present-day equivalent of foster care.

In 1890 there were 60,981 youngsters under the age of sixteen in institutions; by 1923 the number was 204,888. The majority had at least one living parent. Of course, the increase in institutionalization could be attributed in part to a rising population in the United States, but the numbers also reflected a new level of intervention by outsiders into domestic life. Some argued that welfare agencies used state statutes to expand the definitions of poor parenting and child endangerment, and thereby made intervention inevitable. As a result, intervention rose in direct relationship to statutory permission. This particularly affected the poor and nonwhite. Some state laws, wrote one critic, amounted to nothing more than "punitive regulation of adult behavior . . . used to control . . . a community." Some social work professionals agreed, as did some specialists in child development who argued that a child's emotional well-being was as essential as good physical health. A child might not always have clean clothes or three well-balanced meals a day, but knowing that there was someone to whom he or she was of value was more important than physical comforts. A scarcity of material goods did not translate into poor parenting.[4]

Discussions that centered on intervention and its impact on emotional health were essential in the process that brought about the Indian Child Welfare Act of 1978. The catalyst occurred a decade earlier, in 1968, when Devils Lake Sioux in North Dakota took their concerns about local child welfare practices to the Association on American Indian Affairs (AAIA). What followed were widespread reviews and analyses of federal policies, fact-finding studies, and conferences. The result demonstrated what many, including the North Dakota Sioux, already knew or suspected. Nontribal public and private entities were major actors in the lives of Indian children. This was especially true for those living off-reservation when young, unmarried mothers gave up their children for adoption or when off-reservation families came into the social service system after they applied for state assistance in obtaining food, clothing, and/or housing. Once in the system and assigned to a caseworker, adults and children were monitored—even when they returned to the reservation. The outcome was an alarming percentage of children removed from their families, even when there was no extreme crisis such as death of a parent or evidence of abuse or neglect. From surveys conducted in 1969 and again in 1974, the AAIA estimated that between 25 and 35 percent of "all Indian children are separated from their families and placed in foster homes, adoptive homes, or institutions." The dispar-ity between Indian and non-Indian placements was often astounding. In South Dakota, for example, the Indian population in 1960 was 3.6 percent of the total population, but 50 percent of all children in South Dakota foster care were Indian. On a national level, one out of every four children of Native American heritage was separated from family by the mid-1970s, and Indian children were twenty times more likely than non-Indian children to be placed in foster care.[5]

Foster care was not the only form of placement. There was adop-tion. As one example, the Boys and Girls Aid Society of Oregon arranged adoptions, most transracial, of African-American, Asian, and Indian children. Between 1944 and 1977, the society's Indian place-ments accounted for the largest number of transracial adoptions (132) and represented the highest percentage (94 percent) of the minority groups it placed. The same could be said for South Dakota, where 40 percent of all adoptions arranged by the state's department of social welfare in the late 1960s were of Indian children.[6]

One factor in these adoptions had little to do with race or ethnicity. It had everything to do, however, with American society's moral judg-ments. Pregnancy out of wedlock was seldom admitted to in polite company, and if a woman did not quickly marry, she was strongly dis-couraged from keeping her child, who would bear the stigma of being illegitimate. A woman who chose not to marry *and* to keep her child was considered flawed and weak because she rejected society's willing-ness to "rehabilitate" her by letting her put the child up for adoption and "start over" as if nothing had happened. In the 1950s, sociologists began to survey and analyze women who were unwed and pregnant. After administering a battery of tests to residents at homes for unwed moth-ers, one sociologist used his "interpretative impressions" to declare that women who kept children were emotionally and mentally immature. They scored well only on the test that calculated their "femininity," and even that positive showing, said the sociologist, was misleading, since the women really had no "traditional feminine interests, warmth or concern for others." It was a white, middle-class "interpretative impres-sion" that permeated the social worker mind-set. When social pressures combined with poverty and limited economic prospects, a young woman was primed for placing her child up for adoption.[7]

Despite the rates of child placement and concerns among tribal groups, it was not until 1978 that Indian child welfare was addressed in a congressional act. Until then, the subject appeared only in legislative subtexts that dealt with guardianship for minor children, usually on a tribe-by-tribe basis. The Indian Child Welfare Act of 1978 meant to do much more than briefly specify appointment of adult guardians for minors. Its intent was to drastically reverse practices as they applied to Indian children and to clarify past legislation and court decisions relating to tribal versus state jurisdiction. At the core of the 1978 law was the question of tribal rights to direct the care and custody of children; by extension, it recognized the transmission of Indian culture to future generations.

The 1978 law dealt with children, examining the basic question of who had jurisdiction over child welfare and placement cases. The discussion silently circled the larger issue of Indian sovereignty, an overriding concern of U.S. government and Indian relations since the first treaty was signed. In that context, the U.S. Supreme Court long ago recognized that when the federal government and a tribe made treaties, the government was in effect dealing with a foreign entity. Over the years, the dominant issues of sovereignty have been defined by the courts in terms of land control, mineral rights, or hunting and fishing rights. Sovereignty is about much more. It argues for maintaining an entire cultural entity. It involves aspects of social, political, and tribal life. It includes the right to one's children, as well as jurisdictional control over decisions affecting children's lives.

Jurisdiction, like sovereignty, has been considered in the courts many times, in differing contexts, and with mixed messages. Although the 1978 act was the first to directly consider child welfare, it was certainly not a situation in which jurisdiction in and of itself suddenly appeared as a late-twentieth-century issue. Jurisdictional powers and the role of tribal courts have been addressed in federal legislation and court decisions for decades, attempting to specify in which cases and instances federal or tribal authority applies.

Generally, jurisdictional rights have stipulated the circumstances under which federal or tribal courts could determine cases that dealt with crimes or "Indian Offenses" committed within reservation boundaries. For example, the Major Crimes Act of 1885 transferred judicial control over major crimes on Indian reservations from tribal to federal courts, but in the next year the U.S. Supreme Court decision in *United States* v. *Kagama* stated that Indian tribes had "the power of regulating their internal and social relations." Broadly, this was interpreted to mean that if the crime was not one of the "ten" that included murder, tribal courts oversaw the case. This was reinforced later by the Wheeler-Howard Act of 1934, also known as the Indian Reorganization Act (IRA). Controversial, the IRA has been described as a herald of Indian self-determination, a blunt instrument of assimilation, impractical, and visionary. Among its results was the retooling of tribal courts and offense codes while allowing a larger number of persons with Indian identities to become subjects of "the Indian law."[8]

Jurisdictional debate was both strengthened and muddied in 1953 with congressional passage of Public Law 280 (P.L. 280). On one hand, the law placed some limits on state jurisdiction, encouraging stronger tribal control. On the other hand, it conferred jurisdiction over reservation criminal and civil cases to Alaska Territory and five states (California, Minnesota, Nebraska, Oregon—except the Warm Springs Reservation in Oregon—and Wisconsin) and encouraged other states to exercise their options under the law. One reason cited for widening state jurisdictional prerogatives was a lack of tribal police and/or reservation court systems. Nevertheless, it raised concerns that Indians would not receive fair treatment in white courts and, as it happened when South Dakota chose to participate in P.L. 280 in 1963, face increased harassment and human rights violations. Said one South Dakota police chief, "As near as I can figure out, it's about like the Negroes down South. You can't let them [Indians] get the upper hand." Public Law 280 also left open the door for states to oversee civil cases that, by extension, might deprive parents of custodial care. The 1953 legislation was a tangle, which the Indian Civil Rights Act of 1968 tried to rework to eliminate earlier conflicting legislation. The 1968 act did address jurisdiction, and it limited states' claims subject to approval by the tribe in question. The act, however, primarily aimed at aligning U.S. constitutional rights with those provided in tribal courts. It failed to redress the already devastating impact of P.L. 280.[9]

None of these federal laws or U.S. court opinions directly addressed child welfare in terms of tribal, parental, or family custody. A few social work professionals defined the 1953 legislation as a child welfare act. It was not—that is, unless one wished to apply theoretical possibilities to civil cases that might in some way encompass child custody or welfare. The 1953 act was representative of Indian and U.S. government relations in the mid-1900s, a period in which the federal government wanted to get out of "the Indian business." During the

Truman administration, the government began the process of shifting services to the states or tribal governments, and under President Eisenhower the plan culminated in termination of federal supervision over certain tribes. When Congress passed its enabling acts for termination, there was usually language that concerned children. However, if the acts aimed at the Menominees and the Ottawas may serve as examples, child welfare was only addressed by stating that minor children were to have guardians appointed "in courts of competent jurisdiction." The language differed very little from that used in treaties and agreements dating back to the mid-1800s. Termination legislation was hardly a sweeping child welfare act.[10]

Numerous pieces of federal and state legislation, as well as court decisions, spoke to the mechanism of jurisdiction that allowed non-Indian intervention into domestic life. Jurisdiction could, under some circumstances, involve actions under which Indian children became wards of the state, parents lost custody, or children were placed into non-Indian homes. Children could fall into one or more categories. There were true orphans (both parents deceased); half-orphans (one parent living); the destitute who might be orphans or half-orphans or have both living parents; or neglected and abused children within a household dynamic that included parents or close relatives.

The 1953 law (and the later Indian Child Welfare Act of 1978) was intended for tribal citizens, not all who might be identified as having a biological link to a native group. Tribal enrollment was a major qualifier, and in some states residence on a reservation was a consideration. Nontribal jurisdiction over children and families, therefore, was dependent on a number of factors. The 1953 legislation attempted to qualify these, but there was never any overall mandate. For example, juvenile courts in Washington State could not declare children dependent and remove parental custody. Nor could the courts make children wards of the state and, thus, eligible for adoption. On the surface, it seemed that tribal jurisdiction had precedence over nontribal courts. However, the rules for Washington courts held only *if* the child belonged to a tribe living on a trust allotment. That stipulation allowed court access to children who did not fit the criteria. North Dakota's procedures were different. The state rested its practices on reservation residence and tribal enrollment. North Dakota courts could terminate parental rights and place children into social service custody when families were enrolled tribal members but living off-reservation; in these cases, proof of the child's enrollment, not that of parents, was demanded.[11]

Adding to the complexity of jurisdictional rights and child custody was the 1958 Indian Adoption Project (IAP). Initiated by the Bureau of Indian Affairs (BIA) and the Child Welfare League of America, an organization that traced its beginnings to the 1909 White House Conference on care of dependent children, the IAP focused on children who for any number of reasons were adoption candidates. The Child Welfare League was careful to note that it did not see removing children from their families as a "solution for the mass of Indian children suffering from long-standing national neglect and abuse." When, however, choices had to be made about a child's future, adoption seemed a viable alternative to a young person spending his or her childhood in boarding schools or in foster care. In a decade of work the IAP was active on fourteen major reservations in six states: Arizona, Montana, Nevada, North Carolina, South Dakota, and Wyoming. It also operated in Alaska, California, Colorado, Minnesota, Mississippi, New Mexico, Oregon, South Carolina, Washington, and Wisconsin. The choice of sites was partially based on areas where Indian populations increased after the federally supported Voluntary Relocation Program went into effect in the late 1940s. Among the states involved, the top three in placements were Arizona (112), South Dakota (104), and Wisconsin (48). The total number of children in the IPA program was 395. Tribal government approval was a necessary condition for the IAP to operate on a reservation, and tribal approval was given for some adoptions. Nevertheless, few Indian families were encouraged to take in children. The result was predictable. Most placements were with Caucasian families whose own beliefs and values decided how much, if any, exposure to the child's Indian culture continued.[12]

Although the Indian Self-Determination Act of 1975 strengthened and redefined the powers of tribal governments, it was not until the Indian Child Welfare Act of 1978 that federal law dealt directly with children in any way other than court-appointed guardianship or jurisdiction that might tangentially affect a child's fate. In light of the history leading up to the 1978 act, it was not unexpected that the legislation noted unwarranted removal of children from their families and the role of state statutes: "[States] exercising their recognized jurisdiction over Indian child custody proceedings through administrative and judicial bodies, have often failed to recognize the essential tribal relations of Indian people and the cultural and social standards prevailing in Indian communities and families." The 1978 law called a halt to what had been business as usual. The act strengthened tribal jurisdiction and recognized referral of off-reservation situations back to tribal courts and reservation social services. When a child lived off-reservation or in one of the states acting under P.L. 280, state courts were required to transfer jurisdiction to tribal courts. The exception was a situation in which the parents objected. The law also established an order of preference for adoption; priority descended from a member of the child's extended family, a member of the tribe, Indian families not of the same tribe, and, finally, non-Indian adoptive parents. To support the courts and expanded social services, the law directed that funds be allocated to establish or enhance tribal juvenile courts, family support agencies, and child care programs. In effect, this law endorsed the right of a people to maintain their culture through their children.[13]

Public discourse and social service debates before and after passage of the 1978 act reflected the complexities and differing views of the issue. Some social service professionals focused on available reservation-based social services, which varied from nonexistent to highly efficient. Others took a broader view and explained to their uninformed colleagues traditional child-rearing practices in a culture that was struggling to reassert a claim over its children. It was imperative, insisted these proponents, that children experience the community provided by a dual system of biological family and kinship network. In this community, children were in "close contact with many people who praise, advise, guide, urge, warn, scold, but most important, respect children." A child learned that he or she was a "tribal person." This in itself was difficult for non-Indians to understand, since children in white society were regarded as part of a nuclear family that took its identity from a lineal structure of relatives. Those with a grasp of traditional care and upbringing also explained that there was little place for physical punishment. Children learned what was expected of them through the oral traditions, stories, and teachings of relatives and elders.[14]

Elders played an important role in a child's upbringing. The relatively few American Indians involved in the social work profession offered advice to their non-Indian counterparts for recognizing and understanding extended Indian families that were inclusive of several households (even across state boundaries), numerous relatives, and significant non-kin who interacted with the family. Most important, offered John Red Horse, a professor of social work, professionals had to recognize that "care" had a complex meaning. It extended through the generations, denoting "cultural and spiritual maintenance as well as physical and emotional needs satisfied." Social workers for the most part viewed the elderly as persons who were "retired," whose child-rearing years were behind them, and who often were set apart from their families. This mainstream mind-set failed to recognize the importance of tribal elders. As a point of reference, Red Horse offered the example of a Sioux mother in South Dakota who nearly lost custody of her child because the four-year-old often was left in the care of a family elder who, believed social workers, was too old at age sixty-nine to look after a child. Red Horse's point was that elders were supposed to be involved in child rearing. Young parents were not expected to raise their children by themselves. What white society might construe as a grandparent's interference was considered family support in native culture. A child under an older person's care was not a candidate for investigation and possible removal. Nor were the parents guilty of neglect. Elders had an important, traditionally sacred role. They might not be biologically related, but that was unimportant. They were connected through a wide web of family and tribal relationships.[15]

Not all celebrated the 1978 act. Some in the fields of sociology and social work were dismayed. A few trotted out the tired dogma that Indians were themselves children and not yet ready to assume adult responsibilities of self-determination. In fact, prior to passage of the act, one sociologist suggested that only apologists for white aggression believed that tribes regarded themselves as organized and sovereign entities. The "Indians as children" argument was sometimes tied to the assertion that Indian adults were unable to control their own behavior, much less that of their children, who, in any event, were considered excess baggage and a burden. This assessment was strangely reminiscent of that made by John G. Pratt, a Baptist missionary, who in 1838 proclaimed that Indian parents sent their children to school only to be rid of them and the responsibility of child rearing. As far as Pratt could determine, Indian parents did little to nurture their children.[16]

This perception was held by many child care workers in the late twentieth century. One professional suggested that no one really knew how Indian families regarded their children. Perhaps native groups did not have the right mind-set for raising children; perhaps "folklore" practices and ritual placed children in danger; perhaps there were no internal mechanisms for child care and education. Indian family structure was an unknown quantity, proclaimed the professional. This, of course, ignored the almost three hundred years of written record penned by various English, Spanish, French, and Americans who traveled among, lived with, and observed native groups, and it overlooked autobiographies and oral histories provided by Indians who described everyday life, explained native beliefs, and told stories that had passed through generations by oral tradition and art. Nevertheless, many took the position that the 1978 law was premature since no "psychiatric study of American Indian parenting" had yet been made. In other words, until exhaustive studies had filtered tribal life in all its varieties through the professional and academic lens, there was no basis for addressing parental rights or transmission of culture.[17]

Adoption advocates took another tack and accused tribes of using the law to seize jurisdiction over children who had little Indian ancestry and no connection to a reservation. Some also blamed black civil rights activists for the decline in Indian transracial adoptions. It was suggested that if African-Americans had not decried the loss of black identity through white adoption, Indians would never have thought to object to the assault upon their own culture. In 1972 a researcher for the Indian Adoption Project reached a rather prophetic conclusion: "Minority groups may be becoming less favorably disposed to the adoptive placement of their children across racial lines."[18]

There was also concern that the act represented racial preference since it did not include Asian, Hispanic, or African-American children. Countering this characterization were those who pointed out that the law was part of the political relationship that existed between Indian tribes and the federal government. Such a relationship did not exist with other racial or ethnic groups. Prior treaties and laws dealt with Indian resources, their allocation, and their protection. In the case of the Indian Child Welfare Act, tribes' most precious resource— their children—was protected.[19]

A common thread running throughout these arguments was the claim of seeking only the child's best interest. Those involved in social welfare and care of children are avowed to seek the best interest of a child; intervention into family life is supposed to occur on behalf of the child. Clearly, not all involved in child protection and social services believed that the 1978 law was best for children, but there was a strong contingent that did. This included the American Academy of Child Psychiatry, the National Congress of American Indians, various adoption agencies, and tribal representatives from around the country who lobbied for the law. Collectively and individually there was support. Dr. Karl Menninger, highly respected in the field of mental health, supported passage. Urging President Jimmy Carter to sign the act into law, Menninger wrote in a letter: "I am convinced that this legislation addresses many of the serious problems affecting their [Indian peoples'] welfare especially that of the Indian children." Earlier, before a Senate subcommittee, Menninger spoke directly of the ways in which a child's sense of identity is formed. An important consideration was the damage that occurred when children were told that their "language is no good, [and] when you tell him that his color is not right or imply it by surrounding him with people of a different color, habits, and status."[20]

Nevertheless, backlash to the law discounted culture as a "best interest" factor, preferring to point out where families and tribes failed. This was largely done without a hint that the dominant culture had played any part in creating the framework for family or tribal breakdown. One critic was able to cite chapter and verse on alcoholism's role in the dysfunction of families and its relationship to child neglect in the last decades of the twentieth century. The scholar, however, made no mention of the hundreds of years in which whites imported alcohol, encouraged its use among native groups, or used it as a tool in bartering, bribery, and deception. Nor did critics discuss the ways in which Indian families had been told through schools, missionaries, and the government to exist as nuclear units rather than in extended relationships. Nor did they concede that land allotment, termination, and relocation to urban areas (sometimes federally encouraged) contributed to the breakdown of family groups. Numerous factors acted to "civilize" the Indian and, in the echoing words of John H. Oberly, a nineteenth-century commissioner of Indian affairs, to imbue the Indian "with the exalting egotism of American civilization, so that he will say 'I' instead of 'We.'" By the late twentieth century, "'I' instead of 'we'" translated into loss of family network and support.[21]

Certainly, white-directed education did its part in changing domestic relationships. On this point opponents of the 1978 act were willing to concede that the boarding school experience took a toll. Indian boarding schools separated children from their tribal selves. They insulated youngsters and created an environment that, in turn, produced the institutionalized child. Although individuals often developed their own strategies for resisting or subverting the demands made by regimented surroundings, all were susceptible. The consequences of institutionalization were not newfound fodder for discussion. In the nineteenth century and in the early years of the twentieth century, a few voices cautioned against institutionalization and worried about the long-term consequences for children who grew up outside a home environment. They suspected that institutionalization posed inherent dangers to child development, and they warned of the potential lifelong effects on children and adolescents. Among these social workers and reformers were Charles Loring Brace, a minister and founder of the New York Children's Aid Society, and Frank D. Hall, the moving force behind developing North Dakota's child welfare service. From Brace's years of contact with children, in and out of institutions, he believed that the longer a child lived within an institutional setting, "the less likely he is to do well in outside life." Hall concurred: "The child who is permanently in an institution does not develop into an all-round boy or girl as those do who grow up in a family home, but lack independence of action and thought."[22]

Despite warnings and arguments broached by people like Brace and Hall, America rode a high wave of building institutions and peopling them. Beginning in the mid-1800s, institutionalization was increasingly utilized to house, educate, and separate numerous groups from the mass population. One group consisted of Indian youngsters who were gathered into boarding schools on and off the reservations; these may have been institutions of learning, but they were institutions nonetheless.

By the end of the 1920s and Lewis Meriam's *The Problem of Indian Administration* (better known as the Meriam Report), there was ample evidence that the boarding school plan for education produced "a permanent breaking of family ties." Some young people and their families could mend this break, but long periods of separation, the changes education wrought in young people's behavior and thinking, and a family's or community's refusal to welcome returning scholars with open arms all contributed to what was for many an irreparable chasm. Meriam did not use the language of psychology, terminology that was reaching into mainstream culture at the time his report was completed. Nor did he address the attributes of the institutional child. Nevertheless, he described with great accuracy the final result: "Parents and children become strangers."[23]

By the last decades of the 1900s, those in the fields of social work, child development, and education agreed with the assessment of people like Brace, Hall, and Meriam. The boarding school experience often undermined young adults' abilities to establish family relationships and develop parenting skills. Boarding school students did not necessarily leave school with the psychological, social, or emotional tools to be parents, since they had not been parented themselves. Instead, for many of their growing-up years, they were surrounded by adults who were not parents or kin. Many, in fact, had not experienced sustained family contact and had little idea of how parents, children, and relatives interacted. They did not grow up in an environment that nurtured them emotionally, taught the behavior expected of close relatives, or transmitted the social consequences of shunning responsibilities. A telling result was best summed up by novelist Sherman Alexie through his character Victor, who said of parents, especially fathers, leaving their children: "White men have been doing that forever and Indian men have just learned how. That's how assimilation can work."[24]

Those debating the 1978 law spoke of the long-term effects of boarding school life, but they did not consider the other side of the coin. Children were a central part of tribal life. A whole cadre of adults watched over, taught, and cared for a child. When the children were sent away to schools or removed from tribal culture, a very large piece of domestic life disappeared. Ties that bound people together became frayed. When children and teenagers returned to their homes, adjustment was difficult or impossible. For those returning from long stays at Indian boarding schools, there were few employment opportunities that allowed application of acquired skills, and many were ridiculed or ostracized by those who had stayed behind. Often returnees no longer understood the language of their parents. Some attempted to relearn their heritage and integrate it with white education. Others did not, finding it impossible to adjust. An elderly mother, confronted by the change she saw in the younger generation, felt only defeat. Her thoughts were recorded by a boarding school teacher: "Why seek to keep the old things? Let us lose everything that is ours—Our children no longer understand us, nor we them." The link that bonded child to family and to clan and to tribe was weakened by long periods of separation during youngsters' formative years. What could be said of the boarding school experience could later be applied to the large-scale separation of children and families through the actions of welfare agencies and the federal government.[25]

Seldom has literature, fiction or nonfiction, dealt with separation of Indian children from their tribal identities, but a few publications have appeared in the years following the 1978 legislation. Each explores the topic in its own way, presenting powerful images, poignant stories, and shades of sharp-edged humor. While Sherman Alexie's Victor speaks of broken lives and dreams on a reservation, Alexie's John Smith in *Indian Killer* is the tormented child-turned-man in search of a self that disappeared when he was adopted by a Caucasian couple. John Smith lives in two worlds. One is the white world of his everyday life. The other is the Indian world of his imagination, where he sees himself as the Indian child he might have been: "John's grandparents are very traditional people and are teaching John the ways of his tribe. Ancient ways. John is learning to speak his tribal language." Turtle in Barbara Kingsolver's *Pigs in Heaven* is also of two worlds, both of them very real and both capable of upending her already fragile psyche. When the question of child custody is brought to the moment of truth by a Cherokee lawyer committed to upholding the Indian Child Welfare Act, Turtle's future is settled with a compromise that gives the girl connections to both the white mother who adopted her and the Indian community that welcomes her.[26]

Less than happy adjustments await the semibiographical character in *Shadow Catcher* and the nonfictional *Lost Bird of Wounded Knee*. In *Shadow Catcher*, a story of the "shadow-catching," photography-driven Wanamaker Expedition of 1913, Annie Owns the Fire appears as a representation of the real-life Lakota orphan Emma Crow King, who at the request of her dying father was adopted by James McLaughlin and his mixed-blood Sioux wife, Louise Buisson. Annie Owns the Fire bears little resemblance to the real Emma Crow King, who returned from Chilocco Indian School to care for her ailing mother and then married. Rather, Annie Owns the Fire serves as a representation of the Wanamaker Expedition's praise of Indian culture, which at the same time manipulated the Indian for its own purposes. She is the only character who is expected to bridge the Indian and white worlds. As such, she is constantly at odds with white expectations and her desire to teach Indian youngsters about themselves: "I went to a Sun Dance once. . . . I wasn't supposed to be there . . . because I was raised white." For telling students about their Indian selves, Annie is dismissed, moving on to another school and the probability of another firing. Still, she maintains a sense of optimism. Not so for Lost Bird, who as an infant survived the massacre at Wounded Knee, was found alive four days later in the frozen arms of her dead mother, and became a trophy of war. Bartered over by men who wanted to exhibit her in a Wild West show and by Brig. Gen. Leonard W. Colby, who saw the child as "a living symbol of white victory," Lost Bird was adopted by Colby. Her story was one of alienation. She lived a life in which she was exploited, trapped by circumstances, and rejected when she attempted to return to her Lakota world. She died at the age of twenty-nine. Biographical or fictional, these stories are not celebrations of biculturalism but themes of separation approached from differing viewpoints. Nevertheless, by their telling, the characters represent the Indian Child Welfare Act's underlying principle of the child as a tribal person.[27]

The Indian Child Welfare Act of 1978 did not completely end the loss of tribal children. It certainly could not mend what had gone before. It could not make up for a federal policy of acculturation that disrupted family, clan, and tribal life through removal and the reservation system. It could not rectify the separation of children from their parents during boarding school years or the educational environment that intended to do nothing less than drive out "Indianness" and instill mainstream culture. Nor could it wipe out years of culturally insensitive actions on the part of public and private, state and local social services. Nor could it reverse a transgenerational process in which tribal groups and individuals played their own roles in bringing dominant culture into the Indian world. It certainly could not change the myriad of circumstances that altered native cultures. Certainly, it could not change the process that created what had been unheard of in traditional American Indian culture—the institution known as the orphanage.

1

CRUMBLING CULTURE

They knew they were orphans but didn't know what an orphan was.[1]

As Alfred Halfmoon recalled in his memories of growing up in his Shawnee community in Oklahoma during the early 1900s, there were youngsters who were orphans. They did not, however, understand what an orphan was. They certainly were not in orphanages, although orphanages for Indian children had existed in Oklahoma since the 1870s. Halfmoon's recollections of orphaned children precisely demonstrate the contradictions that existed within native culture. On the one hand was the presence of orphanages, which, by their mere existence, said that traditional beliefs were no longer at work. On the other, there were traditional values that protected children.

"Being an orphan wasn't much different than being a regular kid," remembered Halfmoon. The reason was simple. Despite century-long pressures to abandon their traditional ways, the Shawnees in Halfmoon's area stubbornly clung to "the old folks' leadership." Families welcomed the orphaned into their homes and treated them as their own, and there were the "grandmas"—three of them—who looked after everyone. Halfmoon, who was not an orphan, was as likely as a parentless child to spend the night or eat a meal at Grandma Rosie's. Well-worn paths led to each grandmother's house, and the grandmothers told stories and explained ceremonials and old ways of doing things as the youngsters helped at chores such as fetching water or carrying firewood.[2]

To the outside world, a parentless child wandering from house to house, staying with one family after another, could seem to be a child's desperate attempt to find food and lodging. Inside Indian communities the viewpoint was different. The practice was linked to age-old patterns of child care that survived orphanages and state welfare programs. The youngsters remembered by Halfmoon were not alone. Indian artist Woody Crumbo, for example, spent his growing-up years in much the same way Halfmoon described. Born in Oklahoma in 1912, Crumbo was the son of a father of English and French descent and a mother who was Potawatomie. Crumbo was four years old when his father died and the family moved to the Potawatomie Reservation in Kansas. Then, when he was seven years of age, Woody's mother died. He went back to Oklahoma, where he moved in with a Creek family near Sand Springs. For the next ten years, until he reached the age of seventeen, Woody Crumbo lived with several Indian families in the neighborhood. He was an orphan but not without a network of people who looked after him. It was a situation that continued after he began attending Chilocco Indian School and became friends with a group of Kiowas. During school breaks and summer recesses, he lived with his friends' families, and it was through this experience that he came under the influence of Susie Peters, an important figure in resurrecting traditional art forms among Indians in Oklahoma. After a lifetime in which his work was widely recognized, Crumbo was not remembered as a Horatio Alger–type character who rose above his parentless state by his own bootstraps. Rather, he was remembered for his art. Being an orphan was a fact, but one mitigated by the number of people who surrounded him with family.[3]

Broad generalizations fail to adequately depict every aspect of Indian life or to define individual experiences. Each tribal group has its own views of the world and belief systems, as well as organizational structures and clan patterns. Within each group, factional elements define themselves. As contact with Euro-Americans increased in the nineteenth century, these elements were broadly labeled as conservatives or progressives, full-bloods or mixed. Intermarriage and varying responses within clans or families to white culture impacted traditional ways of life. Outward signs of acculturation do not tell all, however. The Cherokees, for example, were considered by themselves and by outsiders as one of the most civilized of all Indian groups. So, too, were the Choctaws. How, then, to explain the continuation of traditional customs, particularly of age-old dance ceremonies, long after the Cherokee Nation was established in Indian Territory? How to explain why a "well educated Choctaw" Christian minister would revert to old beliefs and blame witches for the death of his son? "[He] took his shot gun, went out and killed all three of them [witches]."[4] These may be aberrations, but they are indicative of any society's truth. A community's or an individual's beliefs can deviate from the standard. Still, cultures exhibit collective attitudes and behavior patterns that can and do alter over time, either through internal forces or through contact with outside influences.

In this context, family organization and the value of children within a culture are critical to any discussion concerning the appearance of orphanages for Indian children. As a rule, it can be said that native groups organized themselves around the extended family and valued children. Within an enclave of family and kin, children were nurtured and prepared step by step to assume their place within the framework of tribal life. Undoubtedly, there were children without parents. In any society, wholesale or personal crises have the potential to create the parentless child. Natural disasters, disease and widespread epidemics, warfare, and accidental deaths all take their toll. No group of people is immune, but how a people deals with those left behind tells volumes about a culture's intrinsic values. When the ways in which Indian children were regarded and treated are set beside Euro-America's concept of the orphaned and how to deal with them, a dramatic contrast emerges. Differences, however, did not remain constant as native groups and Euro-Americans made contact and those encounters began to impact Indian culture as a whole.

European settlers, explorers, and missionaries brought to North America their own expectations, values, and codified laws. For Europeans, the New World had no shape or form until they arrived to transplant their ways of thinking, value systems, and behavior patterns. Their cultural baggage included legal definitions and social norms for deciding how to respond to the various situations in which children found themselves. Whether it was the early era of exploration, the colonial period, or the antebellum era, transported European standards were relied upon for guidance in dealing with parentless, destitute, or abandoned children.

Euro-American culture used familiar legal definitions and social responses. In America the framework for federal and state statutes and courts was based primarily on English Common Law. It was the basis for establishing social order and rules for behavior, but when legal terms were transferred into the public area, they often were broadened, if not blurred. Vernacular interpretations and generalizations emerged. This was certainly true for the meaning of orphan. Legally, an orphan was a minor child without living parents, but the public voice added to the word's character and meaning. "Soon," said one observer in the late 1870s, "the word *orphan* became expanded in its significations to include half-orphans, and later, to embrace destitute children having both parents, living, many of whom were in a condition yet more unfortunate than orphanages." It was an expanded definition that became the standard of the mass culture, blending the circumstances of the true orphan with those of the destitute child with living parents. Over decades of contact between white and Indian cultures, this broad meaning insinuated itself into Indian societies. The youngsters in Alfred Halfmoon's community may not have understood what an orphan was, but they knew that there was such a thing as being an orphan. So, too, did adults who were influenced in their thinking by white mainstream culture. Said one member of New Mexico's All-Pueblo Council in 1959, "In my definition, an orphan is any child whose parents are dead or whose parents fail to take care of him."[5]

"Orphan" was just one of the terms that Indian societies came to know. There were others, particularly "guardian" and "ward." In Euro-American society, impoverished, parentless children were left to fend alone if no family member claimed them. Through court action, they became wards of a governmental entity (county, town, or state) that acted as guardian. Some youngsters placed under the guardianship of a governmental unit were indentured to nonrelatives through a legal contract. Others were placed in an institution, and in this case guardianship often was transferred to the institution. Half-orphans were treated in the same manner when family members could not afford another mouth to feed or refused responsibility. For children in the middle and upper classes of white America, nonfamily care and indenture were less likely. For these youngsters, courts of law made them wards of a guardian or guardians who might or might not be relatives.

Nineteenth-century courts in white America, with the help of increased child-related state legislation, slowly assumed a larger role in determining what happened to children. Women might be named guardians of their own children, but it was just as likely for them to be forbidden the right to oversee their children's upbringing and financial needs. Adult males, who were not necessarily relatives, were named guardians and placed in control of children's inherited property and in-

terests. In these situations, a woman's only recourse was to directly petition governmental bodies, such as the state legislature, and ask that
a "private law"—one that applied only to that specific instance—be
passed to grant her guardianship.6 Guardianship, legally defined in civil
law, lasted until the child reached his or her majority. A straightforward arrangement, it applied to all children. A child, an orphan or half-
orphan, became the responsibility of a court-appointed guardian.

For Indians, the federal government applied the terms "ward" and
"guardianship" to both adults and children in various situations. In the
ongoing Indian-federal relationship, Indians were legally defined as
wards of a dominant culture that designated itself as guardian.
Guardianship bore similarities to the relationship set down in the
courts for dependent children and their adult guardians. Defining the
Indian population as children in need of aid and direction, the U.S. government made itself the guardian of native peoples. In 1831 the U.S.
Supreme Court noted in its *Cherokee Nation* v. *Georgia* decision that
the U.S. government and the American Indian had a "peculiar" relationship because tribes were sovereign nations within a sovereign nation. Nevertheless, the tribes were dependent. As such, they were
wards of their guardian—the U.S. government. American Indians were
still identified as a separate and "semi-independent" people by the U.S.
Supreme Court in its *United States* v. *Kagama* decision of 1886, but
the court followed the 1831 ruling. Native peoples, it said, were "wards
of the nation" because they lived under a dominant culture. Dependency replaced their powers of self-determination. By the end of the
1800s, it was argued that guardianship was a necessity because it provided economic protection until formal education enabled tribal groups
"to [economically] compete with their aggressive and avaricious white
competitors." Portrayed as dependent and in need of protection from all
sorts of hostile, outside forces, Indians remained wards. By the twentieth century, court decisions tried to make it clear that guardianship
over Indians was not the same as that over children (or over adults classified as incompetent). Rather, the relationship was similar to that of
an international protectorate. This suggested that federal guardianship
could last indefinitely. That, argued some legal scholars, was ludicrous,
since by its very nature guardianship was meant to end. After all,
guardianship over minor children concluded with the age of majority.7

Guardianship, based on the canons of English Common Law, was
not the same as adoption. Certainly, no federal legislation spoke of

"adopting" Indian groups. Adoption of minor children, in fact, was not a component of the English codes and, therefore, was not readily incorporated into state or territorial statutes. The only exceptions were in areas of the United States that were once under French or Spanish control; these areas were influenced by those countries' codes of law, which allowed for adoption. For the majority of states and territories of the nineteenth century, guardianship, not adoption, was addressed by state statute. This began to change when Massachusetts broke with English law tradition in 1851 and recognized adoption as a legally binding contract between adult and child. This did not replace guardianship. Rather, it provided another option for child protection. Some states followed the Massachusetts lead rather quickly, but others ignored it. Into the twentieth century, adoption was not accepted or recognized by statute in every state or territory, and social work professionals and reformers continued to argue the merits of adoption "as a method of social treatment."[8]

Although most nineteenth-century U.S. territories and states did not recognize adoption, Indian societies did. Adoption was not an issue of legislation sanctioned by codified laws or signed legal documents overseen by lawyers. It was a fiber of tribal life that intertwined the needs of an individual with the group. Adoption was directed by custom, and it was more varied in its application than white America could understand or envision. Adoption crossed age and gender lines. Non-Indians were sometimes adopted into a tribe, and marriage was not a necessary prerequisite for non-Indian adoption into a tribe, clan, or band. Indian children with living parents could be adopted, with parental consent, into another family. This generally occurred when a family wished to replace a child lost to death. Some adoptions were formalized through public events with feasts and gift giving. At other times, there was simply a public announcement of intentions. Guardianship was implicit in adoption. It did not exist as a separate entity, as in Euro-American society.[9]

Adoption was initiated and completed within established tribal structures. It was not a capricious act, nor were the codes of behavior that directed the care and education of a child left parentless. Since it was common for a family group or a designated relative, such as a grandmother, to take in a child who had lost one or both parents, it was almost impossible for a child to be left totally alone and vulnerable. Defined family ties were coupled with the expectation that uncles, aunts, grandparents, or elders would fulfill their moral obligations for specific aspects of child rearing and instruction. This is not to say that white families did not live in extended units; there were often several generations, and perhaps servants and apprentices, living under one roof, and family members were likely to group in close proximity to one another in a neighborhood. These arrangements, however, lacked the culturally understood demands of the Native American's extended kinship patterns. If and how much a Euro-American family cared for a child relative depended more on personal, family, or ethnic values. In Indian families an array of relatives provided a broad support base for the child. Wrote Charles Eastman, a Santee Sioux who was raised by his paternal grandmother after the death of his mother: "It is quite unlikely that a child would have been abandoned in Dakota culture . . . , since the network of relatives would have cared for any child in need." A historian of Sioux life and customs agreed: "Because of the wide range of possible relatives within the family, orphans were a rarity."[10]

In any culture there are exceptions to the rule. Indian life was not static, peopled with simplistic individuals without personal desires, motives, attributes, or faults. Not every individual bowed to group expectations. Some questioned the rules or acted against them. It cannot be said that every parentless child had a protective family network or that every family always lived up to its responsibility. Despite the protective environment promised children, there were instances in which the culture failed them. In that light, it is understandable that stories told among some Indian groups featured orphan characters who were treated as outcasts because they had no kin. There were also stories that spoke of bad parents, almost always an evil stepmother who deceived her husband while trying to kill or abandon his child. Such was the theme in the Seneca story of the boy adopted by a bear after the boy's stepmother left him to die. It was also the story line in the Canadian Athabascan tale of Swan, whose stepmother's lies led to Swan being abandoned by his father on a far-off island.[11] These stories have parallels to those told in Euro-American culture, but similarity of characters does not mean that the stories were the same in their intent or in the lessons taught.

The stories and myths that societies tell themselves are cultural indicators that reinforce and define collective experiences and consciousness. Whether labeled myths, folklore, or popular or classical literature, stories passed from one generation to another through oral tradition or preserved on the printed page are a barometer of social thought and belief. Stories from Indian and Euro-American cultures, whether told for pure entertainment or to teach serious lessons, illustrate the value systems of each and express cultural ideals. They provide a basic context in which to examine and explore differences and similarities. Pointedly or subtly, stories illustrate inherent beliefs and viewpoints. They delineate societies' differing ideas about childhood and about the nature of children, child care, and instruction.

Native American stories evoked tribal mythology that explained human struggles, world origins, and natural forces. Myths from the Old World of Europeans did the same, and just as stories varied among European groups, they differed from tribe to tribe and clan to clan. Both cultures employed oral communication, producing numerous versions of the same story. Only when the tales were written down by Euro-Americans did they demand a definitive beginning, middle, and end. Among Indian clan or tribal groups, differing versions did not diminish the intent of a story, since all the stories attempted to explain and define the world, tribal identity, and the forces that created and controlled existence. Even with variations, there were recurring themes. One was the orphan who lived on the margin of tribal life—until a supernatural being or animal spirit interceded. Although not as prominent as other figures in Indian mythology, the orphan is important. First, the character itself demonstrates that Indian societies recognized that there were circumstances under which a child found him- or herself without family protection. Second, the fate of the orphan presents an important insight into Indian culture, particularly when the characterization of orphans is compared with that found in white literature.[12]

The horned serpent appears in many tales. The Micmacs in what is now Nova Scotia, as well as other native groups across Canada, tell of a horned serpent. So, too, do Seneca stories, including that of the serpent and an orphan. In the "Great Horned Serpent," the Senecas tell of an orphaned girl left by her village on an island to die. She has done nothing wrong. In fact, she has been obedient and a hard worker. Nevertheless, she is unprotected, and for that she is despised. To rid themselves of the girl, the people contrive a way to abandon her on an island where she will be unable to survive. Yet instead of dying, she is rescued by the Great Horned Serpent, a large, snakelike creature with horns. Through the water, the serpent carries the girl on its back and leaves her safely on the shore near her village. In return for the rescue, the girl promises to observe a feast, the Dark Dance, to remember the serpent. She also promises never to divulge the source of her deliverance for, in not knowing, the people will fear her. In that fear, they will honor her. The Dark Dance is observed and soon spreads to other villages; in return, the girl achieves a special place among her people.[13]

This story, of course, explained how and why the Senecas came to have this particular observance. It also taught that every person is important to a group; one person lost diminishes the whole. It provided a moral for those who felt they could not find their place within their own society. The story offered reassurance: it may have been easier for some to carve out a niche for themselves, but it was possible for everyone. Charles Eastman knew the meaning firsthand. When his mother died giving him birth, he was called "The Pitiful Last." Looking back on this, he said: "I had to bear the humiliating name . . . until I should earn a more dignified and appropriate name."[14] The lesson was clear: no matter how lowly one's position or how great one's suffering, the experience was not singular or irreversible. One could overcome.

Not only could one rise above circumstances, but powers and greater understanding could be gained from an experience. Such is the case in two stories; one from the Micmacs, the other from the Senecas. The two begin dissimilarly, but they reach parallel lines in the telling. In both, a boy lives for a time with bears—a mother and two cubs. In the Micmac version, the boy has no parents and wanders from one wigwam to another without anyone really taking responsibility for him. Without supervision, he wanders off and becomes lost in the forest, where the mother bear takes care of him. In the Seneca telling, the boy has parents, a father and a stepmother. The stepmother, evil and self-serving, tricks the boy into entering a cave; her plan is to leave him to die. In each story, the boy is saved by a female bear and sheltered in the animal's den. Neither boy realizes that he is living with bears, not humans. In time, each boy returns to his own people. For the Micmacs and the Senecas the story spoke of relationships between man and animal, and the Micmac version underscores, more than that of the Senecas, the importance of people looking after each other. Each person's talents and powers are important for a group's collective well-being, and it is for the good of the whole that people take responsibility for each other.[15]

An extraordinary set of circumstances rendered a child kinless and a target for derision, and a child without any protection was largely an anomaly in Indian society. Nevertheless, across geographic distances and tribal and clan lines there were stories that included orphan characters or those that approximated the orphan. Among the Chippewas (the Ojibways) is the story of Naanabozho (Nanbojo, or the trickster), who, depending on the particular version, was either one of three children or a single child whose mother died quickly after his birth. Left to be raised by his grandmother, Naanabozho, the trickster, had great powers. Powers were also at the heart of the origin-creation stories of the Iroquois that spoke of the Good Twin and the Bad Twin, who were among those supernatural beings responsible for creating earth and sky. As creators, not mortals, they hardly needed parental or spirit protectors. They were not labeled as orphans since they were not mistreated by earthly antagonists and in need of aid. They were, however, parentless. Their mother died giving birth to them, and the father was mystically present and then as quickly gone.[16]

Whether or not a character was identified clearly in an Indian story as someone without kin, he or she was linked intricately to nature. Whether a creator of nature's wonders or a mortal protected by animals or special spirits, the parentless child interacted with the natural world. It was not a leap of faith to believe that a bear came to a child's rescue. After all, in Indian culture it was natural for human and non-human to act together. As Jesse Cornplanter explained in recounting the story of the orphan girl and the Great Horned Serpent, "My people [Senecas] were living so close to nature that it was a sort of common affair to have someone get some help from some wild animal." Nature, religion, and everyday life blended. Explained Henry Old Coyote, from the Crow, "You can't categorize the social and religious life of an Indian the way white man does, because everything is interwoven."[17]

It was natural for a powerful being to offer support and provide a path toward respect and acceptance. One Crow myth recounted the sorry state of two brothers without kin who were forced to forage for scraps of food, live away from the main camp, and fashion their garments from discards. Their only recourse was to hope that a supernatural being would intervene. The same was true for the male character in another Crow story. Cruelly treated by a chief, this boy without family reacted to his circumstances by going on a vision quest. Watching over the boy was a bear that took pity and gave the youngster powers that, upon his return to the village, allowed him to turn the tables on those who had mistreated him.[18]

The literature of white America drew on Greek, Roman, and Norse mythology, as well as the folklore of ethnic groups, for its images of man and nature. The stories had ceased, however, to resonate through everyday life. Studied from a distance, when they were told at all, myths and folklore ceased to have a direct bearing on how people regarded themselves in relation to nature and its creatures. Nature was a thing to be conquered rather than something that invited coexistence. When child and animal characters did interact, it was in either a fairy tale or a story of adventure.

Converse to Indian stories with orphan characters, white America's literature in the first half of the nineteenth century offered little hope or promise of finding comfort in the physical world. No protection came from a supernatural being. No animal spirit intervened. For that matter, few humans intervened. Orphan characterization was popular in nineteenth-century literature, with all the sentimental imagery a writer could muster. In stories written during the first half of the 1800s, it was common for the orphan to die. As one example, an 1858 issue of the periodical *Ladies' Repository* published a short story revolving around a young girl who huddled outside New York City's Trinity Church. She wore no hat, gloves, or shoes to protect her from the elements. To those who read of her plight, it was unclear if she was a parentless child, a true orphan. It mattered little. The girl served another purpose. With much sentimental drapery and moralistic clamoring, the story made sure that readers understood that the happy ending was in the girl's death in the shadows of the church. She had suffered terribly, but heavenly peace awaited her in the afterlife. It was better to have died a child than to suffer the degradations of street life that would surely mark her for hell. Describing these children of the streets, a late-twentieth-century novelist astutely observed: "For certain religious sensibilities such children fulfilled the ineffable aims of God."[19]

Not all Euro-American literature of the nineteenth century found it necessary to kill off its suffering child characters or to sap readers' emotions with wrenching affectations. Literature in which children were allowed to live became more common when Charlotte Brontë's *Jane Eyre* and the works of Charles Dickens gained a wide readership in America. Out of their own experiences these authors replaced sentimentality with more realism. They examined the barriers that separated the classes, adults who used children for their own ends, and cruel street life. Characters might die but not to illustrate that death was better than an impoverished life.

Less graphic in his depictions than Brontë or Dickens was the American writer Horatio Alger Jr., who firmly believed in the American ideal of transcending social and economic class lines. Alger created down-and-out boy characters who were saved, not sacrificed to the hereafter. The writer, of course, employed unspoken but understood requirements that made his heroes socially acceptable to readers. The character had to be among the "worthy" poor—someone destitute and without adult care because of bad luck, not because of bad habits or disreputable birth. To rise above his humble beginnings, he had to have an inner drive and resolute determination to better himself. Alger summed it up best in his book title *Bound to Rise* and in that book's main character, who represented "those boys . . . who are hampered by poverty and limited advantages" but possessed "worthy ambition." Alger's heroes always proved themselves worthy, helped along the way by a caring adult. The reading audience would not have believed that the character prevailed because of an intervening animal or supernatural spirit.[20]

The works of Alger and others mirrored changes in mainstream society, where the image of orphaned and destitute children was being restructured. Euro-American cultural and social beliefs were based largely on a puritanical heritage that decreed that children were born under a cloud of original sin. This preordained one to hell unless, of course, strict discipline, long doses of sermons, and religious instruction redirected a child toward the good and right path. "The Protestant vision of the child was clear; unless a child was educated to the knowledge of God and virtue, he would be eternally damned for the innate wickedness of his soul." Diametrically opposed to this view was traditional Indian culture, which perceived its children as innocent. Said Black Elk, of the Oglala Sioux: "Often when we are inside the sweat lodge, little children poke their heads inside, and ask the Great Spirit to make their lives pure. We do not chase them away, for we know that little children already have pure hearts."[21]

This was hardly the viewpoint of those Americans whose puritanical roots agreed with the Reverend Jonathan Edwards and his edict

that no child was "too little to die . . . [and] not too little to go to hell."
By the mid-1800s, however, white America began to waver in the belief that children were the inheritors of original sin. Tenets of the Enlightenment worked themselves into mainstream thought. Influential
were eighteenth-century philosophers and educators such as Jean-
Jacques Rousseau and Johann Pestalozzi, who argued that children existed in a natural state of innocence and were incapable of knowing
sin. The idea took time for widespread acceptance, and Euro-American culture never quite applied it to some ethnic groups or dismissed
the suspicion that chronic poverty was the result of sloth and sin,
which tainted the youngest. It was one of America's most enduring
beliefs, and myths, that any able-bodied person who wanted to work
could find a job. This belief was so ingrained that even some of white
society's most respected and enlightened reformers of the Progressive
Era continued to link poverty with laziness and depravity. The sins of
the fathers were those of the children.[22]

Generally, however, white society of the late nineteenth century
began to regard children as clay to be molded. The earlier impression-
able youngsters were removed from corrupting surroundings, the better chance they had of learning socially acceptable behavior. As
innocents, all children were expected to pass through phases of childhood that slowly unlocked their religious and intellectual selves.
Whereas they once were regarded as miniature adults, children of the
post–Civil War period were viewed as innocents who could be shaped
into whatever adults wanted them to be. This belief created a whole
new set of behavior patterns for adults and children. The mother was
the chief guide along the path of childhood, but unlike Indian mothers, she did not always have a wide network of kin to offer advice or
interact with her children. White, middle-class women had their own
traditions to guide them, but they often depended on any number of
clergy, educators, and self-styled experts who dispensed advice from
the pulpit, through child care books, and in women's magazines.

An idealization of children and childhood became more pronounced
after the Civil War, when it seemed that the country had lost its innocence. Adults transferred their hopes to the next generation. An entire
culture of intellectual thought and material goods grew up around children and childhood. The home environment and the best forms of education were widely discussed. When children died, they were
mourned with a new set of Victorian trappings that included memorial

poetry published in popular magazines and commercially produced memory plaques suitable for hanging in the home parlor. Children's books and toys flooded the marketplace. American society developed its own vision of the ideal childhood. In this world, more aware than ever before of children, orphans held a kind of fascination. They were objects that inspired benevolent feelings among those more fortunate. Who could turn away an appeal to help an orphan? They were unencumbered blank slates that could be molded to meet society's designs and expectations. Literary orphans in the latter half of the nineteenth century contrasted with the earlier theme of an orphan or pauper child redeemed by death. Euro-American society's shift in thinking and perception was not an abrupt transition, but as the mind-set altered, white culture believed that it had stumbled onto a revolutionary new set of ideas. Of course, it expected that its evolving values should apply to all cultures it encountered. It began to overlay its ideas on Native American culture, believing, if not insisting, that Indian societies had little social organization, few ideas about child care and instruction, and no sense of its children. As writer Margaret Connell Szasz noted, Euro-Americans made it clear that "their civilization had developed . . . many beliefs, customs, and ways of doing things—that were not only different from native ways but were superior."[23]

While the expanding mainstream culture of white America altered its views of children, Indian culture did not grapple with the subject of a child's inherent nature or the presence of childhood phases. Said Allen Quetone, great-grandson of the Kiowa chief Standing Bear: "Each stage is crucial and . . . the child should be allowed to dwell in each for the appropriate period of time so that every aspect of his being can evolve, just as a plant evolves in the proper time and sequence of seasons."[24]

Indian culture never questioned the innocence of its children or the need to define marked phases of childhood development. Nor did time drastically shift perceptions of children and their innate nature. Children were valued. Their formative years were filled with well-defined customs that addressed behavior, discipline, and training for future roles and responsibilities. Boys and girls emulated adult models, and through play with cooking utensils or hunting implements they gained basic instruction. This was reinforced as the children grew older and were expected to refine their abilities and contribute to household and public life.

Life in Indian communities was lived in the open for all to see. Children did not exist in isolated, nuclear households. All took an interest in a child's upbringing, and if parents failed, they were chastised or ridiculed into behaving properly. The same type of community pressure was used to discipline and train children. It was important for children to learn their group history and beliefs, as well as to learn respect and to take pride in their society. Scolding, ridicule, stories, and following adult examples taught children. Recalled a Creek woman: "When children were bad, they were warned that the Honka Man would mark their arms. He was about the same as the Bogey man is to the white children." For the Sioux, it was the *cici*-man and later *wasieu*, the white man. In most Indian societies, children were not expected to immediately correct a fault or unacceptable behavior; change took time and maturity. "You're bound to make mistakes when you're a child," observed Leon Shenondoah, onetime chief of the Six Nations. "You're learning all these things but you forget sometimes because you're having a good time." This viewpoint made it less likely that whippings were the first response to misbehavior, although this form of discipline varied from tribe to tribe. Some used physical punishment sparingly, others not at all. In many societies, pain was not meted out as punishment. Rather, physical pain occurred in ritualistic testing of young men as a sign of their rite of passage into maturity or in religious ceremonies that displayed men's courage. To discipline the young, methods other than physical punishment were used. Youngsters who failed to respond were sent to an elder, a grandparent, or the mother's oldest brother or uncle. In Creek society, for example, discipline was primarily in the hands of the mother and the clan uncle, who was older, more experienced, and revered. In other groups, one individual was given the task of acting as disciplinarian. This was the system employed by the Warm Springs people in Oregon. The designated person decided on punishment for misdeeds and then spent a great deal of time instructing children through stories that explained why and how certain things were done or avoided.[25]

There was a marked dichotomy between Indian practices and Euro-American perceptions. In fact, white society could not reach a clear consensus on the subject of corporal punishment. Most nineteenth-century child care experts and mothers' advisers were reluctant to call for its outright banishment. They modified the axiom "Spare the rod, spoil the child" by cautioning that whipping was unjust when a child failed to learn a lesson from it. The enlightened parent, said the experts, tried scolding or withholding treats first. Nevertheless, corporal punishment was a generally accepted method of correction and used throughout all socioeconomic strata of society.[26]

When Euro-Americans did not observe physical discipline in Indian groups, they assumed that children had no boundaries, no direction. This was compounded by scenes of children seemingly spending their time in activities that whites could describe only as games, and Euro-American society, at least until the end of the 1800s, was suspicious of play. In a culture where the work ethic was all-important, play activities seemed the antithesis of character-building chores and studious learning. When Indian children were seen swimming, running, riding horses, and playing with small bows and arrows or dolls, their pursuits seemed frivolous to outsiders. In fact, children were learning. Charles Grinnell, writing of the Cheyennes, noted that outsiders observed children and adolescents at their daily activities and decided that if they were not in a schoolhouse, they were not learning or being controlled. This was certainly the viewpoint of the U.S. Indian agent at the Pottawatomie and Great Nemaha Agency in Kansas, who wrote that children were "unaccustomed to any home discipline [and] taught to obey no will but their own." The result was that they did "pretty much as they please[d] about attending school." The report was much the same from the Rosebud Agency, where the agent complained bitterly that parents made "frivolous" excuses to keep their children out of school. Adults preferred that children "spend their time killing small game with a bent stick and a feathered dart." Charles Eastman understood the agents' perception of time ill spent. Recalling his own nineteenth-century boyhood, Eastman wrote that it was common for non-Indians to believe that there was "no systematic education" when, in truth, instruction was "scrupulously adhered to and transmitted from one generation to another."[27]

White America was generally ignorant of Indian societies' social organizations. The common perception was the Indian as warrior. Therefore, those who had contact with Indian groups often expressed surprise at finding a rich domestic life and a strong sense of community. They also were unprepared for the roles taken on by men and women. Tribal government was not necessarily a male domain. Among the Senecas, for example, women could depose leaders who disregarded the public good, proved incompetent, or conducted their duties improperly. Women could nominate rulers and, if circumstances changed, reinstate those once removed from seats of authority.[28]

Female participation in government was no less surprising than the spheres of labor that nineteenth-century white society defined so stringently and narrowly. There were spheres of work in Indian culture. In fact, survival depended on each person performing specific tasks. The difference was, of course, that work was not always divided into the same gender-specific roles as those found in Euro-American society. Indian men did not cultivate fields, as did whites. That was women's responsibility. Women's labor was intensive, and outside observers were inclined to characterize Indian women as subservient beasts of burden. Mary Henderson Eastman, who lived for seven years at Fort Snelling (near present-day Minneapolis) with her husband and children beginning in 1841, was genuinely interested in the Dakota Sioux and recorded her observations and the stories told by a medicine woman named Chequered Cloud. Eastman wrote sympathetically of Indian women whose lives seemed to her an endless round of work, abuse, and deprivations: "She tans the skins of which coats, moccasins, and leggings are to be made for the family; she has to scrape it and prepare it while other cares are pressing upon her. When her child is born, she has no opportunities for rest or quiet. She must paddle the canoe for her husband." Eastman did not draw comparisons between the work of an Indian woman and that of a white woman laboring on a frontier farm or living on the margin of city life and working long hours in a poorly ventilated factory. The Sioux women were better known to Eastman than Euro-American women outside her own socioeconomic class. To her credit, Eastman attempted to learn about the people she encountered, but she was incapable of interpreting her observations in anything other than the context of white, Victorian expectations. When she noted the female labor that went into constructing tipis, for example, she failed to add a telling point about the women. Men had certain rights within the dwelling, but it belonged to the women; this was reinforced by the use of feminine terms to denote parts of the dwelling.[29]

Whether on the Central Plains or in the hills of Georgia, women had to be self-sufficient since men were often away performing their roles of protector and hunter. Economic contributions translated into rights that could not necessarily be found in white America. As a rule, native women owned property, including their homes. They could, and did, own livestock and slaves. They had the right to their children (unlike white women, whose rights usually were curtailed by law and the courts), and a child most often belonged to its mother's clan, not the father's.[30]

Indian societies were complex in their view of children and their relationships to parent, clan, and overall social structure. In the center of domestic life were the women and their children. When a woman died in childbirth, other women made enormous efforts to save the child. Lucy Thompson recalled in *Reminiscences of a Yukon Woman* that a fine powder of sugar pine or hazelnuts was mixed with water to nourish an infant as a substitute for breast milk. A child, said Thompson, could be raised on this preparation, and no family following the old ways was without the powder. Although women worked to save a child's life, they also had the power and the right to practice abortion and infanticide. These options were not taken lightly. Nor were they prominent, but infanticide was particularly acceptable if the newborn suffered some debilitating physical attribute. Lucy Thompson recalled that among the Klamath Indians in the Northwest "it was considered a crime for parents to bring demented or deformed children into the world." Missionaries were appalled by the practice of abortion and infanticide, as well as a woman's right to choose those measures. Bent on abolishing these practices, missionaries preached against them and demanded that women adopt not only the dress of white America but also its attitudes. The missionaries' influence was seen among some tribes in the early decades of the 1800s; in 1826, as illustration, the Cherokees in the Southeast rescinded a woman's traditional right to infanticide.[31]

Missionaries and others who traveled among tribal groups found a number of practices that shocked their sensibilities. Divorce was easy or complicated, depending on the group, but it was an acceptable solution for ending marital conflict. Remarriage or multiple marriages were also acceptable. Serial monogamy was the norm in some societies; polygamy was acceptable in others. Wrote an Indian agent for the Crow Creek and Lower Brule Agency: "Formerly it [polygamy] was a common and tolerated condition." Although no longer common and certainly not tolerated by missionaries or federal employees, polygamy persisted; in the early 1890s, there were still a number of "cases . . . of long standing on the reservation." Observers of Indian life believed that both serial marriages and polygamy signaled social instability and lax morals. In 1872 the Indian agent for the Sisseton and Wahpeton Sioux damned polygamy. The practice, he said, made women worse off than if they had been widows. It made the children "more miserable than if they were orphans." George Catlin, a chronicler of Indian life, believed that polygamy existed simply because the Indian male was "surrounded by temptations which he considers it would be unnatural to resist, where no law or regulation of society stand in the way of enjoyment." Perhaps in Catlin's world multiple marriages could only be explained as a pursuit of pleasure and primal instinct, but where polygamy was practiced in Indian societies, it was done for a reason. Having many wives represented wealth. Plural marriage consolidated political and territorial agreements, and in some societies a widow was taken as a wife to ensure that she enjoyed the bounty of the hunt. No matter the situation, serial monogamy and polygamy existed within stringent social codes of conduct, not for lack of them.[32]

As a rule, nineteenth-century white culture refused to consider the possibility that kinship networks, marital relationships, gender roles, customs that dictated social order, or child-rearing practices represented complex organizational structures. Thus, the dominant culture set out with a sense of duty and an ethnocentric mind-set to bring "civilization" to the Indian. The civilization movement was broad and powerful, but those directly involved in it acted out of diverse motivations. The movement was laced with the contradictory impulses of good intentions and self-interests, ethnocentric arrogance and religious piety. Nevertheless, there were common perceptions of the native populations. The power of words painted Indians as children; perhaps they were destructive children or perhaps childlike, with a limited capacity for complex thought. Such characterizations projected the Indian as incapable of intricate social organization or belief systems. Inherent in depictions of native peoples was the picture of a population that lacked the intellectual means and the social structure to care for, understand, or educate its children. Some individuals argued otherwise, including whites who lived with and traveled among native societies. Henry R. Schoolcraft, who traveled the eastern United States in the early decades of the 1800s, observed that children were set above all else: "If there is a morsel to eat in the lodge, it is given to the children." James McLaughlin wrote, "This trait—love of children—is the most common characteristic of the Indian father and mother. This affection displays itself in lavish form and terms of endearment, and the parents idolize the children, who in their turn show the most unbounded affection for both father and mother." Catholic missionaries, who seldom tolerated native customs, agreed. Time after time they commented favorably on the child-family relationship, and they realized that it was key to any early success in mission schools. Supervisors at a Catholic mission school on the White Earth Reservation in Minnesota, for example, frequently noted that families were satisfied with a school only when its location allowed them to be near their children. It was much the same at St. Catharine's Indian School in New Mexico: "Only those who know what a deep, intense love the old Indian has for his little ones can realize what a sacrifice it is to send them off to school."[33]

Nevertheless, Euro-American society as a whole was not convinced, for the simple reason that acknowledgment of developed and sophisticated native societies weakened white culture's claim of superiority. To suggest that native societies were anything other than backward or savage or childlike threatened federal policies and missionary endeavors. It certainly begged the questions of sovereignty, dependency, and land rights. Indian child dependency did not begin in the 1900s, and solving claims of jurisdiction and control over a child's fate and cultural influences did not begin in the latter decades of the twentieth century with the Indian Child Welfare Act of 1978. During the nineteenth century, a number of transitional periods and events severely hampered Indian culture's ability to care for and retain control over its children.

Brutal conflicts are the most obvious events that made it difficult, if not impossible, for extended families to sustain a stable environment in which to carry out defined responsibilities to children. The list of conflicts, little wars and big ones, would take volumes, but the Tuscaroras offer a simple example. The Tuscaroras, "the most important tribe of North Carolina east of the mountains," numbered at least five thousand before they rose up against the whites in 1711. By the time the tribe's power was broken and the Tuscaroras fled north to join the Five Nations of the Iroquois, four hundred had died in one battle and one thousand in another.[34] The Tuscaroras were forced to flee when they could not rebuff white encroachment. The story was played out time after time, in one locale after another. Displacement reduced the ability of any group to continue its customary economic, political, and domestic life.

In those instances when a people was not wholly displaced by white advancement into their lands, the delicate balance between man and nature was upset by outsiders. In 1892, for example, white hunters along the coast of Alaska nearly exterminated the sea otter, a key component of the natives' livelihood. Starvation and destitution became so widespread that the Methodist Woman's Home Mission Society "voted $10,000 for the care of orphans of Aleutian Islands, . . . [but] there are so many orphans that the Methodist women have not planned large enough."[35] Native food sources were destroyed out of greed for an economic product, through the act of white settlement, and through deliberate calculation. In the two former cases, it can be argued that Euro-American hunters and settlers did not fully comprehend the ecological consequences of their actions. In the latter instance, however, sanctioned destruction of essential plants and animals was meant to drive Indian groups into a restrictive economic pattern of family farms. Intended or not, altered ecosystems could not help but damage traditional ways of life.

The most obvious example of ecological destruction is the buffalo, which was hunted first for its valuable hide. Herd reductions were gradual in the first half of the 1800s, but the signs were there. In 1849–50, employees at the Fort Kearny sutlery began to note a higher incidence of poor hunts among the Pawnees, reporting that one hunting party could not find a single buffalo between the Missouri River and Kearny on the Platte. Outright slaughter of buffalo began when the vast herds stood in the way of the railroads and westward expansion. Slaughter escalated when the government decided to force Plains Indians into submission by destroying the animals on which they depended for spiritual and physical sustenance. Destruction of the buffalo was a form of cultural genocide that, in the short term, starved a people to death. In 1868 a white contractor for mail service in the Dakotas wrote that the Sioux at Devils Lake were in such dire straits that "they have eaten up their own horses and have actually taken by force horses from the Mail Carriers and eaten them, and unless the Government renders them aid immediately they will, as a matter of course, starve by hundreds." In the long term, destruction of food sources meant that diets became dependent on other sources such as government rations. These were often meager, and no matter the quantity or quality forcibly changed a people's dietary habits. The overall health of a population was damaged. A Catholic publication said of the Sioux in 1908: "Formerly when the buffalos roamed the prairies in great numbers the Indians had plenty of meat. This accounts for the fact that the old Indians are like giants in physical stature, while the younger generation is weak and sickly. The condition of their health is, indeed, truly pitiful."[36]

Diseases also dealt debilitating blows. Smallpox decimated populations from the time of white contact. In 1738 smallpox raged in South Carolina, and its reoccurrence in 1759 was said to have destroyed at least half of the Catawbas. One of the most devastating epidemics of smallpox occurred in 1801–2, and there were less widespread outbreaks that claimed substantial numbers. In 1815–16 the Comanches were afflicted, probably losing four thousand out of an approximate population of ten thousand. In a second major outbreak, that of the early 1830s, the Pawnees may have lost half of their population to smallpox. John Dougherty, Indian agent to the Pawnees, provided a graphic description of their suffering:

> I am fully persuaded that one half the whole number of souls of each village have and will be carried off by this cruel and frightful distemper. They were dying so fast, and taken down at once in such large numbers, that they ceased to bury their dead, whose bodies were to be seen in every direction, laying about in the river, lodged on sand-bars, in the hog-weeds . . . and in their old corn caches; others again were dragged off by the hungry dogs of the prairie, where they were torn to pieces by the more hungry wolves and buzzards.

Six years later, smallpox struck the Upper Missouri tribes with such strength that the Mandans were reduced from a population that ranged between sixteen hundred and two thousand to an estimated one hundred. Unidentified diseases also struck localized populations. Wrote a Methodist missionary of the "fever" that afflicted his small mission group in Kansas and the Indians living nearby: "While we were sick at the mission, the Indians were suffering equally as much. In some families as many as five died. But few families escaped disease; and the number of deaths was great in proportion to the number sick. The awful cries of the Indians around the dead sounded in our ears nearly every day."[37]

Venereal diseases, silent and long-term killers, took lives and infected children through congenital transmission. Although there are those who dispute the contention that Europeans introduced venereal diseases to the Americas, numerous nineteenth-century commentators believed that this was a white affliction visited upon the Indians and one that, not so incidentally, was correlated with the importation of alcohol. "[Whites entered] their villages with whisky in day time & night; to make the men drunk & cohabit with the squaws, disseminating venerial [*sic*] diseases among them." Alcohol contributed to destabilizing male and female roles, economic bases, and family life when its use crossed the line of culturally approved drinking and allowed whites to insinuate themselves into tribal life through sale and distribution of liquor. The condition was not peculiar to any native society. One report on coastal groups in Alaska noted that "the worst enemy of the native is the whisky peddler." Given the number of factors at work, it is hardly difficult to determine that when Euro-American values of Christianity and male and female "spheres" were added to the mix, native culture suffered multiple blows. Patterns of extended family and clan networks were disengaged, and cultural underpinnings of family life and child protection were threatened and disrupted. To replace what had been and to deal with the result of contact, a completely alien concept was introduced into Indian culture. This was the institution known as the orphanage.[38]

This is not to say that the orphanage was a tried-and-true fixture in nineteenth-century white America. Nevertheless, the century became, in the words of David Rothman, an era for "the discovery of the asylum." In colonial America there were few institutions of any kind. The poor, including children, usually lived on local charity. It was common for public officials to auction off the poor to local farmers as extra workers. Families cared for mentally or physically disabled relatives at home or placed them in one of the few existing almshouses. By the early nineteenth century, however, charitable organizations and institutions of all sorts sprang up as answers for specific social problems that spilled over into economic and political arenas. There were almshouses, poor farms, workhouses, and pauper jails. Society stigmatized those who were sent to these places, and for society in general these institutions represented a "skeleton in the closet of our domestic commonwealth." Asylums for the insane, as well as institutions for the epileptic, the deaf, and the blind, were more kindly regarded than almshouses or pauper jails. In the public mind, the mentally or physically disabled deserved a touch of pity, and those responsible for their institutionalized care often sought ways to rehabilitate or train inmates rather than simply warehouse them. There were foundling homes for infants and toddlers and juvenile asylums for adolescents and teenagers. Juvenile asylums were difficult to define, since the resident populations in many were a mixture of innocent poor and criminal delinquents. This made juvenile asylums barely distinguishable from reformatories or industrial schools for youthful offenders whose crimes ranged from theft and prostitution to little more than selling newspapers without a license or living on the streets. Among the plethora of institutions to appear was the orphanage. It, along with its child population, was the most sentimentalized of nineteenth-century institutions.[39]

The first orphanage in America was established in Savannah, Georgia, in 1740. This earliest institution did not, however, open the floodgates to commitment of children to orphanages. More typically, when local communities were faced with what to do with dependent children, they fell back on colonial poor laws and relied on almshouses, pauper prisons, or poor farms. Until the 1830s, orphanages were a rarity. During the 1840s and 1850s there was a gradual increase that corresponded to the general growth in America's population and the number within that population who were orphaned, abandoned, or destitute children. Although Euro-American culture pictured itself as spiraling upward in progress, the mid-1800s were uncertain and dangerous times. Children were among the casualties of immigration, industrialization, urbanization, and expanding western settlement. Children were likely to lose parental or extended family protection in the festering squalor of a New York City neighborhood, through a farm or industrial accident, to epidemics such as cholera that swept through urban centers (especially during the mid-1800s), or along the route of the Overland Trail. By the mid-1800s, there were over fifty orphanages east of the Mississippi—from New York to Chicago to Mobile, Alabama. West of the Mississippi, emigration to the far western borders of the continent carried its own price; in 1851, two years after the forty-niners arrived in the gold fields, California opened its first orphan asylum. By the end of the Civil War, orphanages appeared in proportion to the needs of those made orphans or half-orphans by the war. As many orphanages were founded in the 1860s as the combined total of the two preceding decades. By the end of the 1860s, the orphan asylum was firmly established as the premier form of child care in the United States.[40]

Orphanages were advocated as viable alternatives to almshouses (also called poorhouses), pauper jails, and county poor farms where children were housed with adult populations that often included the mentally ill, elderly, physically disabled, and sometimes the criminal fringes of humanity. It was nothing short of "evil," declared one writer, for children to have contact with the sort of people who were sure to transmit moral "contamination." Reformers, clergy, and philanthropists suggested that one had only to visit an almshouse to see the need for something more humane. Wrote one visitor: "Children were packed like sardines in double cradles; were cared for by pauper inmates; and were indentured to people whose credentials could hardly receive a proper investigation." Added to this voice was that of another who offered the thought that nothing was worse than an almshouse, not even jail, for a child. Orphanages, it was argued, provided a safer environment than those institutions where children and adults lived side by side. Furthermore, orphanages were capable of doing a much better job than almshouses of offering the basic educational skills of reading and writing. Without education, many warned, the child inmates would grow up to be society's future dangerous classes. They would threaten social and economic stability through their ignorance, unrest, and antisocial behavior. Orphan asylums provided children from the lowest socioeconomic levels with something they otherwise would not have had—basic, formal education.[41]

During the nineteenth century, most states outlawed commitment of children to poorhouses, since orphanages were preferable to institutions that did little but incarcerate a child. To elevate public perception of the orphanage, it was usually called an asylum. This implied, if not in reality at least in the ideal, that the institution was a place of refuge and protection. And, despite its name, the orphanage—the orphan asylum—was not just for the truly parentless child. Vagrant, destitute, delinquent, and homeless children and adolescents were admitted. There was little attempt to clearly distinguish one from the other. This was certainly the case when parents in dire straits used the orphan asylum to meet their own needs. In a time when there were few social welfare safety nets, adults sought out orphanages when they were desperate to provide for their children during personal and economic crises.

As early as the 1830s, the Orphan Asylum Society of the City of Brooklyn housed both orphans and half-orphans. Interestingly, those with one living parent were in the majority. The parents, often widows, paid fifty cents a week for their children's upkeep. Similarly, when orphanages appeared in the developing cities of what had been the western frontier, the practice continued. The Chicago Protestant Orphan Asylum, established after the great Chicago fire of 1871, took in destitute children whose parents paid a small remittance. These were not isolated events. It became common practice for parents to place children in homes during times of family upheaval or tragedy. Many charities defended the practice on the grounds that it kept the family together, and parents took this function for granted. A widow placing her two sons in New York's Hebrew Orphan Asylum fully intended to retrieve the boys after she established herself as a teacher of piano and violin. When times got better, parents reclaimed their children. When times were bad, children reentered the asylum. For innumerable children, life was a revolving door of home life and institutional stays. Growing-up years were spent in and out of asylums, depending on the ups and downs of a family's fortune.[42]

When orphanages began to appear on Indian reservations, it was not unheard of for these institutions to be used in the same way. Some youngsters were placed in institutions for short stays while parents dealt with economic setbacks, a spouse's death, or marital conflict. Other children spent all or most of their growing-up years in institutions, often regularly visited by their parents, a surviving parent, or relatives. One Chickasaw woman recalled that when her mother died, "[father] sent me to the orphan's home at Lebanon [Oklahoma]. . . . This was a home for both boys and girls of the Chickasaws and Choctaws." On the Pine Ridge Reservation, Isabel Gap Gyongossy was raised by her grandparents, although her parents also lived on the reservation. Her grandfather, a onetime scout for the U.S. Army, believed that she should learn white ways. To that end, she was sent to Holy Rosary Mission School, which accepted both non-orphans and orphans. During the times Isabel's grandparents were away performing in a dance troupe with a Wild West show, she lived at the mission. In her grandfather's eyes, the mission provided both an education for his granddaughter and a home away from home when the grandparents were absent. By the 1930s and the years of the Great Depression, an increasing number of Indian families sought out mission and boarding schools for their children. They considered these as options for the same reasons that non-Indians turned to orphanages.[43]

Institutions for children were not of one type. Some were publicly supported with tax moneys. With little expended for daily upkeep of children or for their education, these institutions often had the worst reputations for shoddy conditions and questionable employee qualifications. More prevalent were privately funded asylums that were supported by religious groups, local churches, nondenominational organizations, or philanthropists. These privately run asylums varied widely in quality, and some were no better than their public counterparts. In the public mind there was an image of the "bad" orphanage that simply warehoused children or replicated the workhouse described in Charles Dickens's *Oliver Twist*. At the other end of the spectrum was the "good" institution that tried to meet children's physical, spiritual, and educational needs. The good orphanage provided sanitary surroundings, a bed, food, and religious and secular education. Trained, responsible staff were on hand or, as in the case of doctors, available when needed. Children had educational and social opportunities that would not have been available if they remained outside the institution.[44]

Private orphanages did not, however, always serve an entire population. A few took in children of all racial, ethnic, and religious backgrounds., but most were in some way restrictive. Jewish charities ran their own Hebrew orphan asylums and, within that realm, sometimes imposed more restrictions by separating German Jews from those of eastern Europe or by forcing the Russian or Polish Jew to assimilate into the German culture. Catholic and Protestant charities also focused on their respective congregations, but it was not always a congenial arrangement. More interested in proselytizing than in recognizing a child's religious heritage, both Catholics and Protestants took in children of other backgrounds and then sniped at one another with accusations of religious interference. Promises to the contrary, both generally ignored a child's religious heritage, seeking instead to instill their own beliefs. As one example, the New York Foundling Hospital, a well-respected and well-run Catholic charity, did not question the religion of a mother who gave birth in the hospital or that of destitute parents who brought a child to the charity. Said one woman, almost eighty years after her placement in the Foundling Hospital: "I went in Jewish. I came out Catholic."[45]

Race, nationality, and sex often defined orphanage populations. As an illustration, among Philadelphia's child institutions was the Home for Destitute Colored Children; Indianapolis had the Colored Orphan Asylum and the German Protestant Orphan Asylum; and in Rochester, New York, was St. Mary's Male Orphan Asylum.[46] These were just a few of the many institutions that served a specific population. Undoubtedly race played a role in segregating black from white children, and asylums for a specific national group or gender were designed to separate children into definable populations. Victorian fears of promiscuity and sexual temptations contributed to male- or female-only institutions. Many also thought it easier to manage a specific population, rather than one with both sexes or multiple racial and/or ethnic heritages.

Separation and segregation also were found in orphanages for Indians. The first Indian orphanages to appear in the 1800s were intended to serve a specific tribe, such as the Cherokees or the Senecas. Unlike a number of Indian boarding schools that congregated youngsters of many tribes in one place, Indian orphanages of the nineteenth century maintained an environment in which children shared a common tribal background. Sometimes there was separation along the lines of gender, although that was not an overall characteristic of Indian orphanages. For one tribe, the Creek, there was also segregation along racial lines; one orphanage served Creek children, and another was for children who were descended from the Creeks' African slaves and/or children who were of mixed Creek and African heritage. Living among children of their own tribal backgrounds or ethnic mix, residents of Indian orphanages were segregated from Indian children not of their tribe as well as from Euro-American children.

In the eyes of most who directed and financed orphanages for a specific group, segregation was desirable. It assured a single, homogeneous population. For this reason, there was a proliferation of urban institutions and charities that did not intend to aid every ethnic, racial, or religious group. All orphanages were not meant for all children. Certainly, Protestant and Catholic institutions played tug-of-war in the game of "rescuing" children and placing them in their respective orphanages. Jewish orphanages existed to care for children of that religion and to keep them out of Protestant and Catholic institutions.

Segregation on the basis of religion was an important factor, but certainly not the only one that determined the composition of a population. For a number of institutions, language and customs were just as important as religion, if not inseparable from it. Some orphanages such as the German Protestant charity in Indiana tried to retain some remnants of old-world heritage against the tide of Americanization. Homogeneous populations shared common ethnic, religious, and/or racial backgrounds. There were understood customs, language, and traditions.

Orphanages often were fenced or walled, suggesting to the casual observer that these segregated the inmates from the surrounding community. For many institutions, walls and fences were defensive. They kept the rest of the world out. Inside these islands of common language or religion or customs, mainstream culture had less opportunity to intrude and dilute traditions. These institutions were able to function in this way because those in charge were of the same religion and heritage as the children taken into the asylum. To some degree this was also true for a number of Indian orphanages where tribal involvement was high, all resident children were of the same tribe, and at least some of the staff were of the same Indian group. This, of course, did not exclude the influence of white civilization, but it created an atmosphere in which ties to tribal identity were not completely severed.

Orphanages in the United States were not carbon copies of one another in size, population served, or financial support. Nor were they all intent on housing children and adolescents until they reached the age of majority. Some offered what they hoped was only temporary shelter. Several charities operated on the principle that housing was short-term, until children could be reunited with parents or placed with a nonrelated family. Sometimes home placement was through indenture, a procedure recognized by state statutes that legally bound a child to an adult for a specific period. Indenture took many forms. Sometimes a youngster was indentured to learn a specific trade, such as carpentry, but often the indenture made the child a simple laborer who worked at the whim of his "employer." Charities also placed out children through adoption when it was allowed by state law. Many placed children in homes through what would be described today as foster care.

The Boston-based New England Home for Little Wanderers used every means at its disposal to make institutionalization a temporary period in a child's life. The charity was committed to the belief that home life was preferable to institutional care, and it sought home placement whenever possible. Placement could be through indenture, adoption (since Massachusetts allowed it under state law), and the relocation plan that became known as the orphan trains, which moved children out of urban environments to rural ones. Other charities, such as the New York Children's Aid Society and the New York Foundling Hospital, also believed in home over institutional life and used a variety of placement methods, including the orphan trains. These two New York institutions and their Boston counterpart displayed a willingness to come to the aid of children from all backgrounds, although the Children's Aid Society was somewhat restrained in its enthusiasm for children and teenagers who were not of western European background. Nevertheless, these philanthropic organizations largely ignored social, racial, and religious prejudices of the times and opened their doors to all.[47]

By the end of the 1800s, children under the care of the New England Home for Little Wanderers represented all religions and most of the immigrant groups from Europe. Also counted among those receiving aid were a number of Indian children from northeastern tribes. The Boston charity was not the first to take in Indian children; nor was it the last. In the early twentieth century the Graham Home, which evolved from the Orphan Asylum Society of New York, admitted Tuscarora Indian children.[48] Obviously, these institutions were not for Indians only. They attempted to serve children and adolescents of many backgrounds, and tribal children became part of a larger, mixed population.

The orphanage, that nineteenth-century institution that in one way or another touched the lives of children from every racial, ethnic, or religious group, first appeared on Indian reservations in the mid-1800s. Although these orphan asylums for Indian children shared similarities with other orphanages, they were exclusively for Indian children and adolescents. They were not, however, found on every reservation or established en masse. In other words, the Bureau of Indian Affairs or religious missions to Indians did not mount an orphanage-building spree at a particular point in time. Nonetheless, orphan asylums appeared, and their presence was a singular indicator of what was happening on a larger scale. The Indian orphanage signaled that an entire culture, made up of diverse tribal societies spanning geographic and territorial boundaries, was losing its battle against a multitude of outside forces to sustain inner life and identity. Orphanages were meant to be beacons of refuge. They were idealized as symbols of benevolent intentions. Those for Indian children were also something else. They were visible testimonials to massive social, economic, and political disintegration within American Indian culture—a culture that had never thought to shut its orphaned away in an institution.

Indian orphanages shared the basic goals of other orphanages—the good orphanages. Those in charge sought to rescue the homeless and save children from the ravages of poverty. They sought to protect the defenseless against life-threatening circumstances and from those who preyed upon the innocent. Unquestionably, child rescuers sought to impress upon children a sense of religion and to provide a basic education with a heavy emphasis on vocational training. In the best of all worlds, the institution was more than a place. It was "home." These were the ideals to which a good orphanage aspired. They were the ideals of Indian orphanages.

2

FIRST SOLUTION: SENECA

The institution is beautifully situated on a farm of 100 acres in the valley of the Cattaraugus Creek on the Cattaraugus Reservation.[1]

In September 1855 the cornerstone was laid for a building on the Cattaraugus Reservation in western New York State. Within one year the building was occupied and known as the Thomas Asylum for Orphan and Destitute Indian Children. In the years to come, the institution housed children and teenagers whose family names included Tallchief, Snow, Jemison, Skye, and Twoguns. The asylum provided youngsters with shelter, religious training, and classroom instruction. Children were provided with various forms of entertainment, recreation, and instruction in art and music. What happened inside the structure directed their lives. Missionaries and philanthropists responsible for the asylum hoped that when youngsters left the institution as young adults, they would influence their communities and elders with the ideas and belief systems learned in the orphanage. It was not by accident that the asylum was situated at a central point on reservation lands. It was intended as a beacon from which white culture would radiate.

Thomas Asylum was a sanctuary for youngsters who had little, if anything, outside the institution. In keeping with the ideals of what an orphanage should be, it was a refuge and a school. As such, it was operated by Euro-Americans who maintained that the fundamental goals for Indian education were conversion and acculturation. These remained constants in any discussion of Indian education, but to more fully understand this focus a broader view of American education must be taken into account.

An emphasis on assimilation and acculturation did not begin and end with education formulas for native groups. It was a key element in what became known as the "common school agenda," which concerned education for all in the United States. Central to the agenda was the belief that education was essential in creating a national identity. After all, in the nation's formative years, people regarded themselves as Virginians or Pennsylvanians or Kentuckians—not necessarily as Americans. If the young country was to survive and expand, nation-building required a cohesive sense of country and national loyalty. People of diverse backgrounds had to develop a shared set of attitudes and values. Reformers such as Horace Mann, who created the Massachusetts Board of Education and became its secretary in 1837, turned to the French Enlightenment for inspiration—much as framers of the American Constitution had done. Out of this borrowing emerged the idea of a secular, common school education, although religion and its lessons of morality were never far beyond the classroom door.

The common school agenda demanded basic language skills and literacy in English. Through a common language came assimilation and acculturation. As early as 1797 the agenda was articulated in essays by Presbyterian minister Samuel Knox and Samuel Harrison Smith, editor of the *National Intelligencer*. The American Philosophical Society in Philadelphia recognized both men for their work. Knox wrote that a national system of common school education would be a "harmonizing" influence for the nation. Smith was more forceful, stating that it was the "duty of a nation to superintend and even coerce the education of children." Their words gained importance when immigration increased in the 1830s and 1840s and the newly arrived, especially the impoverished Irish, were viewed as ignorant and lawless. Poverty and ignorance, warned Mann, could bring a developing country to its knees. Schools had to "purify the thick atmosphere of moral pollution." It became the nation's duty, as a measure of self-preservation, to assimilate and acculturate through education. This became an ongoing crusade. In the late 1850s, for example, the New York Children's Aid Society established night schools; the "Italian School" was for the moral and educational improvement "of the dark-eyed little musicians, male and female," who roamed New York's streets. Another school was "designed to keep the young German girls out of mischief and give them some useful instructions in the evenings." One wonders what sort of mischief German girls could produce to wreak havoc on the larger society. Nevertheless, poor and illiterate immigrants were considered a palpable threat—one warned against time after time. Immigration, wrote one social commentator in the early 1890s, "complicates our moral and political problems."

National identity simply could not develop under the weight of multiculturalism. It should be seriously asked, continued the writer, if "in-sweeping immigration is to foreignize us, or [if] we are to Americanize it?"[2]

It is one of America's myths, perpetuated by the common school agenda, that immigrants wished to become Americans as quickly as possible and to that end changed their names, abandoned ethnic customs, and pushed their children into English-only schools. Immigrants of the 1830s and 1840s were not necessarily so inclined. They did not rush en masse to wrap themselves in American culture. They were as likely to settle in rural areas as in cities, and in both settings they largely maintained their customs and languages through their own schools, newspapers, religious communities, and social organizations. Only with later waves of immigrants, particularly during the late 1800s, was there anything approaching widespread concession to the demands made by American public education. To make their children Americans, parents became more reluctant to teach their children the language and customs of their heritage. To achieve, youngsters often decided that whatever they had to endure in school was worth the price of an education.[3]

Immigrant contact with Euro-American education paralleled the Native American experience, although in reverse chronology. Early in the 1800s, Indian groups accepted, or at least accommodated, education aimed at assimilation and acculturation. As the century wore on, this attitude reversed. The boarding school experience was often so disruptive to cultural cohesiveness that some Indian groups became more skeptical and resistant while immigrants became more receptive to American education. Unlike the immigrant, the Indian by the last decades of the 1800s often experienced the trauma of having children wrenched away, sometimes under military force, to be sent to distant boarding schools. Despite the divergent responses between immigrant and Indian groups to Euro-American education, the educational experiences of immigrant and Indian children bore striking similarities. Youngsters were punished for not speaking English, and many were taunted, even abused, by teachers or classmates for having accents. Names were changed by teachers. Both Indians and immigrants were belittled for their preferences in food and for the way they dressed. Both groups were targeted by the common school agenda, which intended to instill a dominant culture perspective.

Thus, when missionaries, secular educators, and government officials became involved in Indian education, the desire to erase Indianness was not a singular plan. Turning Indians away from their religious beliefs and customs was fueled by a movement that firmly believed in education as a tool for forging a national identity that inculcated patriotism and shared expectations. It was the means through which social unrest could be subdued. In the common school plan there was no room for diversity, multiple languages, or ethnic customs. National identity had but one name, "American." Certainly, while many aspects of education in government-supported Indian schools were debated, the heart of the common school plan was never in question. Agreements for Indian contract schools supported by the government made that abundantly clear: "To instruct pupils as to the duties and privileges of American citizenship, explaining to them the fundamental principles of the Government, and to train them in such a knowledge and appreciation of our common country as will inspire them with a wholesome love of it."[4]

On that September day in 1855 when the Thomas Asylum officially came into being, there was an air of optimism. The institution, in the heart of the reservation, promised to meet the needs of children. It also promised a continuing missionary presence and the introduction of Euro-American education among the Indian nations that made up the Iroquois confederation—the Mohawk, Oneida, Onondaga, Cayuga, Tuscarora, and Seneca. After all, the groups had a long history of contact with Euro-American missionaries. French Jesuits came among the Senecas in 1657, and their later expulsion, for political interference, not religious conversion, hardly dampened the admittance of other religious groups into Indian communities. In the early decades of the 1800s, Tuscaroras, who had been driven out of North Carolina and accepted by the Iroquois confederacy in about 1723, converted to Christianity at a rapid pace. So did the Oneidas. Among the Senecas, Quakers and Presbyterians began to dominate the religious scene, and in 1829 portions of the New Testament were printed in the Seneca language.[5]

There was every reason to believe that the asylum would continue to provide an arena for teaching the tenets of Christianity. At the same time, the asylum was a physical manifestation of Christian charity and the missionary belief that one was obligated to work among non-Christian peoples of the world to convert them to the Bible's message of salvation and a heavenly afterlife. Conditioned by their own culture and background, those responsible for the asylum failed to realize that the institution was a significant marker in the history of Indian-white relations. True, it was a school on a reservation, but it was not just a school. It served a defined child population—the orphaned and destitute. Although those responsible for financing and building the asylum did not acknowledge it, this was the first Indian-only orphanage in the United States or its territories.

For the Senecas, the asylum represented a pivotal and painful realization. It was a visible admission that Indian culture was failing in the care and upbringing of its most vulnerable citizens. One could no longer translate the mythical salvation of the orphan, as in the story of the girl and the Great Horned Serpent, into a meaningful lesson. The hard realities brought about by a number of interrelated factors meant a loss of behavioral systems as the Senecas made the transition to reservation life and exchanged large clan networks for a smaller circle within a nuclear family. When kinship customs could not be acted upon or sustained, the Euro-American definition of an orphan overtook Seneca society.

The Society of Friends, the Quakers, was instrumental in establishing the Thomas Asylum, but this was not the religious group's first contact with the Senecas. The Quakers were longtime observers of, and participants in, the lives of those that made up the Iroquois confederacy. The Quakers had long advocated policies of peace, friendship, and aid. In the late 1700s, at approximately the same time that the confederacy began to disintegrate, Pennsylvania Quakers formed a committee to send technical aid to a large number of tribes in the eastern United States. The Quakers provided implements and teachers to demonstrate the use of these tools in agriculture and the manual arts; for the Iroquois, the latter included missionary-influenced departure from the traditional forms of basket making to designs more suited to European tastes. The Quakers further involved themselves by acting as guardians of Indian interests at a number of treaty signings. In that capacity, Quakers observed the Seneca agreement to the Canandaigua Treaty of 1794, which guaranteed Indian lands in western New York State but did not return all territory lost by treaty in 1788. Too, a few young men, including the son of Seneca leader Cornplanter, began to attend Quaker-run schools in Pennsylvania. This broke with the Senecas' refusal dating back fifty years to allow some of their young men to go to Virginia, where they would be instructed in the "same manner" as white children.[6]

Four years after the Canandaigua Treaty, the Society of Friends took an important step in its relationship with the Senecas. Rather than waiting for Indian students to come to them, the Quakers went to the Indian. A school was opened on Seneca land during the winter of 1798–99. Never successful, it struggled along for ten years with irregular attendance and a student enrollment that never rose above twenty. Finally, the school closed. As unremarkable in reaching the native group was another school established in 1822. Education could only be described as the most rudimentary, and it is doubtful that any real learning or transmission of culture occurred. Tribal leaders and representatives who met with European, Canadian, and American leaders knew English and/or French, but the average adult and child spoke only their native language. For their part, teachers were not skilled linguists. The language barrier was compounded when missionaries met resistance. In the face of a changing political and social climate, some Senecas clung to their ancient customs and beliefs, opposing adaptation or accommodation.[7]

To increase the prospect of success, the Quakers focused on the education of a few young men away from their homes. These Senecas traveled to Philadelphia, where they lived with Quaker families while attending school. It was not unlike the outing system used during the nineteenth century by such large boarding schools as Carlisle, established in 1879, or by smaller institutions such as the boarding schools operated by the Board of Mennonite Missions. Two of the Mennonite missions were in Indian Territory; the other was the Halstead Indian Industrial School in Kansas, which was funded in part by the federal government as a contract school. Although these were Mennonite institutions, there was a Quaker connection. The Society of Friends encouraged Mennonites in Indian Territory and Kansas to spread a "gospel net" over the Cheyennes and Arapahos. Through such missionary work and outing programs, Indian students left their own people. Some of those at Halstead remained and took Mennonite family surnames. In both Quaker and Mennonite programs, youngsters were exposed to life in white homes; taught English (although in the Halstead case the language was most likely German, since the Mennonites did not readily accept mainstream acculturation); and taught standard educational subjects, agriculture, and vocational skills.[8]

The number of Senecas sent to live among the Quakers was small. The relatively few to receive an education away from home were a disappointment to the Quakers, who regarded themselves as protectors of Indian interests. From the Quaker viewpoint, it was essential that Indians learn the ways of the dominant culture. Oral tradition could not compete with the abilities to read and write in English. The Quakers believed that it was a practical case of survival in a world that was slowly reducing the tribal land base and destroying economic and political independence. By the late 1700s, the reservation system was in place with four primary land areas—Tonawanda, Cattaraugus, Buffalo Creek, and Allegany. One historian characterized these reservations as "slums in the wilderness . . . where no traditional Indian culture could long survive."[9] The Quakers were firsthand observers. When age-old formulas for maintaining extended households, solving marital problems, and addressing grievances no longer served, something had to fill the void.

Traditionally, clans were divided into matrilineages that controlled land and offices of authority. Women were included in councils and expected to offer advice in matters of importance rather than hover in the background and follow the male lead. In fact, reluctance to exert authority would have been disastrous in a culture where men were gone for months, even years, to engage in hunting, warfare, or diplomatic missions to other tribes. In the early descriptions of Iroquois life set down by Jesuit missionaries and French explorers, there was disagreement regarding women's roles. Some said that while women had places of authority, these were only honorary. At the other end of the spectrum was Joseph Lafitau, who wrote perhaps the most detailed descriptions of Iroquois life in 1724. Lafitau could not emphasize enough the importance of women: "There is nothing more real than this superiority of the women. It is they who constitute the tribe, keep up the genealogical tree and the order of inheritance, and perpetuate the family. . . . the children belong to them." However much Iroquois culture changed over two centuries, accounts left by Henry R. Schoolcraft and Lewis Henry Morgan influenced late-nineteenth-century feminists. Both Elizabeth Cady Stanton and Matilda Jocelyn Gage, for example, believed that the Iroquois of the past exhibited a model of female equality.[10]

By the 1840s the Iroquois way of life was under siege. The Iroquois had once ranged over millions of acres, but reservation boundaries restricted men from far-flung travels and redefined male and female roles. Arguably, reservation life demanded more adaptation from males than females. Women could fulfill their roles as wives and mothers, but men were less able to act out their preparations to be warriors or hunters, statesmen or religious leaders. Nevertheless, women were affected, too. Traditionally, they owned the land and the fields that they cultivated. The harvests were their harvests. Reservation life upended accepted gender roles that dictated who worked and owned the land. Women lost a basis for their power, and men lost their traditional roles. The consequences were readily apparent to the Quakers, who continued to encourage male education while giving a new emphasis to female schooling. As part of its mission to aid the Senecas in their transition to reservation life, the Society of Friends returned to reservation lands in the 1840s and organized a boarding school for girls. Results, however, were as lackluster as in the Quakers' earlier attempts at reservation schools. The girls' school had a brief and unproductive life.[11]

The Quakers were more successful when a Presbyterian minister, the Reverend Asher Wright, and his wife, Laura, arrived on the scene. They began their mission work in 1831 on the Buffalo Creek Reservation, where the United Foreign Missionary Society had established a church as early as 1823. The Wrights made a concerted effort to learn the language, and in time Wright translated the New Testament into Seneca.[12]

In 1845 the Wrights left Buffalo Creek, not out of choice but because it appeared that the land would go to the Ogden Land Company through a fraudulent treaty signed in 1838 and renegotiated in 1842. It was a turbulent and unsettling period that capped over a decade of dispossession. The Iroquois, already fragmented by population movements to Canadian reservations and earlier alliances with the French, British, or U.S. government, became further separated by dispossession of lands in the United States. In 1831 the Sandusky Senecas sold their reservation and moved to a reserve in Indian Territory, placing some Cayugas and Senecas far from their traditional moorings. In the same period, Eleazer Williams, a Mohawk who became an Episcopal minister, persuaded most of the Oneidas to sell their New York lands and relocate in Wisconsin. Later, in 1848, a small number of Senecas went to Kansas to settle on a promised reserve. They quickly regretted the decision. The open prairie was hardly comparable to forested New York. Kansas was deemed "unhealthy." Twenty-six of the sixty-six Senecas died. Of the survivors, all but two returned to New York. Dispersion of Iroquois, as well as the controversial Buffalo Creek land sale, contributed to a situation in which the formerly self-sufficient and great Iroquois groups were embattled on all fronts and fighting to maintain their sovereignty.[13]

Most of those living on Buffalo Creek vacated the land in 1845 and moved to the Cattaraugus reserve. A number of Senecas and Cayugas, however, left New York altogether and joined kin who earlier had gone to Indian Territory. Not all willingly vacated the land. The Tonawanda Senecas, faced with relocation to Kansas, refused and took legal action. The case went to the U.S. Supreme Court, but a settlement was reached before arguments began. In turn, Tonawanda Senecas used money set aside for their prospective removal to Kansas and purchased back seventy-five hundred acres from the Ogden Land Company. The arrangement was settled in 1857.[14]

Amid the uncertainty of land rights and relocation, the Wrights settled on the Cattaraugus Reservation where they worked for almost ten years before the pivotal summer of 1854. Events leading to creation of Thomas Asylum were set in motion with a singular event—the death of a man. The result was a larger crusade than the Wrights had planned or envisioned. As Laura Wright later recalled, when the man died, he left "a large family of children in extreme want. It was soon ascertained that on this Reservation alone, not less than fifty were in circumstances of great destitution and suffering."[15] There was a pressing need to care for these children. The remedy seemed to be an institution to house the orphaned and destitute. Clearly, the Wrights did not consider the possibility that these children would be cared for by clan or extended family. There were still family groups that followed the old ways, but with each passing year life was more disrupted.

The tribes of the Iroquois had been able to maintain traditional ways of life for decades after contact with Jesuit priests and Protestant missionaries and with English, French, and American military forces and governments. Religious observances, gender roles, and familial connections generally remained intact. This began to dissolve under years of strain and in the face of political and military intrigue with foreign governments, attempts to appease the Americans and their newly formed government, and internal disputes. One tribal voice did not speak for all. There were factional splits and outright animosity, and fighting broke out between tribal divisions and clans. It was impossible to reconcile any number of intertribal controversies. Disputes erupted over land cessions, relations with Indian groups to the west, adoption of white customs, and religion (including that of the Seneca prophet Handsome Lake, who combined some elements of Christianity with ancient tradition).

Men died fighting beside French or British or U.S. soldiers during the Revolutionary War, the War of 1812, and the French and Indian War. They died fighting each other, too. Women and children died. Internal and external warfare, famine, and epidemics took their toll. At the same time, the economic base of combined hunting and agriculture shrank in direct correlation to confinement on reservations. Some built sawmills to supply wood to whites, but these did not make up for the disruption in basic economic independence. Then, there was alcohol. Despite the original Trade and Intercourse Acts of the 1790s that outlawed or limited alcohol exchange in the fur trade, liquor remained a primary token of barter. Waterways that were highways to commerce and trade were also gateways to importation of alcohol. Handsome Lake, who had battled his own taste for alcohol, described the scene following a 1798 trading expedition: "Now that the party is home the men revel in strong drink and are very quarrelsome. Because of this the families become frightened and move away for safety." White merchants did not look to the effects of alcohol, only the business potential. A number petitioned the New York legislature to lift bans that prohibited selling liquor to Indians. There was a ready market on the reservations, and as one historian noted, the Indians "preferred not to drink alone but in large convivial groups." After a night of cavorting, "sodden households woke sometimes to find a member dead, or cut in a brawl, or frozen in the snow outside."[16]

Asher Wright was familiar with the events that swirled around the people he had come to convert. Dispossession, warfare, and disease, including the 1847 typhoid fever epidemic that killed at least seventy, dulled a sense of community and family. One result was destitute and orphaned children. Wright certainly came into contact with these children. In one instance, he penned a brief account of an orphan girl who, as she was dying, asked to be buried beside her mother. Wright could meet that simple request, but he and his wife saw no way to guarantee care for the fifty or so children they identified as needing help in the summer of 1854 unless, of course, they explored the idea

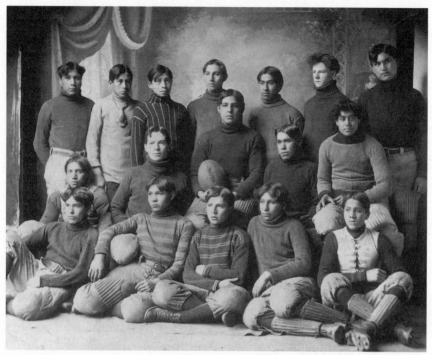

The 1902 football team at Thomas Indian School, established in 1855 in western New York State as the Thomas Asylum for Orphan and Destitute Indian Children. New York State Archives.

of founding an orphan asylum. Given the time period and the growing popularity of orphanages as institutions of child rescue, it seemed an acceptable—if not modern and forward-thinking—choice. For help they turned to the Quakers because of their long association with the Senecas. The Wrights contacted Philip Evan Thomas, who was a Quaker, a successful banker and merchant, and the first president of the Baltimore and Ohio Railroad. Thomas had a keen interest in the Society of Friends' earlier endeavors among the Senecas and visited the Cattaraugus Reservation on several occasions. According to Mrs. Wright, Thomas responded as they hoped. He first dealt with the immediate situation by asking that "a few of the most destitute children be collected and sustained through the approaching winter at his expense." The Wrights took ten children into their household while Thomas and the Society of Friends planned for a long-term solution.[17]

The needs of the Seneca children galvanized Thomas, the Quakers, and the Wrights. They set out to raise funds for a permanent child asylum. The Senecas responded by giving a piece of land for the purpose, and the Wrights appealed to the New York legislature for funds. The governmental body could have denied the request; instead, it appropriated $2,000 for the Thomas Asylum for Orphan and Destitute Indian Children. Thus, "a work growing out of the missionary labor among the Indians . . . [and] one which strongly appeals to the sympathy of the Benevolent, and based on the principle of justice, was begun."[18] The asylum was incorporated as a private but state-aided institution. From its inception, it represented a cooperative effort between the Senecas, a religious group, a philanthropist, and the State of New York.

The loss of the Buffalo Creek Reservation and the aftermath of removal and factional conflicts among the Iroquois sparked the series of events that led to the founding of the Thomas Asylum. The need for the institution was reinforced by the American Civil War, which reached into every niche of life. Casualties of the war could be counted in terms of those left dead on battlefields or maimed, but noncombatant casualties were more difficult to assess. Nevertheless, the cost of war was marked in a number of ways. During the war, eastern cities witnessed a staggering rise in child vagrancy when children simply had no place to go. Fathers were gone to fight or dead from battle or from disease that spread unabated through camps. Mothers, barely able to support themselves or their children, were forced into low-paying jobs. Many turned to prostitution and theft. A startling number, "the mothers, wives, and daughters of men . . . with the armies of the Union," wound up imprisoned. Considering the number of abandoned, destitute, and orphaned children, it was hardly surprising that as many orphanages were founded immediately after the war as had been established during the two previous decades.[19]

Just as Iroquois warriors had fought in earlier American conflicts, they participated in the Civil War. Military service offered men an escape from the confinements of reservation life. It provided an outlet for combat, which by custom was a means through which males gained influence and status among their people. Loyalty to the Union cause was not necessarily the first or only reason to join cavalry and infantry units. Although New York State first refused enlistment on the grounds that Indians were not citizens, it relented in the face of early Union losses. By the end of the war, men of the Iroquois tribes were enlisted in units from New York, Wisconsin, Pennsylvania, and other northeastern states. (Best known of the Iroquois fighters was Ely Samuel Parker, who became an aide to Gen. Ulysses Grant and later Grant-appointed commissioner of Indian affairs.)[20]

One can point to any number of critical events that shaped life for the Iroquois, but the Civil War was a defining point in a cultural transition that determined who would care for the orphaned and the poor. Far away from military engagements and battles, those left behind felt war's fury. Widows and orphans grew in number as men died in battle, from disease, and as prisoners of war. In one example, a Seneca private, William Kennedy, died far from home in the horrors that were the Confederacy's infamous Andersonville prison. Then, there were those who survived but returned home less than whole. Veterans had been ravaged by disease or lost limbs and suffered psychologically from their personal experiences. In the postwar period, both veterans and reservation families became more dependent on outside aid rather than family help. The extensive clan and family ties that once ensured care diminished under the weight of war's impact. People were less willing to look after anyone who was not a close relative. Fading into distant history was the belief that happiness in the spirit world waited for women who raised large families or for childless women who cared for orphans. Postwar conditions did not draw people closer together. Pressure increased for additional relinquishment of Indian land, and those who tried to get by on subsistence farming found it more difficult to survive within a market economy that moved toward supply-and-demand production. Each factor in itself had the potential for creating parentless and/or destitute children. Combined with the price paid for military service, the possibility became fact.[21]

Thomas became a necessity, as well as a part of reservation life. Youngsters, in and out of Thomas, referred to it as "salem," a word that evolved from "asylum." In 1875 the public-private relationship ended, and the asylum became a state institution under the direction of the New York State Board of Charities. Thomas was, after all, a home for the orphaned and destitute and, as such, a charitable institution. A history that briefly noted the asylum simply stated that the change resulted from the efforts of William Letchworth, director of the state board of charities, and Asher Wright, by then in his seventies. There were, however, forces at work other than the two men's "personal appeal." In 1875 the State of New York passed the Children's Law, a sweeping piece of legislation that increased state powers over local authorities in determining placement of destitute and orphaned children. The law required that all children between the ages of two and sixteen who were incarcerated in county poorhouses (also called poor farms or almshouses) be transferred to institutions exclusively for children and adolescents. The law's intent was to remove minors from the poorhouse environment where they were shut away with adults. Although most children resided in poorhouses because their parents were there, the 1875 law separated children from adults no matter their relationship.[22]

There is no evidence that Indian children were cloistered in poorhouses, with or without relatives. Nevertheless, the law had its effect on the native population. The legislation expanded state intervention into the lives of poverty-stricken Indian families. By theorizing that these families, if they lived off the reservation, were likely candidates for the poorhouse, the state made the children prospective Thomas inmates. Theory became reality when the state legislature in 1894 stipulated that indigent Indians could be committed to county poorhouses. By legislative act, money was provided to each county to care for "all poor Indians who are so disabled that they can not maintain themselves." Local authorities were directed to seek out these unfortunates and place them in the local facility. Upon entering the institution, the Indians, adults and children, were "subject to the supervision of the State board of charities."[23]

The Bureau of Indian Affairs, created in 1824 and variously known as the Indian Office, the Indian Department, and the Indian Bureau, was not involved with the asylum's creation or funding. If the state had anything to say about it, it never would. New York argued that Indians within its borders were under state jurisdiction, and it went so far as to try to tax Indian lands (an attempt that was struck down by the U.S. Supreme Court). Undaunted, the state held to its basic argument that U.S. laws concerning Indian relations did not apply to those states that had been among the original thirteen colonies. Following that reasoning, the State of New York in 1875 ensured that at least one federal agency would be limited in its power over the Indian population. It did not seek federal money but instead took full responsibility for operating Thomas Asylum. This was a thorn in the side of the Indian Bureau. John Oberly, who served as superintendent of Indian schools before becoming commissioner of Indian affairs, reported in 1885 that, of all the schools under the Indian Bureau, only those belonging to the Five Civilized Tribes in Indian Territory and those in New York State were beyond the agency's control. Indian schools in New York, with the exception of the small and "most excellent" Quaker-run industrial school on the Allegany Reservation, were state supported. Therefore, although the federal bureau had an Indian agent in New York, Thomas officials were not obligated to report on the physical condition of buildings, student enrollment, or curriculum. It galled Oberly, who concluded his report with the thought "that school reports should be required of them is a proposition which admits no doubt."[24]

Oberly was not the only one to complain. Catholic missionaries were feeling left out, too. Through the work of Jesuit missionaries, the Catholic Church had a long association with tribes in New York. Over time, however, religious orders and missionaries were eclipsed by non-Catholic groups, and Catholics were relegated to a second-class position in their attempts to open schools on the reservations. Establishing churches was as much a problem. Of the six reservations in New York State, only St. Regis on the Canadian border had a Catholic church by the end of the nineteenth century. Frustrated, the Bureau of Catholic Indian Missions took to diatribes. The bureau's publication, *The Indian Sentinel*, became the mouthpiece for condemning the Indians of New York who lived without any Catholic influences. One *Sentinel* article declared that these Indians were the "most thriftless, most drunken, and most immoral Indians in the country."[25] How different things would have been if the Catholic Church dominated. Said a leader of the Board of Catholic Indian Missions in 1906:

> Not very long ago I visited the Cattaraugus Reservation in New York—a reservation in the heart of civilization, surrounded by churches and schools—a reservation that has within it a couple of white towns built on leased land, one of them the large town of Salamanca—a reservation invaded by railroads and trolley cars—yet the Indians of the reservation are pretty much as they were fifty years ago; their language is quite prevalent; the majority of the people are still pagans.[26]

In the 1880s it was estimated that within the continental United States there were approximately thirty-eight thousand Indian children between the ages of six and sixteen. Of this number, about eighty-five hundred were in boarding schools, and almost five thousand attended day schools. These numbers, however, did not account for Indian children in New York State or children of the Five Civilized Tribes in Indian Territory. The Indian Bureau lacked control over institutions in those areas and had limited information on day schools, boarding schools, and orphanages.[27] In fact, when the Indian Bureau noticed orphanages at all, it was in the context of boarding schools. In his 1885 school superintendent's report, Oberly provided an outline of "Boarding-Schools on Reservations." There were basically four types of schools that received part or all of their funding from the federal government: the agency, the contract, mission, and independent. The agency school was government supported, with the Indian agent for the particular agency in charge and responsible for reports to the Indian Bureau; often the agent was referred to as the superintendent, although there was a school superintendent or principal in place for daily operations. The contract schools received money from the government to support a number of students, but usually not all of them. In these instances, the individual or the mission board operating the school had to have another source of revenue to adequately maintain the buildings, buy supplies, and pay staff. Contract schools could encompass mission schools run by denominational groups, as well as independent schools operated by persons not affiliated with any mission board. The reservation boarding schools itemized by Oberly were not to be confused with federally supported off-reservation boarding schools or the independent or mission schools that functioned without federal contracts. If anything, several types of schools operating simultaneously on the same Indian reservation explained why commissioners of Indian affairs such as Thomas Morgan favored disbanding the contract system and why religious groups fought desperately to see that they were not overlooked when contracts were awarded. It also explains why orphanages were not categorized as a separate type of institution. Officially, the orphanage was the same as a boarding school.[28]

The Thomas Asylum and the orphanages that operated in Indian Territory under the Cherokee, Choctaw, Chickasaw, and Creek tribal governments presented unique situations. New York State held firm control over the Seneca orphanage. In Indian Territory, the tribes set up their own school systems, which included orphanages. In both the New York and Indian Territory systems, the federal government was left out of the equation. Governmental officials had to rely on Indian agents, whose reports were often unenlightening. Generalizations failed to note the numbers of students or staff, the subjects taught and textbooks used, the level of vocational instruction, or the presence of clergy. For example, in 1897 the New York agent wrote of the Thomas Asylum: "Extensive improvements have recently been made and more are contemplated in and about the asylum, for which special appropriations have been made by the legislature of the State of New York. The superintendent, Mr. George I. Lincoln, has proved to be an efficient manager of the asylum and farm, and his wife a very competent matron." Exact numbers of students and details about school curriculum and living conditions were left to the imagination.[29]

The point that the complaining Oberly either missed or failed to acknowledge was that the State of New York demanded as much, if not more, from Thomas as did the federal agency in terms of healthy environment and classroom instruction for most of its sponsored schools. In no way did Thomas parallel the conditions described by a newly arrived superintendent at the federally supported Leech Lake Boarding School on the White Earth Reservation in Minnesota. Shock reverberated from the pages of that superintendent's 1892 report. Buildings were in shoddy condition; children were sleeping without sheets or pillows; and provisions were so scarce that Leech Lake pupils were subsisting on potatoes from the school garden, pork and beans, and flour meant to be used for bread. Whether bread baking actually occurred was another matter. There were so few eating utensils that children used "their fingers for forks." In the classrooms there were only a few "torn pieces" of textbooks.[30] Such conditions were unheard of at Thomas, and when instances of inadequately equipped orphanages occurred in Indian Territory, they were never on the scale described by the Leech Lake superintendent. Through a consistent concern for youngsters and their environment, the institutions in both New York and Indian Territory provided a strong argument for nonfederal control of Indian institutions.

The orphanages in New York State and in Indian Territory began as small enclaves of child rescue. The same was true for many non-Indian orphanages. There was a homelike quality, with a few children overseen by one or two adults who, like the Wrights, had taken children into their households. Children had lessons in the parlor, shared meals around the family table, and performed chores that might be expected of any child. In such a domestic setting and close quarters, it was easy for adults to behave as parents rather than as detached caretakers or disciplinarians. Conversely, it created an atmosphere in which children responded as members of a family.

Few orphanages of any type were able to maintain this homey atmosphere when they increased in physical size and added personnel. More buildings for dormitories and classrooms expanded capacity. In rural areas, orphanage grounds took on the appearance of self-contained farm complexes, since livestock, crops, dairy products, and garden produce supplemented institutions' incomes and served as a basic food source for the residents. When child populations increased, the family atmosphere diminished or disappeared altogether. Large numbers of children congregated in one place required additional staff, and more children meant more regulations. To keep order, strict rules were enacted. Orphan asylums of all types—not just those for Indian children—often took on a military air. One critic of orphanages in general pictured them as places where residents were "regulated with mathematical precision, the child seldom seen apart from a line but moved in serried ranks, always marching." It was a case, observed one historian, of orphanages placing "a greater premium on order, discipline, and obedience, [than] on domestic affections."[31] Public rhetoric often presented adult authorities as heads of a large, hearty household. In actuality the child-parent relationship was greatly diluted or was nonexistent.

In 1876, a year after the New York State Board of Charities assumed all responsibility for Thomas Asylum, the institution housed ninety-seven children and adolescents: fifty-one males and forty-six females. The total was almost all the law allowed, since there was a limit on the number admitted. The state's budget called for payment of $100 per capita annually for one hundred inmates. The number suggests that any atmosphere of home and family life was diluted while the trappings of institutional life increased. A rising population made it difficult for children to receive individual attention or emotional support. That was undeniably true at institutions such as the Hudson County Almshouse in New Jersey, where two teachers were responsi-

The occasion for this Thomas Indian School photograph was identified only as "Group of Students in Costume." New York State Archives.

ble for over two hundred children. It was not the way of things at Thomas, where the number of adult supervisors and teachers kept pace with a rising number of residents. In 1855 the adult-to-child ratio at Thomas was about one adult per every seven children. In 1877, when the staff was at nine supervisors and teachers, the ratio was one to eleven. It was an acceptable number, particularly when compared with places like the New Jersey almshouse or, for that matter, public schools, where ratios could be as high as one to fifty.[32]

There were rules at Thomas, and there were punishments for those who failed to obey. Nevertheless, the institution did not shut youngsters away to live out a regimented and dreary existence until their day of release. The routine of classroom and chores was regularly broken by periods of entertainment and recreation. One former resident recalled a number of activities:

Another nice thing at T. I. S. [Thomas Indian School] was the sleigh rides. It gave us a chance to get away for a while, and it was fun. . . . I loved the horses and to hear the bells jingle. We had heavy bear rugs to keep us warm. If they took us in the afternoon,

we were given 25 cents or 50 cents to shop in Gowanda. We
bought things for ourselves and managed to spread the money out
so that we bought our relatives and friends a few presents. The
moonlight sleigh rides were fun also. We'd sing as we rode along.
When we got back to our building, hot chocolate and cookies
were waiting for us.[33]

Some "amusements" took place on the grounds, and others took
Thomas residents out into the Seneca community. Activities could be
as simple as singing songs around the piano, but entertainment also reflected whatever was new or popular at a particular point in time. The
exciting technological innovation of "moving pictures" invaded
Thomas, and just after World War I the institution purchased its own
projector, "a picture machine." Most of the films shown at Thomas
were educational, but the mere presence of a projector and films speaks
to the fact that Thomas brought America's popular culture into the institution. Not all entertainments had an educational bent, however.
Many were just for the sheer pleasure of enjoyment: an afternoon performance by a magician; Christmas and Easter parties; and socials that
often brought the surrounding community into the asylum. Maple
sugar parties were special events. "We had the maple sugar parties right
in the big kitchen. Both boys and girls stirred the syrup until it turned
into candy. The harder we stirred, the harder the candy got. Boy! That
was fun!" Class groups traveled to county fairs and "Indian fairs" on
the reservation. Children enjoyed picnics at Silver Creek. Unlike those
orphan asylums where the oppressive environment shunned anything
that might be considered frills, Thomas invited the outside world in
and, conversely, took children outside their everyday environment.[34]

Thomas fit the image of the "good" orphanage by adding a liberal
dose of recreation to students' lives. Other policies, however, were
much more in line with those of other institutions. Haircuts were routine, just as they were in Indian boarding schools, where haircuts were
often the first order of admission. The seemingly simple act was a
traumatic experience for innumerable Indian students, as well as a
symbolic gesture that they were being cut away from their people. A
Papago at the Phoenix Indian School recalled that the boys with "bald
heads were too ashamed to eat." A girl at another school remembered
that when her braids were cut "I lost my spirit." The practice at
Thomas was not described as a determined effort to drive out Indian-

ness. Haircuts were the norm in all institutions—reformatories, orphanages, and mental asylums—overseen by the state board of charities. They were also the norm in privately operated institutions. The
most patent reason, and a valid concern, was hygiene. Head lice was
a difficult problem to control in close quarters. Nevertheless, the psychological intent at Indian boarding schools cannot be overlooked.
Haircuts erased individuality and said in one snip what a thousand
words could not. Conformity was expected. Conformity also was con-
veyed through dress. Like many other institutions, Thomas insisted
on uniforms for the schoolroom; out of class, uniforms were shed in
favor of denim or cotton workclothes or clothing more appropriate for
the playground. All clothing was provided. Thomas did not request or
expect money from Indian annuities or special appropriations from
the federal government. State funds purchased fabric that could be
made into clothing on-site, and numerous items were acquired ready-
made from other institutions under New York State control. At nom-
inal cost, Thomas purchased items of clothing, including mittens,
shirts, and shoes, made by inmates of the New York State Reformatory, the New York State Training School for Boys, and the New York
State School for the Blind. State-supported institutions were intertwined. Goods produced from manual-labor instruction in one set of
institutions became functional items in another. It was a comple-
mentary arrangement.[35]

English, fundamental to the common school agenda and demanded
at federally supported Indian schools, was the language at Thomas. As
in other places, failure to comply met with punishment: "They tried
to do away with the Indian ways and our language by punishment."
Nevertheless, youngsters found ways to circumvent the rules. While
doing chores, they managed to "sneak conversations in Seneca with
other fellows." At times, they met in secret comradeship. "But we
used to speak our language down behind the Boy Scout cabin. There
was one gas well that was burning back there. Some of the girls at the
kitchen would sneak food to us or we'd swipe it ourselves. Then we'd
cook on that fire." More obvious to the adults, and something they
found impossible to control, was "Salem slang," which emerged from
a mixture of Indian and English. Some youngsters were more profi-
cient in slang than in English, and one former resident recalled that he
paid the price when looking for a job: "They [employers] told him to
learn how to talk English first."[36]

Religion was part and parcel of every child-based institution, and Thomas Asylum was no different. Founded out of missionary reaction to prevailing conditions, Thomas continued to offer the teachings of Christianity after the New York State Board of Charities assumed charge. Thomas, however, was not supervised by a man of the cloth after Asher Wright retired. No missionaries, ministers, or religious orders directed Thomas. Of course, this did not rule out religious instruction, since it was unimaginable that any institution responsible for children would exclude religion. At Thomas, however, religion did not overshadow secular education. There was time for prayer and Sunday school just as there was time to learn conjugation of verbs. On the Sabbath, ministers were called in to conduct services and direct Sunday schools. Quakers could be part of this religious training, but they did not have control. Ministers from a number of denominations served Thomas, and the state purchased Bibles, hymnals, and Sunday school supplies from the Presbyterian Board of Publication and Sabbath School Work. New York State counted these purchases as "educational expenses," no more or less important than buying the Taylor First Reader series or Natural Music Reader books or subscriptions to popular magazines such as *St. Nicholas* and *Youth's Companion*.[37]

To retain the idealized image of the orphanage as a place of refuge and learning, many Thomas superintendents and teachers preferred to label the orphaned and destitute simply as children, pupils, or students. The State of New York classified them differently. This was the case after the state took over the institution and, through the state's board of charities, was the primary entity to intervene in domestic situations and to determine which children were asylum candidates. Under state code, the children were designated as "inmates"—the same term applied to individuals placed in reformatories, mental asylums, or prisons. Children were assigned to the orphanage through "committal," a legal contract signed by the impoverished child's parents or the orphaned child's guardian. Thus, when youngsters traveled to or from Thomas, official reports itemized expenditures as "Transportation of Inmates." The state had its terminology; the asylum's personnel had theirs. Generally they ignored the inmate label and reported the "transportation of children" or the "expenses of children."[38]

The institution changed as resident numbers increased and the physical environment matured. A farm, established to support the institution, was in continual development. Its expansion was, in part, a result of the youngsters' labor. After all, this was part of their education. Classroom instruction went hand in hand with learning a vocation, which, in this scenario, focused on farming. Those in charge believed it only right that these youngsters contribute to their upkeep. Certainly the authorities did not wish for it to appear that these children were living at state expense without offering something in return. However, the Thomas Asylum did not adhere to the edict of "spartan frugality and severity" under which many orphanages operated.[39]

The institution worked for a measure of self-sufficiency, but it was never expected that the labor of its residents would keep the place going. A large cadre of cooks, laundresses, day laborers, and farmhands were employed. When youngsters worked on the farm or at indoor chores, the work was intended to teach skills and introduce a mindset that would serve them when they were adults. "They taught us animal husbandry right there on the farm. . . . There were poultry classes too." The boys learned to grade the eggs, an important skill if one planned to sell eggs at market; and "they also had a lot of pigs. We even had classes on how to slaughter them. . . . I never did like to slaughter them." While learning about agriculture, youngsters were exposed to the work ethic of white society. "I was there for seven to eight years. We used to get our assignments in the morning. If I had to work in the barn, I got up at 4:30 in the morning." Schedules, assignments, and responsibilities were important to the process. After all, "the Indian might have all the knowledge of the books, and he would remain a barbarian . . . [if not] taught to work."[40] Most white Americans agreed that outdoor life on a farm provided the best place to learn and to be exposed to white values of an "honest day's work."

Obviously, Thomas Asylum was in a rural setting because the reservation was rural. For a great many other institutions—private orphanages, reformatories, and state homes for children of non-Indian backgrounds—rural location was by choice, not dictated by circumstance. White Americans in the nineteenth century firmly believed that rural life was wholesome, built character, and was morally superior to the urban environment. Even city dwellers who would live nowhere else suggested that there was a "tendency of city life to corrupt [the] very young." Urban charities that did not have rural centers preached the benefits of country life. Some charities acted on this belief by transporting children to rural homes via the orphan trains, arguing that rural America could save urban children both physically and spiritually. The New York Children's Aid Society believed in the idea so strongly that it not only used the orphan trains but also established a farm school in rural New York to prepare boys for farmwork. The approach for other urban charities was different. A number sponsored Fresh Air programs, which sent children of the lower classes to rural camps or to live with farm families for a few weeks during summer months. Those in the business of child rescue and philanthropy celebrated the opportunities rural institutions offered: fresh air and the great outdoors were healthy; farm folks were full of honest values; work in gardens or the dairy offered life lessons. As one commentator forcefully declared, "They [children and teenagers] must be made to do for themselves. Opportunity and guidance, not charity, are required."[41] What better place to learn to do for oneself than in the country?

Thomas Asylum, as well as Indian orphanages that appeared in other areas, was ideally situated to play out the dominant culture's idealization of rural life. On a more realistic note, placement in a country setting also allowed propagation of the program to turn Indians into American farmers and housewives. For the time period, agriculture seemed the most viable occupation. Despite the rise in industrial manufacturing, the United States was still predominantly rural. National life rested its perceptions of American character on the idealized images of the stalwart farmer, the pioneer woman, the never-say-die homesteader. In the realm of social work, the importance of country life was stressed in any number of ways. Charity workers, including Charles Loring Brace of the New York Children's Aid Society, strongly argued that farm life was a powerful tool for assimilation. Within this forum that celebrated country living, Indian culture was meant to assimilate into the patterns of Euro-American rural life, not urban.

There was a paradox, however. Although Indian orphanages like Thomas were in the country, they were still on reservations. Children were not completely separated from their people or culture. Nor were they mingled with children from tribal groups outside New York. Not unlike orphanages for Jewish or German-speaking children, Indian orphanages, through their location and child populations, were insulated from a larger, more diverse world. When compared with the drastic culture shock experienced by youngsters sent to off-reservation schools, where they were separated by distance from their own people and where their Indian identities were stripped from them as quickly as possible, on-reservation Indian orphanages retained connections to tribal life by their very locations. At Thomas, this was reinforced when the staff included Indian teachers.

The duality of tribal life and an educational system that was Euro-American in content was not necessarily what those in charge intended. Thomas Asylum did not intend for young people to maintain their cultural heritage at the price of ignoring white mainstream ideas. Learning native culture was discouraged. Thomas residents were not meant to live as their ancestors had done. The institution was as dedicated as other forms of Indian education, on or off the reservation, to Americanize and acculturate. To a large degree it seemed to accomplish just that by implementing a curriculum that balanced classroom and vocational studies with recreation, art, music, and violin and piano lessons. When the institution expanded its admission policy in the last decades of the 1800s, it drew youngsters who were not orphaned or destitute but who were attracted by the range of subjects. Two non-orphans, for example, attended Thomas because "their mother wanted them to take music lessons." Vocational studies, too, were more varied than the stereotypical home economics and agriculture format found in non-Indian orphanages—or, for that matter, in government-supported Indian boarding schools. By the early 1900s, Thomas offered beautician and barber training and instruction in metalworking, carpentry, and typesetting. These offered options beyond farm life and added to the possibilities for earning a living after leaving Thomas.[42]

Thomas attempted to do much more under state direction than meet the federal government's expectations of civilizing native peoples through religion and agriculture. During the winter of 1903–4, for example, the institution adopted the kindergarten model for early childhood education. By introducing and developing this program, Thomas followed a growing national trend in education that would not be replicated in a federally supported orphan school for another ten years, when the Cherokee Orphan Training School began a kindergarten that, in its beginnings, left much to be desired. Reporting to the commissioner of Indian affairs, the superintendent at the Cherokee facility noted:

A large proportion of the enrollment is of small children, a great many of them coming to the school at ages of five to eight, in many cases with no knowledge whatever of English. To give these children a proper groundwork on which to build their education, I believe they should have at least a year of kindergarten work. Kindergarten materials have been furnished, and have been used to a certain extent in connection with the work of the primary teacher, but much more satisfactory results could be secured if a regular position of kindergartner should be established.[43]

Thomas had a kindergartner (a teacher for the garden of children) and a curriculum that emulated the early-learning program imported from Germany in the late 1800s. When the kindergarten movement was introduced to America, it was promoted as a form of education for "luckless children" of lower, not upper or middle, classes. It was education for the poor. Race and ethnicity were of little importance. The movement reached out first to those with the least. Kindergartens were expected to make up for family and community environments that placed little emphasis on formal learning. Kindergarten programs began as local attempts, but the movement gained wide attention with the 1893 World's Columbian Exposition in Chicago, where the Children's Building featured a kindergarten. Exposition visitors watched as trained teachers worked with children from Chicago's poorest neighborhoods. Kindergartens promoted early learning and, for non–English speakers, introduced the language of mainstream America. For the poor, the immigrant, and the orphaned, kindergartens promoted acculturation and complemented the common school agenda. Progressive orphanages embraced the concept, and Thomas made a concerted effort to be progressive.[44]

Over the years, Thomas Asylum changed in physical shape and appearance. Major renovations took place in the late 1800s, and in 1900 the institution was rebuilt. Additional portions of the farm were developed and fenced. While some of those living at the asylum were marginally involved in these changes, they were not used as the chief workforce. After all, the State of New York had child labor laws. For renovations and new building programs, the state hired day laborers, carpenters, and plasterers, as well as skilled craftsmen.[45]

A company was hired to fireproof the buildings. Officials well understood the dangers of fire in any institutional setting and the threat

A kindergarten class at Thomas Indian School in the early 1900s.
New York State Archives.

to the lives of inhabitants. Fires in other institutions could be attributed to carelessness, buildings' shoddy conditions, or poor heating and lighting systems, since coal- or wood-burning stoves and kerosene lamps were most often used. Officials also knew that not all fires were accidental. Historically, they were a statement of resistance. In 1859, for example, juvenile inmates at Massachusetts's state reformatory set fire to the institution, and the number of fires at Indian boarding schools was a constant concern for the Indian Bureau. Fires at Fort Stevenson were "of frequent occurrence"; two boys at the Blackfoot Agency, remembering a fire the previous year (1898), decided that if another building burned the school would close for a long time; and two girls nearly succeeded in burning down the girls' dormitory at Carlisle. The list went on. On the White Earth Reservation in Minnesota, "some unknown person or persons" tried to burn the government boarding school in 1888. Editors for the reservation newspaper were appalled—not necessarily because the attempt was made but because of what might have happened if it had succeeded. "There is no doubt that many of the children . . . would have lost their lives, owing to the inadequacy of fire escapes with which the school is not properly supplied." The editors suggested that the children "agitate" and "insist" that proper precautions be taken. There were no guarantees that this would not happen again. The Indian Bureau's response to fires was to see that schools held fire drills and had water buckets and fire escapes—although those were missing at White Earth. The bureau also stiffened punishments for those responsible, including confinement in state reformatories or prisons.[46] No doubt, Thomas officials would send any arsonist to a state reformatory. It was not the threat of punishment, however, that reduced the possibility of intentionally set fires. The New York institution was not a federally run school, and it had considerable Seneca support. It was less a target for calculated forms of resistance.

By the late 1800s, Thomas was no longer an asylum for the orphaned and destitute. When the State of New York began to enforce compulsory education for Indian children, Thomas evolved into a reservation school that took Indian children regardless of their family or economic circumstances. The population expanded somewhat to include youngsters from other New York tribes. In 1905 the asylum was renamed the Thomas Indian School to reflect two significant changes that occurred over the years. First, classroom offerings advanced to include eight grades; when another grade was added in 1930, Thomas had a graded junior high school. Second, by 1905 the student population went beyond the most needy and the orphaned. Not all had been "committed" because they were parentless and/or destitute. Thomas became comparable to Indian boarding schools in the breadth of its population.

This change was reflected in a number of small ways, including official school reports. It can be argued that these sorts of reports provide factual detail such as per capita costs but that they fail to offer descriptive glimpses into an institution's everyday life. That can be true, but seemingly dry ledgers and monthly reports sometimes offer often-overlooked but important signals about staff attitude, physical environment, school activities, and the lives of students.

As the Thomas Asylum evolved into a state-run reservation school, administrators altered descriptions of the population. The children were no longer called inmates, and "Transportation of Inmates" reports dropped the term in favor of simply listing "traveling expenses." Reports also began to note unencumbered, and often unescorted, comings and goings of students to and from school. The institutionalized population was no longer one that had no place to go and no one to see. There was an influx of new students who had homes and families that they were allowed to visit. In fact, the school paid for railroad tickets and sometimes meals for students en route. Financial reports began to contain such notations as "expenses of Flora and Evelyn to Holcomb and Jane to East Concord"; "railroad fare . . . 2 girls, transfer of trunks"; "railroad fare for Jerome Skye to Lawtons from Buffalo and his street car fare total 65 cents." Expenses also were incurred by Emily Lincoln, head matron and later successor to her husband as Thomas superintendent. She traveled to meet young students or see them home. In one instance, she took Salina Maybee and Sophia Gordon to a chautauqua in Buffalo. No doubt, this was considered an educational experience, not one of pure entertainment. Nevertheless, it was a trip away from school. It and student outings to county fairs and picnics clearly demonstrated that students were not confined for the duration of their time at Thomas.[47]

The reports told other stories. Although Jerome and Flora and Evelyn and Jane traveled from here to there and back again, not every child or teenager enjoyed freedom of movement or special opportunities such as a chautauqua. For those who were labeled incorrigible, the story was quite different. In one instance, a teenage boy was removed from Thomas and transferred to the Western House of Refuge, a reformatory established in 1849 and overseen by the state. The boy stayed almost one year. Since those committed to the reformatory stayed until they reached the age of majority, it can be assumed that the young man was released on the basis of age, not necessarily because he mended his ways or was rehabilitated. He was not readmitted to Thomas but was "escorted . . . home to Tuscarora Reservation" by the school superintendent. There was also the case of a Thomas resident remembered by a classmate as "a nice kid but he had a problem." In and out of trouble at Thomas, the young man was sent to the reformatory after "he stole the superintendent's limousine and after that he stole a truck"; as a young man, after he was released from the reformatory, he was imprisoned for murder and executed.[48]

Travel reports from Thomas provide other glimpses at institutional life. Thomas had an infirmary and a medical staff, and at times teenage Thomas residents worked there. "One time Alice [Doxtator] and I were put in charge of the hospital. We had to give out [prelabeled] medicine and change bandages. We took the nurse's place when she went on vacation. If it was anything serious, we were to call a matron and a doctor. Luckily, nothing happened." A doctor and a dentist made routine visits, and expense reports noted the purchase of medical supplies such as quinine tablets, cod liver oil, cough syrup, and disinfectant. Serious cases were transported to a Buffalo hospital. In one instance, the superintendent took two "sick" boys to Buffalo; "sick" was perhaps too mild a term, "as one of them was paralyzed." The cause and the result were not reported, although one wonders if the one boy was the same one who, a resident remembered, was crippled when a teacher allowed a "pile on." "This child was then thrown to the floor and about 30 kids piled on top of him. One of the boys, Deforest Billy from Allegany, was crippled as a result of this punishment." Lack of explanatory narrative was common for institutional reports, leaving one to speculate about the full stories. The same was true for a notation concerning a school nurse who escorted two pupils for examination by a specialist; one of the two required an operation. Neither the illness nor the results of the operation were reported. The presence of facilities and staff at the school, as well as efforts to secure medical help outside Thomas, indicate official concern for health care. Vigilance, however, was not always enough. At Thomas, just as in other institutional settings, there was death. In a one-line report, for example, the Thomas superintendent noted the cost of hiring an undertaker and digging one grave. He did not identify the deceased or the cause of death, and again one is left to speculate. Was the death the same as that witnessed by Florence White, a onetime Thomas student who stayed on to work after 1907? In the hospital, she took care of a dying patient who had tuberculosis and scarlet fever.[49]

How did mortality rates at Thomas compare with those of other New York orphanages or with those at Indian boarding schools? As David Adams noted in *Education for Extinction*, it is impossible to know exact mortality rates or to make statistical comparisons, since there was little data gathering in early Indian boarding schools and the Indian Bureau had no systematic reporting procedure until the end of the nineteenth century. Even then, numbers were questionable, since boarding school superintendents often sent the terminally ill back home. In one case, however, the superintendent for the newly opened Santa Fe Indian School did not act quickly enough and was left with the unhappy task of locating "a suitable place upon the school farm" for a burying ground. Before she could be sent home, a Jicarilla Apache girl died of "acute pulmonary tuberculosis." In future situations, youngsters were returned whenever there was any possibility that they could travel. "One pupil was sent home who died soon afterwards." Government-supported schools had good reason not to report deaths and to remove ill students. In many cases it was difficult enough to convince native groups to send their youngsters to boarding schools, and any reputation for an unhealthy environment only made persuasion more arduous. In that context, schools benefited if mortality rates were suppressed.[50]

Nineteenth-century mortality rates outside Indian boarding schools are as elusive. Before 1900, data gathering was limited to a few urban areas and states that required registration and recording of vital statistics. Therefore, it is difficult to know how Thomas compared with other institutions, even those within the State of New York. The Nursery and Child's Hospital in New York City, for example, reported a mortality rate of only 15 percent. This was remarkably low when one considered that its charges were largely infants and toddlers already experiencing some type of medical problem. On the other hand, the rate was skewed because this was a private hospital that turned away the worst cases. On the other end of the spectrum was Randall's Island, which had the first juvenile reformatory in the United States. Begun by the Quakers and taken over by New York State, the reformatory was acclaimed by such foreign visitors as Charles Dickens, since it was considered a notch above similar institutions in Britain and western Europe. By 1857, Randall's Island held the largest reformatory population in the country, earning it the label of "greatest reform school in the world." Housing both males and females in numbers upwards of two thousand, the institution could not pick and choose its residents on the basis of health, and the sheer numbers created an environment ripe for the spread of contagious diseases. Mortality rates ranged from 60 to 76 percent. Data from Thomas are largely lacking and may, as in the case of Indian boarding schools, reflect the practice of not reporting deaths if they occurred away from the institution. Arguably, however, the rate could not have approached the disastrous percentages represented by Randall's Island. Thomas records simply do not support any conclusion that mortality rates were comparable. They do, however, show that asylum officials worked to reduce the incidence of infectious diseases by stressing personal hygiene and by supplying youngsters with necessary items such as toothbrushes, toilet paper, and soap. In the twentieth century, the school also implemented the cottage system of small residences. These were more homelike than dormitories, and they reduced the spread of infectious diseases by dispersing residents rather than congregating them in large spaces.[51] Nevertheless, the paucity of exact numbers leaves the question hanging, as does the lack of statistics for other Indian orphanages that had their own little graveyards.

Barely suggestive of its importance was the brief Thomas notation of transportation for a girl to an "open-air camp." The girl did not yet have tuberculosis, but she evidently was predisposed to the disease. Nineteenth-century medical wisdom identified tuberculosis as a "constitutional disease" with variances in death rates between ethnic groups explained away as differences of inherent physical superiority. After Robert Koch identified the tuberculosis bacillus in 1882, there was an awakening. Tuberculosis could be combated. To separate the afflicted from the healthy and to aid recovery, fresh air camps and sanitariums became the standard form of treatment. These facilities were not, however, the norm in federal facilities for Indians. Too few doctors in the Indian Medical Service and no concerted efforts to build sanitariums placed native populations at greater risk. In fact, between 1920 and 1925, tuberculosis was estimated to kill Indians at a rate seven times greater than that for non-Indians. Outside the world of Indian reservations, however, there was growing national interest in treating and eradicating tuberculosis because "of the growing conviction that tuberculosis is a fertile cause of poverty." It deprived children of their parents, deprived families of a breadwinner, and left all the makings for lives of destitution. As early as 1902 the New York Charity Organization Society addressed the problem by appointing a standing group within its organization—the Committee on the Prevention of Tuberculosis—that initiated the first public education campaign in the United States "to secure adequate treatment looking to the cure of the poor consumptive." In 1909, largely through this campaign, New York began "fresh air classes" for "pre-tuberculous" children. These youngsters were considered candidates for the disease because they were anemic or showed other signs of poor health; lived in families where tuberculosis was present; or lived in crowded conditions. Since the girl sent to an open-air camp returned to Thomas within a relatively short time, it is most probable that she was identified as "pre-tuberculous" and that school officials took the precaution of treating her before the disease took hold. The difference between the actions of Thomas officials and those at government boarding schools is blatant. Whereas government institutions screened out possible consumptives without providing medical attention and sent the sick home to die, Thomas made an effort to practice preventive medicine by following progressive trends of the time.[52]

By the second decade of the twentieth century, Thomas was no longer referred to or regarded as an institution for only the orphaned and destitute. Nevertheless, it continued to be overseen by the state board of charities, which evolved into the New York State Department of Social Welfare. By 1927 the department administered Thomas, but social workers did not populate Thomas by wholesale removal of children from their families. One policy statement concluded that "as social services to children have increased and have been made available to Indian children as well, the need for institution care has decreased. . . . [Children] are not removed from their homes for poverty alone." When youngsters were removed, social workers attempted to rehabilitate the families without completely cutting child and parent ties. This attitude was significantly different from the long-accepted nineteenth-century edict that child rescue was independent from aid to families.[53]

Most nineteenth-century reformers believed that children were better served if removed from their home environments. It was a question of manipulating a child's surroundings during the formative years. Not yet irreparably damaged, children were salvageable. Adults, said the reformers, were not. Few social welfare workers and reformers linked child and adult welfare, but this deep-rooted belief was modified when professionals began to reach the conclusion that children and families were in crisis. One response came from the 1909 White House Conference on Dependent Children, whose findings argued that families should be kept together. State and local governments could help by providing financial aid and support programs that

kept families together during a mother's illness or a father's unemployment. A major result of the conference was county and state aid-
to-mothers programs that recognized child rescue as part of family
rescue—not separate from it. New York, along with Illinois, Massachusetts, Michigan, Ohio, Oklahoma, and Pennsylvania, mandated
such programs under state law. Of course, not every charity or social
service agency accepted this aid formula. The American Humane Association, founded in 1885, continued to argue that child protection
had nothing to do with family rescue. Nevertheless, reformers accepted the new trend for a number of reasons. The most important
was a rising fear that social and economic changes were threatening
family cohesiveness, even among the sacrosanct white middle class,
which was the icon of stability. Families in crisis first gained wide attention just prior to World War I, and the theme was revisited time
after time during the twentieth century. In 1940, for example, the
White House Conference on Children in a Democracy asked with
trepidation if the "family as an institution is itself disintegrating."
What social ills awaited the national culture if the family unit dis-
solved? These large issues inadvertently affected the Indians residing
in New York as the state's welfare policy of working with the entire
family included Indian households. The outcome was consideration of
the family dynamic rather than removal as a first response.[54]

In the 1900s Thomas still carried out its original mission to house
and educate orphaned and destitute Indian children. That mission expanded over time to include a larger population, and educational opportunities did not end at Thomas. Many who received part of their
education at Thomas left to attend off-reservation boarding schools
such as Haskell Institute in Kansas, Carlisle in Pennsylvania, Hampton Institute in Virginia, and eastern colleges. In 1940 Philip Cowen of
the New York State Department of Education made an extensive study
of Thomas. He lauded the school and recommended enlarging the facility. That assessment was offset six years later, however, when
Willard W. Beatty's *Informal Report on the Thomas Indian School* pictured Thomas as prisonlike. Beatty recommended that youngsters
above the fourth grade attend nearby public schools, despite his concession that Thomas was "probably slightly better" than those
schools. The report had to be considered within the context of surrounding events. New York State wanted to close Thomas because
more effective assimilation would be achieved when Indian youngsters

were forced to attend school with whites. Also, the school's budget could be better used for other Indian-related social service programs.[55]

Many in the Seneca community balked at the prospect of closing Thomas, but responses were as individual as personal experiences. This is borne out by available firsthand accounts, which provide no clear agreement on any aspect of life at Thomas. Food, its quality and quantity, was an important issue for residents in any orphan asylum, and it was no different at Thomas. "The oatmeal was wormy; the salt pork was cooked and served in its own grease. . . . when they tried to mash the potatoes, it would shoot across the room, so the kids called them 'bullets.'" Others recalled that there was plenty of good food to eat. Memories of treatment were equally divided, since, as in most institutions, punishments varied from teacher to teacher and from student to student. One woman recalled that when her coat tore because it was too small, the matron "pulled my ears and hair, and then she sent me to bed. I had to stay in bed all day." As counterpoint to this and the recollection of the "pile on" as punishment was the emphatic pronouncement of one man: "I loved every minute at 'Salem.'" So, too, did a woman who recalled: "Mrs. Brennan [teacher and matron] was also the one to give me my first birthday party . . . and my first birthday cake. . . . The Brennans were like a father and mother to me."[56]

Some former students gladly watched the end of Thomas; their memories of mistreatment, punishment, and work could not let them think otherwise. Others remembered the place fondly. The doors closed on Thomas shortly after it celebrated its centennial year in 1955, despite the work of some Senecas to find alternatives. Some in the Seneca community suggested that Thomas could be turned into a model vocational high school or an Indian college along the same lines as Haskell. Many Senecas regarded Thomas as "theirs" with a genuine sense of pride. Many regarded it as a place that had resisted assimilation. For one hundred years, Thomas, "Salem," kept youngsters close to their people. It had been an obstacle to enforced off-reservation education. True, it introduced mainstream white culture, but its very location on the reservation allowed it to maintain a sense of people and place.[57]

3

ORPHANS AMONG US: CHEROKEE

No. I don't remember my mama and papa. I was orphan. . . . I go to
Cherokee Orphan School.[1]

The orphan Arlie Reeves, who had no memory of her parents, was
among the first to enter the Cherokee Orphan Asylum in Indian Territory. Like mainstream white America, the Cherokees had "discovered" the orphanage, and in the early 1870s, for the first time in the
tribe's history, its leaders conceded that outside forces had substantially altered Cherokee society. Old kinship patterns and family bonds
no longer addressed the needs of all children.

The experience of Arlie Reeves and of the Cherokees in general was
not a peculiar one. Rather, it was representative of hundreds of children and teenagers of the Five Civilized Tribes—Chickasaw, Choctaw,
Creek, Seminole, and Cherokee—and of the tribes' common experiences with Euro-American society. Years of contact with whites, expulsion from tribal homelands in the Southeast, rebuilding in a new
region, and the effects of the American Civil War each contributed to
producing an environment in which orphanages became an acceptable
option for dealing with the parentless and destitute child.

The tribes, however, did not act in concert to establish orphanages
or decide among themselves that these institutions were necessary.
Each of the Five Civilized Tribes, with the exception of the Seminoles,
who did not have the resources, made choices that were true to their
individuality and specific situations. There were no long intertribal
discussions centered on the responsibilities of kin to look after their
relatives. Nor were there recriminations against those who failed to
fall back on age-old traditional forms of child care and protection. In
fact, the old ways had not been the status quo for years, and those who
practiced them were often disparaged for being conservative and backward thinking.

White influence among the Five Civilized Tribes was a reality while the tribes attempted to keep the reins of their own governments and institutions. Influenced, if not assaulted, over decades by white formulas for education and clustering of child populations in boarding schools, tribal leaders found it relatively easy to view orphanages as places of learning rather than as symbols of failed family responsibilities. Thus, the Cherokee Orphan Asylum was funded in 1871, but establishing an orphanage and then making it operational were not the same. The building was provided for, but simple necessities were in short supply, and education was rudimentary during the first years of the asylum's existence. In four years of classroom instruction, Reeves was taught the fundamentals of reading and writing English. Nevertheless, as her spoken memories attest, she was never comfortable with her second language and struggled with its use. When Reeves's four years of study were completed, she did not "graduate." There was no more education to be offered, but this was not a boarding school. It was an orphanage. Reeves had no one waiting for her to come home. She had nowhere to go beyond the asylum. She stayed, doing housekeeping chores. Then, when she was "big enough," she married and left.[2]

The Cherokee Orphan Asylum was funded with $4,000 appropriated by the National Council of the Cherokee. Operations began in a building near Tahlequah, the capital of the Cherokee Nation that sometimes was called the "Athens of the Cherokee Nation," since in the latter decades of the nineteenth century there were as many as six active institutions of learning at one time or another in or near the town. Spearheading the push for the orphanage was the principal chief, William Ross, who greatly favored tribal support of educational facilities within the Cherokee Nation. Although it was a special place with a specific population, the asylum was viewed as a school. As such, it was overseen by the Cherokee Board of Education.[3]

The Cherokee Nation had a constitutional government and departments within that government with explicit responsibilities. As one of those departments, the board of education established schools—day or neighborhood schools, boarding schools within the nation, and the orphan asylum. The board handled the financial accounts; selected youngsters to attend off-reservation boarding schools; organized school districts; hired teachers and superintendents; visited and evaluated schools (this was the responsibility of board members in each district); and made arrangements for contract schools. Remembered

Girls' basketball team, 1920–21, at the Cherokee orphanage in Indian Territory, which was first known as the Cherokee Orphan Asylum, then the Cherokee Orphan Training School, and finally as Sequoyah Orphan Training School. Archives and Manuscripts Division of the Oklahoma Historical Society.

one man: "The Cherokees had good schools. . . . They had schools all over the Nation and the buildings were usually built of logs. The teacher's salary in these schools was not much. They taught English in all the schools."[4]

Ross and others recognized that there were youngsters who, like Arlie Reeves, had no place to live and little chance for formal schooling. There were boys and girls who were orphans, half-orphans, destitute, and/or abandoned. In the last decades of the nineteenth century, Cherokee culture was not what it had been at the beginning of the century. Acculturation, removal from traditional homelands, and the travesty of the American Civil War in Indian Territory created an atmosphere that did not always offer children the protective arms of a wide kin network or clan association. Many adults were not able to meet the needs of dependent relatives. There were desperate cases that only an asylum seemed to serve. Pleading for aid, one woman wrote that she was trying to look after her fifteen-year-old niece and "raise her as she should be." The girl's mother was dead; her father, a white man, had abandoned the teenager, remarried, and left Indian Territory. The aunt feared for the girl's future if she was not taken in by asylum officials and given a structured environment and educational training.

I think that the only thing that can be done with her would be to send her to the Orphan Asylum. Unless this is done with her there is no question but that she will be ruined and go to the dogs. I feel that we Cherokee should look after such people and protect them if we can. I can do nothing with her myself and the only possible way to save her is to send her to the orphanage.[5]

The Cherokee Orphan Asylum was the first institution of its kind for the Cherokee, but the group had substantial experience with white formulas of education dating back to the decades before removal to Indian Territory. Official U.S. publications such as reports by the secretary of the interior stated that the first treaty with any direct reference and federal appropriation for Indian education was made with the Oneida, Tuscarora, and Stockbridge groups in December 1794, but the statement overlooked at least four other actions taken prior to the Indian Civilization Fund Act of 1819 and its allocation of $10,000 annually for support of Indian schools. The first support for Indian education actually began with a bill passed on July 12, 1775, by the Continental Congress appropriating $500 for the education of Indian youth at Dartmouth College, and an 1803 treaty, made with the Kaskaskias of Illinois, provided for a priest to "instruct as many of their children as possible in the rudiments of literature." There also were agreements with native groups in the Southeast; notably, these were made with the Creeks, in August 1790, and with the Cherokees, in the Holston Treaty of 1791. Under both, the federal government supplied tools and, in the case of the Cherokees, four persons to offer instruction in the use of these work implements. At its most basic, this was a governmental attempt to introduce manual-labor training to domesticate the Indian. Men would take up agriculture, supplanting women's traditional role. In turn, females would be turned toward the womanly arts expected of middle-class whites.[6]

During the 1800s the federal government and missionary workers joined hands in bringing Euro-American education, and not so incidentally Christianity, to tribal groups. For the Cherokees, this meant early-nineteenth-century contact with whites working in the mission fields. Among the first missionaries were Baptists who established schools. In the first decades of the 1800s, Humphrey Posey, a minister, opened four schools and employed Indian teachers while he continued itinerant mission work. The schools were haphazard affairs that closed within two years. Posey, undaunted, opened a single school at a mission station in Georgia. By late 1821, white volunteers arrived to serve as teachers. Within a short time, there were approximately seventy students at the school—enough to encourage the opening of another. By comparison, the schools established by Methodist circuit riders were temporary, depending on the circuit being traveled. They were poorly run, since the Methodists placed less emphasis on education and more on conversion; convert numbers, important as indicators of missionary success, were gleaned from the slightest interest shown by the native population in such rituals as baptism or the rousing preaching and religious fervor elicited by camp meetings.[7]

For its part, the government gave its blessing to missionary work. Thomas L. McKenney, superintendent of Indian trade and then first commissioner of Indian affairs in 1824, encouraged missionaries to ask for financial support and to solicit Congress for aid. Those working in the mission fields were in a position to ask. They promised native conversion to Christianity and to the values of white culture. With passage of the "civilization fund" in 1819, mission boards received steady support and financial reinforcement. Posey asked for, and received, $500 to pay the salaries of three white teachers. The government relied on missionaries to do the work of educating Indian groups in vocational areas such as using a plow or a spinning wheel and in the subjects of reading and writing English. Missionaries became a growing and consistent factor in the lives of native populations, and the government saw these ministers and teachers as the perfect instruments for introducing white culture and transforming native societies. The government was only too happy to subsidize mission field efforts. Few questioned the church-state arrangement; the exception, of course, occurred when a religious group felt slighted in the amount of moneys received.[8]

Although missionaries worked to teach the English language, they also attempted to reach the Cherokees with the phonetically based Cherokee alphabet developed and perfected by Sequoyah. For the Cherokee, Sequoyah's innovation provided another means of communication. Within a short time of its appearance, the majority of Cherokees were alphabet literate, and the Cherokees established a newspaper in 1828 to keep the entire tribal group informed. For the missionaries, the alphabet provided an avenue for instruction and conversion.[9]

As a rule, Cherokee leadership accepted the onslaught of white education. Early in their contact with Euro-Americans and the federal government, most influential Cherokee leaders concluded that education provided the means for understanding the outsiders. One could not fight what one did not know, and one could not negotiate without comprehending the other side's words, nuances, and basic beliefs and values. Education was a key to making judgments and dealing with outsiders. Accepting and then employing classroom instruction was a survival tactic.

By the 1830s much of the Cherokee people, as well as members of the Creek, Seminole, Choctaw, and Chickasaw tribes of the Southeast, had incorporated into their lives aspects of what the white world offered. They accommodated Euro-Americans and adopted white-directed education, English, and the plantation-style economy employed by encroaching white settlers. A clear economic hierarchy emerged between those who did and did not adopt the plantation economy and the use of black slave labor. Those Cherokees who did were the rich, as well as among the most educated. Arguments that their wealth depended on the use of slaves as a cheap labor force mirrored the attitudes of white slaveholders. The Cherokees and other tribal groups in the Southeast, therefore, adopted aspects of the federal and dominant-culture vision of what constituted civilization, but the tribal groups also adopted a distinctive regional view of Euro-American life when slave labor in the fields and black servants in homes became common in wealthier Indian households. Within tribal and clan units, socioeconomic boundaries and educational levels widened to create sharp contrasts. At the same time, a number of black slaves who escaped from their white masters found refuge among the southeastern tribes. Some established their own villages. A number were counted as free tribal members, and intermarriage confused the lines of race. Blacks who adopted native culture or who were the offspring of intermarriage often were labeled by whites as "Black Indians." By the 1830s, generalizations that once served to define Cherokee culture were no longer adequate characterizations or representative.[10]

The federal government's push to turn the male hunter and warrior into a farmer had its impact, and white encroachment reduced hunting territories, turning males more and more to farming. At the same time, women were redirected toward the dominant culture's concept of woman's sphere. The domestic arts of spinning and weaving were introduced with help from Washington, which supplied looms and spinning wheels. Women's place in Cherokee culture was undermined when male and female roles radically altered. It was further reconfigured by two emerging factors. The first was the introduction of slavery, which took women out of the fields and moved them into the homes. The second was intermarriage with white males who did not necessarily understand or accept matrilineal or clan customs. Influence exerted by white spouses or neighbors, as well as missionaries and government agents, acted to rearrange traditional gender responsibilities. This may have satisfied Euro-Americans' expectations, but it remained to be seen if the change served Cherokee culture.[11]

The Cherokees in general adopted many aspects of the white culture's attitudes and lifestyles, leading them and the other southeastern groups of Creeks, Choctaws, Chickasaws, and Seminoles to be named the "civilized" tribes, or the Five Civilized Tribes. In their own estimation, the Cherokees viewed themselves as a civilized native people. In a relatively short span of time, they accepted Euro-American education and missionary groups; established a newspaper using a Cherokee-designed alphabet; moved dramatically from a dual economy of hunting and farming to one that was primarily land based; established a political organization patterned after the U.S. branches of government; and adopted non-Indian clothing and work implements. Outwardly, they were worthy of praise from the dominant culture. Inwardly, the price was destablization of internal relationships, traditional culture, and gender roles.[12]

Destablization was magnified by the most dramatic assault on the Cherokees—removal from their traditional homeland. Removal was not, of course, an American creation. The U.S. government had only to look at British patterns of colonization and the dispersion of undesirable elements in British society to the far corners of the earth. The American government had only to consider the British expulsion of Acadian French from Canada or the routine shipment of the poor and the criminal out of the British Isles to colonial outposts such as Australia, Canada, and Capetown. Taking a lesson from British colonialism, the federal government embarked upon its own program to expel a people from their homeland.

Some removal of the Cherokee people occurred prior to 1829, but the 1830s witnessed a federal mandate, under Presidents Jackson and Van Buren, of forced relocation. It was the final and irrevocable solution to the "Indian problem," which in no small way centered on land control rather than on claims that removal was benevolent and in the Indians' best interest. No matter how civilized the Cherokees and the other tribes of the Southeast had become, their application of Euro-American culture to their own lives could not save them from a policy that by the end of Van Buren's administration had relocated major portions of the Five Civilized Tribes, as well as thousands of other eastern Indians—including Potawatomies, Delawares, Iroquois, Osages, and Shawnees—west of the Mississippi River.[13]

If any situation was ripe for creating an orphaned and destitute population of children, it was the removal period in Cherokee history. The relocation process occurred not in one large migration but in stages. Indians were rounded up. Those who attempted to elude relocation and hid in the hills and forests were chased down. Held at collection points, they waited in camps for transport and military escort. Camp life consisted of poor diet, lack of sanitation, overcrowding, and abuse from the soldiers assigned to collect and escort them. The components made for a lethal combination. In the camps, it is estimated (depending upon the source) that from three hundred to two thousand died of pellagra, measles, malaria, smallpox (which became epidemic among the Choctaws), and dysentery.[14]

Camps were worse during summer months, leading one hundred Cherokees to petition Gen. Winfield Scott, military supervisor over Indian "emigration," to put off additional confinements until cooler weather. In part, the petitioners wrote: "We do not want to see our wives and children die. We do not want to die ourselves and leave them widows and orphans."[15] In this instance, the Cherokees used the term "orphan" as Scott would construe the word's meaning: the vernacular, not legal, definition for children without one parent. Clearly, exposure to white, dominant society and its teachings had introduced the concept of orphan and half-orphan to the Cherokees.

Life outside the detention camps was hardly less dangerous or chaotic. Groups were sometimes driven like cattle, and in one instance, a number who refused to be loaded onto boats at the collection point of Ross's Landing at Nashville were summarily forced on board by soldiers. It was little wonder that in the ensuing confusion and panic families became separated, leaving children on their own. On the overland trek, the Trail of Tears, the saga of separation and death continued. One traveler from Maine observed the ordeal and wrote: "We learned from the inhabitants on the road where the Indians passed, that they buried fourteen or fifteen at every stopping place, and they make a journey of ten miles per day only on an average." How many died will never be known. Estimates range from five hundred to two thousand, and one historian speculated that there would have been ten thousand more Cherokees alive in 1840 had it not been for removal. Forced migration created an atmosphere that diminished family and clan connections. "The people became socially disoriented, their town and clan organizations disrupted. Families dwindled and were divided."[16]

In the midst of removal and in its aftermath, the Five Civilized Tribes were haunted with the question of their ability to respond to the needs of children who were, more than ever, the hope for tribal survival. It might be expected that the personal and group tragedies explicit with removal would provide the transitional moment in which the Cherokees, Chickasaws, Choctaws, Creeks, and Seminoles buckled under the burden of parentless children and established orphanages for their care. After all, orphanages already operated in other areas of America, and the first had appeared in Georgia, a part of the Cherokees' land base. Nevertheless, the Cherokees did not choose institutionalization as a solution to their problems. The traumatic events of the 1830s certainly produced orphaned children and tore apart families, but the Cherokees were able to continue caring for children who were without parents or without kin support. They did not build an asylum that separated these children from the rest of Indian society. Over time, the Cherokees assimilated a substantial set of ideas and behaviors from white culture, but they had not adopted the idea of institutionalization.

If removal and its aftermath demonstrated anything, it was the resilience of the Cherokee people. In the land west of the Mississippi, towns were established; a capital was founded in the Cherokee Nation; and farms were laid out. By 1860 over one hundred thousand acres were under cultivation, and livestock numbered almost two hundred thousand. There were homes and businesses. Most certainly there were schools. The Cherokees remained greatly devoted to education, and on December 16, 1841, the Cherokee government passed its first public school act, which established a unique and self-sustained school system. Not long after passage of the act, eleven schools were operational. Within five years there were two seminaries, also called academies; one was for males, the other for females. At the same time, the Cherokees continued to send a small number of young people to schools outside the nation. To support the system, the Cherokees used the perpetual annuity payments for schools agreed to in the removal treaty negotiated in 1835. The Cherokee government contracted with Baptists, Presbyterians, and Methodists to run the nation's schools and provide superintendents and teachers (although the staff was as likely to be Cherokee as Euro-American). Sallie Rogers McSpadden, a graduate of the Cherokee Female Seminary and a teacher at the Cherokee Orphan Asylum, recalled: "Our old Cherokee school system was an Excellent one—and most thorough—all expenses of school supplies such as textbooks and writing materials were met by our Cherokee council."[17]

The system was remarkable on several levels. It was tribally supported and beyond Indian Bureau influence, and thus the Cherokees were not obligated to report to the federal agency—much to the chagrin of officials such as John H. Oberly, who complained that only the tribes in Indian Territory and in New York State were beyond the bureau's reach on matters of education.[18] As a tribe-directed system, the Cherokee Board of Education could, and did, void contracts with a denominational group when staff or subject content did not meet the board's expectations. This placed the missionaries, determined to Christianize and civilize, in the position of often standing with hat in hand asking to be let into the system. They served at the pleasure of the board, leaving them to vie for contract schools.

Not everyone agreed with how schools were organized or, for that matter, with the idea of schooling. To a large extent it was true, as some complained, that wealthier families had an advantage in seeing that their children were chosen to attend off-reservation boarding schools and the two seminaries in the Cherokee Nation. These schools had limited space, and the board of education had final say on who could and could not attend. It was a point of honor and prestige to be chosen for these educational opportunities. Left outside the mainstream of education were the "pagan" Cherokees and the poor. Generally beyond the pull of education was the conservative faction, most of whom were full-bloods. They had not responded well to missionary efforts before removal, and they were the least likely to seek educational opportunities in Indian Territory. Some observers said that conservatives ignored schooling because they kept to traditional child-rearing and instructional practices. If a child wished to attend school, out of curiosity or interest, parents indulged the whim. Others argued that the full-bloods were interested in education, but being among the poorer class of farmers, they needed their children at home to work. They did not have the slave labor used by other tribesmen. Full-bloods were also less likely to seek out formal education because most did not speak English. Their children faced an uphill battle in classrooms where English was the language of instruction. It was not a situation overlooked by the Cherokee Board of Education, which tried to entice families to send youngsters to the tribally funded day or neighborhood schools. On the other hand, it was highly unlikely that a child from the conservative group, one who was not Christianized, or who came from the poorest of the poor would be ushered into the shining lights of education—the nation's seminaries and off-reservation boarding schools. In fact, as late as 1914, there were "many full-blood children who have almost reached maturity without the benefit of school training."[19]

The schools of which the Cherokees were so proud and in which they invested so much both emotionally and financially came to an abrupt halt with the American Civil War. The system simply shut down. It was a casualty of the Cherokee Nation's split over Northern and Southern loyalties, as well as the war within a war that the Cherokees fought among themselves. The onslaught of the Civil War provided the setting and the opportunity for buried feuds and animosities to rise to the surface. Old wounds and grievances over the Treaty of New Echota, which sold away lands in the Southeast, ruptured into open fighting. Lines were drawn between who had and had not supported the treaty of removal, and opposing forces showed themselves when once again accusations surfaced and pointed fingers at tribal leaders who were said to have benefited financially from the removal agreement. Under the banner of North or South there was the opportunity for one side to seek retribution against the other. In essence, the Cherokees fought two civil wars; one pitted Union Cherokees against

Confederate, and one provided the opportunity to settle old scores through internal factional fighting.[20]

Juxtaposed against the backdrop of intertribal warfare was the division of pro-Southerners and pro-Northerners. One has to ask why the Cherokees would support either side. White Southerners had battled the Indians in the Southeast and ultimately helped drive them out, and the federal government, representative of the Union, had ejected the Five Civilized Tribes from their homelands with military force. Despite the many reasons for staying out of the fray, the Cherokees, as well as the other displaced southeastern tribes, chose sides. Officially, the Cherokee government, under Principal Chief John Ross, tried to remain neutral, but it was a lost cause. Pro-Union Cherokees went off to join units, including the Kansas Indian Home Guards; the Third Indian Regiment, a Cherokee unit; and the Indian Brigade, which included two regiments of Cherokees, one regiment of Creeks, and battalions or companies of Comanche, Seminole, Ute, Natchez, Shawnee, Delaware, and Osage recruits. Meanwhile, the Cherokee government sagged under pressure from other tribes in Indian Territory and from Indian agents who were Southern sympathizers. In the end, neutrality was a dream. The Cherokees signed a treaty with the Confederacy, following the Creeks, who were the first to sign. An estimated 8,500 to 13,500 Cherokees were Confederate sympathizers.[21]

Although not all Cherokees approved the treaty with the Confederacy, a number of factors came together to garner sympathy for the Southern cause. One of the most obvious was slavery. When the Cherokees left the Southeast, they did not leave their slaves behind. Neither did the other Five Civilized Tribes at the time of removal. Recalled a Chickasaw woman: "We always kept ten or more slaves before the [Civil] war and had good negro quarters for them. I was born with slaves to wait on me." There were also free blacks living among the Five Civilized Tribes. They so feared being turned over to white slaveholders that they chose to join the move west at the time of removal. For the Cherokees in general, support for the Confederacy was support for the plantation system that relied on slave labor; by 1860 at least four thousand slaves were at work in the Cherokee Nation. Just as fundamental to deciding loyalties was a lingering bitterness toward the federal government, which was compounded when the government abandoned Indian Territory at the beginning of the war. Physically the military was gone, leaving the territory unprotected.

Materially the government seemingly forgot the tribes. Annuity payments were delayed, adding to the suffering already being exacted by a severe drought. Foodstuffs were in short supply. Animals were dying. A growing number of individuals were destitute.[22]

Intertribal fighting and Confederate-Union clashes occurred within the territory. One side raided the homes and neighborhoods of the other. Seven major battles were fought between Union and Southern troops within the boundaries of the Cherokee Nation. Those who decided to stay in their homes and neighborhoods were often burned out and robbed of their property, particularly livestock. It became routine for women and children to hide outdoors rather than risk being caught inside their homes. Those who decided to abandon their homes became refugees, repeating for many the nightmare of removal some thirty years earlier. Those hoping to escape the turmoil flocked to military forts or moved to other tribal territories where conditions were hardly any better. By the end of 1862, approximately two thousand Cherokee refugees, along with slaves and free blacks, camped near Fort Scott in the southeastern corner of Kansas. The Union fort was perhaps the safest place in Kansas, where the 1850s' legacy of "Bleeding Kansas"—a dress rehearsal for the national Civil War—continued into the 1860s with military engagements and guerrilla warfare. Many of those who did not flee to Kansas or to other tribes' lands went to Fort Gibson, Indian Territory, where at least seven thousand Cherokees sought safety. A onetime slave, Dennis Vann, recalled the situation: "Fort Gibson became so crowded with refugees that the Government sent the Vann slaves and others to Franklin County, Kansas." There they stayed in east-central Kansas until after the war, when they returned to Indian Territory at the request of their former mistress.[23]

Displacement, economic losses when crops were not harvested and farms were burned out, starvation, and the onslaught of disease (especially smallpox) in overcrowded and unsanitary refugee camps demoralized and decimated the general population. Death in battle, by ambush, and through assassination took the lives of men engaged in retribution over the removal agreement. By the beginning of 1863, at least one-third of the Cherokee women were widows, and one-fourth of the children were parentless. After four years of war and civil chaos, Indian Territory was, wrote one woman, "in a worse condition than it was in 1838. . . . Many fathers coming home found their once beautiful homes leveled to the ground by the cruel torch of war and their families suffering for the bare necessities of life—and in many sad instances the father did not return."[24]

The war disrupted life to the point that, as in the larger scope of events in the states and territories, the population of orphaned and destitute children increased. It has been estimated that there were at least twelve hundred Cherokee war orphans. For the Cherokees, the situation was different from that of removal. After relocation, the Cherokees relied on extended families or nonfamily friends and neighbors to shelter and care for children. From an education annuity, an Orphan Fund of $50,000 guaranteed by the removal treaty signed at New Echota, the Cherokee Nation paid volunteer families a per diem fee to care for homeless children. Of this fee, a portion was earmarked for education to ensure that youngsters were not kept at home and used as cheap labor. The Cherokee solution for child placement was not a unique arrangement in the larger world of charitable institutions. Outside Indian Territory, other organizations did the same. The New York Foundling Hospital, for example, placed infants and toddlers in private homes. In both the Cherokee and New York cases, placements were similar to what later developed into foster care.[25]

Effects of the Civil War in Indian Territory brought child care to a breaking point. There were simply too many family and clan groups unable emotionally or economically to carry out their age-old responsibilities to children. In some cases, there was no family left. The number of orphaned children precluded the possibility that volunteer families could be found for all who needed a home. The Cherokees, like the Senecas in New York, found themselves in a position where it seemed that only an orphanage would answer the need to house and educate orphaned and destitute children. The Cherokee response was a microcosm of the national scene as the post–Civil War era witnessed a boom in orphan asylums.

At the close of hostilities, the Cherokee government turned to rebuilding the nation. High on the list for restoring national life was resurrecting its school system. One of the schools was the Cherokee Orphan Asylum. Dating back to the 1835 treaty agreement, annuity moneys existed for education. The Orphan Fund was separate from the "permanent school fund" of $160,000, but the existence of both exhibited an intention to educate all children. In 1866 the needs of the orphaned were even more pressing, and the Cherokee National Council began to redirect the Orphan Fund from home care and existing educational opportunities to establishing an institution just for orphaned youngsters. Added to the fund were unclaimed bonuses and back pay due deceased Cherokees who had served in the Union army. When the Cherokee National Council realized the full impact of the war, it accepted the fact that the Orphan Fund would remain a necessary annuity for years to come. On November 29, 1871, the fund became a standing appropriation to provide for "parentless children." Thus, the Cherokee Orphan Asylum had its beginnings, although there was no groundswell among the nation's citizens demanding such an institution. The council, with the help of the asylum's first superintendent, the Reverend Watt A. Duncan, found itself having to explain the asylum. Through a letter published in the *Cherokee Advocate,* Duncan observed, "The Orphan Asylum is a new thing in our country. There has been but little said about it. And some people seem not to understand what it is." The reverend went on to explain that the national council had decided that an asylum was better than the "old orphan system" and that the Cherokees should be proud of this advancement in civilized conduct. Whether or not the Cherokees knew it, wrote Duncan, "Our little Nation is not wholly out of sight. . . . They [white Americans] want to see what we are going to do by way of improvement."26

The asylum was another symbol of the Cherokees' acculturation process and of the nation's willingness to "improve" itself with white institutions. On a personal level, however, the newly opened Cherokee Orphan Asylum was viewed and remembered in very different ways. A white teacher employed in the Creek school system recalled that her father, a Congregational missionary in Kansas, and his followers decided to help the Cherokees with the orphan home. After all, "[they] were in need of everything for the children." The minister and his flock gathered clothing, food, books, bedding, furniture, and other "necessary articles." They then persuaded the Missouri, Kansas, and Texas Railroad (the "Katy") to ship the goods free of charge. No doubt the items were welcome, since beginning an institution from scratch demanded more items than Cherokee finances would allow, and the number of orphans exceeded the amount of money available for their care. While adults gathered contributions and listed the number of needed plates, bedding, and reading primers, children saw the environment from an entirely different perspective. A lasting memory for

one girl who entered the asylum soon after it opened was not the mis-
matched furniture, pieces of donated clothing, or life in the classroom.
Instead, almost sixty years after the fact, the onetime inhabitant recalled with a touch of wonder: "I remember the first cook stove I ever
saw; it was in the Cherokee Orphanage."[27]

The Cherokee Board of Education contracted with the Methodists,
and the Reverend Watt A. Duncan became the first superintendent to
oversee the orphanage. His three young daughters attended classes
alongside the Indian children. Duncan's wife acted as matron, directing every facet of the children's life. It was not unusual for a husband
and wife to team as superintendent and matron, and since both positions were salaried by the Cherokee Board of Education, the couple
added to their modest income, which averaged $100 a month for su-
perintendent and $50 for head matron. Within five years of opening,
the asylum had four male teachers (including Duncan, who also
served as instructor) and six female teachers. In addition, a number of
adults were employed as either full- or part-time cooks, laundresses,
and handymen.[28]

One immediate and apparent difference between the asylum and
the Cherokees' male and female seminaries was the population. Unlike the seminaries, which separated boys and girls, the asylum was
coeducational. There was simply not enough money to create two orphan homes that would separate the sexes, and the Cherokee government was unwilling to use non–Orphan Fund moneys to accomplish
gender segregation. Thus, five years after the home's founding, its population had an equal number of males and females: eighty boys and
eighty girls. Despite the fact that the population had grown to 160,
Duncan and his family attempted to maintain a homelike atmosphere
in which residents were treated as members of a large, integrated family. One teenager, Cornelia Chandler, whose mother died when Cornelia was nine and whose father died when she was fourteen, fondly
remembered the reverend. As a testimony to his efforts, she said: "He
was more than a teacher, he was our daddy."[29]

In 1877, at the age of nine, George French entered the institution,
staying until 1886. Of that time, he said: "The boys and girls [approx-
imately 125] went to school together, all stayed in the same building,
boarded and roomed in the same house. We played ball and we boys
would hunt and fish on Saturdays. . . . We had Saturday evening to
ourselves."[30] His recollections were as straightforward as the girl's

memory of seeing a cookstove or Cornelia's characterization of the home's superintendent. These were not rousing endorsements of the place in which they lived, but neither were they harsh assessments that spoke of severe discipline and strict control, as was so often the case with those who recalled experiences at Indian boarding schools. This is not to say that all children fit easily into orphanage life or learned to accommodate themselves to their surroundings. Nevertheless, recorded memories reveal a level of acceptance and an attempt to focus on what was good or pleasant.

Several factors influenced this reaction. The first was the population. The children and adolescents were all Cherokees, although in one instance a superintendent who followed Duncan reported that two sisters, age eleven and nine, might be Shawnees; the superintendent could not say "positively." Nevertheless, the population was overwhelmingly from one group. This was distinctly different from Indian boarding schools away from reservations, where many diverse tribal groups attempted to acclimate themselves both to the white authorities and to classmates with dissimilar backgrounds. It was also different from those urban orphanages where populations represented many ethnic groups. There was a certain solidarity in sharing a common background in the Cherokee Orphan Asylum, where "pupils" were much alike in tribal heritage and personal history. They were either parentless or had a living relative unable to provide care. When there was a living parent, that parent was so reduced in circumstances that room and board at the asylum was a luxury compared with what awaited outside. Also, despite lessons in American and world history that presented a decidedly Euro-American worldview, there was a sense of tribal identity. The children were not mixed with other native groups or with non-Indian children. English was taught, and the Cherokees generally identified with dominant-culture education, but the children were not surrounded by an all-white set of authority figures. The white superintendent may have represented the patriarchal "daddy," and the head matron may have taken on maternal duties in her day-to-day contact with the children. Nevertheless, their ability to create an environment totally devoted to acculturation was minimized by a number of factors.[31]

Youngsters were not placed in white homes to work and to live, as was done so often at federal boarding schools. Nor were they indentured to white adults as laborers or apprentices, as was the case for poor American-born and immigrant children. They certainly were not put up for adoption. Although it was true that "orphans presented an excellent opportunity for missionaries and others intent on 'civilizing,'"[32] white influence was softened by the presence of Cherokee teachers and support staff who were hired and fired by the Cherokee Board of Education. Youngsters did not see white faces every day. Sometimes they saw no white faces at all.

During some time periods, no Caucasian teachers were employed at the home. In 1902–3, for example, the staff was made up of seven teachers, the superintendent, and two medical officers, all of whom were Cherokee. At the time, this representation was comparable to the female seminary, where, out of a staff of twelve, only the "principal teacher" (the superintendent) was white. Orphan home employees were less comparable, however, to the Cherokee Male Seminary, where four staff members were white and five were Cherokee. For the orphan asylum, as well as other educational facilities in the Cherokee Nation, teachers were not excluded on the basis of race, but the number of Cherokee teachers increased as the post–Civil War school system produced capable young men and women who willingly took teaching positions in Cherokee institutions. Two of those employed at the orphan home in 1902–3, for example, were Mary Elizabeth Gulager, who graduated from the Cherokee Female Seminary in 1900, and Cherokee "Cherrie" Vashti Edmondson, who graduated from the seminary and then taught there before joining the staff at the orphan home.[33]

Still, the Cherokee teachers were a paradox. They were Cherokees teaching their own people, but they represented white education. They offered a measure of reassurance to youngsters that they were somehow still connected to their own people. Nonetheless, multiculturalism was not encouraged or expected by a number of teachers who, by virtue of their own educations, were role models for adopting white culture. Over the years, these teachers included some of the best educated the Cherokees had to offer, such as S. F. Parks and W. W. Hastings. Parks graduated from the Cherokee Male Seminary and then the law school at Cumberland University in Lebanon, Tennessee. He taught for a brief period at the orphan home and then began his law practice, later acting as an attorney for the nation and assisting in the Indian roll compilation for land allotment under the direction of the Dawes Commission. W. W. Hastings, also a graduate of the Cherokee Male Seminary, studied at Vanderbilt University and then taught before holding many positions, eventually being named principal chief in the late 1930s when he opposed the Indian Reorganization Act.[34]

Orphanage memories suggest another factor in the lives of children at the asylum. Many learned to wear the institutional cloak so well that it was difficult to shed later in life. Once in an institutional environment, some found it impossible to adjust to the outside world. Sallie Jones, parentless and living with an uncle before entering the orphanage, left as a young woman but spent most of her adult life in one institutional setting or another. Before her marriage and after its failure, she worked as a matron at various Cherokee schools and at the Chickasaw Bloomfield School. Many found that institutions offered them a predictable routine and a sense of security that they were unable to find elsewhere. Whatever the emotional or psychological influence, there were individuals who as adults found ways to reenact their earlier institutional experience. Some sought out the institution through criminal activity that led to incarceration. Others followed paths that took them into institutions as staff. This was in no way a condition found only among Indian children. There were innumerable examples from many sources, including Caucasian youngsters placed in rural homes through the relocation practice of the orphan trains. For some, the impact of institutional life during their formative years was so strong that it could not be dismissed as simply a phase in one's life.[35]

The location of the Cherokee Orphan Asylum at Tahlequah was of short duration. In 1875 the asylum was moved northwest of Tahlequah to Mays County near Pryor Creek. The orphanage and 1,280 acres of surrounding land were labeled the "Orphan Asylum Reservation." A three-story brick building was constructed. It contained classrooms, dormitories, and necessary space for a dining hall, kitchen area, and laundry.[36]

The amount of property was essential if the institution was to emulate other orphanages in country settings. First, the institution had to achieve a measure of self-support from crops, livestock, and gardens. Self-sufficiency would remove some of the financial burden of feeding all those mouths. The farm made it possible for boys to learn the arts of animal husbandry and crop cultivation. Produce from the garden, dairy products, and animal products from slaughter made it possible for girls to learn cooking and methods of food preservation such as canning. Intended or not, the farm and its uses made this institution no different from innumerable Indian boarding schools or orphanages for non-Indian children.

Space was always a consideration, even when the orphanage moved and the physical size increased to accommodate 250 (a maximum capacity that bordered on overcrowding). The board of education decided who would go to the asylum, just as it determined who would attend Cherokee Nation seminaries and off-reservation schools. Obviously, priority cases were the true orphans such as Henry Payne, orphaned at the age of eight, or the five children referred to in a letter urging Principal Chief Samuel Mayes to see that the youngsters went to the orphan asylum despite the willingness of families to take them in. "Mrs. Catharine Duncan died at my house with heart failure. Mrs. Duncan was left a widow by the death of her husband 2 years ago. She leaves 5 children ages 2, 4, 8, 11, 14. They have no relatives able to cair [sic] for them." The letter writer was looking after the children and thought that "good homes can be procured for them in the county." However, it was the writer's desire and the hope of "other friends" to place the children in the home, where "they would get a better education." The last suggests that the letter writer regarded the orphan home as a school, and as such, it was more desirable than a neighborhood school.[37]

Second in line for admittance were those with one living parent, particularly if that parent was a destitute mother. These children were more apt to spend a shorter time in the orphanage. Arch Nelms, as one example, spent only one year, 1889, in the asylum before returning to his mother and aunts. As in other orphanage situations, when circumstances improved for the parent, the child went home. Sometimes a widowed mother and her child came to the orphanage together. It was not unheard of for the board of education to give the mother employment to get her back on her feet financially and, at the same time, give her children shelter and education. This was the situation for Susanna Adair Davis. With two children to support after her full-blood Cherokee husband was shot in the line of duty as a law officer, she was employed as one of the matrons. In charge of forty-six boys, ranging in age from six to ten, Davis worked at the orphan asylum for four years, earning twenty dollars a month. Meanwhile, her children were allowed to live and study at the institution. Over the years a few children, such as Florence Caleb, attended classes because the parents

Uniform attire was not standard at Indian orphanages; an exception was the Cherokee orphanage after the turn of the century. Archives and Manuscripts Division of the Oklahoma Historical Society.

were employed as teachers. In Florence's case, her mother was an instructor at the orphanage.[38]

For the board of education, responsible for placing youngsters in the asylum, decisions were not always easy. First, there was only so much space, meaning that potential candidates were scrutinized to ensure that a relative was not using the orphanage to avoid his or her responsibilities. Second, some of those meeting the criteria for placement were likely to be difficult and disruptive in the institutional setting. Administrators, no matter the institution, preferred compliant, well-behaved residents. When confronted with potential troublemakers, officials balked. Troublesome to the Cherokees were those youngsters who, if they had lived in some disreputable section of a metropolitan area such as New York City's Five Points, would have been adjudged delinquent and carted off to an industrial school or reformatory. The Cherokees did not have a youth correctional facility, however, although there was a jail for adult offenders.

One case facing the Cherokee Board of Education was that of the Palmer boys, who were prime candidates for future imprisonment if something was not done to intercede. The boys, whose mother was "absolutely destitute" and living on the charity offered by her local community, were out of control. In her situation the mother could not provide any parental authority, and in traditional society it would not have been her role but rather that of her brother or a clan elder to do so. Without a male relative to direct them and with the mother unable to provide much of a home life, the boys ran wild. One concerned man wrote: "They are the worst boys I ever saw and will be sure to land in the penitentiary if something is not done for them. If you [Indian agent] will issue an order to place them in the orphan asylum or school at Prior [*sic*] Creek, I.T. and send it to me I will endeavor to have them sent there." The Indian agent did not have the authority, but he quickly passed the request on to those who did. He directed his own appeal to Principal Chief Mayes: "I am willing *personally* to give something out of my own pocket to assist in getting them a place where they may be sheltered from want and not be exposed to temptation and crime." In this small saga of an impoverished mother and two boys likely to end up on the wrong side of the law, there were no accompanying materials to indicate if indeed the Palmer boys were admitted to the asylum. Their names did not appear on subsequent listings of residents. Considering the reputation that preceded them, it is possible that access was denied. Or they may have arrived and then bolted or been placed in one of the Cherokee Nation's boarding schools or its jail.[39]

Clearly, the orphanage demanded school board attention. It most certainly demanded operational money. Consistently more was spent than allocated, even when the farm contributed to the larder and when the orphanage sold a portion of its crops for income. Money became so tight that teachers were required to pay $7.50 per month for room and board; failure to do so meant dismissal. Within the larger community, local merchants as well as those outside the Cherokee Nation often clamored for payment. When funds were exceptionally low, the board might approve appropriations from the general school fund, but largely it relied on the Orphan Fund to support the institution.[40] It was never enough. This did not mean that the Cherokee school system as a whole was in financial trouble. Ample funds supported the seminaries and other Cherokee Nation schools and paid for off-reservation scholars, but it was rare for moneys to be transferred from one account to another. This left the orphan asylum at the bottom rung of appropriations.

By the end of the century, the Cherokee Orphan Asylum was providing good classroom instruction, although this was largely a result of teachers' dedication rather than having a wealth of teaching materials or well-appointed classrooms. Twenty-five years of shoestring economics left the institution with innumerable problems that scandalized the board after members made a three-day visit in 1900. The visit and the report that followed were engineered by James Allen Thompson, board president and superintendent of the orphan asylum. Thompson wanted the Cherokee government to acknowledge that the home needed major improvements. There were rotting porches, sagging and collapsing floors, and old rusted pipes that provided woefully inadequate drainage. Added to the physical deterioration was a general lack of almost everything. "In dormitories we found no chairs, no tables, no water and slop basins, no towels, no combs and no mirrors and no bath or wash rooms. The sick rooms were poorly ventilated and not properly cared for, and the medical superintendent is neglecting the Sanitary conditions of same."[41]

The report accurately assessed the physical state of the asylum structure, but it may have overstated the scarcity of items, since tribal records demonstrate an ongoing routine of making purchases for goods and services. It also may have overdramatized neglect by the medical officer. After all, medical personnel were not assigned exclusively to the orphanage. For example, Dr. C. M. Ross, a grandson of Principal Chief John Ross and a graduate of the Cherokee Male Seminary, returned to the Cherokee Nation with a medical degree from Missouri Medical College in St. Louis. He established a private practice while also serving as medical superintendent for four Cherokee institutions—the Cherokee Female Seminary, the male seminary, the Cherokee Insane Asylum, and the orphan asylum. He routinely visited each and responded to medical emergencies. Nevertheless, it was impossible to attend to emergencies in more than one place at the same time. Weather, as well as travel distance, sometimes slowed his ability to respond. In one instance, a student at the Cherokee Female Seminary lay seriously ill with pneumonia. Sleet covered the landscape, making it impossible for staff to send for help or for the doctor, if he had known, to reach the patient. A teacher, Narcissa Owen, did what staff often did—took charge. Owen made up a home remedy for a potato poultice—hot boiled potato slices mixed with earth (she improvised by taking dirt from a flower pot). The dirt acted as insulation and kept the poultice hot, much as a clay pot would hold the heat of food. In about three hours the girl's fever "had gone down entirely and she went to sleep. . . . After a few hours she was thoroughly relieved." None of those who acted as medical superintendents, including Walter Thompson Adair, the first Cherokee graduate of a medical school, were untrained practitioners. It was the position itself that demanded more than was humanly possible. The medical officer for the four Cherokee institutions received a salary that averaged $1,500 per year, but the officer had to supply all of his own medical supplies. Expenditures for the orphan asylum made this abundantly clear. Little money went into outfitting a dispensary or sickroom, and often the most basic of supplies such as bandages or disinfectant were lacking.[42]

Not discussed before, during, or after the 1900 report were the number of children who died at the asylum. They were simply left unacknowledged. These deaths were less likely a sign of outright neglect than an indicator of numerous factors that placed the institutionalized at risk. Children and adolescents were more likely to enter an orphanage undernourished and possibly already suffering from pellagra, tuberculosis, or other diseases. Even when these maladies were diagnosed and treated, life inside an institution was no guarantee of improved health. Contagious diseases such as measles and chicken pox spread at rapid rates among youngsters crowded into dormitories and classrooms. When the incidence of smallpox was particularly high in the Cherokee Nation in 1882 and 1901, many children—not only at the orphanage but also at the Cherokee seminaries—contracted the disease. No institution could escape the fact that children died. The Cherokee Orphan Asylum could not guarantee, any more than any other institution with a child population, that all its charges would survive to adulthood. Thus, as one former asylum inhabitant remembered, "If any of the children died, they were buried at the School Cemetery."[43]

To correct the many deficiencies outlined by the 1900 report, the Cherokee Council approved a large expenditure out of non–Orphan Fund accounts. Contractors and day laborers were hired to rebuild porches and flooring, replace the old roof with one of metal, and place new fencing around pasture and livestock pens. There seemed to be a thousand and one incidentals purchased for everyday use. Purchase orders bulged with itemized lists: water dippers; globes for kerosene

lamps; boxes of soap; one dozen "fine" combs; pie plates; eating utensils; and foodstuffs such as sugar and baking powder that could not be
homegrown. School supplies such as tablets, pencils, and crayons
were purchased, and Thompson enhanced the curriculum by purchas-
ing up-to-date textbooks from the American Book Company in
Chicago. Subjects ranged from beginner's reading primers to texts on
algebra, agriculture, physics, geography, history, and Latin. Clearly,
the intention was to offer the same subjects that were available at the
Cherokees' male and female seminaries. Classroom offerings combined the components of common school, classical, and manual-labor
education into a well-rounded curriculum.[44]

Finally, and as important, acceptance of secondhand clothing from
kind benefactors or having children wear whatever was at hand came
to an end. Thompson, a graduate of the Cherokee Male Seminary and
Cumberland University in Lebanon, Tennessee, had years of experience
as a teacher and school superintendent in both the Cherokee and the
Choctaw school systems. A product of his own educational experience
and familiar with boarding school procedures, Thompson instituted
uniform dress at the Cherokee orphanage. To that end, caps and shoes
were purchased, as well as yard goods, buttons, and thread. Local seam-
stresses, including girls at the Cherokee Female Seminary, applied their
skills and needles to creating the appropriate clothing. One quarterly
bill alone included charges for over three hundred yards of fabric.[45]

Considering the money expended at the orphan asylum and the
labor demanded for improving the structure, it was an unspeakable
tragedy when the asylum burned on November 17, 1903. There was
speculation that the fire was intentionally set—but not by students.
Two distinct factions within the nation had been at odds with tribal
leaders since the orphanage opened. The first group included aligned
political opponents who accused some leaders, including Principal
Chief Ross, of misusing Orphan Fund money for their own gain. The
second group constituted the freedmen who believed, with good reason, that their orphans were not being cared for as conscientiously as
other orphans in the Cherokee Nation. Either group may have had a
motive for setting the fire, but speculation and gossip never crossed
the line of outright accusation or quite believing that anyone would
put the children at risk. The insurance company, located in Brooklyn,
New York, unequivocally stated that there was no arsonist, since the
fire originated between the third floor ceiling and the roof. Unfortu-

nately, damage was total. The fire, fanned by a strong northwest wind, spread quickly. With no modern fire-fighting equipment, "vigorous efforts" by staff and children to douse the fire with buckets of water was an exercise in futility. Within an hour, the roof caved in, destroying the building's interior and its contents.[46]

None of the adults or the 149 children were injured, but the youngsters with no place to turn were again homeless. In the hours after the fire, the community of Pryor Creek rallied to care for the children, and the board of education met to decide its immediate response and long-term plan. There was no doubt that the Cherokee Orphan Asylum would continue, but in the interim places had to be found for the children and adolescents. Fifteen of the older boys and sixteen of the girls were transferred to the Cherokee seminaries. The remaining children, two teachers, a nurse, and five other asylum employees went to the Whitaker Orphan Home, a nondenominational, privately run orphanage at Pryor Creek.[47]

The home was established by W. T. Whitaker and his wife, who arrived in Oklahoma with the opening of the Cherokee Strip to white settlement. Whitaker later wrote that when he and his wife came to the area, they wanted to find a way to help those in need. He consulted with the Reverend Watt A. Duncan, first superintendent of the Cherokee Orphan Asylum, for advice on opening an orphanage. With about $100 of Whitaker's own money and donations collected from subscriptions "ranging from 10 cents and up," a simple building was constructed, and twenty-one white children, boys and girls, entered the Whitaker Orphan Home in 1897. Since the Whitakers were not connected with any church-supported charity, they scrambled to keep the orphanage operational. Whitaker recalled that soon after the place opened he went to Pryor Creek to buy coats for seven little girls at the home, but before the purchases were made, he was located by the manager of the train depot. At the station was a box addressed to Whitaker. The scene that followed at the orphanage brought tears to the eyes and whoops of joy: "When I opened the box every child in the home was standing around the box, wanting to find out what was in it. When I opened it, the first thing on top was coats for the little girls." The box and its donated contents came from women in a Missouri Eastern Star lodge.[48]

When the Cherokee Board of Education placed the majority of its orphan asylum children in the Whitaker Home, the youngsters were for the first time exposed to an environment that accommodated both Indian and white children. The number of Caucasian children was not large, however, and Whitaker had no reason for excluding either group of children from the home. There is no doubt that he welcomed the Cherokees out of a heartfelt concern for their welfare. Nevertheless, the financial aid promised by the Cherokee Board of Education was a strong incentive. While the children were housed at the Whitaker Home, the owner received a per diem per child on a par with what the Cherokee government paid when children were in the Cherokee Orphan Asylum. Whitaker was equally pleased by an unexpected bonus. During the six months the Cherokees resided at the home, the superintendent of the Cherokee orphanage set about making the Whitaker home "more comfortable." A small room was converted into a kitchen, fireplace grates and windows were repaired, and the barn was "put into a condition whereby it could be used." In all, concluded the Cherokee superintendent, "We took good care of it [the home], and left it in a much better condition than we found it."[49]

Soon after the refugees from the fire arrived, a few additional Cherokee orphans took up residence at the Whitaker Home. Among them were Martha Goins and her two younger sisters. Their father, a Cherokee, died in 1900; their mother, a Caucasian, died in 1903. Martha stayed at the Whitaker orphanage for a short time and then was transferred to Chilocco Indian School, where she remained for three years. She then returned to Whitaker and stayed until 1908, when she married a young man who "was also an inmate of the home." Although she spent a relatively short period of her life at Whitaker, Martha Goins, in her reminiscence, made it clear that she considered the Whitaker Orphan Home as the place where she and her sisters "were reared and educated."[50]

The children from the Cherokee Orphan Asylum could have remained at the Whitaker orphanage. The director was more than willing, but the Cherokee Board of Education had other plans. It did not intend to allow outside charity to replace a tribally controlled institution or to intermingle white and Indian children. The board's solution was simple. All it required was a reshuffling. In early December 1903 the Cherokee council approved a $10,000 appropriation (added to the $7,333 received from the insurance claim) to make "comfortable and convenient quarters" in the building being used as the Cherokee Insane Asylum. The insane asylum, located about five miles outside Tahlequah, never had more than twenty inmates, and these could be transferred with little problem to the building used as the Cherokee Nation's jail. Once the inmates were moved, the insane asylum would be "repaired and equipped in such a manner as will enable them [orphanage staff] to properly care for the orphan children."[51]

The Cherokee Insane Asylum, officially called the Asylum for the Insane, Deaf, Dumb and Blind, was another symbol of the Cherokees' adoption of Euro-American institutions. For the Cherokees it announced that they had attained a high degree of civilization on two levels. First, they were following white culture in building asylums. Second, a population of poor "unfortunates" in need of an asylum was proof that the Cherokees were civilized because many nineteenth-century reformers believed that insanity was the price a culture paid for civilization. The higher incidence of insanity in a society, the greater its advancement. These same reformers argued with great conviction that in areas where Indians or members of the "negro race" were the chief occupants, there was little or no insanity. Therefore, by having an insane asylum, the Cherokees proved that they were civilized.[52]

Cherokee asylum inmates ranged from the adolescent to the elderly. Since some were blind or deaf, not all were adjudged to be insane. Those who were, however, were believed to be better off if removed from the environment that had evidently brought on their mental illness. At this time in American society, institutionalization was not seen as simply shutting the mentally ill away. It was considered a way to cure the problem while often protecting the larger world from uncontrollable rage or acts of violence. One visitor to the Cherokee Insane Asylum, Narcissa Owen, certainly approved the idea, and years after the fact she still seemed to be shaking her head over the chance encounter with someone she had known during childhood: "One of the inmates recognized me and said, 'Don't you remember that school at Mose Daniel's? . . . I burned up that schoolhouse to see the big fire.'" Owen did remember. The fire forced her to walk an extra half mile to attend another school.[53]

When white settlers entered Indian Territory during and after the land rush, they found themselves without the institutions to which they had grown accustomed. This included an insane asylum, and a number of newly arrived settlers petitioned Indian agent Dew M. Wisdom to allow white "unfortunates" into the Cherokee institution. The Cherokees found themselves in an uncustomary position. The nation had an infrastructure of schools, governmental organizations, and established institutions. The incoming whites did not, sending them begging to the Cherokees for help. Their appeals went unheard. The Cherokees chose to keep the insane asylum for their own people. For its part, Oklahoma's territorial government solved the problem in the short term by transporting white "unfortunates" to an Illinois institution; when that proved too costly, it contracted with a Missouri hospital to operate an insane asylum in the territory.[54]

For the Cherokees the insane asylum building adequately solved the problem of what to do about an orphanage. Repairs were less costly than rebuilding, and the Cherokee council believed that the solution offered a good opportunity to move the orphanage back to the vicinity of Tahlequah. The asylum already had a farm on which crops and gardens were cultivated and livestock raised. It was the same type of environment necessary for an orphanage. The only problem was what to do with the inmates of the insane asylum. In the short term, they could remain in the nation's jail, but this was not a satisfactory solution for the future. The U.S. government, through its intervention into Cherokee life under the Dawes Commission, provided the answer. Inmates of the insane asylum were transferred. Minors who were categorized as "deaf and dumb" were sent to an institution in Illinois, with the federal government paying a per diem per pupil. Under a U.S. congressional act passed in April 1904, adult inmates were sent to Canton, South Dakota, where an insane asylum had been built in 1899 to serve Indian tribes other than the Cherokees. Meanwhile, the Cherokee Insane Asylum was converted for use as an orphanage. The physical plant was expanded, and one of its interior components—"the box," used to hold the most violent of mentally unsound inmates—was removed.[55]

When children entered the newly renovated institution in May 1904, the Cherokee government was struggling to retain its control over the asylum. In 1887 the U.S. Congress passed the General Allotment Act, generally referred to as the Dawes Act. This was amended and extended by an 1891 amendment, and in 1893 the Dawes Commission was created to implement allotment of Indian lands in severalty and to dissolve the governments of the Five Civilized Tribes. The Cherokees staved off the commission and dissolution, but in 1901 the

Costumed girls at the Cherokee home participate in a Maypole dance, 1921. Archives and Manuscripts Division of the Oklahoma Historical Society.

Cherokee Nation and the Dawes Commission came to terms over the asylum and the Orphan Fund. They agreed that the fund would be directed by the U.S. secretary of the interior and that the Cherokee Orphan Asylum would continue to operate only until land allotment was completed. Despite this, the Cherokee government still retained some control when the new orphan home opened in 1904. By the next year, however, the Cherokees were only nominally involved. The U.S. inspector for Indian Territory visited the asylum, declared it operational with 106 resident children, and between June 1904 and June 1905 spent over $12,000 from the Orphan Fund. The expenditure was double the amount normally spent in a fiscal year by the Cherokees. The federal government intended to deplete the fund as quickly as possible. At the same time, the Cherokee government was pressured to divest itself of the old orphan asylum site at Pryor Creek. On this point, the Cherokees demonstrated considerable reluctance, and the land was not sold until 1909.[56]

Tribal dissolution and land allotment set down by the Dawes Commission meant that school systems operated by the Five Civilized Tribes were dismantled. The federal government decided how tribal funds were spent for education, which Indian schools in Oklahoma remained open, and accessibility to out-of-state boarding schools. Most of the Cherokee neighborhood or day schools closed their doors. This changed the educational options available to Indian youngsters, who could attend the few boarding schools remaining in Oklahoma or enroll in boarding schools such as Haskell Institute in Kansas. They could attend Oklahoma's public schools, where, said one report, "a large number" of students, especially mixed-bloods, could be found.[57]

For the Cherokees, there was another choice. Although the federal government gave every indication that it would close the Cherokee Orphan Asylum, it did not. After tribal dissolution, the Cherokee orphanage remained open under the Indian Bureau, which found the transfer from tribal to federal direction relatively smooth because James Allen Thompson had insisted on changes such as uniforms and a curriculum comparable to that of the Cherokee male and female seminaries. At the time the federal government stepped in, orphan home operations already shared many similarities with federal boarding schools. The orphan home did not, however, have every component. There was no disciplinarian on staff, and there was no systematic punishment for failure to speak English. There certainly was no outing system until federal officials took control. The home changed in tone, but one constant remained. As a survivor of tribal dissolution, the Cherokee Orphan Asylum continued to offer shelter and an education to a specific group of children, adolescents, and teenagers.

4

AFTER THE WAR: CHICKASAW

This was a home for both boys and girls of the Chickasaws and
Choctaws. Our sleeping rooms were upstairs, and the classrooms and
dining were on the first floor.[1]

During the Civil War the Chickasaws sided with the Confederacy,
partly because the mixed-blood leaders owned slaves and partly because the Chickasaws had no reason to support a government that
forced their removal and then was slow to carry out treaty promises.
The Chickasaws, numbering fewer than five thousand at the beginning of hostilities, were not safe from conditions created by the Civil
War. There were refugees, lost homes, and broken families. Among the
refugees were approximately 225 men, women, and children who
chose to remain neutral; they joined Creeks, Seminoles, and Cherokees who fled to Kansas. Fighting in Kansas, however, forced many to
move again, seeking protection at Fort Gibson in Indian Territory or
Fort Smith, Arkansas. Life for these refugees was an unsettled round
of relocation and the haunting fear that when they returned home
there would be nothing left. Pro-Confederate Chickasaws who stayed
in their neighborhoods fared little better when they were confronted
with fleeing Cherokees who sought refuge among the Chickasaws and
vied for provisions and resources. To alleviate some of the deprivations, white Confederates allowed the Indians to take rations from
Confederate stores. One report estimated that almost eight hundred
Chickasaw women and children received this aid while "their men
were away fighting." Among the Chickasaws there were orphaned
children and youngsters whose families barely subsisted on handouts.[2]

At the close of the war, the Chickasaws emerged from the chaos determined to rebuild. This included reopening the nation's school system, which was established during the 1850s. There had not been an
orphanage within the system prior to the war, but in the postwar period the Chickasaw Nation opened an orphan asylum as a place of

refuge and learning. Meant primarily for Chickasaw children, the new orphan home also took in a few Choctaws. This was not because the Choctaws did not develop their own orphan asylums. They did, but the Choctaw institutions appeared at a later date and without the immediacy exhibited by the Cherokees and Chickasaws to care for those made destitute and orphaned by the war.

Admittance of Choctaw youngsters to the Chickasaw orphanage was based on three preexisting conditions of the Choctaw-Chickasaw relationship: Choctaw families and children lived in Chickasaw territory; the two tribes were in close geographic proximity; and the two had a long interrelated history. Some historians, ethnographers, and archaeologists believe that at one time the Chicaksaws were an inseparable entity within the Choctaw people. The two clearly were more similar than different in language and cultural attributes. However, by the time of contact with the Spanish, French, and later British and Americans, the Chickasaws were identified as a separate people, occupying portions of Kentucky, Tennessee, Alabama, and Mississippi. They were never, however, as populous as the Choctaws.

Both groups had their own Trail of Tears, and removal bound the Chickasaws and Choctaws when they were assigned one shared western territory. An agreement signed at Doaksville, Indian Territory, on January 17, 1837, stipulated that the Chickasaws would settle in the Choctaw Nation with the rights of Choctaw citizenship. The agreement also created the Chickasaw District, land to be held in common by the two tribes. The Doaksville arrangement produced an environment in which the Chickasaws were slow to establish schools in Indian Territory. Major Ethan Allen Hitchcok, investigating fraud among contractors providing rations, believed that money received by the Chickasaws from sale of Mississippi land was the cause. Hitchcok offered the opinion that the tribe settled among the Choctaws and showed no interest in moving to the Chickasaw District as long as their money lasted. Others believed that the Chickasaws were reluctant to finance schools as long as they remained in a subservient position within the Choctaw Nation. They saw no reason to build on land of another tribe. It took pressure from missionaries and from government officials, including the Indian agent for the Chickasaws, for the tribe to set up schools. In 1844 tribal leaders agreed to construct a schoolhouse, but none was forthcoming despite the Indian agent's report that the tribe was "very anxious" to have its children educated.

Finally, the first school in the Chickasaw District—the Chickasaw Manual Labor Academy (later called the Chickasaw Male Academy), a two-story stone building—opened in 1851. Operated under the direction of the Methodist Episcopal Church, South, the academy was coeducational until the Wapanucka Female Manual Labor School (later called the Wapanucka Institute) was established in 1852. The first schools in the Chickasaw District nicely conformed to the federal government's idea of acceptable education: "Schools on the manual-labor plan are the only schools that will do much good in any nation of Indians. To give them an education without learning them to work, either as farmers or mechanics, is of but little use to them."[3]

Nineteenth-century Euro-American society relied on basically three education models: the school curriculum that included reading, writing, arithmetic, American history, and geography; classical education, provided either by tutors or by private schools or colleges, which extended basic education into studies of classical literature, music and art, and languages such as Latin; and working apprenticeships that taught youngsters a skilled trade such as carpentry or typesetting. From these emerged the manual-labor model, which combined common school education and apprenticeships to form the basis of education endorsed by the common school agenda.

From their first contacts with Euro-Americans, Indian groups were introduced to manual-labor education. Along with classes in English and Christianity, tribes were supplied with work implements and taught to use them. The instruction became more formalized with the organization of schools. Manual-labor, or vocational, training became the norm in most educational settings. The majority of Indian youth were exposed only to the manual-labor model. The exceptions were those who attended eastern schools, where they were given the education necessary to establish careers as doctors, lawyers, ministers, and political leaders.

The manual-labor form of instruction was strikingly similar to that for immigrants and poor whites, although the rationale differed. Vocational training for Indian youth was intended to civilize them; the same training for non-Indian youngsters was meant to educate them before their poverty and unrest could disrupt the social order. One proponent of vocational education suggested that manual-labor training would teach cooperation and leadership, and in the best of all worlds it would be balanced with a curriculum that included math, literacy in the English language, and student activities such as debate clubs and literary societies.⁴ This combination began to appear in public schools at the turn of the century, but in the nineteenth century vocational training for non-Indian groups most often occurred through indenture; in industrial schools established by private charities or state agencies; in most orphanages; in urban settlement houses; and in reformatories and juvenile asylums where manual-labor training was regarded as rehabilitation.

The settings for manual-labor instruction were not lost on the Indian Bureau. The number of non-Indian institutions using this type of education suggested that there were even greater possibilities for application in Indian schools. Agricultural training was a centerpiece in the majority of Indian schools because farming was regarded as the great civilizer, and domestic training was pictured as the one avenue through which girls could learn "true womanhood." Thomas Morgan, commissioner of Indian affairs from 1889 to 1893, agreed, but he wanted to do more. Morgan, characterized by historian Francis Paul Prucha as "the first significant national figure in the history of American Indian education," was in tune with progressive educational trends of his time. He was also a fervent believer in education's ability to assimilate diverse groups into a national culture of patriotism and American identity. Manual-labor education was touted as being capable of achieving assimilation and stemming unrest among immigrants who found America to be not a place of opportunity but a land of bigotry and racism. With the possibilities promised by manual labor in mind, Morgan made an extensive study of such training in juvenile reformatories where manual labor dominated. Facilities in Kansas, Indiana, and Maine were studied, as well as the industrial programs of the New York Juvenile Asylum and the Rhode Island Home and School and Orphan Asylum. Morgan's objective was to determine if programs in those institutions could be used as a blueprint for establishing "suitable" Indian training schools with one hundred students per institution. Morgan envisioned Indian boarding schools that were modern models of manual-labor instruction, producing graduates who possessed trade skills and were able to work at vocations other than farming and homemaking. No doubt, Morgan was influenced by the growing vocational education movement in the United States. Certainly his inquiries came at a time when this movement was gaining momentum, and they also emphasized the important place of vocational training in Indian education. Practices in reform schools and orphanages had a great deal in common with Indian institutions of learning. The correlation made by Morgan suggests much more than finding ways to enhance and expand manual-labor training. Articulated or not, Indian schools in general were considered similar to reformatories or orphanages in the ways young people were congregated together, marked for acculturation, and educated for their futures.[5]

The Chickasaws emphasized vocational training, too, but not necessarily as a means to achieve assimilation or acculturation. It was a practical approach. There was a need for leaders who were trained in the "academies" and off-reservation boarding schools and colleges, but there was as much need for young men and women who could adequately engage in the many occupations necessary to build up the Chickasaw Nation in Indian Territory. Carpentry, construction of buildings and bridges, operation of printing presses, and "modern" homemaking practices taught in home economics classes were just some of the identified needs of a nation bent on self-sufficiency.

Before the Chickasaws were removed from their traditional homeland, their earliest encounters with white education were combinations of common school and training in agriculture. In 1820 the first school opened near Cotton Gin Port on the Tombigbee River in present-day northeastern Mississippi. Under direction of the Missionary Board of the Cumberland Presbyterian Church, the school was supervised by the Reverend Robert Bell, and an "agriculturalist" was employed for training adults. Two years later, when twenty-eight students were enrolled and the board provided proof of its work, it received $500 from the federal government. This was not the extent of Chickasaw education. A few young men attended schools away from home. Of those enrolled, most were mixed-blood sons of prominent families and tribal leaders. The earliest known instance of a youth sent away to school was Pitman Colbert's attendance at a Maryland school in 1803; by the mid-1820s, a number of young men were students at the Baptist-supported Choctaw Academy in Scott County, Kentucky. A version of a prep school, it was intended to serve as a training ground for the next generation of Indian leaders. Although there was a decided Baptist influence, the curriculum did not narrowly focus on religion or basic instruction. It was not a religious seminary. Studies encompassed mathematics, reading, writing, grammar, some science, and music. The environment commingled Chickasaws and Creeks, Choctaws and Pawnees, Potawatomies and Seminoles.[6]

After removal, the Chickasaws continued to finance off-reservation education for some males, but in 1848 the Chickasaws quit the Choctaw Academy in favor of sending students to Delaware College in Newark, Delaware, and Plainfield Academy in Norwich, Connecticut, where Chickasaw youth sometimes lived with white families. The move was the result of Chickasaw, as well as Choctaw and Creek, complaints that the Choctaw Academy was a corrupting influence. Some young men returned from the academy with white vices rather than skills to help their people, and time spent away from home sometimes wrecked young men's emotional ties to their families. In one instance two Choctaws committed suicide upon their return to Indian Territory; one found his relatives in dire poverty, and the other was faced with the death of his mother and an alienated father. If anything, experiences with the Choctaw Academy made tribal governments in Indian Territory more committed to building up their own schools.[7]

Considering the Chickasaws' long involvement with eastern schools, one could easily wonder why they did not consider placing the orphaned in eastern institutions. There were certainly any number to choose from after the Civil War, yet that option was never considered. After the war, the tribe continued to send some of its young people to schools away from home territory, but most youngsters remained in the nation. Circumstances had changed for the Chickasaws. In 1855 the tribe won separation from the Choctaws. The Chickasaws gained the right to self-government, and the boundaries of the Chickasaw Nation were clearly defined. With a renewed sense of tribal identity and control over the tribe's resources, including its children, tribal leaders chose to establish a school system. After the Civil War, that system had an orphanage. Choctaw children inside the boundaries of the Chickasaw Nation were allowed admittance, but by the late 1880s the Choctaws had their own orphanages, and the Chickasaw government stipulated that its institution was "for Chickasaw orphans only."[8]

The orphanage was known by several names. Its first official title was the Lebanon Institute, since it was located near the town of

Teachers and residents of the Chickasaw Orphan Home near Lebanon, Indian Territory, ca. 1896–97. Archives and Manuscripts Division of the Oklahoma Historical Society.

Lebanon in the Chickasaw Nation. Many, however, simply referred to it as the Lebanon Orphan School. Then, in 1879, it was formally designated the Chickasaw Orphan Home. By the turn of the century it was the Chickasaw Orphan Home and Manual Labor School. By whatever name, the home was for both boys and girls. One youngster, who was not sure of his birth date but believed that it was 1858, was among the first to reside in the orphanage. He recalled: "As far back as I can remember the Chickasaw Orphan's Home was located one mile east of the present town of Lebanon. The first teacher I remember at the school was Ned [Nat] Smith. . . . [There were] usually 60 or 70 students."[9]

The numbers varied from fifty to just over one hundred, and the applications for admittance almost always exceeded available space. The Chickasaw government easily and efficiently dealt with the situation. For those orphans and half-orphans turned away from the Lebanon home, space was found within the nation's boarding schools. It was a telling solution. The orphanage was intended to be a "first class boarding school [with] scholarship to be of first class grade . . . for males and females."[10] It was for a recognized group within the population, but since it was considered a place of education, children and teenagers could be moved to another Chickasaw-supported school when the situation demanded. Education had the highest priority. No white, middle-class sentimentality seeped into the authorities' thinking about "poor" orphans. No social dicta demanded that the orphan be segregated from the non-orphan when there was no room in the home. The lives of youngsters at Lebanon represented special circumstances, but the children were not to be deprived of the classroom. They were scholars.

From extant material it is difficult, if not impossible, to determine the exact opening date of the home. One historian, writing of the post–Civil War period, stated that four Chickasaw academies "reopened" in 1876 and that one of the four was the Lebanon orphanage. The implication is that all were operational prior to the Civil War. Nevertheless, there is no clear evidence that the orphan home existed before the war, although the Chickasaws had their own Orphan Fund dating from the time of removal. It is more likely that the 1876 date was used as a reference to the time in which the Chickasaw government began to fully appropriate moneys on a regular basis to all forms of education. Becoming completely functional was a slow process. It began soon after the U.S. government resumed annuity payments in 1867 and eleven neighborhood schools opened. These were followed by the four academies in question—the Chickasaw Male Academy, Bloomfield Female Academy, Wapanucka Institute, and Lebanon Institute. All opened before the 1876 date, although the settings were generally ramshackle. Classes were conducted in school buildings that were in various states of disrepair after being damaged while in use as military camps or hospitals. (The prewar Colbert Institute was not among those used; the building was burned to the ground during the war.) Despite the distractions and makeshift surroundings, students were in attendance and teachers were at their desks.[11]

In the atmosphere of rebuilding and reinstituting a measure of normalcy in the nation, the opening date for the Chickasaw Orphan Home remains unclear. Based on available material and calculated dates, it seems that the home may have opened as early as 1868. It most certainly existed in 1870, predating the Cherokee orphanage by one year, if not longer. A steady flow of funds did not support the institution until 1876, however. In that year the Chickasaw government fully funded all its educational facilities. Orphan home appropriations came from the tribe's Orphan Fund. Overall supervision of the home rested with the governor of the nation, the Chickasaw superintendent of public instruction, and a trustee who inspected the school periodically. In the beginning, the Chickasaws chose not to contract with a missionary group for running the orphan school. Daily supervision of the home and its sixty orphan residents was in the hands of Capt. Nat Smith (a Civil War veteran) and his wife.[12]

One historical overview of Chickasaw education strongly suggests that the home remained a noncontract institution until 1904. In fact, contracts were let out in the 1870s. By 1876 Captain Smith was no longer in charge of the home, although he was still a teacher there. Supervision was in the hands of the Reverend R. S. Bell, remembered by one early resident of the home as "a good man" whom the children liked. Bell's church affiliation is unclear. One resident later recalled that the orphan home was under contract with the Cumberland Presbyterian Church, but this personal memory may have become confused over time and the orphan home mistakenly jumbled with a proposal submitted to the Chickasaw government for another orphanage. In 1889 a missionary identified as the Reverend J. J. Reed was authorized by the Presbyterian Church of the United States to negotiate with the Chickasaws for a contract orphanage in Tishomingo County. This orphan home was intended for girls between the ages of eight and twenty; if there were not enough orphans to fill the facility, non-orphans would be admitted. The Chickasaw government approved the proposal, but there is no evidence to indicate that the place ever advanced beyond the planning stage. In fact, the reverend in question was John Jeremiah Read, superintendent of the Choctaw-run Spencer Academy for boys. Name spellings on school and tribal documents were sometimes casual affairs, more phonetic than exact, and in all probability the minister who proposed an orphanage for the Chickasaws was the same man who supervised the Choctaw school where, soon after Read's arrival, an outbreak of pneumonia took the lives of a number of students and that of Read's young daughter.[13]

There was a Presbyterian interest in building orphanages in the Chickasaw Nation, and this may have clouded recollections associated with the orphan home. It is more likely, based on the strong presence of Methodists among the Chickasaws and the fact that later superintendents were Methodists, that Chickasaw Orphan Home contracts were let to that denomination. Clearly, whatever early intentions the Chickasaws entertained for operating the orphan home themselves were of short duration.

In the summer of 1876 the *Vindicator,* a newspaper based in Atoka, carried an account of that year's examination of pupils at the Chickasaw Orphan Home. It was with a sense of pride that the reporter noted the number of interested observers and the students' conduct: "When we arrived at the Academy there were many of the citizens of the Nation present. . . . When the examination commenced we were all invited to the school room by Professor Lindsay [teacher], . . . where we witnessed a most thorough and rigid examination."[14]

Following student recitations and responses to questions posed, Jessie Bell, wife of the superintendent, spoke to the youngsters, impressing upon them their future responsibilities as representatives and citizens of the Chickasaw Nation. The children were being educated to fulfill a much-needed role. They were told that

> they would have to protect their tribal rights under treaties with
> the Federal Government, and to compete with educated, saga-
> cious and unscrupulous white men . . . that they should remem-
> ber that the appropriations made by their Legislature to educate
> them was interest on purchase money paid to their tribe by the
> Federal Government for old homes in Mississippi.[15]

They were not to forget that their traditional home was somewhere else or that the tribe had been forced to leave. Neither were the students to shirk their duties to the Chickasaw people. No doubt Bell's charge to the youngsters was a reminder of young men such as Holmes Colbert and Allen Wright (both onetime Delaware College students) who used their education to serve the Chickasaws with distinction. Their achievements were many. Colbert, at the age of twenty-six, drafted the Chickasaw constitution; Wright became governor of the nation and compiled a dictionary of the Chickasaw language. Pride in tribal heritage was reinforced at the summer examination when one speaker addressed the audience in both English and Chickasaw. The bilingual presentation was no doubt for members of the audience who spoke no English, but it was also representative of the way in which the home was conducted.[16]

Few children entered the home with a command of the English language. In fact, one estimate of English speakers among the Choctaws and Chickasaws claimed that 70 percent of those attending neighborhood and boarding schools spoke no English.[17] At the orphan home, English was the language of the classroom, and teachers were expected to enforce the rule. Outside the walls of learning, however, youngsters used Chickasaw to communicate. They did so freely, knowing that they would not be punished or humiliated as was the norm in off-reservation and federally directed boarding schools. The bilingual nature of the Chickasaw home did not change over time. It was still in place in 1906 when Carrie Wilcox and her husband, superintendent of the home, arrived. With amusement, rather than condescending disapproval, Wilcox recalled that both students and teachers used the Chickasaw language: "I was well liked by the children. They would pat my arm, then laugh and run away. I asked the teachers what they said when they did this. They replied, 'Fish belly.' I suppose because my arms were soft and white, while theirs were brown."[18]

Considering the paucity of materials on daily conduct, it is impossible to say if Wilcox's attitude was the norm, but she certainly was not alone. A teacher in Choctaw schools witnessed, if not encouraged, the same bilingual environment noted by Wilcox at the Chickasaw home. It was not a case of teachers simply overlooking a youngster's lapse into his or her native tongue. Teachers risked their jobs, since teaching certificates usually stipulated that they were not to allow students to speak their own language. Failure to comply meant loss of teaching credentials and unemployment. The certificate of the teacher at the Choctaw school was no different, but the woman found her own way to compromise the rule.

> I enforced that in the school room, but did not try on the play ground. Some of those little fellows were away from home for the first time in their life [sic], and were so homesick that it would have been rank cruelty to have kept them from talking to each other in their native tongue. So I just didn't hear them.[19]

The use of native language and of English in Indian schools and orphanages, especially in those operated by the Five Civilized Tribes, presents a view of Indian education that does not always conform to evidence demonstrated in studies of life in off-reservation boarding schools, where use of English was strongly enforced and noncompliant students punished. Location and population were key factors in the differences. First, orphanages were not off-reservation. Nor did their populations represent a multilanguage environment. Delawares were not mixed with Chickasaws. Choctaws did not live or study side by side with Senecas. Grouping Choctaws with Chickasaws at the orphan home did not represent a large problem in terms of language, since the linguistic base of the two shared great similarities. Off-reservation boarding school directors, on the other hand, argued that English brought a common language to an otherwise multilingual environment. Orphanages for one native group, however, had no reason to make the same claim.

In tribally run orphanages, bilingual communication was compatible with the objectives of education. As demonstrated by the Chickasaw Orphan Home exercises of 1876, adults watched proudly as students conversed in English. At the same time, they were addressed in Chickasaw and admonished to be future leaders. Children were expected to learn English. It was an economic asset, and, by learning white culture through reading and writing English, the children would become mediators between the two worlds.[20] These future actors in the life of their tribe would be somewhat different from those who had gone away to Indian boarding schools. Through their use of English and the world introduced by that language, children in orphanages were affected by the dominant culture. Arguably, however, their lack of long-term contact with Euro-American families, all-white faculties, and non-Indian communities made them less susceptible to accepting and adapting all the dominant culture's value systems and thought patterns. It was one thing to be exposed to a foreign culture; it was quite another to live it. These children were far more likely to adapt to their own culture, which itself was in a state of evolution.

Orphanages overseen by the Five Civilized tribes in Indian Territory were little affected by the English-only order issued by John D. C. Atkins, commissioner of Indian affairs from 1885 to 1888. In fact, the Chickasaws generally ignored it. Instruction already was in English, and the Chickasaw government was not obligated to report the conduct of its schools to the Indian Bureau. Of course, this was not the situation where schools were not tribally supported. At the government contract school for the Poncas in Indian Territory, for example, English-only was a standing rule. When it met with resistance, the Indian agent for the Poncas was told by his superiors to be more assertive. The agent promised to make the desired changes, but following Atkins's directive would not be easy. "The Ponca children are bright enough . . . but they partake very much of the nature of their fathers in the point of a sullen reluctance to speak more of the English language than will exactly do. The rule on this point will be stricter with them."[21]

At some Indian agencies, the order was taken to the extreme by officials who extended the English-only edict from the classroom to private homes, church services, and community gatherings. Needless to say, the order was not well received on a number of fronts. Among those upset with the policy were some missionaries. The Reverend Isaac McCoy, for example, encouraged Baptist missions in Kansas to instruct Shawnee Indians in their own language, believing that native groups "improved" more readily when they were introduced to religion and white thinking through their native tongue. McCoy used the Five Civilized Tribes as the best example of this approach. Atkins's position also flew in the face of those clerics who had developed orthographies or translated the Bible or portions of the Scriptures into native languages. Even those Indians who believed that English was a necessary tool for dealing with the white world and for advancing native peoples beyond "the superstition of . . . ancestors" were appalled.[22] Opined the editors of the Chippewa publication *The Progress:*

> So far as we can see, nothing in his [Atkins's] policy during his term of office has been marked by wise statesmanship, benevolence, or even shrewd policy. . . . For one thing we may mention his (in)famous ruling on the use of the native tongue in Indian schools, of whatever sort. We do not find fault with his effort to restrain the use of the spoken language in educational institutions, but it was going beyond reason to arbitrarily decree that instruction of any sort not be in the vernacular.[23]

The Indian Bureau and its superintendent of Indian schools, an office established in 1881, exerted little influence on the Chickasaws' bilingual environment, but the Chickasaws accepted the idea of manual-labor instruction. The nation's first boarding schools incorporated this form of training, and the orphanage continued the plan. Training in agriculture and the manual arts was part of each learning day. The home had a farm that developed and improved over the years. By 1900 the farm boasted one hundred hogs, thirty-four cattle, four mules, one horse, a small apple orchard, and fields of crops, primarily corn. Boys milked the cows, cut wood that was used as heating and cooking fuel, and raised gardens. Girls learned to can food for winter use, and both boys and girls worked at grinding wheat and corn into flour and meal. Girls also did inside chores, washing dishes, and ironing. They learned by doing, but the little evidence offered from the reminiscences of onetime residents suggests that the youngsters were not overworked or overburdened. One girl recalled that heavier outside work and the canning were done by the "larger," older girls. Younger children helped but were not pushed into performing tasks that were beyond their years. Another former resident remembered that girls did not do all the indoor work because "a woman was hired by the Chickasaw Government to do the laundry. A negro and a white woman did the cooking." Handymen were employed for maintenance work.[24]

Issues of language and incorporation of vocational education illuminate the orphan home's practices. Nevertheless, they do little to tell us about those who lived and studied in an environment that Carrie Wilcox described as an "altogether lovely setting" with grounds "shaded by beautiful trees." Today, most of the names of the onetime inhabitants of the Chickasaw Orphan Home are lost in the passage of years. Only in a few instances are there glimpses, primarily in the few student lists that remain from the superintendent's reports to the Chickasaw superintendent of schools. The names stare back from the page, providing one clear message. Relatives, siblings or cousins, resided together in the home. In one year's listing, as illustration, over 50 percent of the surnames represented two or more youngsters with the same last names; the largest number with the same name, Keel, was six.[25]

The children were both full-bloods and mixed-bloods. Overton Lavers, for example, was "$\frac{1}{2}$ Chickasaw Indian," and Susan Lewis was a full-blood. Some of those admitted into the orphanage had kin, reluctant or unable to provide care. One girl attended neighborhood schools for five years, but when her mother died, "[father] sent me to the orphan's home at Lebanon." The burden of trying to work and care for a family of five children alone was simply too great for him, and there evidently were no aunts or grandparents to come to the rescue. Other children were without any relatives. They moved from one household to another in local communities until coming to the orphanage.[26]

Their appearances upon arrival told who did and did not have family, as well as revealing without a word the abject poverty in which some had existed. "Some of the girls and boys would come to the school with suit cases and trunks and some with their clothing sewed on them." For the latter, what they wore was all they had. Clothes were sewn on to keep them from falling in tatters at the children's feet. It was a condition found in non-orphanages, too. A teacher at a neighborhood school later recalled that there was one boy "who was so offensively dirty and so much in need of a bath that I sent his mother a note asking her to give him a bath. Her reply was that his clothes were sewed on and she wouldn't remove them."[27]

In an orphanage one might expect destitution to be the common denominator, exhibited by a number of factors such as inadequate or dirty clothing. Nevertheless, there were distinctions between haves and have-nots. One matron at the orphan home expressed the hopeful thought that "on the playground all were equal," but it is the nature of congregated children to divide into cliques that often are based on age, physical strength, and social and economic distinctions. Sharon Skolnick (Okee-Chee), a ward of Murrow Indian Orphanage in the 1950s, recalled a condition of childhood that transcended time and place. There were insiders and outsiders, bullies and victims. "Dolls seldom ended up with their intended owners; instead, a small clique of the biggest, toughest girls housed impressive collections under their beds. . . . I knew the outcome was preordained: I would receive a beating as fair exchange for . . . [my] worn little rag doll."[28] Whether authorities recognized it or chose to look the other way, there was a child hierarchy within orphanages. The matron at the Chickasaw orphanage may have chosen to believe that all were equal, but it is doubtful that the orphanage was an exception to the fact that children make up their own rules and establish their own social orders beyond the prying eyes of adult authority.

Skolnick's doll suggests another avenue for approaching assimilationist education aimed at young Indian girls, particularly in the late 1800s and early 1900s. Whether in Euro-American or Indian cultures, dolls served as playthings and teaching tools. Dolls for Indian girls were made from a variety of materials and displayed various degrees of sophistication in construction and decoration. A child of the Seneca Nation recalled that she had rag and corn husk dolls, made by her grandmother. In Euro-American society dolls also were largely handmade. This changed after the Civil War, when refined techniques allowed the first early forms of mass production, and manufactured dolls became more common in white American culture. Availability and the aspirations of a growing white middle class to emulate the upper class in material goods prompted a justification for store-bought playthings. Little girls would learn social conventions through the doll tea party, and when girls visited each other with their dolls, they emulated the Victorian ritual of home visiting among women. During the Victorian era, dolls became a reflection of one's social and economic status in white culture. They also were part of Indian orphanage life. At the Thomas home in New York, dolls were purchased in lots, sometimes numbering twenty to twenty-five dolls at a time. Extant expense reports from orphanages tell the story, as do visual images. Consider a photograph from the Creek Orphan Home that pictures ten young girls holding their dolls. These are not homemade dolls wearing hand-sewn dresses or with heads adorned with horsehair braids. The dolls have china heads with white faces and Caucasian features. The dolls held by the Creek youngsters were playthings, but playthings with a purpose. Doll play was a means for transmitting social values. The expected roles of mother and caregiver, as well as passivity, were learned. For Indian girls, Euro-American dolls were reflections of the culture they were expected to accept. The impact and influence of these playthings are impossible to determine, since studies indicate that Euro-American girls often subverted doll play's intended purpose by using dolls to express aggression and unladylike behavior. For example, "Funerals were especially popular, with Becky [doll] ever the willing victim." Although data on doll play among Indian children are unavailable, it might be suggested that if white girls acted out scenarios in ways never intended by adults, Indian girls did the same. Nevertheless, the presence of these dolls in Indian orphanages is itself a commentary on the ways, many of them silent, that reinforced acculturation.[29]

For the vast majority of children and teenagers who entered the Chickasaw orphanage, enrollment lists are the only sign that their personal experiences included a stay. Only rarely is more learned. Aaron Hamilton, whose name appears on a list from 1904, was interviewed in 1937. It is only through the short manuscript of his reminiscence that he becomes more than a name on a list. Orphaned by the age of five, Hamilton did not immediately go to the orphanage. Instead, his grandparents took him into their home, which Aaron remembered as a "box house with shingle roof." He began school at a Baptist mission near Anadarko, but at the age of twelve he was taken in by an aunt who almost immediately placed him in the orphanage. Since Hamilton did not elaborate, one is left to wonder at the possible reasons for this turn of events in his life. Perhaps the grandparents died or became physically unable to continue looking after the boy. Perhaps the aunt was the only other relative, but in a traditional household it would not have been the responsibility of a female relative to oversee a young man reaching the age of puberty. Or perhaps the reason was economic. In the orphanage the adolescent would receive room, board, and an education. Whatever the circumstances, Hamilton's stay lasted only two years. His aunt may have reclaimed him or another family member stepped in. He did not say, but after his relatively short stay at the home, Hamilton began attending a neighborhood school at Sulphur Springs.[30]

Susan Lewis, also without parents, was taken in by a relative. In her situation it was an uncle, a minister and her mother's brother. Then, paralleling Hamilton's story, the girl was sent at the age of twelve to the orphanage, where she stayed for five years, until she was considered a young adult who should be out on her own. Where she went or what she did after leaving, Susan did not record, but from her reminiscences it is clear that she married. For her, as well as other young women entering an adult world, marriage was the most obvious step and possible choice.[31]

Among the memories of Susan Lewis was the Methodist minister W. S. Derrick, who served as superintendent: "He [Derrick] was greatly loved by the children. We had good food, and were well treated while he was in charge." As Lewis implied, the atmosphere was not always so benevolent. The superintendent set the tone for an institution whether it was an orphanage, a reformatory, or an Indian boarding school. A case in point was the government-supported Santa Fe

Indian School, where the first superintendent used handcuffs to teach "object lessons" to errant students, and a later superintendent took it upon himself to lecture the U.S. commissioner of Indian Affairs on the three things families expected for their children—that they be well-fed and well-clothed, and that they "must not be punished." The superintendent believed that he should respect the parents' wishes.[32] No matter the overall statement of goals, an institution embodied an administrator's outlook. For the Chickasaw home, this was clearly apparent. Derrick's tenure was bracketed by a predecessor who left in disgrace and a successor whose performance could only be described as mediocre.

In March 1881 the predecessor, the Reverend R. N. Saunders, was brought before the Chickasaw superintendent of public instruction and the board of trustees to face charges that he had attempted "to seduce certain School girls under his charge." The primary witness, Emma, was a girl in her teens who testified that Saunders came to her bed in the middle of the night, in a room shared with five other girls, and offered Emma one dollar if she would sleep with him. The girl refused, called out to her friend Sophia, lit a candle, and found the man gone. Emma did not see the man, but she identified Saunders from his voice. Sophia fetched the home's matron, who, investigators decided, must have believed the girls, since she told Saunders's wife. In his defense, the superintendent brought forth numerous witnesses who spoke of the man's good character. Saunders also sought to discredit a black woman employed at the orphanage who spoke against him. In all, the investigators took the girls' story of events seriously, particularly after it was learned that Mrs. Saunders attempted to keep the girls quiet. "She told us not to say anything about it." Saunders's case was not helped either when it was revealed that he was accused of seducing a young woman not connected with the orphanage. The investigators did not find Saunders guilty. After all, this was not a court of law. They did, however, immediately dismiss him. The Chickasaws simply could not allow one of their institutions to be tainted with scandal or allow rumors that mistreatment of children was condoned.[33]

Stories of sexual misconduct were not limited to this case. At the federally supported Santa Fe Indian School, for example, a superintendent vehemently protested accusations that a girl was molested there. The superintendent conceded that the girl was sexually assaulted, but, he was quick to add, the crime was committed at the Jicarillo Subagency, not at the school. One had to consider the source, said the superintendent. The man spreading the story was hardly of good character; he was "awaiting his trial for the murder of Mrs. Barnaby." At the government-supported Manual Labor Boarding School for Sioux at the Sisseton Agency in South Dakota, misconduct on the part of the school's "missionary lady" was not overt but highly suggestive. She not only allowed social evenings with young men to degenerate into "kissing bees" but also encouraged boys and girls at the school to play games that the principal could only describe as "loose." She was dismissed, as was the cook whose son, a foulmouthed bully, exposed himself to daughters of one of the boarding school's Indian domestics.[34]

The Chickasaw, Sisseton, and Santa Fe reports and investigations relating to sexual misbehavior were hardly intended for wide public broadcast. Officials reporting on the government schools did so through correspondence, knowing that these revelations would not appear in official publications or in reports by the commissioner of Indian affairs. These were local matters to be dealt with quietly. This side of institutional life, whatever the institution, was almost never talked about or brought before a public forum. For that reason, Indian Bureau reports and the Chickasaw response stand out precisely because they straightforwardly dealt with incidents during a period when most institutions overlooked abuse, especially when it meant confronting administrators in a position of power.

When the general public was told of sexual misconduct in institutions, the discussions almost always focused on the behavior between adult inmates in almshouses or insane asylums. The possibility that adult caretakers could, or would, take advantage of child residents was ignored. Therefore, state departments of charities and local newspapers were likely to follow the line of reporting found in one Illinois newspaper that was aghast at conditions in the local poorhouse: "It has been charged that male and female inmates of the institution are very, very naughty, and indulge in acts which are forbidden by the laws of the church and state." This was the best reason, argued charity work professionals, to keep the sexes separated. If they could not be kept in different institutions, they should at least be separated within the same place with alternating mealtimes and common areas designated as male or female only.[35]

Although separation of sexes overlooked the possibility that children would fall prey to their caretakers, segregation by gender was a

major concern in child institutions and the primary reason for establishing male- or female-only orphanages. Nevertheless, when charitable groups and state departments of charities looked at the costs of
maintaining separate facilities, finances outweighed fears of sexual
impropriety among residents. The majority of orphanages were for
both sexes, who were segregated as much as possible.

At the Chickasaw home, Derrick replaced Saunders, stepping into a
situation that demanded a rebuilding of trust between the Chickasaws
and the white mission group contracting for the orphan home. He
more than adequately met the challenge. On one hand, Derrick's commitment to Christian-based instruction could be portrayed as intense,
even zealous. His reports were filled with religious references and
praise to God: "He Who has declared himself to be a father to the fatherless has overshadowed the Orphans Home with the wings of his
infinite love and mercy." On the other hand, the reverend did not lose
sight of earthly necessities or simply pray that all would be provided.
He actively pushed the Chickasaw government to maintain the physical environment and expend money toward daily needs. When he
spent more money than approved, his reasoning was direct and un-
compromising: "Our school must keep pace with the times. It becomes necessary to avail ourselves of the advantages of modern
improvements." In one fiscal year alone, Derrick refurnished the dormitories with iron enameled bedsteads. This would hardly seem
worth comment except for the fact that enameled surfaces were easier to clean and, therefore, produced a more sanitary environment.
The reverend also purchased new tables, chairs, and dinnerware for
the dining room, and he refused to cut back on foodstuffs such as
sugar or such necessary items as utensils and children's clothing when
prices increased. Rather than chastise Derrick, the Chickasaws agreed
and in January 1901 appropriated $10,000 for maintenance and equip-
ment instead of the usual $8,500 from the Orphan Fund.[36]

While Derrick's actions may seem small, his attempts to improve
living conditions, maintain a healthy diet, and create a more sanitary
environment contributed to better health among the children. The
reverend did not bluntly state the influence of his efforts, but he implied as much in his 1900 report. Although surrounding neighborhoods had been "visited by contagious and loathsome diseases, . . . not
a life has been lost during the year [at the orphanage]." Derrick did not
name the diseases, but typhoid was a recurring problem during the

1890s, reaching epidemic levels in some areas. It did not strike the Chickasaw home, but in 1890 it took the lives of four girls not so far away in the Choctaws' Wheelock orphanage, where an additional three deaths were not related to typhoid but the result of the "effects of tapeworms," consumption, and heart failure, respectively. The four typhoid deaths were labeled a "small mortality" by the Wheelock superintendent considering that the home required a doctor's attendance for almost two months and that there were thirty-two cases, including the superintendent's illness. Besides typhoid, smallpox was widespread during 1899–1900 and took the lives of children at the Creek Orphan Home. A teacher at the time remembered that a doctor was called, but "two boys died one night while I was alone in the room with them." The high incidence of smallpox led the Choctaws to establish a "smallpox camp" near Atoka to quarantine those afflicted, and doctors were called in to vaccinate the general population. Although there is no record that Chickasaw orphanage residents were vaccinated before or after the general outbreak in Indian Territory, lack of documentation does not suggest that this preventive measure was overlooked. After all, the children escaped the epidemic. However, they were not safe from disease and death. Mortality records are missing for the Chickasaw home. The only suggestion of death is a small cemetery on what was once orphanage property. Since the cemetery dates from the early 1870s, one might conclude that its sixty-five graves represent orphanage children. However, stones still standing in the 1930s marked a number of graves for the elderly and a few infants, suggesting that this was also a community cemetery. It is therefore impossible to ascertain the number of burials directly related to the orphanage.[37]

The reminiscence of Susan Lewis implies that when Derrick left, as he did in either late 1903 or early 1904, the climate altered dramatically. It was not just this resident's perception. There were changes, and none were for the better. The basis for change was not tribal neglect. Rather, it was the Dawes Commission, which in March 1893 was authorized by Congress to take steps toward dissolution of the Five Civilized Tribes as separate national entities. Dissolution, in turn, would pave the way for territorial status, and eventually statehood, for Oklahoma. Members of the commission, Henry L. Dawes, Meredith H. Kidd, and Archibald S. McKennon, went to Indian Territory to meet with representatives of an intertribal council (the Seminoles did not send a representative but sided with the council). Although the tribes resisted the commission's plans, land surveys were conducted and tribal roles were compiled with the object of allotting land in severalty. In 1898 tribal courts were ordered to cease functioning, and all cases, civil and criminal, went to U.S. courts. In 1898 the tribes also received instructions that no act passed by their governments would be considered valid unless approved by the president of the United States.

Under the Curtis Act, adopted by the U.S. Congress on June 28, 1898, the Indian Bureau took supervisory control of Creek and Cherokee education and complete control over Choctaw schools. Tribal governments had struggled against federal interference for some time. Even after passage of the Curtis Act and later enabling acts, tribal governments did not slip quietly away. Bill No. 42, passed by the Choctaw government, when it no longer had the status to act as a legislative body, provides a good reference for the general mood of the Five Civilized Tribes: "The secretary of the interior has not only taken unlawful possession of said school property [of Spencer Academy], but while in the custody the same has been destroyed [by fire] by the Negligence of the custodian in charge thereof. . . . In addition . . . funds belonging to the Choctaw Nation have been misappropriated . . . [by paying] John D. Benedict."[38]

Benedict was the first U.S. superintendent of schools appointed for Indian Territory. He had little appreciation for the school systems developed by the tribes in Indian Territory, and he was intent on shutting down schools as quickly as possible. Under Benedict was a school superintendent for each Indian nation, except for the Seminole. John M. Simpson was the first superintendent assigned to the Chickasaw Nation, but the nation exhibited such intense animosity that Simpson's role was reduced when the Chickasaws managed to retain control of their own school system. The nation's actions came at a price. The Chickasaws had signed the Atoka Agreement of 1894, which provided for allotting tribal lands, terminating the governments of the Five Civilized Tribes, and specified that the Choctaws and Chickasaws would share in the royalties from the coal and asphalt taken from their lands. This money would be used to support education within the two tribes. When, however, the Chickasaws struggled to maintain control of their schools, the nation's share of coal and asphalt royalties was withheld by the federal government. The Chickasaws were forced to continue funding schools out of tribal moneys.

There was never enough, and payment warrants issued by the Chickasaws became worthless. Realizing that schools, including the orphan home, were in danger of closing or being severely reduced in quality, the Chickasaw government offered a compromise. The federal government could examine schools on a regular basis and set the requirements for teacher qualifications. Although one history of the Chickasaws maintained that after 1898 tribal government was nothing but an "empty shell," it still managed to keep a large measure of control over education into the first decade of the twentieth century.[39]

Considering the Chickasaws' determination to maintain tribally directed education, the changes that occurred at the orphan home after Derrick's departure can be understood in the larger context of tribal versus federal control. Decline in the quality of life at the home was largely a result of the Chickasaws' preoccupation with staving off the federal government while still maintaining supervision of the entire school system. Decline also was helped along by mismanagement at the institutional level. While dealing with the political climate, the Chickasaw government decided to terminate its contract with the Methodists. This eliminated an interested, and sometimes interfering, third party in the triangle of missionaries, federal authorities, and tribe. With the Methodists out of the picture, the Chickasaws decided to contract with an individual not directly associated with any church organization. In 1904 Vinnie Ream Turman, who already acted as principal and teacher at the home, received the contract. She and her husband, L. M. Turman, attempted to maintain the status quo, but that was all. They did little in the way of seeing that repairs were made or suggesting that the Chickasaws expend additional funds for upkeep. In fact, the Turmans most likely were not up to the task of overseeing the home's complex operation of education, everyday child supervision, and fiduciary responsibilities. Mrs. Turman was ill, and neither she nor her husband was a skilled financial manager, as a review of their reports indicates. In these reports, numbers simply do not match. For example, in 1904 the Turmans reported the average enrollment at 103, and for each student $5 was spent on clothing. This resulted in a total expenditure of $750, but according to the ledgers, the Turmans actually spent $235 more than goods received.[40]

There is no evidence that the Turmans willfully misused funds or that sloppy accounting was censured by the superintendent of schools or the home's trustee. Nevertheless, the Turmans' tenure proved a low point. Buildings fell into disrepair, supplies ran low, and maintenance was slipshod. Under federal pressure to relinquish control over its schools, the orphan home was on the brink of closure in 1906. Given the circumstances, it was little wonder that the Chickasaw superintendent of education and tribal government failed to attend to conditions at the home or supervise the caretakers more vigorously. Just when it seemed most certain that the home would close, however, the government pulled back from its demands. In any case, the Chickasaws already had decided to keep the home open. They felt that it could not be abandoned. It was an absolute necessity.[41]

During the time that the institution's future remained uncertain, Vinnie Ream Turman died while "[at] her post striving to educate and enlighten the Chickasaw orphan children."[42] Her husband, along with the couple's daughter, who attended the school with the other children, stayed for perhaps another year. When it was decided to keep the place open, Turman left. Wilcox entered the picture as the next—and last—superintendent.

In hindsight, Wilcox fades into the background when placed beside his wife, the home's matron. Carrie Wilcox was a powerhouse of activity, and she had no compunction about saying what she thought. Appalled by conditions, she did not mince words when complaining to Chickasaw authorities or U.S. Superintendent John D. Benedict: "Beds have to be moved from one side of the room to the other when it rains." It was as if there was no roof at all when the water ran in. She expected repairs to be made immediately. And, while the roof was being mended, something could be done about the dormitories, which were infested with lice. "That room where the boys have slept," she wrote, "are full of them." Mattresses and bedding had not been cleaned properly in some time. Wilcox asked Benedict for permission to burn the lot, but her tone left no doubt that she intended to carry out the plan, with or without permission.[43]

The descriptions left by Carrie Wilcox provide a sad commentary on the home's condition, particularly in light of the pride and careful maintenance that prevailed in years past. The institution began as a three-story frame building that encompassed classrooms, dormitories, and the necessary dining area, kitchen, and laundry. In 1896, appropriations paid for completing "a very modern three-story brick building," which allowed classrooms to be separated into one building, with sleeping quarters and living space in the other. Heat was provided by fireplaces, and as a reminder of those who had served as examples of Chickasaw leadership, rooms were named for former tribal governors. The dormitories were not long spaces with beds lined against the walls. Younger children were quartered away from adolescents. Considering the expense of expanding the orphan home, it was almost incomprehensible that within ten years of its new construction the place became so dilapidated. That it had was not a mark on the Chickasaws' interest in schooling or lack of dedication to the orphaned and destitute. Prevailing conditions were a visual narrative of Chickasaw resistance to federal intervention and statehood politics.[44]

It was not just the expense of building a new structure that made the decline tragic. The curriculum and caliber of teaching had improved steadily until the institution could proclaim itself a "graded" school. Under Derrick's leadership, classes were organized for the work of a particular year's course of study, grades one through eight. This change reflected mainstream America's interest in graded schools, which educators touted as progressive and an ideal educational model for all American schools. At the time the Chickasaw orphanage became a graded school, these types of schools were hardly the standard, especially in rural sections of the United States. Yet Derrick successfully implemented the model at the orphanage. The reverend was generally cautious in claiming great strides among pupils, saying that they made "reasonable" progress, but a note of pride crept into his announcement that in 1899 the institution had its first "graduate" from the graded school.[45]

During Derrick's tenure as superintendent, the home's name became the Chickasaw Orphan Home and Manual Labor School, and the institution's population reflected a growing number of half-orphans, as well as a few children with both parents living. Two main factors were responsible for this slight shift in population. First, the home's original purpose was to care for children orphaned by the Civil War, but those youngsters were becoming young adults and leaving. There were still children in need, but not in such dramatic numbers as seen immediately after the war. A second reason for the change in population was the general attitude of the Chickasaws. They had never attached a social stigma to being an orphan or rigidly separated these children from others. When there was no room available at the orphan home, children were placed in one of the Chickasaw boarding schools. Conversely, when there was not a full quota of orphans at the Lebanon facility, remaining space was filled by half-orphans and children with living parents. Records, particularly those from the turn of the century, indicate that the home's population consistently numbered between 100 and 150. Approximately two-fifths of the residents during this time were labeled "not orphans." Still, Carrie Wilcox mused that there seemed "to be a great number of poor and orphan children in the Nation."[46]

Superintendent Wilcox and his wife were caught up in forces beyond their control, and it was their lot to face the end of an era for Chickasaw education. Since the 1870s the Five Civilized Tribes had fought a continuing holding battle against federal control of their affairs. Tribes saw this outside influence as an attempt to impose foreign rule on their status as nations. Nevertheless, the outsiders could not be held at bay forever. In coming to terms with federal and territorial intervention, the Chickasaw government attempted to stave off total lack of control with its own measures. In 1904 the Chickasaws passed legislation that allowed "parents, guardians and others having legal custody of Chickasaw children to send such children to any reputable white or Indian schools, in Indian Territory or elsewhere." The Chickasaw superintendent of schools would issue warrants, or certificates, to pay for each child's educational costs, no matter the choice of school. At best, tribal government could only attempt to avoid the inevitable. In March 1906 all functions of tribal government, courts, and schools were terminated by the Curtis Act. It was an immeasurable blow to the Chickasaws, as well as the other tribal nations in Oklahoma. Their school systems, long a source of pride, were no longer theirs. The federal government finally achieved something it had wanted for a very long time—control over Indian education among the Five Civilized Tribes.[47]

To allow some flow in education while the Curtis Act was implemented, federal authorities kept a number of schools operational while Chickasaw neighborhood schools were consolidated with white schools or closed. Boarding schools continued until tribal funds for education were depleted. When the money ran out, students began attending white public schools or went to Carter Seminary (formerly Bloomfield Academy), Chilocco Indian School, or Haskell Institute. A very small number entered or continued to attend St. Elizabeth's School, established in the Chickasaw Nation in 1887. Operated by the

Sisters of St. Francis, the school was funded by Katharine Drexel, a Philadelphia heiress who founded a religious order and gave her fortune to the building of mission schools throughout the western United States. St. Elizabeth's School accommodated fifty girls. Not all were Chickasaws; Choctaw, Potawatomie, and Creek girls, ranging in age from seven to eighteen, also attended. The school, as well as other Catholic mission schools such as St. Mary's Academy at the Sac and Fox Agency or the St. Louis School for the Osage, was not a safe haven from federal plans. Nationally, Catholic schools serving Indian populations were in a precarious position as the federal government withdrew contracts of financial support and began to investigate landownership during the allotment period. St. Elizabeth's School came under particular scrutiny when the government decided to investigate if the Chickasaw government's sale of school land to the mission was illegal. If the government proved its case, the school would be closed and the land allotted. These machinations were a form of harassment against Catholic missions during a time of deep anti-Catholic feeling within the bureau, but for the children being served by St. Elizabeth's and other Catholic missions, threat of closure meant that they, too, would be thrown into the turbulent quest for an alternative place of education. Of course, the government intended that students would either enter public schools or attend one of its Indian boarding schools.[48]

The Chickasaw Orphan Home and Manual Labor School was categorized as a boarding school and, as such, continued to operate during the interim period. By 1906, however, the home no longer operated year-round. There was no school during the summer, and children were expected to go home. Support staff, including the laundry worker, cook, and handyman, were dismissed. A distressed Carrie Wilcox wrote to John D. Benedict: "Who is going to care for, cook, and work for the children left here? . . . There is as near as I can learn some 20 or 25 that say they have no home but this and are going to stay here." In addition, one Indian man asked permission to send his four wards for the summer and have them stay on when school began in the fall. Wilcox was not going to turn the children out and lock the doors. Her letter concluded, "I see no way but to keep the children for they have no homes—this is their home."[49]

It would not be their home for much longer. The federal government, which never acknowledged that the place served as an orphanage, phased it out. By 1910 it no longer existed. Some youngsters went to Indian boarding schools supported by the federal government, and some were placed in privately run orphanages within the state, such as the Baptist-supported Murrow or Presbyterian Goodland. A very few became wards of the state, while others simply wandered away from the institutional setting. In one instance, Kate Barnard, Oklahoma's first commissioner of charities and corrections, found "children of full blood Indians living like little animals in open fields without clothing." The court-appointed guardian responsible for them was using the children's allotments for other purposes. No one was looking after any aspect of the children's welfare, least of all finding an orphanage for their care.[50]

When the federal government phased out tribal control and enforced allotment, it introduced the nightmare of child guardianship. Under the Dawes Act, tribal rolls were compiled, identifying individuals eligible for allotment of property. Graft began when the rolls fell into the wrong hands. Rumors of theft turned into confirmations bannered by headlines like that appearing in the *New York Tribune:* "Creek and Seminole Roll Theft Scandal." Rolls listed each person entitled to an allotment, and the shyster looking for a way to profit from dissolution used the rolls to find children and then become their court-appointed guardian. Unintentionally the federal government aided this scam when, in 1908, minors were removed from federal protection and given over to the probate courts, which then assigned guardians to the youngsters. There was a general belief, and as it turned out one that was well-founded, that the Dawes Commission knew of the situation but did little about it. Matters were exacerbated when officials offered their own interpretations of the law or did not abide by it. In one instance an Indian agent tried, but failed, to divest three Cherokee children of their land in favor of a woman who felt that she had some claim to the property. In another case the U.S. Department of the Interior advised a father that he might be the *"natural* guardian" of his son, but he was not the *"legal* guardian." Parenthood did not ensure guardianship. The federal attitude was a harbinger of things to come. Parents did not then, or later, have a basic right to oversee their children. The cycle of federal, court, and individual intervention that led to passage of the Indian Child Welfare Act of 1978 did not begin with tribal dissolution. Nevertheless, allotment and approval of court-appointed guardianship made it far easier for non-Indian determination over children's lives.[51]

Division of property through allotment provided every minor on the rolls with his or her own estate, which varied in value from an average acreage of farmland to wealth if there was oil or other minerals on the property. The situation was ripe for the unscrupulous, the "professional" guardian who applied to the court and became the person in charge of a minor's property. Most of these guardians were not satisfied with only one or two wards but made a business out of finding children and cashing in on their allotments. Orphaned children became a valuable commodity, sought out for financial gain rather than out of benevolent concern.

Kate Barnard made it her crusade to stop the unprincipled guardian. Barnard's own childhood experiences made her especially sensitive to the needs of orphaned and destitute children. Born in Nebraska and raised by relatives after her mother's death, Barnard had little contact with her father until he took her to Oklahoma Territory and his homestead. All too quickly it became apparent that Kate was wanted only for her labor. She was left alone and nearly destitute while her father spent most of his time away finding whatever work he could. She left the life of a single female homesteader and worked her way into a position helping destitute children newly arrived in the territory. Along the way, she became involved with the American Federation of Labor. Hailed by some as Oklahoma's Jane Addams, Barnard was the first elected commissioner of charities and corrections when the office was created by the Oklahoma Constitutional Convention.[52]

For Barnard, guardianship fraud was easy to find, but dealing with it was another matter. Her office was at most only a three-person operation, and the task of protecting children from pilfering guardians was overwhelming. She conceded that for every case she successfully won in court, there were many others that went unchallenged. Among her cases in 1910 were those of 11 full-blood children and 16 mixed-bloods whose guardians were not providing their wards with "any part of their maintenance from their estates." Barnard went to court, had the guardianships voided, and transferred the children's affairs to the Board of Control of the Oklahoma State Home. In 1912 she reported an increase in prosecuted cases: 8 cases representing 12 children in Pontotoc County; 9 cases representing 15 children in Haskell County; 12 cases representing 21 children in Tulsa County. The list went on.

In 1912 alone, she appeared in court for over 1,200 cases, amounting to over $1 million in estates due the children. Certainly not all were dependent orphans, but the watershed of fraud took aim at those who had no kin or those with adult relatives who themselves were cheated out of their allotments.[53]

Guardianship fraud was not carried out in secret or closed court proceedings. It was common knowledge. Wrote a correspondent for the *Weekly Chieftain* in Vinita:

> If there is anything in this world more justly entitled, than any other, to protection against all the forms of imposition and wrong, it is the orphan. . . . The man who could conceive the idea of capitalizing the pathetic exigencies of orphanage, certainly had a business eye of the most unusual penetration. And yet there were not a few thrifty geniuses who hit upon the scheme of hunting out and gathering up Indian orphans, and under the pretense of benevolently caring for their infantile wants, secure[d], through the help of federal courts, personal control and use of their allotments until the little ones become of age. The profit which a guardian might receive from such a business is too manifest to need explanation.[54]

There were lesser schemes, too, although these were more speculative than the tangible results gained by preying guardians. In 1903 the U.S. Department of the Interior reported that a number of individuals in Indian Territory were making "crude attempts . . . growing out of ill-advised individual ambition" to establish schools. Looking to the future, these entrepreneurs in education hoped to entice Indian and African Indian students who were about to lose their educational facilities through federal closure. One example cited by the 1903 report was "a private enterprise school run by semi literate negro whose industrial plan" for education was to raise cotton. The school's pupils— at the time of the report there were only three Creek freedmen— received no classroom instruction. The school was bogus. The "superintendent/teacher" only wanted youngsters as a source of cheap child labor.[55]

Some in the Indian Bureau, including Commissioner of Indian Affairs Cato Sells, attempted to draw attention to the problems, particularly guardianship fraud. Nevertheless, the federal government, prompted by influential Oklahoma whites, was generally oblivious. Cheated orphans and misused children were Oklahoma's mess. After all, "large expenditures were made from Federal, tribal, and private funds for the maintenance of orphans' homes." The government offered the opinion that orphans had contributed nothing to their own support while enjoying shelter, food, clothing, and education at others' expense. Furthermore, with the exception of the last Cherokees and Seminoles to get their allotments, the government argued that there were few children who could not be supported from their own estates. In the push toward statehood, most whites in Oklahoma agreed with the government's position, but some voices disputed generally accepted perceptions. "[There is] no more erroneous belief than that the Indians are all fabulously wealthy. . . . to be an Indian, of whatever tribe simply means to be the possessor of rich oil land, fine farm land and a big bank account with Uncle Sam." One writer tried to remind readers that children were cheated by guardians, many were poor, and there were youngsters who had no relatives. "While the territory trips merrily into statehood, some of her red-skinned citizens are in dire distress . . . , and the cry of the orphan may be heard."[56]

Throughout the nineteenth century, the federal government recognized the presence of orphans, as white culture understood the definition. Individual Indian agents made references to orphans and orphanages in their reports to the commissioner of Indian affairs, and those reports were published as part of the commissioner's larger annual reports. Orphans also were recognized when the Orphan Fund was established for the southeastern tribes upon their removal, and orphans were named in the Dawes Act of 1887 as a group entitled to land allotments. Yet the federal government did not officially recognize orphanages for Indian children. They were invisible, hidden behind the curtain of Indian boarding schools.

Having set up the allotments, divested tribes of their control over orphanages and the orphans themselves, and established a court system that allowed allotments to be plundered, the government only sporadically addressed the result of its actions. Commissioner Sells pursued an investigation of the probate courts, and the Oklahoma legislature reacted by passing new rules to protect minors' property. By 1914, however, those rules were overturned, and the old probate system continued to perpetuate the frauds. The Indian Bureau had little authority to do anything other than cajole federal and state lawmakers for stronger legislation and to conduct investigations to make their case. Sells's one victory was short-lived, and his successor as commissioner of Indian affairs, Charles Burke, fared little better. In 1923 Burke ordered a study. At the same time, a private investigation was made by Gertrude Bonnin, a founder of the Society of American Indians; Matthew Sniffen, of the Indian Rights Association; and Charles H. Fabens, of the American Indian Defense Association.[57] Included in Bonnin's report was the wrenching story of a defrauded Choctaw girl who was oil rich but living an impoverished life:

> Little *Ledcie Stechi*, a Choctaw minor, seven years old, owned rich oil property in McCurtain County. She lived with her old grandmother in a small shack in the hills. . . . They lived in dire poverty, without proper food or clothing and surrounded by filth and dirt. . . . In April, 1923, they were brought to Idabel, the County seat. . . . A medical examination showed she [Ledcie] was undernourished and poisoned by malaria. After five weeks of medical treatment and nourishment, Ledcie gained 11 pounds. Her health improved, and she was placed by an employee of the Indian Service in Wheelock Academy, an Indian school. Mr. Whiteman, evidently fearing to lose his grasp on his ward, demanded the child, and Ledcie Stechi, child of much abuse, was returned to the custody of her guardian 24 hours after she was taken to the school where she would have had good care. . . . A month later, on the 14th of August, word was brought to the hills that Ledcie was dead.[58]

The investigations of Bonnin and others put a face on the fraud taking place, and the reaction was reminiscent of that seen under Sells's administration. New legislation was passed to protect Indians from the excesses of probate courts and guardians. The new laws, however, were largely ineffectual. In any event, by the mid-1920s, the damage was done. Families had been devastated, individuals impoverished, and children victimized. For her part, Kate Barnard prosecuted case after case during her time in office. As she wrote, "Some guardians were good and honest, but very few; quite a number were bad and dishonest. . . . About a quarter of a million dollars have been collected illegally from the various orphans by various guardians."[59] This was money that the youngsters would never see upon reaching their majority.

Dissolution was a dramatic transitional point for tribal governments, land titles, and the final push to turn extended Indian families into separate, nuclear units. It was also a transitional period for Indian children. Federal control of tribal institutions in Oklahoma meant that orphans would no longer reside within a tribal nation. They would no longer experience the degree of insulation from whites or from other tribes that they had known. As important, dissolution robbed adult and child alike. When the Indian Rights Association in the 1920s researched fraud and corruption perpetrated against the Five Civilized Tribes, it found a systematic pattern of fraud, exorbitant legal fees, and loss of property through probate court proceedings. Families that once possessed the means to care for their children became dependent, and the incredible tangle of guardianship fraud placed a larger number of children into that category labeled as orphans. They were not necessarily parentless, but by virtue of their new destitution, they fit the broad public definition of an orphan child. "Poverty" was synonymous with "orphan."

5

THE MISSIONARIES: CHOCTAW AND CREEK

There shall be fifty (50) orphan boys at Armstrong Academy, and fifty girls at Wheelock Seminary. During vacation such as have no relative or proper friends to visit will be cared for by the respective Superintendents.[1]

The Chickasaws and Choctaws were never far apart geographically, culturally, or linguistically. Their close relationship often bound them together when dealing with federal representatives and making treaties, and Presbyterian missionaries categorized the two as one when, in 1827, they organized the Association for Missionaries in the Choctaw and Chickasaw Nations. Yet, for all their common bonds, the Choctaws and Chickasaws did not approach orphanages in the same way. Nor did the Choctaws establish orphanages in the immediate post–Civil War period as did the Cherokees and Chickasaws. If the Choctaw orphanages had any close correlation it was to Creek institutions that appeared during the same time period as the Choctaw.

After the Civil War a few Choctaw children entered the Chickasaw Orphan Home, but, on the whole, the Choctaw government did not recognize a need for an orphanage. Instead, it, like the National Council of the Muskogee Nation (Creeks), used the Orphan Fund to support orphans' education in boarding or neighborhood schools. For children's everyday care, families took the orphaned and destitute into their homes. By traditional custom, adoption was common and simply announced when a child ate from the family bowl. Among the families sheltering orphans, a number settled in clusters near schools. One teacher recalled that whites aided in this settlement; in one instance, a couple employed as instructors built "camp houses" for families while their children attended school. At the Presbyterian Good Land Mission (the original spelling was later compounded into Goodland), "many families moved close by" for access to church services and a school.[2]

White culture might conclude that the lack of an orphanage meant that there were no parentless children—an impossibility—or that the Indians were neglectful and uncaring. Euro-Americans unfamiliar with child care practice in Indian culture would assume that dependent Indian children were treated as those in white culture sometimes were, left on their own to fend for themselves. Those who worked for years in the mission field among the Choctaws knew that this was not the case. Still, the missionaries were products of their own cultural expectations. If the Choctaw government would not use its Orphan Fund to finance an orphanage, missionaries would step in and do it themselves.

What emerged from this white push for orphanages was a multiplicity of institutions in the Choctaw Nation, presenting an outward image that the Choctaws were more interested in the "discovery of the asylum" than they actually were. It was not so much a case of the Choctaws wanting an orphan asylum as it was of missionary insistence. Religious groups were at the forefront nationally in sponsoring and organizing orphanages. It seemed only natural that Christian charity for the orphaned would be extended in the Choctaw Nation. Of the mission groups, the Presbyterians had a vested interest in establishing an orphanage, since it would provide another avenue for entering into a contractual agreement with the Choctaws. Tribal leaders eventually acquiesced, but their habit of opening and then closing contract schools was testimony to a rather halfhearted acceptance. The orphanage was an unfamiliar institution to all native groups, and the idea never seemed to settle well with the Choctaw people. Given that, it is ironic that eventually more orphanages were established in the Choctaw Nation than in any other Indian nation or on any Indian reservation. Additionally, three of those located on Choctaw land survived in some form after tribal dissolution shredded the institutional systems of the Five Civilized Tribes.

The first inclination toward an orphanage among the Choctaws was not tribally initiated or part of the nation's school system. Rather, it was an outgrowth of a classroom set up in 1850 at the Presbyterian Good Land Mission. As one history of the place explained it, "A minister's wife [Mrs. Oliver Porter Stark] gathered a group of Indian children into a side room of the log house that was the Presbyterian manse. . . . And there she began to teach." Among these children were an indeterminate number of orphans, but they were not distinguished from non-orphans. The mission, established in 1848, was first supported by the American Board of Commissioners for Foreign Missions, a Presbyterian and Congregational group. With the American Civil War and the Choctaws' support of slavery, however, the American Board withdrew its support of Goodland, and the Southern Presbyterian Church Executive Committee of Foreign Missions took over until 1894. Despite the split over slavery, Presbyterian interest in Goodland represented a continuation of religious work among the Choctaws, dating back to the early 1800s.[3]

In 1818 the American Board, which a year earlier began work among the Cherokees, chose Cyrus Kingsbury to open a mission among the Choctaws. In August of that year, Kingsbury established the mission station he named Eliot in honor of John Eliot, a missionary who served among the Algonquins during the mid-1600s. (Documents from the period variously gave the spelling as Eliot or Elliot.) Situated on the Yalobusha River, the mission quickly developed with the help of Indian workers. By the end of 1819, it had a boarding school, a farm that provided both sustenance and a hands-on teaching environment in the agricultural arts, and a blacksmith shop. For the mission's continued improvement, the Choctaws committed $3,000 a year. Kingsbury so impressed a number of individuals that he was invited by David Folsom, a mixed-blood, and John Pitchlynn, a white married to a Choctaw woman, to build another mission. In 1820 the Mayhew mission station was sited near present-day Columbus, Mississippi. The American Board, pleased with Kingsbury's success, sent additional helpers. Among them was Cyrus Byington, who first served as a teacher but, with the help of missionary Alfred Wright, worked to devise an orthography for writing the Choctaw language. To perfect his skills and knowledge, Byington enlisted the aid of David Folsom, who provided language instruction and wrote Byington's sermons in Choctaw. By 1824 Byington was able to spread the gospel in the Choctaws' native tongue, and the language was used in the classroom to enable students to make a smoother transition to English.[4]

The Choctaws accepted the missionaries and pledged monetary support for the mission school. Enthusiasm was tempered, however, when families were expected to leave their children in the hands of missionaries who intended to keep youngsters out of their home environments for as long as possible. Too, the missionaries lectured parents on their lax discipline, and when missionaries doled out physical punishment in the classroom, they expected it to continue when children were at home. Corporal punishment and keeping children from their parents for extended periods were complete reversals of Choctaw custom. Children learned by imitating adults. They had generous amounts of freedom, and when they misbehaved, ridicule was the method of correction.[5]

At issue, too, was the school environment. Children were given "American" names that teachers could pronounce. This was common practice in mission fields around the world, and not so coincidentally, name changes also were part of school life for immigrant children in urban areas of the United States. On a practical level, teachers argued that these changes made their lives easier, since they would not have to stumble over unfamiliar pronunciations. Embarrassed by teacher reaction and degrading comments about their strange-sounding names, students took new names to fit in. At many Indian boarding schools, children altered their names before teachers had a chance to shame them in front of a class. Through ridicule and pressure, name changing was a fact of assimilationist education. New names gave children, whether Indian or immigrant, an American identity and impressed upon them the expectation that they adopt the values and attitudes of teachers who represented the dominant society. Added to this Americanization process was manual-labor instruction, a means toward acculturation. At the Choctaw missions, acculturation was a long-term goal. In the immediate present, manual-labor training was often just a ruse for using child labor to sustain the missions' gardens, crops, and buildings. Some Choctaws objected. If manual labor was to be part of the curriculum, the Choctaws wanted it to be in the "mechanical trades" such as blacksmithing.[6] Clearly, the Choctaws saw a benefit in some forms of this instruction. It could produce skilled workers for jobs that would be essential as the tribe had further contact with whites and adopted some aspects of their lifestyles. The Choctaws were not, however, willing to allow their children to be used as replacement labor for white adults or to have them directed en masse to agriculture.

Despite the ebb and flow of tensions between the Choctaw people and the missionaries, the overall relationship was congenial. The dedication of many sent by the American Board was such that they gained respect and, in turn, found it difficult to think of themselves in any place other than with the Choctaws. Such was the relationship that when the period of removal came, a number of mission workers moved west with the Choctaws. The most prominent were Cyrus Kingsbury, Cyrus Byington, and Ebenezer Hotchkin, but there were also Methodists and Baptists who worked among the tribe and made the move.

Choctaw removal was pushed along by both the federal government and the State of Mississippi. In 1826 the United States attempted and failed to secure all of the Choctaw lands in Mississippi. Then, in 1829, the state made its bid for tribal lands by extending state law over areas held by the Chickasaws and Choctaws. Mississippi abolished tribal governments in 1830, and tribes received state citizenship. With the federal removal act of 1830 and the Treaty of Dancing Rabbit Creek, the Choctaws began emigrating in 1831. George Gaines, general supervisor for Choctaw removal, planned to move about one-third of the population each year, from 1831 through 1833. The primary collection points were at Memphis and Vicksburg, where encamped Choctaws faced extreme food shortages. Relocation was a disaster of mismanagement. There were not enough steamboats to transport the people by water; there were few wagons to carry them overland; and scant supplies accentuated the suffering. Choctaws died of a variety of causes. During the winter of 1831–32, those transported up the Arkansas River to the military Arkansas Post were unloaded and caught in an unbelievably severe blizzard. Without shelter and proper clothing, Choctaws froze to death or later died of pneumonia. In the summer of 1832, deaths were attributed to dysentery and to cholera that raged along the lower Mississippi River Valley. The only federal official who seemed genuinely concerned for the Indians was Francis W. Armstrong, Indian agent, who diverted about one thousand Choctaws from cholera-ridden Vicksburg, took control of a steamboat, and saw that the overcrowded vessel delivered its passengers to Arkansas Post.[7]

Choctaw life and economy in the years leading up to the period of removal had evolved into a society largely delineated along the lines of plantation-style farming that used slave labor. Those most often following this type of agricultural model were more apt to live as nuclear families, to be of mixed-blood background, and to educate their sons and daughters at white-directed schools. In fact, young Choctaw men attending Plainfield Academy in Connecticut were described by one observer as "gather[ing] under the old elm tree where they would sing and talk of their plantations, their homes, and slaves until the church-bell rang at nine o'clock when they were to retire." Those not using slave labor for production of cash crops were usually full-bloods who continued to live in villagelike communal settings and were less likely to accept missionary-inspired education. The pattern continued after removal. Mixed-bloods generally represented the aristocracy of the tribe, although some full-blood families were included in this social stratum. Those who adopted plantation-style agriculture in Mississippi continued this way of life in their new homes. They settled in areas conducive to livestock raising and large-scale production of corn and cotton. Slaves, who traveled with their owners during removal, remained a labor force. Most full-bloods, on the other hand, settled in the "timber region" and engaged in subsistence farming. With few towns and a scattered population, little changed over time in the area remote from the center of tribal affairs. In 1912, for example, a federal report stated: "There are more full bloods in the hills in this part of the state than any other and so far as I can learn have practically no school facilities." The disparity between social and economic groups was apparent:

> My parents were just poor Indians. . . . I learned to read and write some. . . . Some of the children went to school until they could read in a book called a history. When they got so they could read in this book the superintendent of the Choctaw tribe would send them back east to the states to college. Just children of the better-to-do people got to go and get an education. . . . People with money and education lived better than we did.[8]

The Choctaws, like the other tribes removed from the Southeast, had a multilayered system of education. A few male and female students were selected to attend eastern schools; their expenses were paid through the nation's education funds. Some well-to-do families financed their children's educations without tribal support. Within the nation, the school system consisted of boarding and neighborhood schools that began almost as soon as the Choctaws reached their new territory. The missionaries who accompanied them, along with Indian agent Francis W. Armstrong, encouraged schools. By the end of 1836 the American Board operated eleven mission schools, and the Choctaw Nation supported eight boarding and twenty-two neighborhood schools funded through treaty annuities. In addition, a handful of students attended eastern institutions, including five "very interesting and promising boys" enrolled at Delaware College.[9]

The Choctaw school system was overseen by a board made up of a superintendent and three district trustees. (The number of trustees was later reduced, and the tribe's principal chief was added to the board.) The board chose students for boarding school and off-reservation education. Those selected for schooling in the States had to be enrolled in a school within the Choctaw Nation and had to pass a physical examination to ensure, most of all, that they did not have tuberculosis; later syphilis was added to the examination. To assure a degree of fairness, selections were made "from the various Districts as nearly as may be in proportion to the school population of each and the number of each sex shall be kept equal." The school board maintained direct control over all schools within the system. It hired and fired teachers whose conduct was expected to be moral and temperate, and the board reserved the right to initiate or void contracts made with the American Board and the later Board of Home Missions.[10]

Within the school system there were orphans and half-orphans. A few were officially noticed in relation to their mothers when the Treaty of Dancing Rabbit Creek included a supplement that specified land distribution to four widows (two the wives of chiefs) and their "fatherless children." Orphaned children were a fact of life that could touch anyone. John Turnbull, superintendent of education in the Choctaw Nation for several years, was no stranger to parentless children. Some of his grandchildren were orphans. They, along with "several other orphans," were raised in the Turnbull household. Parents and relatives were lost during removal or through diseases that took lives in Oklahoma. Malaria and dysentery were common, and in some families tuberculosis affected every adult.[11]

Added to death by disease, realigned kinship patterns destabilized the family structure that protected children within a wide framework of relatives. In traditional society, children belonged to the mother and her kin: "The mother was always considered entitled to the pos-

session & controul of the children. . . . The mother could only be con-
trouled in the management of them by her oldest uncle & by him only
when She treated them badly. She could give them away . . . to any
person who would receive & adopt them. . . . Any person having a
family or owning a house could adopt any child." That changed with
the shift in relationships that began prior to removal. The plantation
lifestyle and intermarriage with whites reconfigured traditional relationships. Clan networks were exchanged for nuclear families. Across
the continent, this type of change occurred when tribes were restricted to reservations, but the Choctaws, as well as others of the
Five Civilized Tribes, slipped into this pattern of nuclear families
through their own economic and marital choices. The maternal line
of family and clan responsibilities weakened after removal—helped
along by the Choctaw Marriage Law of 1852. This statute specified
that, in cases of divorce, property was to be divided equally. No longer
did the husband simply leave the home and return to his own relatives, and no longer were children considered to be the mother's. Custody of children was decided by seven "disinterested" persons. The
law was a result of intermarriage with whites, whose understanding
of inheritance and custody was based on male, not female, lineage and
control. It was much more a reflection of male rights provided under
English Common Law than it was of traditional Choctaw society.
Thus, with the 1852 law it was quite possible for maternal responsibilities to be subordinated and for children to lose ties to their maternal relatives.[12]

Still, orphans in the nation were not separated into a distinct group,
although "orphan" was sometimes used as a descriptive term. In one
instance, for example, a Choctaw pardoned from jail was described as
a young man "who being an orphan boy and destitute was falsely con-
victed [of murder]."[13] The Choctaws clearly understood the Euro-
American definition for the word. Nonetheless, the nation's removal
from its home area and its later Civil War experiences did not create
an atmosphere in which an orphanage seemed necessary.

When compared with other tribes in Indian Territory, the Choctaw
people came through the Civil War years in relatively fair condition.
The Choctaws in military units saw less fighting, resulting in fewer casualties and a correspondingly lower number of widows and orphans.

Too, the nation was not plunged into the internal warfare experienced by the Cherokees. The largest problem for the Choctaws was depletion of food stores. This was exacerbated by an influx of refugee civilians from other tribes and, in the war's last two years, Confederate Creeks and Cherokees who entered Choctaw lands before advancing Union troops. Deprivations led to destitution, malnutrition, and the spread of disease as populations were crowded into a limited space. Still, the Choctaws did not experience the death, destruction, and destitution that rained down on other tribes in the territory.[14]

The number of orphaned and destitute children apparent in other tribal groups at the end of the war were not found in the Choctaw Nation. Those without familial support were either taken in by nonrelatives or placed in the Chickasaw Orphan Home. Nevertheless, the tribal government eventually established orphanages. In 1882 the government designated for the first time an institution as a place for orphans. The timing seemed dictated by outside forces more than by a true need for an orphanage. The Presbyterian Goodland Mission was still operational, and orphans lived at the mission with nearby families. At the same time, Baptists had their own plans for an orphanage. In the 1870s Frank Ross, a Choctaw who attended a Baptist theological seminary and then became a missionary among his people, attempted to establish an orphan home. He and his Caucasian wife, Emma Jean, gathered about ten children into their home. The children were fed and clothed through donations from church and missionary societies, and they received rudimentary instruction. Mrs. Ross recalled years later: "I taught the little Indian children to speak English. They were anxious to learn and very obedient." According to Mrs. Ross, "the children loved the home so much, some claimed to be orphans just to be taken in." Be that as it may, the orphanage did not thrive. The Ross experiment closed after two years. The couple was unable to gain a Choctaw contract or to elicit support from the Baptist Board of Missions. The board had its own plans, spurred on by the Reverend Joseph S. Murrow, a major figure in Baptist mission work in Indian Territory. Murrow was a board trustee for Indian University (later known as Bacone), which was first located in the Cherokee Nation and then relocated to the Creek Nation through Murrow's persistent efforts to gain Creek approval and monetary support. For Baptist work among the Chickasaws and Choctaws, Murrow wanted the board of missions to establish an academy near Atoka. Although he did not indicate it early on, the institution would accept orphaned children. Murrow's hopes were later realized in the form of the Atoka Baptist Seminary, which evolved into an "orphan academy."[15]

With both Baptist and Presbyterian orphan home programs, the Choctaws did not seem to need more. Nevertheless, the tribal government established one. The opening of the Choctaws' orphanage in 1882 correlated to the realignment and relocation of Choctaw boarding schools. Creation of an orphan asylum came at the pivotal point when the nation decided to move Spencer Academy, a boarding school established in 1844, from near Doaksville to Kiamitia County. This presented an opportunity to establish an orphan home without the expense of constructing a new building. Once the Spencer Academy buildings were vacated and students moved to the new site, the abandoned boarding school became an orphanage. Referred to as "Old Spencer," the new orphanage was only temporary. The long-term plan was to have two orphan homes—one for males, one for females.

Separation of the sexes was common for boarding schools funded by the Five Civilized Tribes, but it was atypical for Indian orphanages. Using the Orphan Fund as the primary, and sometimes only, source of money, it was not economically feasible to support two orphanages. Nonetheless, the Choctaws created a system in which boys and girls were separated—a decision that was heartily approved by white missionaries and teachers. In fact, W. S. Derrick of the Chickasaw Orphan Home urged tribal leaders to consider separate orphanages for their children. Although Derrick acknowledged that many, in and out of Indian Territory, favored coeducation, he did not. "One of the greatest troubles we have in school originates from having boys and girls together. There are things we do not wish to record here that might be spoken of. I do request that for the welfare and reputation of the school you [Chickasaw Board of Education] devise at once for the separation of the sex[es]."[16]

Whereas the Chickasaws did not separate boys and girls, the Choctaws would. For the time being, however, boys and girls were gathered into Old Spencer, and W. H. Robe and his wife were placed in charge. The criteria for child placement were determined by the Choctaw National Council. Children had to be from six to twelve years of age and either true orphans or half-orphans. County judges, who were in charge of probate cases, decided on a child's eligibility, and a whole family of children could be admitted. The last was an important addendum, since it was a departure from eligibility rules for boarding schools, where admittance was limited to one pupil per family. Once in the orphan home, girls could remain until they reached the age of sixteen; boys stayed until their eighteenth birthday.[17]

The age limits were the same as those for the nation's boarding schools, and as in those schools, instruction was strictly in English. This in itself was distasteful to some missionaries such as Cyrus Byington, who strongly argued for bilingual instruction. The approach had been successful in the mission schools of Mississippi and, to Byington's way of thinking, English-only instruction separated the generations and made youngsters think only of material improvement over the spiritual. Nevertheless, English was the means of communication.[18]

Youngsters had barely settled into Old Spencer when the plan for separate male and female facilities was put into motion. In 1883 Armstrong Academy, a boarding school established in 1846 and named for Indian agent Francis W. Armstrong, was slated for relocation. The nation's capital was being moved from Chahta Tamaha (sometimes referred to as Choctaw City) to Tuskahoma, and Armstrong Academy was following the capital. When the academy building was vacated at Chahta Tamaha, the Armstrong Orphan Home School for Boys took over the abandoned site. The home was variously called Armstrong Orphan School, Armstrong Orphan Male School, and Armstrong Orphan Home School, with the latter becoming the official name assigned through Choctaw legislation in 1883.[19]

The Choctaw government directed that the Armstrong Orphan Home School be placed under contract with "the same terms and conditions as are made in similar contracts for other Academies in the Nation." The contract was to be made with the Presbyterians. It also decreed that the home accommodate fifty boys. One-third were to be selected for admittance by February 1884. To ensure fairness, each district in the nation was to be represented as equally as possible. This was an important feature. Neither the Choctaw National Council nor the probate judges who made the selections wanted to be accused of favoritism. With that in mind, future superintendents of the home carefully detailed the number of boys in relation to the counties they represented. True to the desired objective, the home's population adequately represented each district and the counties within those districts. The numbers varied only slightly in relation to population density in the respective counties.[20]

As for the girls at Old Spencer, their new residence would be at Wheelock, which was referred to as both an academy and a seminary for girls. Founded as a day or neighborhood school in 1832 by the Reverend Alfred Wright, Wheelock was supported by the American Board of Commissioners of Foreign Missions. Wright named the school for the Reverend Eleazer Wheelock, who founded Dartmouth College, the first such institution to receive federal funds for Indian education. The Wheelock school was located near the military road that ran between Fort Smith, Arkansas, and Fort Towson, Indian Territory. The land was hilly and much of it heavily wooded, with streams meandering through the area. It was described by more than one observer as one of the most beautiful sites chosen for an Indian school.[21]

Wheelock's early history reflected the struggles to establish schools in the Choctaw Nation after removal. Although some families moved close to the day school, it served a limited number. To add more students and provide educational opportunities for those living in remote areas of the timber region, a dormitory for girls was built five years after the school began. In 1842 the Choctaws appropriated funds to pay the educational expenses of twenty-four girls. The appropriation met with general disapproval among the Choctaws, not because it paid for girls' education but because the funds came from money received from a sale of land to the Chickasaws. Most Choctaws opposed using the sale moneys for educational purposes. Nevertheless, the money was spent for building a school system, and that included enlarging Wheelock. From that point on, the Choctaws and the American Board supported Wheelock as a cooperative venture. This came to a halt with the beginning of the Civil War. The school closed, and before it could reopen, Wheelock was destroyed by fire in 1869. Interest in the site was not renewed until the early 1880s, when the Choctaws began to plan for separate orphanages for males and females, and the American Board decided to build an orphan home on the Wheelock site. It seemed a fitting continuation of the school's prewar focus on girls from poor families who might otherwise receive no education.[22]

Girls living at Old Spencer were transferred to Wheelock, along with the superintendent and matron, Mr. and Mrs. W. H. Robe. Two years later, Robe resigned and his son, R. C. Robe, became Wheelock superintendent. It was R. C. Robe's task to see that buildings were

*The Choctaw-supported Wheelock Female Orphan Academy near
Millerton, Indian Territory, ca. 1885. Archives and Manuscripts
Division of the Oklahoma Historical Society.*

completed and gardens developed. He also set about improving the
quality of "helpers . . . when before we were obliged to have either
colored women or inferior white women." Robe did not, however, select only Choctaw women to fill the positions. A longtime employee
in charge of overseeing girls at their chores of making apple butter or
soap was a black woman, Lottie Cole, known affectionately to the
girls as "Aunt." In time, Robe reported that his changes brought in
workers who took a personal interest in the youngsters' welfare.[23]

The girls from Old Spencer, as well as those who later went to
Wheelock, were not all true orphans. Some were half-orphans or destitute girls with both parents living. The Choctaws had firmly adopted
white, dominant society's popular, not legal, definition of an orphan,
and the female seminary was an example of an institution that carried
the name of orphan home but took in more than the true orphan.

Life for Wheelock residents was multidimensional, with both the
conventional forms of education and extras not commonly associated
with orphanages. Girls were expected to work at making soap or preserving food; it was not uncommon for them to "assist" in canning
two to three hundred gallons of fruit for nonseasonal use. These
chores constituted the girls' vocational home economics instruction,
and academics encompassed reading, writing, arithmetic, and U.S.

history. Robe, however, wanted more. On one occasion he asked for a piano after a number of girls showed an interest in music. This delighted Robe, who thought "there is nothing that has a more refining influence over young people than music, painting and drawing. . . , and such things as appeal to the philosophy of taste and cultivate the faculties of the true, beautiful, and good." A piano, textbooks purchased from the American Book Company, and an upgrade of staff contributed to an environment that attempted to meet a number of needs. At the same time, Wheelock residents were never to forget the lessons of frugality. Almost all the girls' clothing and personal necessities came from missionary societies or church congregations, which often "adopted" one or two girls as their projects. When individual girls found themselves lacking personal items or wishing for a special treat, they earned money by working for the employees. Cleaning a teacher's room, ironing clothes, or brushing a teacher's hair brought a few cents. The girls also learned the axiom "Waste not, want not." Recalled one former resident: "One way of impressing the girls with the fact that they must eat all food taken on their plates was to leave on each plate for the next meal all uneaten food."[24]

The boys and girls at Old Spencer were relocated to their respective new homes within a short span of time. What remained at Old Spencer in usable furnishings and equipment was dispersed to other schools within the nation. When the place was completely abandoned, the Choctaw government sold "old Spencer Academy to the highest bidder." It had outlived its purpose, and the need for extensive repairs made it a liability rather than an asset.[25]

Both Wheelock and the Armstrong Orphan Home School were located in rural settings. Both included farmland, although Wheelock's occupants were not expected to cultivate the school's "very profitable hay meadow" or to learn farming methods. The story was different for the boys at the Armstrong home, where the farm provided the basis for instruction in agriculture. Armstrong's was not, however, a model farm. Most outbuildings needed some kind of repair on a regular basis, and the crops cultivated on the farm's 150 acres did not represent cash crops but primarily feed for the few livestock. After all, a small number of cattle and hogs, four mules, four horses, and one pony were not a collective picture of large-scale animal husbandry. The Armstrong farm provided some basic foodstuffs, and youngsters worked at chores that maintained the operation. This was their training in agriculture.

Of more interest to the nation's council was manual-labor instruction that emphasized carpentry and blacksmithing, although a recurring problem was having enough tools with which to teach and learn. It was not a situation limited to the home. The superintendent of the re-located Spencer Academy, Alfred Docking, complained to John P. Turnbull of the Choctaw Board of Education that attempts to teach carpentry and other trades were severely hindered by "too few tools." Taking the Choctaws to task, Docking asked: "Shall the Choctaw Na-tion be behind [in vocational education]? Or shall she not rather make ready for the growing demand and with her white sister reap for her children the grand harvest of results in industrial progress!" The state-ment presented an interesting paradox. For almost a century, the pre-vailing intent of education had been to turn Indians into farmers, but Docking, certainly aware of America's industrialization, suggested that the Choctaws consider their industrial growth, not agricultural. In their own way, the Choctaws had been doing exactly that since their first contact with white education and their demand for more emphasis on the mechanical trades.[26]

When not engaged in vocational training, the boys, dressed in suits of trousers, shirts, coats, and vests, received academic instruction. Since education at the orphan home was based on the common school model, vocational and agricultural training took part of the time and classroom studies took the rest. Subjects varied widely, based on the student's age, ability, interest, and exposure to learning in neighbor-hood schools. In 1889 there were thirty-seven boys living at the home (not the full complement of fifty). Of these, seven were in their first reader, learning to spell and to write on their slates. Meanwhile, other students were in the second, third, and fourth readers, learning some arithmetic, penmanship, and geography. More advanced students were instructed in English grammar, writing, spelling, arithmetic (in-cluding decimals and long division), geography, and "Scripture Read-ing—Moral Philosophy." One of the thirty-seven students was in a category all his own. He was studying the full range of subjects offered to other students, plus U.S. history and "High Arithmetic," which in-cluded percentages and basic bookkeeping. This was not a graded school but one in which students progressed at their own pace. It was quite possible for a young man to reach his eighteenth birthday and to never have achieved the level of "High Arithmetic" or the ability to read a textbook on U.S. history.[27]

There is no direct evidence that corporal punishment was used at the home. In other words, there is no testimony from former residents. Nevertheless, its presence is strongly implied. Since missionaries at the Presbyterian missions in Mississippi insisted on physical punishment for misbehavior, there is little reason to believe that they altered their methods in Oklahoma. There were rules to be obeyed and punishments to be meted out, as C. J. Ralston suggested when he took charge of the Armstrong home in 1890. Ralston assured the Choctaw school board that "Our Motto is Justice to All." It was both a promise of equal rights within the school and a threat of the consequences when rules were disobeyed. Continued Ralston, "I require implicit obedience and faithfulness to every duty." Having said that, the superintendent added that six boys had "completed their time and were honorably dismissed." The impression left by Ralston was that the boys had been released from a reformatory, not an orphanage. In fact, the superintendent may not have seen much difference between the two.[28]

The superintendent's statement of dismissal suggests a basic but important question: What happened to those who were dismissed? One wonders if they were prepared to live outside the institution. In 1901, members of the Atoka Commercial Club offered the following observation: "The Choctaw orphans . . . are well cared for and are given excellent instruction, not only in the usual branches of an English Education, but also in the Industries most suited to their needs. . . . As the older ones go out from the school, they are received into the best society and are well able to care for themselves." For most young women the next step beyond the institution was marriage, but some sought more education. During Wheelock's long history, its "graduates" went on to study at Indian boarding schools outside the nation, and many obtained college degrees. It was the same experience for a young woman, a onetime resident of Murrow's Baptist Orphan School at Atoka, who attended Oklahoma Baptist University after leaving the orphanage. For her, the desire to seek more education was encouraged by an older brother, a Baptist minister.[29]

Ralston had a difficult time at Armstrong Orphan Home School. Matters came to a head when the Choctaw National Council expressed dissatisfaction with the home's management. In 1892, only two years after Ralston's tenure began, the Choctaws terminated the mission contract, and Ralston was directed to turn the home over to the Choctaw government. Peevishly, he defended himself and his methods: "I have endeavored to do all in my power to advance the interest of the boys in every direction." He saw his job as one of helping people until they could help themselves. For lack of better results, Ralston blamed the boys, who seemed to show no signs of wanting to advance. His attitude reflected a broader viewpoint being adopted at the time by reformers who blamed their lack of success on native groups rather than their self-created expectations. On the local level, the Choctaw government was not moved. It enacted a plan first used by the national council in 1885 when, unhappy with operations at the Spencer and New Hope academies, it canceled contracts and placed the schools under control of the board of trustees. Clearly, the Choctaw National Council and the nation's school board paid close attention to school management, and when circumstances did not meet their expectations, contracts were terminated.[30]

In the orphan home situation, the national council intended to continue the institution under Choctaw direction, as it had done with Spencer and New Hope. Instead, Armstrong was closed and the boys transferred to Armstrong Academy at Tuskahoma. This once again placed the orphan and non-orphan side by side. A few of the boys listed in the orphan home records of 1889 became residents of the academy in 1894. If anything, their records offer witness to uneven academic progress, and perhaps to Ralston's management style. Cornelius Hayes, for example, was working in the fourth reader and first-level geography and arithmetic textbooks in 1889 at the orphan home; by 1894, when he arrived at the boarding school, he had advanced only to the next reading level. Making more rapid progress was Eastman Williams, who began the first reader and learned to write on his slate in 1889; by 1894 he was ready for the fourth reader. Armstrong Academy's superintendent offered the view in 1894 that the "boys all seem satisfied with the management and every thing [sic] is favorable for great accomplishments in the direction of educational work."[31]

Like the Chickasaw Orphan Home, Armstrong Academy was a graded school, and like the Chickasaw home, the academy attempted to follow the progressive ideals of reform education. Graded schools were supposed to be better than the classroom in which students of the same age worked at different levels. Although numerous surveys conducted in the early 1900s never proved that graded schools were superior, they were argued to be so. Thus, Armstrong was a product of late-nineteenth-century reform thinking. As such, it attempted to provide a well-rounded school environment. Life was not a drudgery of manual labor and academics. There was time for recreation. Equipment for sports and games, including a croquet set, was purchased. Although by itself a croquet set may seem a simple, even inappropriate, example of play equipment for Indian youngsters, its presence, and that of other recreational items, indicated the new importance placed on leisure time and play.[32]

The Choctaws, members of the other Five Civilized Tribes, and those responsible for Thomas in New York State had something to prove. They could provide care and educational facilities as good as, if not better than, those under federal direction, where the play element often lagged behind. At the Santa Fe Indian School, for example, drills that promised "perfect military precision" overshadowed the school's "instructive amusements and recreations" of baseball for boys and tennis for girls. Government schools often cited the lack of money for equipment as the reason for little play activity. Indian orphanages had financial problems, too, but each adapted as best it could the progressive ideals that combined play with education.[33]

Basic to the play-recreation movement was the tenet that a child's environment could be manipulated to produce socially acceptable behavior and attitudes. Whereas earlier thought had adhered to the Calvinist belief that human nature could be subjugated only with threats of hell in the hereafter and physical punishment in the present, social reformers of the late 1800s argued that human nature could be altered by shaping a child's environment through the social interaction offered by playtime. The last decades of the nineteenth century saw monumental scientific advances. Science was able to control more diseases and was being used to develop new technologies for manufacturing. Why not use a scientific approach to manipulate and standardize a child's environment and thus yield productive future citizens? One element in that environment was organized play. Experts in the field of child development believed that recreation, organized and directed by adults, not the children themselves, was important for mental, social, and physical well-being. Too, it taught youngsters to be part of a team. By extension, that team was America. Play could take many forms—organized sports teams, choirs or glee clubs, agricultural clubs such as 4-H, or supervised games on a play-ground. No matter its form, play was important for altering the worst impulses of human nature. In fact, organized activities were argued to be a strong deterrent to juvenile delinquency, and in any of its applications, play was praised for its abilities to restructure a child's behavior patterns for the public good. Time only reinforced what the nineteenth-century reformers preached. For example, the 1940 White House Conference on Children in a Democracy concluded: "Recreation for children in a democracy should reflect, therefore, in its program, organization, and operation those values which are implicit in the democratic way of life."[34]

Given the social and reformist climate of the late nineteenth century, it is not surprising that orphan homes among the Five Civilized Tribes and in New York adopted play-recreation as a sign that they were on the leading edge of progressive thought. Thomas in New York purchased croquet sets and seesaws to fit out the playground, and it routinely ordered the necessary equipment and uniforms for baseball, lacrosse, and football. It was the same in other institutions. The Cherokee and Creek orphan homes had their football and baseball teams, and Cherokee girls had a basketball team after the turn of the century. The latter reflected popular culture's emerging "Outdoor Girl," a contradiction to Victorian ideals of womanhood. The Outdoor Girl participated in activities once considered unladylike. She exercised her mind and her body. As part of the movement to direct play for youngsters, reformers took into consideration the benefits for girls. Organized recreation was as important for structuring the female environment as it was for directing that of males.[35]

While the Choctaws could point to a number of progressive indicators, the tribal government still had to oversee school and orphan home management. The Choctaw takeover of the Armstrong orphan home was repeated at Wheelock in 1894. The contract with the Presbyterians was voided, and the Choctaw government decided to run the institution with a superintendent of its own choosing. Thus, E. H. Wilson, "a member of a prominent Choctaw family," was put in charge. The arrangement worked for five years, but then Wilson's tenure was terminated. The Choctaw government sought a new superintendent "who shall give all his time and attention to the management of the school." The implication was that Wilson had other interests that distracted him from the daily supervision of Wheelock, which by that time was variously referred to as Wheelock Academy, Wheelock Female Seminary, Wheelock Female Orphan Academy, and Wheelock Orphan Seminary.[36]

Termination of some contracts did not imply that the Choctaws cut all ties to mission groups. Tribal government simply took an active interest. It felt perfectly capable of running its own institutions. In doing so, the Choctaw government attempted to give itself a stronger position in the face of federal plans to dissolve tribal governments and institutions in Indian Territory. As for the Presbyterians, their reaction to losing Armstrong and then Wheelock was to redefine Goodland Mission as the Goodland Indian Orphanage and School. Since the mission's inception in 1848, a number of orphaned children had lived in or near it, but when Presbyterians lost their contracts at the Choctaws' orphanages, greater efforts went into Goodland. In 1894 the Home Mission Committee began soliciting donations that contributed to building a log dormitory for approximately twenty boys. The dormitory was described as "one large room of hewn oak, with a stick-and-mud chimney; a loft over head, to which the boys climbed a ladder when it was time to sleep; a side room which was used as a kitchen and dining room; and a front porch." Among those responsible for gathering donations and building the dormitory were Choctaw elders Wilson Jones, Bartwell McCann, and Wall Hayes. The elders represented the trend of conversion among the Choctaws after removal; with Presbyterian encouragement, most ministers and all church elders were Indian. The Goodland elders took their responsibilities seriously. To provision the home, the elders, as well as members of Goodland's church congregation, hitched up a wagon and traveled the countryside asking for donations. Families contributed foodstuffs such as cornmeal, flour, potatoes, and sugar. They also provided fuel for heat and oil for lamps.[37]

The orphanage had barely begun when McCann and Hayes died, both of pneumonia, leaving Goodland without two of its most faithful workers. Then poor crop years made it extremely difficult for the local population to support the orphanage with donations. In 1898 the dormitory closed, and children were placed in private homes. To keep Goodland open as some sort of educational center, a Presbyterian minister, the Reverend Gibbons, and his wife operated a day school there until 1901. In that year the reverend and Silas L. Bacon, a full-blood Choctaw who was an Indian elder in the church and a minister, persuaded the Choctaw National Council to reopen the orphanage under contract. The government agreed, but it made stipulations. Bacon, who served on the Choctaw National Council for several terms, would act as superintendent. He, not the Presbyterians, would be the contractor. The council would pay thirty-six dollars per year for each child—up to a total of forty. The money came from mineral leases agreed to by the Choctaw government in its negotiations with the federal government. In making the agreement, the Choctaws effectively maintained control. The dormitory reopened, but its space was limited. To accommodate the overflow, Bacon housed a number of orphans in his home. A girl who stayed in the Bacon household later recalled that she was too young to remember the deaths of her parents but that she was taken in by Eliza Alfred Bacon (the minister's second wife), and "there I lived until I became of age and married."[38]

Bacon, himself an orphan, was raised by his grandmother, Betsy Pitchlynn. As a child he attended school at the Goodland Mission. Later he attended Spencer Academy (not the orphanage of Old Spencer), and in 1900 he was ordained as a Presbyterian minister. Despite his education, Bacon believed himself limited in the white world. His English was not fluent, and he self-consciously apologized for improper spellings and misuse of words. Perhaps for that reason he worked diligently to see that youngsters received more academic training than vocational. He was portrayed by one teacher at the orphanage as "a wonderful fullbood educator." Because of his religious conversion and the influence of Presbyterian ministers at Spencer Academy, Bacon also strongly advocated Bible studies as part of the curriculum.[39]

If anything emerges from the descriptions of Bacon, it is of a good man dedicated to caring for orphaned children and seeing to their spiritual and material needs. The orphanage in its first years maintained only the barest of necessities for day-to-day living; by 1903 there were only about fifteen boys and girls in residence. Nevertheless, if there was any orphanage that truly exhibited a homelike atmosphere for children, Bacon's Goodland was the prime example. There were no uniforms or strict work regimes other than the chores in which youngsters learned by doing. Bacon and his wife were father and mother. Under their supervision the home grew. The Bacons donated

The Reverend Silas Bacon (lower right corner), his wife (second from left, standing), and Choctaw youngsters at Goodland Indian Orphanage and School, Hugo, Oklahoma, ca. 1926. Archives and Manuscripts Division of the Oklahoma Historical Society.

their allotment to ensure that it would. Four dormitories as well as other buildings were constructed. Money came from private donations, from home mission funds and, as a final gesture from the dispersal of Choctaw funds at the time of dissolution, $10,000 from the Choctaw National Council. Bacon served the orphanage for twenty years before his health rapidly declined. He was replaced by Samuel Bailey Spring, who was a teacher, church elder, and one-quarter Choctaw. In 1922 Bacon died of tuberculosis; his wife preceded him in death by just a few months. They were buried in the cemetery at Goodland Mission, with a headstone that read: "Both freely gave their time and talents, impoverishing themselves for the needy orphans of their race."[40]

Just as the Choctaw government gave some monetary support to Goodland, it did the same for the orphanage that emerged from Murrow's Atoka Baptist Academy, which in the late 1800s was referred to in official Choctaw documents as the Baptist Orphan School. County judges selected youngsters for the orphan school, just as they selected residents for Armstrong and Wheelock. However, at the Baptist orphanage, the Choctaws made no demands for separation of the sexes. Money, ranging from $2,750 to $5,500 per year, was appropriated to support thirty boys and twenty girls at the facility. The orphanage also served as a school for the children of newly arrived white settlers during the interim between settlement and organization of white school systems. Settlers could send their children to school at the orphanage by paying $1.50 per month.[41]

The Baptist Orphan School at Atoka, as well as Choctaw support for it, was slated to end during the period of tribal dissolution. Nevertheless, the Choctaws continued to appropriate money and to sign contracts. It seemed that the best defense against federal plans was to act as if they did not exist. Such actions had little hope of success, and on April 14, 1899, the Choctaws were advised by federal officials that the Chickasaw and Choctaw agreements for allotments and ultimate dissolution of tribal governments did not allow the Choctaws to continue making contracts without approval from the U.S. secretary of the interior. Local residents of Atoka stepped in to support the Baptist institution, petitioning the federal government to keep the orphan home. Some went farther, suggesting that instead of being closed, the home should be expanded to include a larger number of Choctaw orphans. Instead of maintaining fifty places allowed at the home, they asked that the number be increased to one hundred. "We are reliably informed that there are many Choctaw orphans throughout the country who are unable to gain admission into any of the schools thus far established and whose friends desire that they be admitted."[42]

There were not more true orphans, but there were more destitute children because guardianship fraud was divesting youngsters of their allotments. Still, the federal government found no reason to keep the Atoka home operating. Aided by the Choctaws and Chickasaws, Joseph S. Murrow once again stepped in. He was the initial driving force behind establishing the Atoka Baptist Academy, and for years he attempted to break down tribal barriers in religious work, organizing the Choctaw and Chickasaw Baptist Association in 1872. When the federal government effectively ended Choctaw financial support of the Baptist orphanage, Murrow devised an alternative. In November 1902 the Murrow Indian Orphans' Home was incorporated in U.S. district court. Articles of incorporation stated that the home was intended for "destitute orphan children of full-blood Indian Parentage, from any or all tribes of Indians resident in the United States," as well as for destitute and orphaned children whose heritage was "not more than one-half white blood." This included youngsters whose backgrounds were a mix of Indian and black. One girl, of Choctaw freedmen descent, lost her parents and grandmother by the age of seven. Her older brother, unable to care for the girl alone, placed her in the orphanage until he was able to support her through his work as a Baptist preacher.[43]

According to the articles of incorporation, it was the home's duty to "to instill into their [children's] minds and hearts moral and religious instruction" and to offer basic academic and industrial training. Although it was expected that English would be the language of the home, organizers believed that English was also essential, since the home was intended for children of any Indian tribe—not just the Choctaws—and a multiplicity of native languages would create barriers between the students. The English-only policy made a lasting impression. Left alone after the deaths of her parents and then the death of the grandmother who cared for her, a former resident of the home commented: "When I was eleven years old . . . I was taken to the Baptist Orphan's Home. . . . I did not know a word of English when I was taken to Atoka, but now [1937] I do not know many words of my own language. We were not allowed to speak our language at the school and so we younger children almost forgot our own language."[44]

The Choctaws and Chickasaws passed resolutions supporting the Murrow Indian Orphans' Home as a worthy undertaking. The tribes also joined in asking the U.S. Congress to approve setting aside land for the purpose of building a new orphanage, rather than use the site at Atoka: "A suitable amount of land should be donated, in a legal manner, in aiding the maintenance of this institution in order to enable its management to properly care for the unfortunate members of the Choctaw and Chickasaw tribes of Indians in after years." In all, the donated land amounted to 1,790 acres about twenty-five miles north of Atoka. By 1905 the plan was approved, and by 1906 the acreage included 3,200 acres. Most was in farmland, but there was ample space for a 40-acre orchard and land for gardens and housing. Baptist missions continued to support the orphanage through donations of goods and money, but children's expenses—approximately thirty-six dollars per quarter—were paid out of the children's allotments. Whatever was left over went into each child's trust fund, which was turned over at the age of majority. Meanwhile, children and teenagers lived in the orphanage, were educated, and not so incidentally did most of the labor necessary to maintain and develop the institution. No one could accuse the inhabitants of malingering.[45]

Since the presence of orphanages and their histories within Indian populations were largely overlooked, it is not surprising that one writer, searching for something to boast about in the new state of Oklahoma, claimed that the Murrow orphanage was "the only Indian orphan home in the United States." Perhaps another writer was more accurate in saying that Joseph Murrow "considered the founding of the Orphan's Home the last and best effort of his sixty years of service to the Indians."[46]

It was certainly one of his most difficult efforts. The home was plagued with financial problems. So, too, was the American Baptist college of Bacone Indian University. First established at Tahlequah in 1879, the school was known as Indian University. The Baptist goal was to have a university for all Indians, although in its early years the offerings were equivalent to a high school curriculum. The Reverend Almon C. Bacone, for whom the school was named, was among the organizers and the first president; Joseph Murrow was president of the board of trustees. The school was moved from the Cherokee Nation to Muskogee when the Creek Nation agreed in 1881 to give land, money for construction, and funds for student support. The Creeks' reasoning was basic. A few students were supported through tribal funds for advanced educational opportunities in the States, but the tribe could not accommodate all who wanted this education, and most Creek families could not personally afford to send their young people away to school. There was a pressing need for something closer to home. "There are some who wish their daughters Educated and their financial condition will not admit of their sending their Daughters to the States." The Baptist college was a solution to the dilemma.[47]

When the Creeks accepted Bacone Indian University into their territory, there were no orphanages in the Creek Nation. Yet within ten years of Bacone's appearance, there were two Creek orphanages. The appearance of one did not hinge on the other, but by the early 1900s, Murrow's Baptist orphanage in the Choctaw Nation and Bacone University in the Creek Nation came together to create Murrow Indian Orphanage.

Given the fact that up to 1891 the Creeks had not found it necessary to establish an orphanage, one has to wonder why the nation bothered. Crucial transitional points—the Civil War and/or missionary influence—that led to organization of orphanages among other tribal groups did not produce the same response among the Creeks. In fact, the appearance and growth of orphan homes in the Creek Nation bear no correlation to any striking pivotal moment save one—the prospect of white encroachment in Indian Territory and the gathering clouds of tribal dissolution and allotment. Orphans were certainly known in Creek society. After all, the orphans "adopted" by Andrew Jackson and Peggy Eaton were survivors of the Creek Wars, and at the time of removal from the Southeast, 573 orphans were counted as recipients of twenty sections of land to be used for their benefit.[48] The Creeks, however, did not consider orphanages until long after forced removal and wars disrupted tribal life and age-old family patterns. The timing for creating orphanages sets the tribe apart from others, but the contrast with other tribes is most dramatic in the types of orphanages established. The Creek government created one orphanage for Creek children and another for Creek freedmen.

The stories of the Creek Orphan Home and the Creek Colored Orphan Home begin with fire. Considering the number of fires that ravaged buildings in the Creek Nation, this is not surprising. In fact, any detailed history of the Creek school system should contain a chapter on the incidence of fires that destroyed mission and school buildings. Fire destroyed outbuildings at the Coweta Mission School (also called the Coweta National Boarding School). Asbury Manual Labor School burned in the early 1870s, was rebuilt, and burned again in 1881. Tullahassee Manual Labor School, established by the Presbyterians and described as one of the Creeks' "most effective educational institutions," burned in 1880. In each case it was believed that local arsonists were to blame. It was the burning of Tullahassee that inadvertently led to the creation of the Creek Colored Orphan Home, which had its own experiences with fire. The beginning date for the Creek Orphan Home, located near Okmulgee, is unclear, but in 1891 it was rebuilt after a fire. Recalled one of the men who worked on the project, "It was originally a frame structure and it is thought that some of the inmates were instrumental in its being burned. We reconstructed this asylum of native stone and brick that was near by."[49]

When Tullahassee Manual Labor School was destroyed by fire in December 1880, the federal government made a special appropriation of $5,000 to assist in rebuilding the school at a new location. The rebuilt institution was named Wealaka Manual Labor School. What remained of the fire-ruined Tullahassee the National Council of the Muskogee Nation decided "to turn over to the Colored people of the Nation," since the site was "in the midst of a colored settlement." The freedmen would receive the farm, orchard, buildings (damaged and undamaged), and $3,191.66 to rebuild the main structure. At first the freedmen resisted. One spokesman, after traveling to all black settlements in the Creek Nation, informed the national council: "[I] have had a chance to ascertain the sentiments of the people, . . . and I am fully satisfied that a very large majority of the colored people do not want the old remains." They wanted instead to make some exchange for the old agency building, located at what was called Agency Hill or Union Hill. There was every reason to want this building and not what was left of burned Tullahassee. The agency building was vacant but in fairly good repair, and it was in close proximity to all black settlements. Nevertheless, the national council persisted, and the freedmen finally agreed. In November 1883, Tullahassee was rebuilt and opened as a boarding school for Creek freedmen, capable of accommodating fifty students. Still, the black community had been heard. When the Creek government decided to establish an orphanage for Creek children, an orphanage for the "colored Creeks" also opened. The site chosen for the orphanage was Agency Hill.[50]

A onetime resident of the Creek Colored Orphan Home was George McIntosh, whose heritage was a mix of Creek and African. Said McIntosh, "On the colored side [of my family] were slaves of John McInstosh," who brought his slaves with him at the time of removal. As with other tribes in the Southeast, the Creeks had their own history of slavery. Before removal, federal officials took a census that counted nine hundred Negro slaves in Creek territory. The number failed, however, to reflect anything close to the true demographics of the African population. There were free blacks, some of whom were considered to be tribal members, and mestizos, who as the offspring of intermarriage blurred Indian and African, slave and free. Left unrecorded, too, were the number of black Seminoles who with the Seminole Indians were attached at the time of removal to the diverse ethnic and linguistic groups that made up the loose confederation of groups called the Creek. With every Creek and Seminole group traveling west at the time of removal, there were black slaves and mestizo Creeks and Seminoles.[51]

The Civil War brought hardship and death, and the Creeks and Seminoles were as divided as the other Five Civilized Tribes when it came to loyalties. One postwar report estimated that at least 1,700 Creeks enlisted in the Union army. Meanwhile, many Creek and Seminole civilians attempted to flee the conflict, in one well-reported instance suffering horrific conditions in freezing weather along the Verdigris River in Kansas. Among these refugees were 3,168 Creeks, 777 Seminoles, 53 Creek slaves, and 38 free Creek blacks. Despite common suffering and a general support of the Union by Creeks and Seminoles, they, along with the other Five Civilized Tribes, underwent Reconstruction after the war. All slaves were freed and allowed to decide if they wanted to remain in Indian Territory. Reconstruction also addressed blacks who had always been free and those with African and Creek or Seminole heritages. In 1867, rolls were prepared to designate those who were Creek freedmen and entitled to the same benefits afforded other tribal members. The procedure was basically the same for other tribes during Reconstruction, although no roll of Chickasaw freemen was ever taken, and Choctaws still living in Mississippi were ignored.[52]

Not all responded in the same way to their freedmen. The Cherokees, for example, established schools for freedmen and much later, in 1889, in the face of some dissension within the nation's government, opened the Cherokee Colored High School. (This was summarily closed by the federal government in 1911.) The Cherokee Nation, however, refused to establish an orphanage for freedmen despite heated protests that they should have a share of the Orphan Fund. The Chickasaws never considered an orphanage for blacks or youngsters of mixed black and Indian heritage. Chickasaw schools were restricted. Freedmen education was left to the Baptists, and when, in 1882, the federal government promised money to the Chickasaws if they provided schools, the tribe's response was to ask that all freedmen be removed from the nation. As Lomawaima pointed out in the study of Chilocco Indian School, many tribes were hostile to people of African ancestry. In part, many members of the Five Civilized Tribes retained the old plantation-slaveholder mind-set, but on a national level boarding schools excluded students suspected of being of mixed black and Indian heritage on the basis that blacks were trying to pass as Indians and get benefits to which they were not entitled. At the Santa Fe Indian School, for example, the superintendent informed the commissioner of Indian affairs that he would admit two brothers, whose mother was Ute and father a Negro, only if the commissioner ordered him to do so. After all, "they look to me to be full blood negroes, and will be a bad element in this school."[53]

The Creeks took another tack. A handful of day schools served black communities, and there was a boarding school for freedmen. The Creeks had a dual, segregated system. If there was to be an orphanage for Creek children, the Creek freedmen would have one, too. From its beginning, the Creek Colored Orphan Home housed a number of children with the McIntosh surname. They were not necessarily siblings, but they were certainly descendants of those slaves who took their names from the many McIntosh family members who were slaveholders. The orphanage housed both boys and girls, and if any were of Seminole African descent rather than Creek African, the records never gave that indication. Instead, there were only the numbers, divided by how many of each sex resided at the orphanage. Numbers varied from twenty-five to fifty-five, although officially there was only enough room for fifty. References to this orphanage are meager, offering few intimate insights into the lives of these children or the routine of their days. The language of the home was English, which most often was the language of the children, rather than Creek. In fact, one of the continuing arguments Creek leaders offered for not doing more for freedmen education in general was that freedmen already spoke English and were, therefore, at less disadvantage than the Creeks for dealing with white society. The argument is borne out by records from the two Creek orphanages; while almost none of those in the Creek Orphan Home were conversant in English, all of those in the Creek Colored Orphan Home were. Too, there were personal testimonies to the situation: "The Indians owned slaves and sometimes a slave could talk English, in which event the Indian would take him as an Interpreter when he would go to trade with the horsetraders . . . or to other places." If anything emerges from existing documents, however, it is the battle to finance the institution and provide youngsters with basic necessities. Money came out of the Creek Orphan Fund, but less was allocated for the home than for the Creek Orphan Home. This meant that consistently the superintendent spent more than allowed, leading him at one point to remind the Creek Board of Education: "As you know the students are orphans . . . and no one to help them so I have furnished some clothing to those most in need." Still, the superintendent remained optimistic: "No sickness of account. My teachers are diligent in the school room. Children are contented and I think are progressing satisfactorily in there [sic] studies."[54]

The Creek Colored Orphan Home came out of the Creek government's acceptance of the principle that institutions for Creek freedmen were to mirror those for Creek children. It would not have appeared at all, however, if the Creek government had been able to carry out its original plan of accommodating Creek orphans at the newly constructed Wealaka Manual Labor School. The Creeks hoped to follow the Choctaw plan that originally attempted to integrate orphans into the general populations of boarding schools. Therefore, the National Council of the Muskogee Nation directed that fifty orphans be added to the one hundred students already at Wealaka. The superintendent and others were appalled. The boarding school could house only one hundred. There was no room for fifty more; at best, the superintendent could find space for ten. The council was asked to reconsider, and, like the Choctaws before them, the Creeks realized that there were two choices—either expand the nation's boarding schools to accommodate orphans or build an institution just for this group of youngsters.[55]

Neither the Creek Orphan Home nor the home for Creek freedmen operated under contract with a religious group. The American Baptists donated hymnals and Bibles, and Sunday services leaned toward Baptist or Methodist doctrine, but the orphanages were overseen by the Creek government. In both institutions, superintendents were chosen on the basis of their loyalty to the government, prominence within the nation, and education. Alexander Lawrence Posey, as just one example, served for a short time as Creek Orphan Home superintendent. Called the "Creek Poet" for his literary prowess, he was educated at Indian University (Bacone) and was a member of the House of Warriors, the lower branch of the Creek legislature. Although Posey was more than capable of acting as superintendent, the federal government called the Creeks' choices for superintendents political favoritism and condemned it. The practice, said the government, only guaranteed poorly run schools. Of course, this was a matter of viewpoint. For the Creeks, placement of their own people ensured loyalty to the tribal government's expectations for education—not white expectations. Too, while the Creek government chose superintendents from a specific group within the nation, staff was racially mixed. Teachers, matrons, and other employees such as cooks and handymen were as likely to be Caucasian or black as Indian.[56]

At the Creek Orphan Home, supervision was largely in the hands of a respected and politically involved family. The first superintendent,

*The Creek Orphan Home near Okmulgee, Indian Territory, 1901.
Seated to the far right are Johnson Tiger, superintendent, and his
wife, Lena, matron. Archives and Manuscripts Division of the
Oklahoma Historical Society.*

Moty Tiger (the name was also spelled Monti and Montey), was described by one teacher as "the best manager of any of the superintendents." Others would have high praise for Tiger's successors, who, with
the exception of short tenures by Peter Ewing and Posey, were Tiger's
sons. First, there was George and then Johnson Tiger, a graduate of Bacone College (the former Indian University), who did not follow a Baptist calling but became an elder in the Creek Methodist Church. While
George was director, Johnson and his wife, Lena, taught at the home,
and Johnson preached there on Sundays. In a later reminiscence, Lena
Benson Tiger made a point of mentioning clan affiliation: she belonged
to the Bird Clan, her husband to the Alligator Clan. Acculturation had
not totally drained the Creeks of their past. Despite decades of white
contact, some age-old tribal characteristics held on, even in the face of
orphaned children whom nobody claimed.[57]

The orphanage blended white education and religion with traditional ways of life. The home emphasized academics over manual
labor. Superintendents made perfunctory statements about girls wash-

ing and ironing and boys working on the farm, but more space was reserved for reporting on the classroom, where geography, arithmetic, algebra, grammar, and history were taught. "Twenty recitations by six classes are heard and taught daily in the advanced department"; in the primary department were three classes. No matter the level, there was English—not as a means of Americanization but as a tool for survival in the white world fast closing in around Indian Territory. So important was English that teachers were required to routinely report on students' progress, since almost none of the children knew the language when they entered the home. The spring report for 1896, for example, noted 30 boys and 25 girls in the home; of these, 6 could "understand and speak English." Two years later, with 31 males and 27 females, teachers reported that 22 were English literate. How teachers gauged fluency was probably arbitrary rather than based on any test standards, but the rise in numbers suggests the intensity with which English was pursued. At the same time, Indian culture was maintained in small but important ways. Recalled a former employee, "I used to cook for the Creek Orphan's Home east of Okmulgee. Sofkey and Blue dumplings were two of the dishes I prepared." Softkee, considered a Choctaw traditional dish, was prepared in much the same way as hominy. Blue dumpling preparation also began with shelled corn "treated with wood ashes or lye as for hominy." The dumplings *(char-tar-haka)* were an ideal food for an institution; they were filling and could be used over a period of days. Said Lena Tiger, who advanced from teacher to home matron, "Blue dumpling is eaten as bread and will keep for days without getting stale, when heated in hot water or sliced and fried." Susan Tiger, wife of George, summed up the home's atmosphere by noting that it was little different from other Creek schools and that "the food was about what most home-cooking was like."[58]

Although the Creek government was slow to establish orphanages, their importance was stressed during the period of tribal dissolution. There were orphans in the nation who lived in circumstances unimagined within traditional culture. In his journal, Alexander Posey noted:

While at town this afternoon, I picked up a poor little orphan boy; who has been tossed hither and thither, like a weed on a wide sea, without father or mother to cling to many years. I brought him back with me [to the orphan home], and he is the happiest boy

Holding their china-head dolls, girls from the Creek Orphan Home sit with matron Lena Tiger, 1901. Archives and Manuscripts Division of the Oklahoma Historical Society.

this side of paradise. He has a home now and some one to look to for food and raiment.[59]

During the period of dissolution, federal officials demanded that the Creek government cease and desist from issuing new purchase warrants to pay school system debts. Finances were in disarray largely because unscrupulous whites issued fraudulent warrants for which they demanded payment. The unbelievable tangle was somewhat alleviated in 1897 when the federal government appropriated long-requested funds to defray the nation's public debt. This came at another cost to the Creek Nation, whose boarding schools were forced to close until finances were righted. The only exceptions were the orphanages, which remained operational during the crisis. Once the nation's school system was back on its feet financially and all its schools reopened, the orphanages continued. Sometimes they did so under formidable circumstances. The Creek Colored Orphan Home lost a dormitory to fire and "labored under great difficulty" to accept more children. The Creek Orphan Home constantly dealt with the problem of resident children being swindled by guardians. Despite problems, a federal report of 1903 offered the opinion that the Creek Orphan Home's record "has been very creditable to its young Indian superintendent [Johnson Tiger]. Orphan children are sent here more to find a home than to go to school, and are younger and more dependent than in other schools." A close observer simply stated that "the Orphan Home at Okmulgee was a wonderful place."[60]

6

TRIBAL DISSOLUTION: OKLAHOMA

The friends of orphan children wrote us saying that, "our school was their only chance."[1]

A result of tribal dissolution and allotment in Oklahoma was closure of some Indian orphanages and restructuring of those that remained operational. Control over tribal orphanages was taken up by federal management that decided which, if any, orphanages continued under the broad tent of government-supported Indian schools. At the same time, church-sponsored institutions such as Murrow and Goodland and the privately run Whitaker continued. Out of dissolution emerged dual institutions—federal and nonfederal orphanages for Indian children. In a few instances this meant that children and adolescents of one tribe continued to be surrounded by others of their own heritage. For other Indian youngsters, however, the institutional landscape altered dramatically as they were congregated into settings more interested in their Indianness than in tribal affiliation. This was a pivotal moment in the history of Indian orphanages in Oklahoma. Unlike the Thomas School in New York, where residents shared a common heritage, twentieth-century Indian orphanages in Oklahoma began to intermingle children in a pan-Indian environment.

Acculturation remained a goal of orphanages in Oklahoma, but assimilation was less emphasized. Henry Dawes approached dissolution from the viewpoint that Indian culture should conform to a white model of civilization without blending into it. Indian Bureau school officials took a similar view, "endeavoring to fit these girls and boys for life among their own people." In Oklahoma this was underscored by the white culture's inclination to exclude rather than include. Whites and Indians attended public schools together, but African-Americans, including those of Indian extraction, were segregated. In the majority of orphan homes that appeared in rapid order after statehood, children of Indian and Indian African ancestry were unwelcome. Indian freedmen were excluded from the Whitaker home, too, but the institution accommodated both Indian and white children. It was to this home that Kate Barnard directed an impoverished white woman who begged for help in finding a place to house and educate her children, since there was no private or state institution exclusively for white children yet in operation. That quickly changed. Indeed, Oklahoma became a microcosm of the nation's mania for institution building. Within ten years of statehood, there were at least eight orphanages for Caucasian children, and one has to wonder if all these institutions were necessary, since the orphaned population could not have demanded such a number.[2] It is more probable that adults in Oklahoma used orphan homes in the same way that people did in other states—as temporary housing when times were hard or at specific periods of family upheaval. Too, various religious groups established their own orphanages to ensure that a dependent child's religious heritage was not compromised.

Although total dissolution of tribal governments was supposed to be completed in 1906, it was not. Dissolution was an excruciating bureaucratic process that at times bordered on the absurd. When the Creek Nation, for example, was ordered to turn over school materials, each item was counted. When six typewriter ribbons were turned in, not the four listed on an inventory of property, and when the number of thumbtacks differed by twelve, federal officials commanded the Creek superintendent of schools to explain. If anything, this mind-numbing exercise illustrates the federal government's intent to shred any reminder that tribal governments had once been at work. While the counters fussed over how many thumbtacks the Indians actually owned, the larger issues of restructuring tribal funds and divesting governments of their powers remained, and resistance continued. John Benedict's report on the Creeks could have applied to any of the tribes: "The Creek Council is composed largely of dissatisfied Indians who have been opposed to all the steps taken by the U.S. Government toward allotment of lands, and have just passed a resolution opposing statehood of any kind."[3]

Of considerable concern to all nations under the dissolution mandate was the fate of their school systems, and Benedict played a key role in determining closures. He had no intention of keeping the systems intact and little interest in maintaining every tribal school. Behind him was the force of the Dawes Commission that had earlier denounced the Indian nations as incapable of governing themselves. For his part, Benedict reduced the generality to the specifics of schooling. To bolster the government's image as experts in Indian education, Benedict widely broadcast the opinion that Indian superintendents and teachers were incompetent. "Very few of those engaged in the school work in these nations," he said, "have ever had any professional training." Benedict engaged in outright disinformation for, as he knew, there was substantial evidence to the contrary. Those employed at tribal schools were not only educated; many were graduates of white institutions, and there was the testimony of outsiders brought in to conduct teacher training institutes, or "normals." One letter to the U.S. secretary of the interior complimented the "skillful primary teacher" at the Armstrong home for orphan boys; another commented on the "superior scholarship" displayed by all teachers in the Choctaw Nation. While Benedict was quick to charge that instruction had been poor in tribally supported schools, he was reluctant to admit that when the government took control, it tried to retain Indian instructors but had a difficult time keeping competent superintendents and teachers because of poor pay. Johnson Tiger, for example, quit the Creek Orphan Home because the salary was inadequate.[4]

Anxious to hurry Oklahoma statehood along, members of the U.S. Congress made their own damning statements. One senator called for a congressional investigation, since it was common knowledge, he said, that tribal schools were "conducted loosely." "Pupils who are afflicted with tuberculosis and other diseases are admitted to the detriment of the health of inmates of the schools, resulting in an appalling mortality." If that was not reason enough to condemn the schools, one had only to look at "the inter-mixture of the sexes [that] results in a lowering of the standard of morality."[5] One could always rely on the whisper of sexual improprieties to gain audience attention. It made little difference that there was no basis for suggesting that tribal boarding schools were riddled with disease and death or that sexual misbehavior was condoned. These schools were an obstacle to dismantling Indian governments and securing Oklahoma statehood. Pubic indictments of the schools were meant to spur speedy closure.

Congressional condemnation supported Benedict's work, which set about castigating Indian schools on several counts. He portrayed them as being in "deplorable condition," poorly maintained, and struc-

*After the Civil War, the Five Civilized Tribes reacted to their
freedmen in different ways. The Creeks funded a boarding school
at Tullahassee (shown here in 1890), and then supported the Creek
Colored Orphan Home at another location. Archives and
Manuscripts Division of the Oklahoma Historical Society.*

turally unsound. He attacked the selection of teachers and superintendents, maintaining that favoritism played the largest role. He criticized Creek schools in particular for not utilizing their farms to a
greater extent and thus providing more on-site support to schools and
their residents. While he attacked tribal education in general and took
special aim at the Creeks, Benedict waffled when it came to closing
all orphan homes, as well as boarding schools such as Jones Academy,
where a minority of the residents were orphan and half-orphan boys.
Although Benedict attacked the Creeks, he expressed particular concern for closing Creek orphanages. "In my opinion," he wrote, "the
Creek Orphan Home and the Creek Colored Orphan Home should not
be discontinued, because there would be no provision whatever for
maintaining these Indian and Negro children belonging to the Creek
Nation." At the time there were sixty-two at the Creek Orphan Home
and fifty-three at the home for Creek freedmen.[6] Saved, too, were the
Cherokee orphanage and Wheelock Female Orphan Academy, although the Indian Bureau never intended to be in the business of running orphanages. If, however, the bureau regarded these homes as
boarding schools, albeit special ones, the personal circumstances of
the child population were easily overlooked.

Under Benedict's directive the Creek orphan homes continued to operate, and the Creek superintendent of schools stayed at his job through 1906. It was to the Creek superintendent that A. H. Mike, superintendent of the Creek Colored Orphan Home, applied for reappointment and suggested staff for the upcoming year: "For teacher Miss Mary L. Roberts, normal graduate Lincoln Institute who is also a musician. . . . As the cook we had last year did not do her work satisfactorily I beg to be privileged to secure one." To all appearances it was business as usual, but behind the scenes the Indian Bureau had control. All schools still in operation, orphan home or not, were inspected by federal officials. Would-be teachers were required to attend training institutes, and teachers on staff had to demonstrate that their classroom curriculum adhered to prescribed courses of instruction. Payment warrants for everything—whether salaries, expenditures for food and clothing, or miscellaneous supplies from a hardware store—were approved by Benedict. Teachers' quarterly reports went into Benedict's hands, and one has to wonder at the man's response to a 1905 report from the Creek Colored Orphan Home. Perhaps to appease the federal official or the government's insistence on Americanization, a teacher added civics to the list of subjects taught. Of the thirty-five orphan home residents, however, only one was listed as studying the subject of government and citizenship.[7]

Despite Benedict's early approval for retaining the Creek orphan homes and official inspections that classified the Creek Orphan Home as an "excellent" school, both Creek orphanages were eventually terminated. First the Creek Orphan Home closed. Then, in 1909, the Creek Colored Orphan Home and the land it retained for farm and pasture were sold to the city of Muskogee "for park purposes"; the $4,500 garnered from the sale was deposited to the credit of the Creek tribe. While former residents of the Creek Orphan Home were dispersed to Indian boarding schools or to private orphanages for Indian children, closure of the Creek Colored Orphan Home led one entrepreneur to hope that his "college" for Creeks and Seminoles with African ancestry would receive more students—and federal payment for taking the older residents of the Creek Colored Orphan Home. The college's stated purpose was to produce farmers, mechanics, and housewives, but it advertised a classical education: "There being many negroes who feel that any school without Latin in its curriculum must be a failure." The federal government, however, was not yet

The "Baseball Nine" of the Creek Orphan Home, 1904. Archives and Manuscripts Division of the Oklahoma Historical Society.

ready to relinquish its interests in Creek freedmen. Tullahassee, once a school for blacks in the Creek Nation, became the Tullahassee Orphan Boarding School. All those placed there had to be Creek freedmen, descendants of those whose names appeared on the roll prepared in 1867, and they had to be "less than 1/8 Indian." As in other institutions, there is reason to believe that not all living and studying at Tullahassee were orphans or even half-orphans. Closure of tribal schools sent students scrambling to find a place to receive an education, leading many who did not fit the orphan criteria to seek admittance at those institutions intended to be orphan schools. Wrote the superintendent at Wheelock Female Orphan Academy in 1912: "It is generally understood by the Indians that the boarding schools are full and it is no use to apply. However we have had seventy applicants the past year that we could not accept for lack of room." The superintendent at the Cherokee orphan home faced a constant problem in weeding out those who were not "needy and deserving children" but who wanted admittance because the school was close to home or because they did not want to attend a public school. It was the same at Tullahassee, where at least fifty prospective students were turned away. These youngsters and teenagers were a little more desperate, since they had fewer options in the outside world, where Oklahoma's public schools were segregated along black and white lines, and "separate but equal" was just a phrase.[8]

"Needy and deserving" were bandied about as the criteria for entrance to an orphan school, but under a congressional directive those admitted had to be "orphan children of the restricted class." The directive emerged in 1907 when Congress lifted most limitations on the sale of land allotted to the Five Civilized Tribes. Under the 1907 act, various classes of allottees—adult Cherokee and Seminole freedmen, all mixed-bloods for whom restrictions had been removed, and all Creeks except full-bloods, for example—were free to sell surplus land or portions of it. In the complicated formula were "restricted" Indians, who could not sell their land without federal approval. Essentially, the restricted class was made up of those of one-half or more Indian blood. As a group, restricted Indians remained under federal protection, and thus government-supported orphan schools were supposed to be just for them. Theory was not played out in the field, however. Orphans, half-orphans, and destitute children of the restricted class had priority for admittance to an orphan school, but superintendents overlooked the criteria when they believed a youngster was deserving. There were occasions, too, when the Oklahoma State Board of Charities and Corrections intervened on behalf of youngsters. When one concerned man saw the Cherokee orphan school as the only hope for a group of siblings whose mother was dead and father was serving a prison term, he asked the state board to contact the superintendent and argue for admittance on the grounds that the children's condition was "more deplorable than if they were orphans." On a national level, Indian Bureau officials would have seen this as state interference, but not so at the federally run facilities in Oklahoma.[9]

Superintendents used their discretionary powers to admit, as well as to dismiss. Under federal control, one of the authorities in the orphan schools was a "disciplinarian"—someone not seen before in these institutions. Youngsters who fit the criteria but whose behavior was disruptive were labeled as incorrigible and turned out. One boy at the Cherokee facility, for example, was removed and sent to his unrelated guardian because his behavior was "a constant evil example to smaller children." A girl was sent to her father. Her "dangerous temper and murderous attitude toward her mates" could not be controlled. There was no place for her in the institution, even if she fit the guidelines for admittance. Thus, local officials bent the letter of the law.[10]

In 1916 the federal government slightly changed its emphasis to include all orphans or half-orphans—if there was room for them. It was a decision with which orphan school officials agreed. Wrote the superintendent of the Cherokee Orphan Training School in 1919: "Our requirement for eligibility to enroll here is that one of the parents is dead." The Cherokee institution primarily served Cherokee children, but when there was room, children of other tribal groups were accepted. In 1920, for example, the training school housed 176 Cherokees and 5 Choctaws; in 1921, there were 183 Cherokees, 7 Choctaws, and 2 Shawnees. With Cherokee students always in the large majority, the institution never reflected a pan-Indian atmosphere similar to that found at boarding schools such as Chilocco or Haskell.[11]

Tullahassee Orphan Boarding School operated for only a short time. The government found the place too costly to run. The buildings were dilapidated and "almost unfit for use." With seventy-five to eighty residents at any given time, overcrowding was a constant problem. By 1914 the school superintendent gave up. He suggested that the government not waste money on repair and maintenance and that arrangements be made to place resident teenagers in other educational institutions. The most appropriate were Tuskegee Institute; Hampton Institute, which seemed perfect because it accepted both Indian and African-American students and received government subsidies that at the time averaged about $167 per student; or Oklahoma's all-black Langston University. These options would provide "better training" at less cost to the government. The Indian Bureau readily agreed. Some of those at Tullahassee went to Tuskegee, Hampton, or Langston. Most of the orphaned and dependent, however, were transferred to the all-purpose, all-encompassing Taft Institution, which was described by Oklahoma's commissioner of charities and corrections as the "Industrial Institute for the Deaf, Blind and Orphans of the Colored Race." The Creek freedmen were placed in an environment where they were not considered in any way as Indian; they were for all intents and purposes "Colored."[12]

Taft Institution emphasized industrial training, but Kate Barnard, commissioner of the state board of charities and corrections, was quick to advocate that the institution provide agricultural-based education:

> It must be remembered that orphan children, graduated out of our institutions will be thrown on their own resources. . . . [I]t is still the duty of the state to teach every child some useful trade to enable it to earn an honest living. The Negro race has made its best advancement under environments that lie close to the soil. Therefore, the dependent Negro children should be taught thoroughly all branches of farm industry. . . . Of course this does not contemplate that no mechanical or mannual [sic] trades be taught, but in the main these Negro children should be made fitted for household and farm work.[13]

In fact, Barnard believed that all dependent children, no matter their race, were better served if trained for farm life, rather than employment in the trades. Hers was the American ideal of rural living, underscored with a sense of practicality: "I believe that farm life is healthier and better in every way for people who have not the prospects of financial help to put them in business in towns and cities." Officials at the Indian Bureau agreed, although in the early twentieth century the bureau's educational model shifted from the nineteenth century's emphasis on agriculture and a smattering of vocational training to a design that placed greater emphasis on home economics as a science and training in skilled industrial or mechanical trades. Said a 1907 report to Francis Leupp, commissioner of Indian affairs: "Endeavor has been made to carry out your policy of giving industrial training and household economy a foremost place in Indian education, and it has been our constant aim to impress upon superintendents and employees the importance of having all instruction practical."[14]

At the Cherokee Orphan Home, renamed the Cherokee Orphan Training School when the federal government took complete control in 1909, the Indian Bureau expanded the manual-labor model to include a wider range of offerings in domestic science and trade skills. To facilitate this expansion, Hervey B. Peairs, chief supervisor of education for the Indian Bureau from 1910 to 1921, endeavored to raise teacher enthusiasm for the "educational ideals" of vocational training. Teacher normals addressed the subject, and instructors were directed to study such texts as *Examples of Industrial Education* and *Domestic Art in Woman's Education.* The reference point in these attempts to educate teachers was the bureau's concept of an ideal program that married practical training to Americanization and acculturation.[15]

Despite its planning, the Indian Bureau faced a difficult reality. Promised tools and materials failed to arrive at the orphan schools. The superintendent at the Cherokee facility found it difficult to locate and then keep capable instructors, particularly in the domestic courses. It was much the same at the Creek Colored Orphan Home before its closure. Try as he might to please federal inspectors, Superintendent A. H. Mike had only enough money to hire a carpentry teacher for one month, and he could not find any blacksmith willing to teach for the salary offered. As for the domestic science department, the superintendent could only say that "the young ladies and girls are doing nicely" despite an instructor who was "a novice in her position." All in all, school superintendents accountable to the Indian Bureau would have agreed with Mike's summation: "Our industrial work for boys is progressing as well as could be expected circumstances and instructor[s] considered." It was a situation that continued in government Indian schools throughout the 1920s, when Charles Burke, commissioner of Indian affairs, admitted that most vocational teachers carried the title "in name only." Considering the situation, superintendents' comments take on new meaning when placed within the context of obstacles to be faced and overcome. When, for example, the Cherokee orphan school superintendent noted that a "typewriting class" was offered in what was hoped to be an entire curriculum of business courses, it was more than a simple statement. It was a point of pride. Equipment and space for all practical training remained limited, but the superintendent found a way to meet the interests of students who expressed "a desire to take up a business training."[16]

Vocational training of the early twentieth century was made up of "modern" innovations that promised a number of desired outcomes. Certainly, it was expected to instill a cooperative spirit and teach students to solve concrete problems. It promised future employment and economic opportunities, as well as self-assurance as farmers or homemakers capable of following the contemporary movement of placing farming and home management on a scientific footing rather than following custom. One report from the Cherokee orphan school noted that boys proved the value of their training when they left the institution and were sought as farm laborers "by the most progressive farmers in the vicinity." Another said: "We have been told by residents of the community that it is easy to recognize an Indian home where children have attended this school. They state that it is cleaner, the food better prepared and the farm more productive." Boys and girls, with little or no contact with outside influences, were excellent candidates for education in scientific farming and domestic science. Boys were beyond the reach of those who practiced old-fashioned farming methods or who found little to recommend in learning a trade. Girls had not been exposed to "a home where the Mother is the drudge and beast of burden," opined one Indian Bureau home economics expert. In fact, most girls had little idea of domestic life in a noninstitutional setting.[17] A resident at New York's Thomas, for example, recalled the surprise she and a friend experienced when they were allowed to visit the friend's aunt:

> She said, I'll make a pie and cake. Alice and I wanted to watch her because we had been learning to do those things in homemaking class. She started with the cake first. There was a bowl, a cup, and a saucer in front of her. Then she started. She took the saucer and dipped it into the flour and put so many saucers of flour in her bowl. Alice and I looked at each other! Here we were taught to measure carefully—leveling each spoon with a knife. We were also taught to sift it several times. She didn't do that! She just put it in the sifter with a pinch of baking soda and a little baking powder. She did use a spoon to measure her lard. Alice and I stood there with our eyes and mouths wide open. We were wondering what kind of cake it was going to be! She made her pie the same way. And you know? It was the best cake and pie that we ever had![18]

At government-run orphan schools, vocational instruction attempted to bridge the nineteenth-century concept of manual-labor instruction and the twentieth century's expansive vocational training. For young women, the list of domestic subjects widened to include lessons in child care. Adolescent girls and teenagers were introduced to domestic science when working in institutions' laundries and kitchens. Through classroom instruction, they were schooled in modern-day canning and cooking methods and taught to sew and mend, and in the late 1920s the Cherokee orphan school used an outing system that placed girls in homes of white families for summer work. These venues allowed young women, future wives and mothers, to interact with children, albeit on a limited scale. There was more that could be done, however, to incorporate the national domestic education movement's interest in child health, nutrition, and early child development.

As a science in which young women learned to be home managers, domestic education looked at child care as systematic child management. Edna N. White of Ohio State University pioneered child management as a component of domestic science education, and a number of university and college programs took up the idea. At Kansas State Agricultural College, for example, elementary school youngsters served as a study group for college students charged with investigating nutrition and child development. At Iowa State College a "practice cottage," or home management house, provided home economics majors a firsthand opportunity to work with young children and apply the findings of contemporary studies that examined the relationship between physical and mental development. Iowa students compared the motor, language, and social skills of the children in their practice cottage with those of youngsters of the same age-group in orphanages, finding that those at the practice cottage lagged in language development but were "superior" in physical and emotional health. How this was determined was not explained, and one may wonder how emotional health in particular was gauged. Still, these college programs were considered to be on the cutting edge of domestic education, and high school courses began to incorporate the same methodology with individual and group projects. In one case, a teenager evaluated her younger sisters' diet and determined that iron and certain vitamins were substandard. She commented, "I solved the problem by making out menus that included the right amount." Implicitly, these lessons demonstrated the interdependence of good nutrition, physical health, and mental development.[19]

To a limited degree, firsthand child management studies were introduced at orphan schools. Child care and its companion, home nursing, were taught in the classroom and through practical applications. At the Cherokee facility, for example, girls learned nursing skills by working in the children's "sick" wards.[20] Government Indian schools offered these lessons because they were part of the domestic and vocational movement of the early 1900s, but for young women living in orphan schools the lessons may have been more essential and useful than the Indian Bureau knew. Growing up in an atmosphere where, for all intents and purposes, they were unparented, these young women lacked role models. Regimentation at these schools also limited contact between age-groups, making it difficult for older girls to interact with younger children. One might reasonably argue that classroom instruction was a poor substitute for personal experience, but for want of any point of reference, it filled a void in the absence of kin networks and extended families.

One historian, writing specifically of domestic instruction at Chilocco, observed that vocational training was out of step with the times. The point requires clarification. It was not out of step with an education movement that was touted and encouraged throughout the nation's school systems and in special training programs that were not limited to Indian education. During the first thirty years of the twentieth century, rural and urban high schools began to offer several courses of study that addressed students' personal interests and needs. There was the classical program for those heading on to advanced education; commercial for those planning to work as bookkeepers, as clerical staff, or in other office positions; normal for would-be teachers; and vocational and agriculture for practical training that might include further education in college. For domestic training, there were also special schools such as the Vocational School for Girls in Baltimore, Maryland, that offered young women unable to finish grammar or high school "an opportunity to fit themselves by special training in a trade or occupation which will serve them materially." Urban settlement houses and benevolent associations also concentrated on the vocational. The Civic Service House in Boston and its Vocation Bureau trained immigrants and helped them find employment. Home economics instruction was a staple in night schools sponsored by New York's Young Woman's Christian Association, and home extension programs for rural women of all ethnic and racial backgrounds gained a national following, as well as federal funding through the Smith-Lever Act of 1914.[21]

There was ample reason to advocate vocational instruction in Indian schools. Nevertheless, the Chilocco example is not without substance. Vocational training *was* out of step with many Indian groups' expectations for educational opportunities that prepared students for college and nontrade professional careers. Quite simply, by the early twentieth century, Indians had been exposed to decades of agricultural, domestic, and industrial training. A number had gone on to college and specialized schooling. They, however, were hardly the majority. Indian spokesmen and friends of Indian interests argued that it was time to redirect education's emphasis. Henry Roe Cloud, a Winnebago leader and educator, spoke for many at the 1914 Lake Mohonk Conference when he criticized the federal government for emphasizing vocational training at the expense of academic preparation. For this educator, vocational instruction was a second-class education. Whether or not he knew it, there were numerous voices that agreed, but not from the same viewpoint. Vocational education offered training for skilled employment, and the component of home economics strengthened women's domestic abilities. Nonetheless, "vocational" carried a social stigma, implying education for the lower classes and the disadvantaged. Therefore, young women who pursued vocational domestic training were apt to be stereotyped as lacking the intelligence or ability to study subjects covered in the classical mode of education. For this reason, proponents of domestic education often found it difficult to persuade young women of any background that this was indeed a form of education. "The fact is that domestic industries are held in contempt by many women," wrote one vocational supporter. One could add that it also was held in contempt by a number of Indian leaders who saw vocational education as the government's attempt to educate but not elevate.[22]

A companion to vocational training's goals of education for life and Americanization was the movement to structure youngsters' leisure time. Thomas School in New York was a shining example of progressive reformers' efforts to organize sports and supervise games on the playground. The same elements were apparent in the tribal orphanages in Oklahoma, and they were expanded under federal control to include a wider variety of sports and youth clubs. At Wheelock there was a Camp Fire Girls organization. At the Cherokee facility, renamed Sequoyah Orphan Training School in 1925 to honor the creator of the Cherokee alphabet, there was a 4-H club. In the 1920s, 4-H was the preeminent national club organization for rural young people. Its aim was to inculcate youngsters with "an intelligent point of view and a favorable attitude toward the business of farming and home making." At the Cherokee orphan school, it was a fitting complement to home economics and agricultural training. When the club formed, thirty boys and thirty girls immediately joined. Club participation demanded that each member demonstrate what he or she learned. Thus, there were individual presentations at club meetings and local competitions. Members of the Cherokee 4-H club learned more than the intended lessons, however. They did so well in competitions and in winning prizes that, according to one participant, "we were thrown out of the county 4-H Club work." Caucasian 4-H participants found it difficult to concede that they could be beaten. On the other hand, local sports teams seemed to enjoy the challenge of meeting Cherokee teams on the playing field. In 1928 it was noted: "The relation existing between our school and public schools is the very best, foot ball, baseball, and all forms of athletics are played between the schools and friendly visits are exchanged."[23]

As part of the acculturation process, celebrations were held for American holidays. The Fourth of July and the birthdays of Lincoln and Washington were favorites. American flags flew, and special programs that usually included student recitations were the order of the day. School plays and pageants that reflected either America's popular culture or its literary traditions were standard. At Wheelock, for example, students presented an annual stage performance. One year it was the operetta *Snow White and the Seven Dwarfs* (performed before an audience of seven hundred). Another year it was *A Midsummer Night's Dream*.[24]

In the early 1930s the orphan schools in Oklahoma opened a little corner for native culture. The Cherokee facility (Sequoyah) and Wheelock began to offer some work in native arts and crafts. This reflected the Indian Bureau's overall directive that Indian boarding schools add native customs, traditional stories, and arts to school curriculum. It was a plan that directly contradicted nineteenth-century arguments that to civilize the Indian all Indianness had to be erased. The plan also parted company with the common school education offered to immigrants. There were no suggestions that immigrant children should be allowed to explore their unique backgrounds. Ethnic and racial differences were suppressed, not celebrated.

Before the turn of the century, there were suggestions that schools incorporate native cultural studies as a way to draw out students and

A flag-draped Wheelock, with the faculty on the porch, during a Fourth of July celebration. Archives and Manuscripts Division of the Oklahoma Historical Society.

encourage their interest in education. However, it was not until the tenure of Commissioner of Indian Affairs Francis Leupp, 1905–9, that the program took hold. Leupp was convinced that there was a place for Indian art and music in education. Schools had a role in preserving cultural heritage, not destroying it. Out of this conviction, Indian education received a new direction. Places such as Carlisle, Haskell, and Chilocco established native arts programs.[25]

The program took hold at other boarding schools, too. Implementation, however, was not uniform. Nor were the programs necessarily interpreted as preservation of a culture. Some school authorities classified the arts programs as vocational training, and Hervey B. Peairs, the Indian Bureau's chief supervisor of education, encouraged this point of view. He noted, for example, the Navajo Boarding School, where a skilled Navajo weaver was employed to instruct students. The employee's job was not to reintroduce blanket weaving to the students but to refine their skills in order to compete in the marketplace. After all, blanket weaving was "a paying industry." The attitude was much the same at Sequoyah. The "certain handcrafts" studied, said one superintendent, "might provide a basis for a vocation." If they did not, at least students were well occupied.[26]

Whereas students at the Navajo school were instructed in an art form that was intrinsically part of their culture and still being practiced, instruction at other government schools was often an amalgamation of many Indian societies. When students at Haskell were asked to tell stories from their particular tribes, some were at a loss and borrowed stories from other students or combined stories from several Indian societies into one. Still, they were stories told by Indians, and the Indian Bureau published some of those gathered at Haskell in a bulletin with the notation that they "were told by the Indian children at Haskell Institute, as they had been told by the old men and women of their tribe." Evidently no one questioned the possibility that these stories were not old or traditional but simply stories made up on the spot or gathered from a number of sources. Whatever the stories' makeup, poignant and to the point was the ending given by one of the storytellers: "This is told by one of the old Indians and now the old Indians are nearly all gone. Maybe they are now in the land of the spirits."[27]

At schools like Haskell, where many tribes were represented, tribal cultures sometimes blurred. Haskell's dance exhibitions and contests displayed the diversity of Indian groups attending the school, and stage presentations that included *Hiawatha* were meant to convey a pan-Indian environment. Both had something to do with Indian life, but they hardly represented the same cultural traditions or values. Dances offered an opportunity to reclaim some semblance of pride in tribal culture. By the early 1900s, however, *Hiawatha* was a symbol of white America's belief that the Indian was a quickly vanishing race. During the time period, sentimental and romantic images of Indian life and individuals appeared in print, early moving pictures, and in literature. One has to wonder if students were aware that Hiawatha was a traditional story that told of a messenger of the Great Spirit, sent down to earth in human form as a prophet. Henry R. Schoolcraft, who recorded native customs and stories, wrote: "The general myth, is recognized in the legend of the Iroquois, under the name of Hiawatha, and Tarenyawazon. . . . Mr. Longfellow has given prominence to it, and to its chief episodes, by selecting and generalizing such traits as appeared best susceptible of poetic uses." Longfellow's *Hiawatha* was resurrected in the early twentieth century as a piece of popular culture that represented "the mystery and magic surrounding the life of the Red man" whose time was almost done.[28]

Youngsters at Indian orphan schools were presented with the same sorts of confusing messages about what was "Indian." At the Presbyterian-directed Goodland in Oklahoma, students received fine arts training when Joe N. Kagey joined the teaching staff in 1913. These studies blended white culture's definition for what constituted fine arts with native arts and crafts. Kagey's influence was felt after he left in 1917 as student activities continued to intermingle white and Indian themes. During the 1920s, Goodland's superintendent, Samuel Bailey Spring, encouraged musical activities and arranged student tours to perform before audiences in such cities as St. Louis, New Orleans, and Denver. It was Spring's way of introducing some students to the outside world while at the same time garnering financial support for the institution. Adding "greatly to the effectiveness of the concerts and special music" were costumes designed by one of the teachers to replicate traditional clothing. At home on the Goodland "campus," residents gave performances, too. Among the most ambitious was *Pushmataha's Vision*, a play written by Spring, who was one-fourth Choctaw. The production commemorated the Choctaw chief Pushmataha, who chose to throw in his lot with the U.S. government and join Andrew Jackson in the war against the Creeks and later in the Battle of New Orleans against the British.[29]

One has to wonder if the play was historically accurate, just as one has to wonder if the native arts taught at Sequoyah and Wheelock were authentic. At these government-directed orphan schools, native arts included basket making, reed work, beadwork, pottery, and "bark crafts." These would be expected as representative of tribal traditions. Since school authorities viewed these activities as vocational, however, native arts also incorporated Euro-American folk crafts or arts. At Sequoyah these included lace making and rug making; at Wheelock, there was rug making, too, with particular attention to hooked rugs. For those in charge of the programs, rug making was considered particularly important because it, like Navajo blanket weaving, was a paying industry. Rural women throughout the southern tier of states were encouraged through home extension programs to develop home industries based on the making and selling of braided and hooked rugs. Very possibly, Indian girls, in their preparation for farm life, could learn to do the same.[30]

Goodland Indian Orphanage and School commencement exercises in 1923, Hugo, Oklahoma. Youngsters performed Pushmataha's Vision, *a play written by the home's superintendent to commemorate the Choctaw chief who fought with Andrew Jackson. Archives and Manuscripts Division of the Oklahoma Historical Society.*

By the mid-1920s, Sequoyah and Wheelock had become mirror images of other government-supported boarding schools. Any uniqueness they once had as tribally directed institutions for orphans was gone. As just two of many Indian boarding schools under the Indian Bureau, both Sequoyah and Wheelock exhibited the same programs and problems found elsewhere in the system. At the same time, their operations exhibited greater differences from New York State's Thomas Indian School. Whereas the Oklahoma orphanages and Thomas shared similarities during the nineteenth century, these were less evident in the twentieth century. Thomas, for example, was well supplied with textbooks and leisure-time reading materials, but the Indian Bureau could not provide the same for Wheelock, Sequoyah, or most of its other funded schools. When Wheelock requested up-to-date encyclopedias, works of well-known American and English poets, and "reference books for the more advanced classes," there was no guarantee that the materials would be supplied.[31]

Educational materials were just one concern. Overcrowding was a constant problem in all Indian boarding schools. At Jones Academy near Hartshorne, Oklahoma, for example, the number of enrolled students forced continued use of a boys' dormitory after it was condemned. (It was still in use in 1939, and appropriations to build a new one were cut from the budget in 1940.) Overcrowding was common at the orphan schools, too. At Sequoyah, employees were housed in the dormitories with students, creating a "highly unsatisfactory" situation for all. There was too little money for building separate quarters on a large scale, and only slowly were staff provided their own spaces. In 1931, for example, the superintendent happily reported: "We were able also to complete a four room cottage for the use of the financial clerk and his wife who is a teacher. This addition relieved crowded conditions in the large boys' dormitory where they were formerly quartered." Circumstances were not as bad at Wheelock. Officials there refused to take in more than could be housed comfortably. This, it was believed, led to an environment that suggested some semblance of family. "We endeavor to make this a school-home for our pupils. A home in that we restrict them as little as possible consistent with good order." Keeping the resident population within a manageable number also contributed to better health in an institutional setting.[32]

The early twentieth century saw an increased emphasis on reporting the status of health care. In part, this was a result of the Progressive Era's interest in the social sciences, which emphasized quantitative studies of specific populations. Anything and everything was counted and analyzed. The U.S. Woman's Bureau, under the U.S. Department of Labor, for example, surveyed specific regions for information on maternal and child mortality, as well as work-related injuries of women and children in the labor force. In this sense, the Indian Bureau was following the new, scientific approach to data collecting, and sometimes it became collecting for its own sake without a carefully detailed goal in mind. The bureau did, however, have at least one goal. By tallying numbers it hoped to improve its image and to demonstrate a sensitivity to disease and death. Among the longtime factors in resistance to government boarding schools were the spread of diseases such as tuberculosis and student death.

Undeniably, any institutional setting was ready-made for the spread of communicable diseases, and the Indian Bureau worked to erase the unhealthy label attached to boarding schools. Nevertheless, what emerges from the records for the Cherokee orphanage and from Wheelock, the two institutions with the most extant health care records, is a contradictory image of concerted medical attention and lax procedures. Vaccinations against smallpox and typhoid were routine, although this did not ensure total eradication. At the Cherokee institution, for example, a small number of deaths were attributed to typhoid fever, and the culprit, poor drinking water or a human carrier, could not be identified. Too, tuberculosis continued to be a real threat. Unlike smallpox, which caused mass epidemics among Indian populations from the time of contact, tuberculosis was fairly rare among native groups in the early 1800s. Its virulence, however, was stronger when a group had its first experience with the disease; organs that were unaffected in Caucasians were attacked by the infection. In later contact, however, the disease became the type more common among non-Indians, one that rested in the lungs. By the first decade of the twentieth century, the federal government considered tuberculosis one of the major health risks facing Indians, and the bureau emphasized plans for prevention and treatment. In truth, however, orphan schools were ill prepared for dealing with it. After the deaths of four girls in a short span of time at Wheelock, the superintendent wrote the Indian Bureau that "our physician should be better equipped for testing the lungs and there should be some way provided for the analysis of sputum so that the cases may be discovered in their incipiency and the girls sent to a sanitorium if possible." At the time of his writing, the superintendent was particularly saddened by the death of a "child [who] has been a general favorite and has no other home than this having refused for three years to go to the home of her nearest relatives, owing to their ill-treatment of her." Added to the Wheelock experience was that of the Cherokee orphan school, where tuberculosis took lives and where the superintendent bemoaned a lack of "facilities for caring for such cases." There was no separate ward for students with any contagious or communicable disease. This in itself contributed to the spread of tuberculosis, as well as influenza, malaria, and measles.[33]

Early in the twentieth century, diseases of the eye drew considerable attention, and doctors from the Indian Health Service devoted considerable time to identifying conjunctivitis, commonly referred to as pinkeye, and trachoma, which could begin as a mild case of conjunctivitis but progress, if left untreated, to scarring of the eyelids, clouding of the cornea, and blindness. Highly contagious viral and bacterial forms of these eye diseases spread rapidly among children, leading to local epidemics. Therefore, it is understandable that boarding school superintendents sighed with relief when, as in the case of the Santa Fe Indian School, it could be said: "Notwithstanding the large number of cases of sore eyes the sight has not been lost in a single instance." Sequoyah had its own "large number of cases," as did Wheelock. In 1914 Wheelock reported that the "trachoma situation has not improved very much this year"; there were at least forty cases. The numbers were consistent with those at the Cherokee institution, where trachoma threatened the sight of 38 to 54 percent of the school's population during the early decades of the twentieth century. In fact, when the number stood at 38 percent in 1917, the superintendent noted it as a decrease from previous years. Incidence of eye problems was such that in 1913 a medical expert was asked to visit the Cherokee Orphan Training School. Out of 72 examinations that year, 39 cases of trachoma were found, as were 6 of conjunctivitis and 3 of "defective vision." The last was not identified as an early sign of eye disease and may have indicated a need for corrective glasses. Some of the most critical trachoma cases identified in 1913 were treated through an operation that cut away granular material that formed on the eyelids and the soft scar tissue it produced. This procedure was used by Indian Health Service physicians until 1927, but it was not until the late 1930s that sulfanilamide was discovered and used to bring trachoma under control. Although operations reduced the possibility of blindness, they were reactive responses, not preventive. Prevention had to begin with personal hygiene and clean surroundings. Yet there is no indication that staff vigorously enacted or enforced simple procedures. Frequent laundering of linens, particularly pillowcases and towels, discouraging youngsters from sharing handkerchiefs and towels, and insisting on frequent hand washing could have reduced epidemics of pinkeye and its progression into trachoma.[34]

One could argue that at the time science was just beginning to understand the relationship between bacteria, disease, and sanitation. However, even if scientific medical knowledge was unsure of the causes of conjunctivitis and trachoma and how they and other infectious diseases spread, greater emphasis on commonsense practices of personal hygiene and maintaining sanitary surroundings could have reduced the incidence of many diseases.

It was not until the late 1920s that significant improvements occurred, although they were not always uniformly applied. To heighten sanitation in the Cherokee home's domestic science kitchen and storage area, terrazzo floors were installed, making it easier to maintain clean surroundings—at least in one portion of the learning environment. As important, a small "hospital" that consisted of two wards—one for boys, one for girls—was added. Too, by 1933 plans were in the making for a cottage-style dormitory for boys. Both the hospital wards and the smaller cottage living arrangement could reduce the spread of contagious diseases. These were certainly improvements, but some components of health care remained substandard. The home's administrator continued to complain that the machine used to sterilize medical equipment was outmoded and unreliable. On the bright side, however, two nurses were hired to live at the school and, "we are happy to state, are registered with the State Board of Nurses." A physician and a dentist were on call, and operations for cases of appendicitis and diseased tonsils were performed at a nearby hospital; following the medical propensity of the time to remove tonsils and adenoids, fifty children underwent the operation in 1928. Improved sanitation measures and quarantine in "sick" wards may explain the decline in reported eye problems and the spread of fevers and measles.[35]

Wheelock, which remained open until 1955, took a new medical turn in the late 1920s when officials became concerned with venereal diseases. Queried by his superiors, the superintendent in 1929 answered that he did not know if any of the girls had syphilis or gonorrhea, but "undoubtedly there is some." In the fall of that year each girl was given a Wassermann test and checked for gonorrhea. These tests became part of the routine physical examination. In 1930, examinations indicated 16 percent of the population had syphilis, although the stage of progression was not identified. "Drugs were dispensed for treatment." Since penicillin was not used as a treatment until the 1940s, the drugs were most likely arsenical compounds, which were sometimes used in combination with other substances such as bismuth, iodine, or mercury. Testing for venereal diseases does not suggest that school officials suspected Wheelock residents of being sexually active. It does suggest that government officials, as well as the general public, were more willing to discuss venereal diseases. After World War I, syphilis became a topic for open discourse through newspaper and magazine articles, radio shows, and the movies (although many of the latter were army training films). As one historian noted, these were publicity campaigns meant to put the public "in a state of alert." The girls at Wheelock were tested because of heightened awareness, and that awareness possibly saved their lives. Unknown to them, they suffered from congenital syphilis, transmitted while still in their mothers' wombs. In a larger context but left unspoken was the fact that these girls were victims of a disease that had silently plagued and killed Indians for centuries.[36]

Besides the federally supported orphan schools in Oklahoma, there were the denominational orphanages of Goodland and Murrow, which had, in the face of severe financial obstacles, managed to survive and operate. Money, however, remained an ongoing concern, and each institution approached the situation separately. When both the Murrow orphanage and Bacone College experienced fiscal problems in the early 1900s, the prudent course was to cut expenses by moving the home to Bacone. Murrow and the college maintained separate identities, but the home was supported through funds provided to Bacone through the American Baptist Home Mission Society. Money, however, remained tight. In September 1912 the home's superintendent reported that the greatest problem facing the orphanage was finances, and this placed limitations on accepting children. There were a great many applicants because the home accepted youngsters from any Indian tribe, and Murrow directors knew of numerous children who should be "in some such institution." Despite the need, many were turned away because they had no funds "to pay even a small fee." Only a few children could be supported for free; the remainder had to be able to pay out of their allotment moneys or tribal annuities. This in itself was a problem, since innumerable court-appointed guardians absconded with children's allotment funds. In one case it was said that a guardian rented his ward's land, took the money, and disappeared. Too, a number of children were not parentless, but the parents had not been appointed legal guardians, and many were as dependent as their children for assistance.[37]

Finances also kept Goodland from accepting every prospective resident. Superintendent Spring estimated that there were twelve hundred applications each year for two hundred places. Usually, however, the actual number at Goodland was three hundred. This meant considerable overcrowding, even when two dormitories were added. It also meant having little to eat. One recollection of the home proudly noted that during the summers over two thousand gallons of tomatoes and hundreds of gallons of fruit were canned and that there was "meat enough for the Goodland family." Nevertheless, a primary memory for many former residents was hunger. Money was stretched to the limit. The federal government paid for about one-fourth of those at Goodland. The Indian Presbytery and, after 1933, the Presbyterian Synod gave small amounts of money. Additionally, after 1911 some state money went to support youngsters placed in the home by the Oklahoma Department of Charities and Corrections. There was never enough money, however, and Spring was reluctant to reduce the number of residents. He justified conditions by arguing that there was a great need for the facility and no other was available in that part of the state.[38]

Spring, a product of the Choctaws' Spencer Academy and a graduate of Southwestern Presbyterian College in Tennessee, had been a member of both the Choctaw Board of Education and the Choctaw Council. He was devoted to Goodland and attempted to offset the institution's deficiencies by the will of his own personality and the deep conviction that those at Goodland deserved some simple pleasures of childhood. There were sports teams, musical programs, and, when possible, a 4-H club. Recalled one former resident: "He even knew the rules for the children's games; and many a child has called to him asking, 'Oh, Mr. Spring, is she over the line?'" To the children the superintendent also gave himself, providing personal attention. "We always felt free to talk over any question with him," remembered one girl. "Not once did he turn a child away, saying 'I'm too busy to see you now.' And we always left those meetings with our problems solved, with something to work on, some encouragement, and some praise."[39]

Money remained a continuing issue for Goodland, as well as Murrow. While Goodland garnered a small amount of money from the Indian Presbytery, which itself was poor, Bacone College benefited itself and the Murrow orphanage by appealing to Indians who had managed to retain their allotments. Their contributions to an endowment fund would support the college's attempt to educate more young people and, not so coincidentally, American Baptist Home Mission Society funds supplied to the college would go further in sustaining the Murrow home. The response was overwhelming. Between 1920 and 1925 almost $1 million filled Bacone's endowment fund. In light of Indian victimization at the hands of guardians, attorneys, and Oklahoma probate courts, Commissioner of Indian Affairs Burke endorsed Bacone's plan. If nothing else, it put money that might otherwise be lost or wasted to good use. The college gained funds, but at a cost. Because Indians seemed so willing to give money to the cause, religious groups began to solicit funds in a frenzy that could only be described as a raid on Indians' good intentions. If Baptists were going to receive Indian contributions, other denominations wanted their share, too. As a result, Burke fought to disengage himself from accusations of favoring Baptists over other religious groups, and Bacone was forced to examine the long-term damage its image would suffer if it appeared too eager to take money from a people who were still considered by the American public as naive and easily tricked.[40]

After the Murrow home relocated to Bacone, there were forty residents in September 1911. Within a year's time, however, the number was reduced to thirty. There were no deaths. In fact, the only reported health concerns at Murrow were conjunctivitis and trachoma. The reduction in residents came when youngsters left the home. Eight of the ten who left were reclaimed by relatives, even when they were not the legal guardians: "These two are half brother and sister. . . . [T]hey entered the home but were taken out again by their grandmother." The two not removed by kin or guardians were runaways. One, a male, was described as almost an adult and had "formed bad habits"; the other boy, fifteen years old, was characterized as discontented and eager "to get out to the life he has been accustomed to before."[41]

The reports of children leaving are significant for one topic they do not address. There are no references to placing children in homes through adoption or today's equivalent of foster care. Charitable institutions in the United States, from the largest such as the New England Home for Little Wanderers and the New York Foundling Hospital, as well as small charities such as White Hall Orphan's Home Society in Illinois, had placed out children for years. The practice was continued by some Oklahoma charities after statehood. On the one hand, it was considered benevolent, since it took children out of institutions and placed them in homes. Conversely, not all homes were loving, and some institutions engaged in placements for the sole purpose of keeping resident populations low. Placing out was only as good as those responsible for it, and in a few cases charities were little more than clearinghouses for placing children. By the early 1920s, for example, the Oklahoma Department of Charities and Corrections condemned one institution, the Cornish Orphan's Home, for dispensing children into homes without adequately investigating the families or evaluating the homes and children's well-being after placement. Neither Goodland nor Murrow followed the placing-out practice. Murrow, in fact, was adamant that its charges remain until they reached the age or eighteen. Murrow maintained this practice until midcentury, when it began to allow adoption of its charges, making some attempt to place children in Indian homes or homes where one of the adults was of Indian heritage.[42]

Murrow emphasized the necessity of residents earning their keep through work that sustained the institution and offered a foundation of training in domestic science and agriculture. This prepared girls to "manage homes of their own when they have them later." They did most of the laundry, and to supplement clothing received from donations made by Baptist churches in several states, they learned to sew so that in time they could make "their own plain dresses." They learned to cook, and in the summer they canned fruit and made apple butter and jelly. Most of the canned goods went into the common larder, but the girls were given an added incentive for their labor. Each was allowed to put aside a small amount for personal use. Boys and girls had their own chickens to raise. For girls this was an important commodity, since in rural America farm women made money by selling eggs and dressed chickens at market. While girls concentrated on homemaking and raising poultry, boys learned "by practical experience the care of stock, handling of farm machinery and the best methods of farm cultivation." They were put on the path to becoming scientific farmers. The idea of being a scientific farmer was not new, but by the 1890s there was a national movement that encouraged farmers to rely on science as a guide for using seed suitable to soil and moisture, improved strains of livestock, modern machinery, and controlled soil treatments. Farmers of all racial and ethnic groups were touched by the wave of scientific farming education. University-sponsored farm extension programs, the U.S. Department of Agriculture, agricultural bulletins and newspapers, and radio stations with large rural listening audiences all played a role in spreading the word of better farming. Since the federal government had always advanced the plan to turn Indians into farmers, scientific farming had Indian Bureau approval. Additionally, it was argued that for allotment to succeed Indians had to learn to be good farmers.[43]

Farms on orphanage lands were ever present, but orphanages varied widely on whether youngsters were actually taught and how much they were expected to do. The labor of Murrow residents supported the institution while the youngsters also learned basic skills that would serve them in the future. The home's managers, as well as those at other Indian orphanages, clearly expected that once youngsters left the home they would live in rural surroundings. This, of course, ignored Oklahoma's potential to develop urban centers or the possibility that onetime home residents would move to urban areas in other states. It also overlooked the larger national picture and changes in demographics. In 1920 the U.S. census showed that for the first time in the country's history, urban residents outnumbered the rural. Orphan school residents were prepared to live in a constricting rural environment that throughout the twentieth century witnessed a steady drop in population and work opportunities.[44]

Goodland also depended on its farm, but the emphasis differed from Murrow, or for that matter from Sequoyah and Wheelock. There was no suggestion that Goodland's farm and farm kitchen served to teach agriculture or home economics. The farm was first and foremost a lifeline for keeping the institution open. Its importance became critical in 1930 after Superintendent Spring died of tuberculosis. During his time at Goodland, Spring juggled money problems against accepting as many residents as possible. Presbyterian support was meager, and at the time of Spring's death the institution faced a debt of $30,000 that threatened to close the orphanage. Rather than shut the doors, the next superintendent, the Reverend E. D. Miller, who was not of Indian ancestry, tried to solve the financial mess by making Goodland totally self-supporting. Increased crop and garden production, dairy cattle, and poultry reduced the number of items that had to be purchased, and hogs raised on the farm were sold for cash. Out of desperation, Miller made residents *the* labor force. A former resident recalled a routine that never varied: "At seven o'clock six mornings a week the horn of the school truck is honked vigorously, and one or another group of boys is off to the farm." Meanwhile, girls were working in the laundry, cooking, or dusting. Each boy had to work one full day each week on the farm. Girls worked the gardens, looked after the chickens, and canned produce. During the summer, when there were no classes, residents spent all day, every day except Sundays, laboring outdoors or in the kitchen. Many residents, who ranged from six to twenty-four years of age, were overworked. While the amount of labor demanded of residents was extreme, it corresponded to a basic nineteenth-century tenet of many orphanages: youngsters should become accustomed to hard work, as well as to a level of poverty. The superintendent thought this a small price to pay if the institution managed to remain open and provide residents with the all-important religious training that had been the home's cornerstone since its beginning. The place of religion could not be overemphasized. After all, Goodland's motto was "The Highest Aim of This Home Is to Glorify Christ."[45]

This was the way of life for residents of Goodland during the 1930s and 1940s. Miller's operational formula mitigated some of the financial problems, as did his plan that consolidated the orphanage with a rural school district and transferred about sixty students from a one-room country school to Goodland as day students. Miller proclaimed that this was a good learning experience for Goodland residents, since it would promote assimilation into the local community. More practically, Goodland no longer had to pay teachers' salaries; the local school board did that. As a way to gain money, Goodland also began to accept, for a fee from the state, teenagers who otherwise would have been ordered by a court of law to a reformatory. Goodland stepped beyond the boundary of the unstated, but understood, orphanage rule that residents be accepted on the basis of their "worthiness." It was a poor bargain. Thefts became a problem, older boys burned a building, and more youngsters ran away, including some who could not endure bullying at the hands of unrepentant juvenile delinquents.[46]

The institution was still in debt when Oscar Gardner, a mixed-blood minister, took over in 1946. For Gardner, the cumulative result of almost twenty years of scrimping was sadly apparent. Said a biography of Gardner:

He was faced with the physical and spiritual welfare of two hundred boys and girls. The institution was in debt $13,000. The buildings were old and inadequate. The water supply was precarious. The farm operation was losing money. The staff was unhappy with the change of leadership and it was discovered that they were taking food home while the children were going hungry. Discipline was administered sporadically and ineffectively by staff members. Income from churches and individuals was low. Some health problems among the children were appalling.⁴⁷

Goodland's farm and domestic work was not based on any model for education, other than the basic precept that it provided practical experience. It undoubtedly taught residents the hard lessons of survival—theirs and the institution's. Goodland could not argue that students' work was part of a vocational plan, as did government boarding schools or the privately run Whitaker home, which by 1912 presented training options that ranged from agricultural to skilled trades. W. T. Whitaker struggled to establish and then maintain his orphanage. His perseverance kept the place going. While the Indian nations managed to hold on to their institutions during dissolution, the Whitaker home's population was almost entirely Caucasian. As Indian orphan schools closed under federal direction, however, the U.S. government began to pay Whitaker twelve dollars a month for each orphaned and/or dependent Indian child accepted at the orphanage. By 1907 there were fifty-four Indian children living in the home. Some were true orphans; others were separated from their families by poverty and guardianship mismanagement. With the number of Indian residents rising, the institution proudly proclaimed itself "The Only Home in Indian Territory Caring for Both White and Indian Children."⁴⁸

With Oklahoma statehood and the building of an infrastructure that included institutions, W. T. Whitaker hatched his own grand plans. Already an established orphanage, the Whitaker home was in the ideal position, so the proprietor argued, to be named a state institution. Whitaker eventually won the argument, but not before he faced accusations of incompetence. Reports began to circulate that the orphanage was overcrowded and, worse, that boys and girls slept in the same rooms, leading to all sorts of illicit activities. Kate Barnard was quick to investigate, and she rebutted that the worst rumors, those of promiscuity, were unfounded. The sexes not only slept in separate buildings but also had separate playgrounds. The lesser charge of overcrowding was true, however. This was only temporary, responded Barnard. The Whitaker orphanage was about to be transferred to the state, and new buildings were under construction. These would allow the home to incorporate the innovative plan of cottage living, which removed dormitory-style barracks.[49]

Whitaker got his wish, but it was a hollow victory. Once the orphanage was transferred to the state and renamed the Oklahoma State Home, the home's founder was dismissed. The home continued to accommodate both white and Indian children, although the number of Indian children averaged only about 5 percent of the total population. In 1910, for example, the institution housed 103 whites, 11 full-blood Indians, and 16 mixed-bloods. All the Indian children had guardians, but none of the children "were receiving any part of their maintenance from their estates." Barnard went to court and had the guardianships transferred to the state, and minors were admitted to the state home only when courts declared them dependent on public support. Not all the children were parentless. Some had one living parent who could not care for the child, and one Indian child, a three-year-old boy of "Creek extraction," was in the home because his condition showed "evidence of serious neglect." The state, through its department of charities and corrections, had the obligation, and the right, to intercede on the child's behalf, assume guardianship, and at times approve adoption or foster family placement. Residents of the state orphanage could be adopted. There was no question here of tribal rights to a child. At the time, that was never a consideration.[50]

To gain more leverage for the department of charities and corrections in fighting guardianship fraud and to maintain the legal right to intervene in cases where the department felt there was parental neglect, Barnard persuaded Oklahoma lawmakers to amend the Session Laws of 1907–8 to designate the commissioner of charities and corrections as "next friend" for all minors who were orphans or in some way dependents. The latter included youngsters who were physically or mentally handicapped, who were dependent because of lack of family support, or who were adjudged to be delinquent and placed as inmates in any public institution maintained by the state. Barnard took her "next friend" status seriously, often reducing it to one-on-one interactions with youngsters. On one occasion she tried to explain to a youngster at the Whitaker home the need for regimentation. Barnard was responsible for the boy's placement in the home, but instead of being grateful for his rescue, he chafed under the rules and regulations. Barnard tried to ease the situation with an adult explanation: "No one is perfectly free because everyone has rights that all are bound to respect, so that when more than one person exists in a place, each must be prepared to conform to the others good. . . . When all the boys and girls are obedient and conform to the rules, they cannot fail to be happy." Barnard was practical enough to know that in the real world many would fail to be happy, but she also knew that an institution could function only when individuality was subordinated.[51]

State boards and individuals responsible for institutions generally reported on facilities in terms of the physical plant, cost of maintenance, and itemized purchases of goods and services. The subtle relationships between adult authority and resident populations were largely neglected. Thus, it is from the official viewpoint of institutional comments and recommendations that most information comes to us. Child residents left a sparse or nonexistent written record, and they seldom emerged from the paper morass of official accounting.

One exception was Barnard's 1912 report, which offered brief sketches of Indian residents at the state home. Joe, a fourteen-year-old full-blood Cherokee, was "a boy of considerable personal pride." Carrie was a fourteen-year-old Cherokee whose "levity interfered with progress in school," but to her credit she was "good at housekeeping" and "graceful in form and movement." Fourteen-year-old Ruth, a Creek, was loud and "indolent" when working in her cottage but an excellent student in the classroom. Amos, a six-year-old Choctaw, had a "happy disposition" but was not eager to learn, and three Cherokee sisters were rather "slow" in the classroom but displayed artistic abilities, determination, and "lovable" personalities. From Barnard's notations, it is clear that teenagers made up most of the home's Indian population and that a few were studying at grade levels below that expected for their age. Ernest, a fourteen-year-old Cherokee, was "strong in body" but "exceedingly slow" in his third-grade studies. In some cases, as in that of thirteen-year-old Clint, who had "an excellent mind," Barnard chalked up poor performance to little previous school experience. All in all, Barnard characterized Indian residents as genial and capable of learning. She specifically remarked upon ten youngsters who had "excellent," "quick and active," or "very good" minds. Given Barnard's personal experiences as a neglected child who rose to a post of importance in adulthood, her remarks are not those of a white woman surprised that Indians had the ability to learn. She was sympathetic to the children's situation, and her comments were crafted to inform those who read her report that efforts at the state home were not wasted on Indians.[52]

After tribal dissolution, there were four types of orphan home facilities in Oklahoma: the Whitaker facility, turned into the state orphan home; Taft, which received state support, for African-Indian and black youngsters; the denominational orphanages of Murrow and Goodland; and the two federally supported Indian boarding schools of Sequoyah and Wheelock. The makeup of each institution's population, as well as the entity supporting the institution, determined the amount of integration between Indian and non-Indian children and the degree of interaction between youngsters of different tribal groups. The state orphan home, for example, commingled Caucasian and Indian children, although the latter remained in the minority. Where Indian children and teenagers were in the majority, there was a level of insulation from non-Indian life.

All-Indian populations did not, however, always ensure a sense of solidarity. This was particularly true at Murrow, where youngsters of any tribal background were accepted and where staff and residents were likely to apply their own perceptions of each Indian group. "Jack was a Comanche, so it was only natural that he was our top horse wrangler. . . . he was the perfect image of the Comanche riders who ruled the southern plains on horseback," recalled a onetime Murrow resident who knew firsthand how easy it was to be stereotyped. "I was Apache. People looked scared when they heard that. Even here, at the Murrow Indian Orphanage. I'm talking about the Indian staff at an Indian orphanage. They bought the whole Geronimo story, the crazed terror of the frontier."[53]

Over time, each institution continued to rely on its nineteenth-century roots to serve the population for which it had been established. Orphanage directors understood that children came to them because of homes broken by divorce, illness, death, and alcoholism, but, with the exception of the state home, there was little effort to join the twentieth century's charitable and social work movement to initiate multipurpose programs that reached nuclear or extended families or found places for children within the homes of relatives or nonrelated Indian families. These children and teenagers were at the margins of society. The immediate problem for institutions was seeing that care and education were provided. The single-minded goal was child rescue. It was not the concern of orphan homes to address or correct underlying systemic social and economic ills. Oscar Gardner of the Goodland orphanage articulated the general feeling that it was not the responsibility of charitable institutions to rehabilitate families for the good of the children. If state social workers wanted to take on the task, so be it, but this was not a role for institutions that cared for orphans, half-orphans, or children so destitute that they were little different from orphans.[54]

The point was taken. In the first half of the twentieth century, social workers began to play a larger role in Indian communities. There were state workers, as well as a small number of field-workers employed by the Indian Bureau. There was some attempt to work with families and to improve living conditions and health care, but the likely first response to domestic problems or crises in Indian homes was long-term child removal. This differed from the viewpoint of social welfare workers involved at Thomas in New York, but it fit into a general feeling within many social welfare agencies that "some sort of intervention" was demanded in any case, Caucasian or nonwhite, where there was evidence of "submarginal incomes," poor or inadequate housing, physical or mental illness, alcoholism, or a family member arrested for a crime.[55]

Indian Bureau employees often identified problems earlier than state workers, and in concert with state workers they decided the immediate and long-term outcome for the children involved. As a rule, the state placed children and teenagers in an orphan home. Placements were not always in the state-run orphanage. Federal and denominational facilities also received their share. To the casual observer, orphan homes continued to serve the populations for which they had been created, but the institutions in Oklahoma no longer operated with total independence. Social workers, social service mandates, and the courts played a role in deciding who was and was not a candidate for residence in the orphan homes.

7

CATHOLIC OUTPOSTS:
OJIBWAY AND SIOUX

The first orphan [was], Mary Carleton. This Mary Carleton was a
Navajo Indian baby, found on the battlefield and brought to the Sisters
by General Carleton himself. . . . General Carleton, with General Sherman and Colonel Meline, assigned rations for eighteen orphan children
at the Asylum.[1]

Perhaps the first recorded instance of an Indian child entering an orphanage in the Catholic mission field of the American West occurred
in 1865 when Gen. James H. Carleton, military commander of New
Mexico, brought the infant christened Mary Carleton to the Sisters of
Mercy in Santa Fe. The Sisters, who numbered only four, were recent
arrivals to the Southwest, asked by Jean-Baptiste Lemay, vicariate
apostolic of New Mexico, to come and establish a hospital. At the
same time that the Sisters went about their task of opening a hospital, they opened an orphanage. It and its residents were described by
Sister Blandina Segale in 1878, over ten years after it opened: "Each
girl had a spoon, a broken ironstone china cup and plate to match,
while some had old pie plates. Each girl is served a piece of bread and
water to drink for dinner, weak coffee for breakfast, and weak tea for
supper. . . . You must remember this is a pioneer mission, poorest of
the poor, and working among the poor." In 1880 the orphanage became an industrial school for orphan girls. Variously known as the
Home and Industrial School for Orphans and St. Vincent Orphanage
for Girls, it received monetary support from the territorial government after substantial lobbying on the part of the Sisters.[2]

Carleton and the U.S. military in New Mexico were charged with
subjugating Navajo and Apache Indians "whom we are endeavoring,"
wrote Carleton, "to establish upon a reservation and teach to till the
earth for support." The federal government expected these nomadic

groups to become sedentary farmers. However, in the Southwest, as in land areas assigned the Sioux, some regions simply refused to be turned into "one of the most magnificent farms in the United States." As Navajos and Apaches were rounded up and forced into confinement at Bosque Redondo, an agricultural "calamity" added to an already desperate situation. The few crops planted by the Indians were "totally destroyed" by insects.[3] Relocation, replete with armed resistance, and the disastrous attempt at crop cultivation provided all the makings for disease, starvation, death, and cultural genocide. The stage seemed set for another orphanage to rise to the occasion of caring for Indian children. This was provided by the orphan asylum established by the Sisters of Mercy, but the fact that the first child taken into the orphanage was Navajo did not in any way suggest that this was intended for Indian children alone. The mission's prime objective was Santa Fe's population of Mexicans and Anglos. Therefore, the Catholic Church and its representatives placed most of their energies and resources in the effort to serve Mexican and white parishioners. When, and if, Indian children entered the orphanage, they were in the minority.

To find Catholic orphanages that focused only on Indian children, one must go to the Northern Plains and look among the Catholic outposts of mission work among the Ojibways and the Sioux. In the Dakotas and Minnesota there was, as in New Mexico, a Catholic presence with a long history in Indian-white relations. Unlike New Mexico, however, there were instances in which Indian orphans were cared for separately from other racial or ethnic groups. To begin an exploration of Catholic work for orphans on the Northern Plains, the best place to consider is Wounded Knee.

When the killing stopped at Wounded Knee, 153 men, women, and children were known to be dead, but the exact number was undoubtedly much higher. Left uncounted were the wounded who crawled away, hid, and later died. Among those who survived the volleys of gunshots and then freezing temperatures and blizzard were children. Some were found by the Sioux, others by the military. Lost Bird, the infant girl found shielded by the frozen body of her mother, was claimed by Gen. Leonard Colby. A number of those orphaned, infants and older children, were taken to Pine Ridge, placed temporarily in the Reverend Charles Cook's Episcopal mission, and later taken into the homes of Indian families that Charles Eastman described as "Christian."[4] Eastman, a Santee Sioux who attended Dartmouth and then Boston University School of Medicine, was at the mission and cared for the wounded. He left the following account.

> We tore out the pews and covered the floor with hay and quilts. There we laid the poor creatures side by side in rows, and the night was devoted to caring for them as best we could. Many were frightfully torn by pieces of shells, and the suffering was terrible. . . . In spite of all our efforts, we lost the greater part of them, but a few recovered, including several children who had lost all their relatives and who were adopted into kind Christian families.[5]

A number of Wounded Knee survivors also found refuge at Holy Rosary Mission, about five miles north of Pine Ridge, where Indians and whites alike sought safety in the troubled days leading up to and after the massacre. In fact, a few days prior to the massacre, the mission's priest, Father John Jutz, encountered a number of Sioux led by a chief Jutz identified as Two Strike. The Indians came to the mission rather than the agency because, in Jutz's words, they were afraid of the soldiers and of being punished for killing some cattle, and they wanted to be near the agency to get rations. What the priest was not told, or failed to mention in his letter to superiors, was that about one week earlier Two Strike and the men with him skirmished with whites at French Creek over stolen horses. Whether or not the priest knew all the details was unimportant; he attempted to intervene with the military on behalf of Two Strike. As a result, Jutz felt himself successful, since fears seemed to have been allayed and the Indian group agreed to bring men, women, and children to the agency. Writing of the events, Jutz informed the head of the Catholic Bureau of Indian Missions: "The result of this mission I shall let you know as soon as they come back." Tragically, Indians arriving later at Holy Rosary were those who survived Wounded Knee. The children were taken in and cared for by Jutz and the Franciscan Sisters at the mission.[6]

Wounded Knee is the marker for the demise of the Sioux culture, but the Sioux way of life was already under siege. White encroachment, the reservation system, and allotment mandated through the Dawes Act of 1887 contributed to a chain of events that acted to break the spirit and starve the soul of a people who were strong, aggressive, and proud. The Sioux Nation was made up of geographically situated groups that shared the Siouan language: the major divisions were the Oglalas; the Sichangus, called the Burnt Thighs and now known as the Brules; the Miniconjous; the Oohenonpas, commonly called the Two Kettles; the Hunkpapas; the Sihasapas; and the Itazipchos, called the Sans Arcs by early French trappers and traders. Added to these were the Mdewakantons; the Wahpetons; the Wahpekutes; the Sissetons; the Yanktons; the Yanktonais; and the Tetons. Dialect differences divided the Sioux into three groupings: Dakota (also called Santee), Nakota, and Lakota. The Sioux Nation ranged over a territory that shifted with war and conquest but which by the mid-1700s encompassed part or all of present-day Minnesota, the Dakotas, Nebraska, Montana, and Wyoming. The groups within the Siouan peoples relied largely on an economy dominated by horse ownership and the hunt. Maintaining this economy depended on control over large tracts of territory, leading the Sioux to engage in both defensive and aggressive acts of war against other native groups.

As a nation made up of several geographically scattered divisions, the Sioux encountered the U.S. Army at different times and in various ways. Many encounters were not direct military confrontations but the result of U.S. troops guarding Mandans, Arikaras, Gros Ventres, Pawnees, and Poncas from Sioux attacks. With forced removal of the Sioux to reservation lands, however, soldier and Indian met as guardian and ward. Siouan groups faced their own "trail of tears," which began a spiral of death and disengaged families. One example was the removal of Santee Sioux who were gathered at Fort Snelling in Minnesota for transport to the Crow Creek Agency in South Dakota. Taken down the Mississippi River and then up the Missouri, the Santee faced considerable deprivations. There was much sickness and sixteen deaths on the transport boat, where "they were so crowded that there was not room enough for all of them to lie down at the same time." Food was "not more than about one-half of [a] soldier's rations" and consisted primarily of "hard bread and mess pork not cooked." Then, "for six weeks after they arrived at Crow Creek they died at the average rate of three or four a day," with the total number of deaths within the first six weeks estimated to be 150. Once deposited in their new environment, the Santee faced further starvation and little or no medical care. They were, however, where the government and the soldiers wanted them—on a reservation.[7]

Military and Sioux also met when the federal government said that the Sioux needed protection. In 1875, U.S. troops went to the Black Hills, where, ostensibly, they were to protect the Sioux after George Armstrong Custer's 1874 expedition found gold and miners began streaming to the area. The Fort Laramie Treaty of 1868 guaranteed the Black Hills, sacred land, to the Sioux, but the discovery of gold changed all that. The military halted miners only because the federal government wanted to keep the peace long enough to pressure the Sioux into relinquishing the land. At the time, approximately ten thousand Sioux already lived on reservations. They were not directly involved in the Black Hills conflict, with the exception of those who "jumped" the reservations and joined the Sioux in the west territory. In 1876 a summer campaign was mounted by the U.S. military to drive all Sioux to reservation lands. General George Crook defeated Indian forces at the Rosebud River, but whatever victory he could claim was mitigated by the decimation of Custer. It was an Indian victory that Charles Eastman described as "the last effective defense of the Black Hills by the Sioux." The all-out U.S. campaign that followed and the massacre at Wounded Knee were the final blows to Sioux freedom.[8]

Added to actions of the U.S. government, military, and gold seekers in the Black Hills were those that changed Sioux culture internally. Alcohol was introduced into Sioux society during the eighteenth century, but its impact was insignificant until the 1850s, when white advancement into Indian country brought purveyors of alcohol and more reasons for whites to use liquor as a bartering tool. There is some suggestion that alcohol consumption dropped immediately after groups were forced onto reservations because the consumers were separated from their suppliers. Nonetheless, there is adequate evidence that the liquor continued to flow. In 1868, not long after the Sisseton and Wahpeton Sioux took up reservation life, the agent at the Sisseton Agency noted unauthorized trading places that made whiskey readily available. The result was "demoralizing tendencies" among the Sioux. Time did not improve the situation. In 1880, agent reports continued to comment on the alcohol problem: "We have been troubled of late by our Indians procuring whiskey. . . . I am able to state that only a small part of our Indians want whiskey or will drink it under ordinary circumstances but that small part cause a great amount of trouble sometimes." As the agent implied, not everyone wanted or drank alcohol. Some attributed this to the Indians' own abilities to resist the temptations of drink. As one nugget of proof, the Sisseton, South Dakota, newspaper noted in 1903 that a "large body of Indians" from the local reservation were en route to a convention of the Young Men's Christian Temperance Union. Others attributed alcohol resistance to missionary influence. When approximately forty Sioux representatives from the Presbyterian-supported Goodwill Mission traveled to the Standing Rock Reservation for a church convention, the Sisseton newspaper credited the Reverend C. R. Crawford. The "aged Indian missionary . . . has lived to see the wild and reckless Sioux converted to civilization and Christianity."9

The road to conversion was not easy or complete—no matter what the Sisseton newspaper reported. Missionaries, Protestant and Catholic, demonstrated various degrees of patience and tolerance for traditional culture. Many learned the language in order to preach and teach, and they welcomed Indian converts who wished to become ministers or members of religious orders. A handful of clerics and Indian agents, among them Methodist agent H. J. Armstrong, who was born and raised among the Crows, argued that native peoples had a right to their own religion. Nevertheless, the collective white majority condemned religious practices and claimed victories of conversion whenever they could because conversion was often a difficult process. The distances to travel, as well as the small number of missions and too few missionaries, created an environment that made it easy for converts to slip back into their old ways. For this reason, missionaries specifically targeted the Sun Dance. Augustin Ravoux, who left France in 1838 for the American missions and was sent among the Sioux in 1840, ran out of words to denounce the Sun Dance, but his message was clear: "Horrible and almost incredible are the penances and tortures some Indians inflicted upon themselves to please their gods and obtain their favors." Ravoux, and missionaries who followed, saw the power of the Sun Dance and the supreme significance it held for the Sioux. The ceremony allowed men to demonstrate their bravery through self-inflicted pain; as important, it brought people together in a sense of tribal unity to seek harmony and *wakan*, everything that was sacred. Thus, whenever converts came to Christianity—and stayed—there was reason for missionary rejoicing. A priest at the Rosebud Agency gladly proclaimed in 1902 that "the power of the Medicine man is broken, at least for our more than 2000 Catholics."[10]

Religion was one obstacle to civilization and acculturation. Family structure was another. Missionaries, along with Indian agents, railed against polygamy. The agent at the Sisseton Agency thought that the federal government should find a means to make it clear that polygamy was against the laws of the United States. Withholding rations was an option. The agent was in a bind: he found it impossible to "harmonize the differences" between two factions that loosely represented the conservatives who resisted change and the progressives who accepted or accommodated it. Chief Gabriel Renville made reconciliation more difficult, since his own domestic living arrangement was polygamous. Although a Christian and of mixed Indian and white heritage, and therefore someone expected to be a progressive, Renville was wont to take the Indians "back to their sacred ways. . . . [He] loves the ways of the Indians better." Besides giving dances that reinforced the old ways, he refused to part with any of his three wives. "There is not a fullblood Sioux here that has as many as he has," declared the Sisseton agent.[11]

Renville did not fit stereotypical expectations of white culture. Because they had a quantum of Caucasian ancestry, mixed-bloods were believed to be intellectually and socially superior to full-bloods and more ready to accept acculturation. The agent's denouncement of Renville underscored the tenor of white-Indian relations on the Northern Plains after the Civil War. Whether it was President Grant's Peace Policy or the later Dawes Act and Nelson Act, the mood was one of white impatience. Mixed-bloods who followed their own voices were regarded with suspicion. Renville was just one example of a mixed-blood who had somehow taken a wrong turn.

How many other Renvilles were there? A number of governmental and religious authorities wondered. The director of the Bureau of Catholic Indian Missions, for example, asked the priest at Holy Rosary Mission for exact numbers of Catholic, Protestant, and Episcopalian Indians (the Episcopalians were considered the Catholics' primary rival for converts); along with this count, the director wanted to know the number of "pagan" Indians and how many onetime Carlisle students were on the Pine Ridge Reservation. In the high-stakes game of saving souls and keeping missions and schools financed during a time of increased friction between the Indian Bureau and Catholics, it was useful to know how many Indian supporters could be relied upon. Carlisle students, educated in a Protestant environment, could be articulate obstacles to Catholic mission work.[12]

There were similar suspicions of mixed-bloods and educated Indians on the Ojibway White Earth Reservation, where the Catholics established St. Benedict's Orphan School. The White Earth agent, T. J. Sheehan, attempted to remove all mixed-bloods from the reservation while at the same time trying to shut down *The Progress*, a newspaper edited by Theodore Hudon Beaulieu and published by Augustus Hudon Beaulieu. Mixed-bloods of French and Ojibway descent, the two represented the métis (mixed-bloods) who acted as cultural intermediaries on the reservation. With their opening edition of *The Progress*, they promised to "advocate constantly, . . . making known abroad and at home, what is for the best interests of the tribe." The newspapermen favored assimilation and thus supported U.S. policy, as well as the views of white and Indian reformers. Nevertheless, they did not completely abandon Indian life, from time to time publishing articles about the old ways. An announcement of upcoming features promised stories from "several centenarians on the reservation" who would tell of when wild game and fish were in abundance and there were no Indian agents, game laws, or police courts "to keep clear of." One story began: "My grandson you have asked me to tell you the customs of our ancestors and the origin of the Indians. It is your wish and I shall tell you our beliefs." The paper closed after the first issue, but Sheehan's victory was short-lived. A U.S. Senate committee hearing vindicated the Beaulieus—in part because they *were* mixed-bloods and nicely fit the committee's racist view that Indians with white ancestry were superior in intelligence to full-bloods. In the aftermath of *The Progress* controversy, Sheehan sheepishly commented that the incident made the Beaulieus "good Indians." To which the newspapermen rejoined: "Well now, really, that's generous! . . . We have strong hopes . . . to civilize, and make a good Democratic Irishman [out of Sheehan]."[13]

People like the Beaulieus and Renville were enigmas—at once both progressive leaders and conservative traditionalists. When Sheehan used a heavy hand to suppress them, his tactics backfired. The same outcome would be quite possible if the Sisseton agent pressured

Renville to give up two of his wives. The agent left the problem to others who had higher civil or moral authority. Certainly, Protestant and Catholic missionaries brought all the influence they could muster to eliminate plural marriages. Polygamous arrangements shocked Euro-American sensibilities and ran counter to Christian teachings that stressed the sanctity of vows between husband and wife and the implied protection of family. For the Catholics, a subtle approach emerged that allowed them to reduce polygamy and, at the same time, bring converts into the church. First marriages were annulled if couples came forward and agreed to be married in the church. It was a relatively simple formality but one with large implications. Wrote a cleric from the Rosebud Agency: "The dance house was their Courthouse: a vigorous beating of the big drum separated them in the eyes of the people—without any fees to the Lawyers." After a number of years, however, the priest was able to say that "the consciences of some Halfbreeds awoke first. . . . Since 1891 the marriages according to the rules of the Church prevailed." The nuclear family of one male and one female in a household gradually replaced the plural configuration of the past.[14]

The hunt economy was destroyed when buffalo herds were intentionally diminished and when men were restricted to the reservation. The extended family was effectively undermined by outsiders' insistence that men take a role in agriculture, which by tradition was female. Although Indian agents gave optimistic reports on the progress of turning the Sioux into farmers, there was more hope than substantial proof. Resistance remained a barrier, but acceptance was problematic, too. The rewards promised by federal officials and reformers were offset when natural forces brought disaster. The Sisseton and Wahpeton Sioux bands, overseen by the Sisseton Agency established in 1867, were distanced from military conflicts farther west. Forced to the edge of southwestern Minnesota and into the northeastern corner of South Dakota, the Sissetons and Wahpetons were kindly viewed by most whites who observed or interacted with them. The Episcopalian bishop of Minnesota, the Reverend Henry B. Whipple, regarded them as "the finest body of Indians that I ever knew." When the two groups were accused of taking part in outbreaks of violence in Minnesota during 1862, their innocence was defended by whites. They were, said

Euro-Americans, "farmer Indians" who demonstrated a willingness to try agriculture. This was due in part to the land on which they lived. Compared with soil elsewhere, that around Sisseton was fertile, and "ordinarily there was sufficient moisture."[15]

Whites hailed the bands for their willingness to engage in farming, but the Sissetons and Wahpetons faced starvation and destitution for their efforts. In 1867, after taking up reservation life, "they labored faithful with the hoe and plough to have their patches of ground ready for the seed." Just as the crops began to show promise, however, "the grasshoppers appeared by the millions and devoured the crops." The result was a people on the point of starvation. The agent at the Sisseton Agency estimated that four to six hundred Indians were in dire straits. Some families attempted to revert to their old ways and hunt buffalo, but this proved unsuccessful. The buffalo were not to be found. Under the circumstances, a number of "prominent" whites decided to take action. There was general agreement, even on the part of the Indian agent, that no one could wait for the government to act. Whipple gathered "liberal donations of goods [that] were made for the benefit of the Indians." Despite this early catastrophe and continued suffering through the winter of 1868, when there were a "great many deaths, caused by their great want of food," the Sissetons and Wahpetons continued in their attempts to farm. And grasshoppers continued to plague them. In the 1870s, drought and grasshoppers descended upon the Great Plains. The "hoppers" swarmed over animals and people; some people swore that their clothing was eaten right off their backs. Nothing was spared. Drought and suffering were repeated in the 1880s and 1890s. "During the 18th, 19th, and 20th of October [1895] sand and dust storms, with low temperature and the wind at 50 miles per hour, prevailed over Minnesota, the Dakotas, and Manitoba, and the inconveniences of such a blizzard were intensified by the alkaline character of the dust." Everyone was affected—Wahpeton, Sisseton, newly arrived immigrant, established white settler. The difference, of course, was that the would-be settler could leave, although many needed charitable aid to do so. The Sioux could not leave, with or without help. Leaving the reservation meant being labeled hostile and subjected to a forced return.[16]

It seemed that those willing to try agriculture were thwarted at every turn. Although Commissioner of Indian Affairs Morgan warned that any attempt to deal with the Indian en masse would fail because no two tribes lived under exactly the same conditions and no two reservations were the same, the federal government and self-styled "friends of the Indian" focused on turning Indians into crop farmers. The most vocal of these "friends" were those who met at Lake Mohonk at the request of Quakers and members of the Board of Indian Commissioners. These reformers and interested observers believed that farming, coupled with allotment, would bring about civilization and acculturation by forcing Indians to shed tribal community for individual self-sufficiency. The theory, however, overlooked Morgan's warning. An inflexible position that emphasized crop farming over stock raising was disastrous for the Sioux because there was no consideration given to soil quality or yearly amounts of rainfall, which were at acceptable levels in eastern regions of the Northern Plains but less so in the west. The priest at St. Francis Mission on the Rosebud Reservation compared the situation of the Sioux with that of white settlers: "The white farmers in the vicinity, who tried to make their living by farming alone, nearly all gave up and left their homesteads; those who combined farming & cattle raising do fairly well." It seemed obvious that "with a little farming & gardening, but mainly cattle raising our Sioux can, in time, be made selfsupporting [*sic*]." The basic obstacle, however, to any agricultural pursuit was the lack of water. Wrote the priest: "No one can blame them [the Sioux] for not taking to agriculture, after their efforts in that line proved failures, owning to scarcity of seasonable rain." What had the authorities expected when much of the western land allotted the Sioux was tableland devoid of water? Allottees were left "without any running water or even wells for 30 & more miles." The government made no effort to help those who tried to dig wells.[17]

When Sioux allotment was still not completed in 1902, the priest at Rosebud again emphasized the need for usable land: "Without water, however, no man nor beast can live on these long stretched table land[s].. . . . Hense [*sic*] they [Sioux] hang around the Creeks, & their 'allotments' are in those places practically useless." It was a scenario that enticed some to strike out on their own and join Wild West shows. The work provided a living, but it detached people from their communities and families. Allotment, endorsed by the Indian Bureau and reformers attending the Lake Mohonk conferences, played out its potential for replacing tribal community with individualism at a tremendous cost.[18]

The consequences of armed conflict, allotment, and reservation life produced a population of children who were orphaned or so destitute that white mainstream society would label their circumstances akin to those of an orphan. Given the conditions, one might expect that a plethora of reformers and religious leaders would demand financial support to establish orphan asylums and that these asylums would quickly appear to look after children who had no safety net of parents and/or extended family. There was, however, no strong and immediate effort to establish orphan asylums for Sioux children. Orphaned youngsters were funneled into the general populations of boarding or mission schools. Some wandered from one Indian camp to another on the reservations. During the last decades of the 1800s and the first half of the twentieth century, only a few efforts emerged to establish orphanages for Sioux children. These attempts came from Catholic missionaries who largely acted alone and without organized help from their superiors.

The dearth of asylum building among the Sioux runs counter to the entire makeup of rapid institutional development in America during the last decades of the nineteenth century. Why the Sioux were largely overlooked when disaster after disaster conspired to produce an orphaned population can be answered in several ways. First, the 1862 Sioux uprising in Minnesota and the later defeat of Custer at the Battle of Greasy Grass (Little Big Horn) did little to promote general public sympathy for the Sioux. It was difficult, if not impossible, for white society to accept the idea that orphaned and impoverished Sioux children were "worthy," and worthiness was a prerequisite for benevolent charity to children. Support for orphanages rested on public opinion, and public perception of the Sioux as warlike and savage made it nearly impossible to elicit compassion or interest in Sioux children.

A second factor, encouraged by the ultimate suppression of the Sioux, was white culture's growing interest in the Indian as a part of America's past—not its present. During much of the nineteenth century, any number of whites, from government officials to ethnographers, predicted the imminent demise of America's first people. As groups were removed and confined before white advancement, the dominant culture began to bemoan the loss of native peoples and to reframe their experiences. Poetry, short stories, and even the decorative arts began to create a particular vision of the Indian. Rodman Wanamaker, a prominent businessman who was infatuated with the idea of anything Indian, made plans in 1909 to build a monument in New York Harbor. It would include a three-story museum, topped by a seventy-foot pedestal on which stood a sixty-foot-high statue of an Indian, resplendent in robes and war bonnet. The statue would welcome newcomers to America, just as Wanamaker envisioned the red man welcoming the first Europeans centuries before. Wanamaker's project never materialized, but its intent spoke volumes about America's willingness to romanticize the Indian while detaching itself from the truth. Another prime example was Joseph K. Dixon's verbose memorial written at the time that the Indian Bureau organized the "last council" of tribal leaders at Wounded Knee in 1909: "Every Indian boy and girl owns a pony, from which they are almost inseparable, and which they ride with fearless abandon. While men are off in search of game the women make bead work of a most bewitching order, meanwhile watching the papoose." As far as Dixon, as well as the general public, was concerned, all was well in Indian country.[19]

A last contributing factor to the dearth of orphanage building was the overall state of educational facilities among the Sioux. The Sioux Nation did not have established school systems with orphan homes like those of the Five Civilized Tribes. Nor was the Sioux Nation likely to have the same number of on-reservation day and boarding schools as those found in Indian Territory. In the immediate post–Civil War years, when schools were established among the Sioux, there was considerable controversy about the direction of Indian education in general, and this influenced education for the Sioux. One faction in the education debate was devoted to the model championed by Richard Henry Pratt, who began recruiting Sioux students for his Carlisle Institute in 1879. Pratt was adamant that his plan was the best option, since it completely separated Indian youngsters from their home environments. Pratt, however, had detractors. Among them were the Beaulieus on the White Earth Reservation, who wrote that Pratt's "success in the training of Indian children has been due more to the disciplining roles of his educational establishment and because he has there the power to enforce his views." Gertrude Simmons Bonnin, a Yankton Sioux, agreed. Her own experience told her that Indians showed greater interest and more achievement in education without Carlisle's military-style discipline. Bonnin also questioned America's willingness to educate foreign immigrants while Indian education remained under dispute. Meanwhile, some suggested that the question was moot, since Indians, particularly the wild tribes of the Plains, were incapable of learning. William W. Corlett, a Wyoming congressman, went a step farther and employed social Darwinism to suggest that there was no point in educating a race that was doomed to extinction.[20]

The debate over schools and education did little to promote large-scale programs among the Sioux. There were no school–orphan homes in the Sioux Nation prior to federal intervention through allotment and government boarding and day schools. Without school–orphan homes there was no reason for federal authorities to consider them and to make decisions about which to keep and which to close. The government did not have to deal with either tribally supported orphan homes or those established by religious groups, since those groups most active among the Sioux had not established orphanages. Presbyterians and Baptists, so prevalent among the Five Civilized Tribes and responsible for building orphanages in Indian Territory, were weak or nonexistent forces among the Sioux. So, too, were the Quakers, responsible for the beginnings of Thomas Indian School in New York State. The most visible missionaries among the Sioux were Episcopalian and Catholic. The Episcopalians' work in the north-central territories began in the early 1860s among the Oneidas in Wisconsin and the Ojibways (the Chippewas) in Minnesota. By 1871, through the work of the Reverend Henry B. Whipple, a special missionary jurisdiction called Niobrara was established to include the Indian reservations in present-day South Dakota and western Nebraska.[21] The Episcopalians were not, however, orphanage builders, and though Catholics were, missionaries were constrained by economics and lack of personnel.

Nationally Catholics were active in building and supporting orphanages, but it was almost impossible to build and then staff such institutions on reservations of the Northern Plains. Just at the time the Sioux and Ojibways were faced with reservation life and allotment, the Catholics faced difficulties in keeping what missions they had. It was nearly impossible to support orphanages as separate entities from mission schools. The situation was largely a result of the government contract system that granted funds to mission boards at a per student ratio, with the number of funded students determined by the Indian Bureau. Thus, missions might ask for money to support one hundred students but receive funds for only half that number, and it was routine for mission boards and their on-site workers to request additional funds for building maintenance and expansion. The superintendent of the Presbyterian contract manual-labor school at Sisseton, for example, nudged the commissioner of Indian affairs for more money in March 1880 with a gentle reminder that the school operated in complete compliance with the "plans of the government for the elevation of the Indians." When that failed to move the Indian Bureau, the superintendent sent the commissioner a list of needed repairs and a peevish observation: "This is a twenty two thousand dollar building without a bath tub or bath room: I think we should have one and tubs in it."[22]

The Presbyterian superintendent was in competition with every other school contractor for financial support. In the late 1880s, Catholics received the bulk of contracts and funds. During the contract year of 1892–93, as illustration, the government made contracts with fifty-one Catholic schools, from California and New Mexico to Michigan and Indiana. The total dollar amount was $363,349. The second closest in contracts were the Presbyterians, who received a total of $44,850 for eight contract schools. After the Presbyterians came the Episcopalians, Unitarians, and Congregationalists with four schools apiece; the Methodists with two; and the Lutherans, Mennonites, and Quakers with one school each. It was little wonder that anti-Catholic feelings developed among Protestant mission groups or that Pratt accused Father John Jutz at Holy Rosary Mission of spreading anti-Protestant rumors. A letter sent from Carlisle stated: "The outrageous and ridiculously untrue things that you, and men of your cloth, say against the government, its schools and its officials, are becoming pretty well understood." As the Catholics continued to receive contracts, there was a general mud-slinging campaign. It was not one-sided. Church clerics were as contentious as their Protestant counterparts. Leading the charge was the Bureau of Catholic Indian Missions, established in 1874, and the bureau's director, the Reverend Joseph A. Stephan, who had been a Catholic agent among the Sioux under Grant's Peace Policy. From the bureau's publication *The Indian Sentinel* flowed a stream of accusations and name-calling. Anyone not in total support of Catholic mission work was a target. Said the *Sentinel* of Massachusetts senator Henry Cabot Lodge: "Senator Lodge is not only a bigot, but he appears to delight in being as conspicuous as possible in his anti-Catholic work." At the center of the controversy was the Indian Bureau.[23]

It was common practice for religious leaders and denominational politics to play a role in Indian affairs and to attempt to influence governmental policies. Mission groups, Protestant and Catholic, believed they had a perfect right to be involved, since from the beginning of the government's Indian civilization movement religious groups received federal support. Church and state were tightly linked when dealing with Indian affairs. Quakers under Grant's Peace Policy were given a major role in selecting Indian agents and superintendents in the Northern and Central Plains. Catholics denounced Commissioner Morgan and various congressmen while lobbying to keep the contract system in place. Bishop Henry B. Whipple, the Episcopalian who established a mission among the Sioux in 1860, felt within his rights to scathingly condemn U.S. policy when the government seemed too slow in its response to Indian welfare: "What depths of woe we have brought this people [Sioux] by our shameless wars. I tell you men would fear to raise the cry of extermination lest Gods justice fell on ourselves." Whipple called down the wrath of God on a "guilty nation" for "every act of oppression [and] every crime against humanity." In the bishop's eyes the government had adopted nothing less than "a robber ethics 'dead men tell no tales.'" Whether well-intentioned or self-serving, church groups and individuals were part and parcel of government policy. Under the shadow of anti-Catholic rhetoric and Indian Bureau outlook, Catholic missions began to lose their contracts or have them reduced. After 1895, government appropriations for Catholic missions dropped every year by at least 20 percent. To make up the difference, priests and religious orders went begging for private donations and more funds from church dioceses.[24]

As operating funds constricted over a period of time, it was impossible for the Bureau of Catholic Indian Missions to support any idea of Catholic orphanages for Indian children. Orphans, half-orphans, and destitute children could be looked after only at mission schools. Therefore, one of the first recorded instances of Sioux children being identified specifically as orphans and placed in a Catholic mission because of their parentless status occurred not in the United States but in Canada.

After the Minnesota uprising in 1862, a number of Sioux crossed the northern border and took refuge in Canada. Among them was four-year-old Charles Eastman, whose father was taken by U.S. authorities. Since

U.S. retaliation for the uprising was swift and merciless, the refugee Sioux rightfully feared reprisals if they returned to the United States. The refugees were still not safe, however. They were set upon by the Salteux, who considered the Sioux invaders and competitors for the limited number of buffalo that remained. There were few places to turn. The Gray Nuns at St. Boniface near Winnipeg gave what food they could to the Sioux, fearing Salteaux retaliation for their charity. The nuns also took in Sioux orphans and gave shelter to a number of youngsters who were given up by desperate and starving families. In the face of grim realities, parents went to St. Boniface and offered to exchange their children for buffalo meat. The children would be safely delivered into a refuge where they would be fed and housed, and Sioux adults would have food to sustain them a little longer. The nuns took what youngsters they could, and rather quickly the number of children at St. Boniface reached forty, with expectations that there would soon be one hundred. Eastman was not among these children; he was raised by relatives, but just a small turn of fate could have placed him alongside others at St. Boniface.25

Over twenty years later, two Catholic missions with Indian orphan populations appeared almost simultaneously in the United States. The first was St. Benedict's Orphan School on the White Earth Reservation for the Ojibways, who were referred to in federal records as the Chippewas or Chippeways. (Today the term is still used at times by the tribal group.) The second was Holy Rosary Mission on the Pine Ridge Reservation for the Sioux. The two missions shared common characteristics: both received government contracts, both were long-lived institutions, and both served orphaned and non-orphaned children. In one written communiqué, hampered somewhat by her struggle with English, Sister Lioba Braun explained the following about St. Benedict's Orphan School:

> Our school not only [is] a home for Orphans [and] Half orphans but a kind of a home school for other children on the Reservation is not to [sic] far away from the Parents that Satisfies Parents— children I can state that since 6 years not a single child run away during the fiscal year. Not enough room especially for all those who want to begin schooling.26

In 1878 three Benedictines—Father Aloysius Hermanutz, Sister Philomene Ketten, and Sister Lioba Braun—arrived on the White

Earth Reservation. They, as well as many other Catholic missionaries who served in Minnesota and the Dakotas, were of German background and had grown up with German as their first language. As Sister Braun's letter indicates, their exertions to master English left little time or energy to learn the language of their Ojibway students. Father Hermanutz, however, sought common ground by learning the basics of the tribal language. The priest, born in Germany, later recalled: "My total ignorance of the Chippewa language was the first great difficulty to overcome. . . . I had only a short compendium of grammar and a dictionary of the Chippewa language and no one to direct me." There was nothing for the priest to do but teach himself. "But I applied myself. . . . after three months of hard study I essayed my first sermon in Chippewa."[27]

The Ojibways' economic and political foundation was based on bands, each of which operated with almost total independence from the other. Religious and ceremonial observances were in the hands of various societies, and tribal identity rested on the extended family relationships of each clan. This altered when the reservation system was laid out in 1867 with seven land reserves. Federal officials and reformers such as Henry Whipple formulated a plan that concentrated the Ojibways into select areas in Minnesota. It was for the best, they argued, because the Ojibways would be protected from white encroachment and outside pressures that included alcohol. The reserves held good farmland, offering the Ojibways a greater chance for economic success as agriculturists. When the Benedictines arrived, the White Earth Reservation was just over ten years old.[28]

The Catholics were not the first religious presence on the reservation. Initially, Congregationalists received control under Grant's Peace Policy, but in 1874 they turned it over to the Episcopalians in exchange for another agency. This brought the Episcopal minister the Reverend John Johnson Emmegahblowh, an Ojibway. Described by *The Progress* as "venerable and well-beloved," Emmegahblowh constantly clashed with the Catholic priest Ignatius Tomazin, who arrived at White Earth in 1873. The two men's contest for power and souls was so disruptive that eventually both were removed by their superiors. The charged atmosphere they left behind greeted the St. Benedict Mission founders, who could not even stake a claim as the first to establish a school. The reservation's first school opened in 1870 under the direction of Julia Spears, whose brother was involved in organizing the first removals of the Ojibways to White Earth. Then, in 1871, a federally supported industrial school opened with twenty-five boys and twenty-five girls. The latter were instructed by Hattie Cook, a niece of the Indian agent, who was employed under an 1863 treaty provision that specified, "Female members of the family of any Government employee residing on the reservation who shall teach Indian girls domestic economy shall be allowed and paid ten dollars per month while so engaged." The Catholics had to begin simply with a day school, competing for students. As it turned out, the missionaries also had to compete for federal contracts. They were successful through support from the Bureau of Catholic Indian Missions.[29]

The Benedictines had ambitious plans to expand the day school into a boarding school and to increase classroom capacity. Major help came after the Drexel sisters—Katharine, Louise, and Elizabeth—made a mission tour through the Dakotas and Minnesota. Katharine Drexel, who funded numerous missions and schools and later founded her own religious order, Sisters of the Blessed Sacrament for Colored and for Indians, provided St. Benedict's Mission with enough funds to construct a new school building. It was not to be just any sort of a building. In 1889 *The Progress* reported that local clay was being tested to determine its quality for making bricks with which to construct a three-story structure. All was being done "under the auspices of and through the benign minificence [sic] of those noble lady philanthropists, the Drexel sisters of Philadelphia." The missionaries got their new building, but they still struggled to support its work. Up to 200 could be accommodated, but when St. Benedict's opened, the government paid for only 25 to 30 students. This remained the status quo until 1903, when the number increased dramatically to 90, with the total number of St. Benedict residents at 150.[30]

The new mission school, christened St. Benedict's Orphan Boarding School, began as a coeducational facility. In fact, Theodore Beaulieu of *The Progress* informed Joseph A. Stephan, director of the Bureau of Catholic Indian Missions, that the "young men" organized a musical club and band to cultivate "a higher and better appreciation of music." Music remained a part of life at St. Benedict's, but the young men did not. Mission workers decided to accept only girls who ranged in age from six to seventeen. By 1891 there were 120 residents. Their education leaned heavily toward religious instruction and preparation for becoming farm wives. Girls learned to knit, crochet, and spin, and

*In 1892, residents and staff of St. Benedict's Orphan Boarding
School, on the White Earth Reservation, pose in front of the build-
ing funded by Katharine Drexel (canonized on October 1, 2000).
Minnesota Historical Society.*

to sew both by hand and with a sewing machine. The average day included an hour and a half of "needlework and chores" in the afternoon. There was also an hour-long "work detail" in the morning
when girls did chores in the laundry, kitchen, and garden. As for outside work, Sister Lioba Braun commented that "the facilities for instruction in farming are simple." The girls had cows, pigs, sheep, and
poultry to look after, and on occasion they learned to kill and dress
chickens and to butcher. Recalled a nun who joined the teaching staff:
"Butchering was always a great time. We killed as many as 40 hogs at
one time. There were tubs of sausage meat ground and ready for the
casings by evening. After the work was done, the cook fried pans of
sausage. . . . all everyone could eat and what fun we had." Although
Catholic publicists broadcast the notion that church policy reflected
Commissioner Leupp's wishes to preserve Indian art and music, St.
Benedict's daily itinerary offers little evidence to support that this was
the case at the orphan school. The only concessions seemed to have
been beadwork instruction during "needlework time" and occasional
allowances for girls to dress in Ojibway beaded clothing.[31]

Youngsters in a classroom at St. Benedict's Orphan Boarding School on the White Earth Reservation in Minnesota, ca. 1900. Minnesota Historical Society, St. Benedict's Convent Archives photograph.

Between 1900 and 1920, off-reservation boarding schools became the norm for Ojibway students. While Leupp advocated preservation of Indian culture in schools, he also approved use of force when parents resisted. Children were rounded up by reservation police for transport to these schools. A small number, which included some later runaways, went to the Catholic contract school of St. Joseph Normal School in Rensselaer, Indiana, and there were reports that orphans were among the youngsters sent to Flandreau Boarding School in South Dakota. In the face of enforced off-reservation schooling, St. Benedict's remained fast, however. As a Catholic presence on the reservation, it received support from the church and expanded in staff. As an orphan school on the reservation, it kept the resident population, which averaged one hundred, close to a tribal community. It is difficult to know how many were true orphans. On one occasion, a supervisor reported: "We have our crowd of ninety-four and expect about ten more this week. . . . Our children are nearly all orphans who otherwise have no one to look after them and we feel obliged to give them a home also." Since the word "orphan" was broadly used, it is probable that a portion of the resident population came from destitute and/or broken families. The sisters seemed to accept existing conditions without wondering how extended clan families had reached the point of being unable or unwilling to care for children.[32]

On the other hand, Father Simon Lampee, who worked among the Ojibways for twenty-one years, gave the situation some thought and developed a concise list of reasons. The main cause of family breakdown, decided the priest, was marriage outside the church. Men and women who lived together as husband and wife without being married in the church did not understand the obligations of marriage and therefore felt free to separate "even if they have children." Although this did not necessarily produce abandoned children, it was proof enough for Lampee that adults felt little responsibility for their offspring. Closer to the mark as a contributing factor was Lampee's reference to alcohol. "Irreligious white men" and whiskey corrupted the Indians, while "drunkenness and shiftlessness on the part of the husband" broke up countless marriages. The priest, however, did not place all the blame on men who drank. Secure in his paternalistic view of what constituted admirable female qualities, the priest lamented the "insubordination and laziness" of wives. As incontrovertible proof of women's laziness one only had to taste their "insipid" bread. It was too much trouble for them to "prepare anything tastefully and properly." Only "Catholic wedlock" could bring "a wonderful change" in women's behavior, improve the family at large, and, evidently, improve homemaking skills. Father Hermanutz was equally critical of women. He blamed them for keeping children out of school and pictured non-Christian women as stubborn and vicious, capable of crippling or killing their children in fits of rage.[33]

There were grains of truth in these explanations for family breakdown. Alcoholism was a contributing factor to marital separation and family upheaval. Nevertheless, the priests were so grounded in their duty to convert that they were incapable of addressing the cause and effect of events that unfolded before them. After the reservation system was in place, the Ojibways faced the turbulent period of allotment, when a combination of timber interests, politicians, and local banks near White Earth Reservation acted to defraud the Indians. Homelessness increased, but neither priest spoke of this or the ensuing poverty. In fact, Lampee believed that the Indians were spoiled by too much money. Neither priest addressed the rise in tuberculosis, venereal disease, and trachoma that accompanied destitution. Disease and death stalked Ojibway reservations. Despite vaccinations against smallpox, the disease periodically appeared in specific localities, and mortality rates spiked during influenza epidemics. Homelessness, destitution, and disease were the stories behind the residents of St. Benedict's, and disease continued to follow the girls. The year 1901 was particularly bad for the orphan school. Hard on the heels of sixty-five cases of measles followed numerous cases of mumps, whooping cough, influenza, and pneumonia from which two girls died. Nonetheless, St. Benedict's was a refuge from the multitude of reasons that brought the loss of family and clan support.[34]

In the first decades of the twentieth century, a new factor in family discord crept onto the scene. Families began to relocate to urban centers, particularly Minneapolis and St. Paul. When Ojibways left the reservations, they joined the ranks of the underpaid, and often unemployed, urban poor. By relocating, families created the circumstances that brought their children to the attention of state and local welfare agencies, which removed them from their homes for any number of reasons—neglect, truancy, delinquency—but the true culprit was poverty. By this time in the early 1900s, Minnesota's social welfare system had a national reputation as being on the cutting edge. The state made its mark in the 1860s by establishing the House of Refuge (a reformatory) just eighteen years after the leader in child rescue, Massachusetts, established one. From that time on, Minnesota enjoyed a reputation for innovative child care and child protection strategies. It was ahead of most states in adapting to new thinking and trends. Perhaps it was for this reason that social workers reacted as they did. In numerous cases, Indian children removed from their urban households were not placed in state homes or private orphanages. Rather, they were returned to White Earth Reservation and placed in the care of the sisters at St. Benedict's. The youngsters were separated from their families, but not from a tribal environment.[35]

Holy Rosary Mission, founded in 1887, was similar to St. Benedict's in several respects, but it was not officially labeled as a Catholic orphanage for Indian children. Rather, it was a mission school. The mission was founded through the efforts of the Reverend Martin Marty, who arrived in Dakota Territory in 1876 after the Catholic Church, through Grant's Peace Policy, was allowed to open missions at Standing Rock and Devils Lake. It was Marty's task to establish more. The opportunity came in 1881, when the federal government suspended its policy of one missionary group per reservation and when Congress granted Catholics access to Pine Ridge Reservation in 1884. Marty was following in the steps of Pierre-Jean De Smet, who pioneered Catholic missionary work among tribes in Illinois and Missouri and then made contact with the Sioux in 1839. De Smet encountered a number of Sioux chiefs, including Struck by the Ree, who implored the missionary for more priests to come among them, preach, and educate the children.[36]

For the school on the Pine Ridge Reservation, Marty asked Jesuits to accept the work as managers and Franciscan Sisters to manage the school's domestic operations and oversee the anticipated female population. Father John Jutz arrived on the Pine Ridge Reservation late in 1885 and chose a desirable site for the school on White Clay Creek. Constructed with $40,000 given by Katharine Drexel, the building could accommodate 200 students. The mission, which became a contract school with federal funds for operational support, opened with 72 students. In March 1890, ten months before Wounded Knee, Father Jutz reported 140 students. There was a wide fluctuation in monthly attendance, however, reducing the yearly average to 128; it was not until 1904 that attendance reached an average of 200. School officials found it difficult to hold students. "Many inducements were employed to attract them to the Government schools," said the Jesuits. In actuality, the situation was more complicated and came to a head in 1896 when the acting Indian agent ruled that the mission could not enroll more students than those stipulated in its contract—unless a student was unable to attend a government day school. Commissioner of Indian Affairs Daniel M. Browning supported the agent. Browning believed that the agent had a duty to build up government day schools; parents did not have the right to decide which school—government or mission—their children could attend. Catholic officials on a national and local level fought the ruling. Holy Rosary officials pressed their view: "The average attendance shows that the pupils did not change often and therefore must have felt at home at the Mission. . . . the Holy Rosary Mission School has been very successful in its work of educating Indian children entrusted to its care, a fact which at all times has been readily acknowledged by all fair-minded visitors and inspectors of the school."[37]

As in other Indian schools, as well as Indian orphanages, Holy Rosary instruction included the vocational and agricultural. Shops and a sawmill provided carpentry training. One of the Sisters, described as "an artist in every kind of needlework," took the girls in tow to teach the domestic arts of sewing, embroidery, and crochet. Girls worked in the kitchen and laundry, and both boys and girls had outside chores. Thirty acres of farm and gardens were planted in potatoes, turnips, corn, oats, and various vegetables. Hogs, sheep, beef cattle, and milk cows were looked after by the students. Isabel Gap Gyongossy, who was not an orphan, remembered her days at Holy Rosary during the 1920s. She recalled the physical work and school assignments, and in looking back she was thankful that the priest and Sisters were "hard" on students. It better prepared her for the future. Not all, of course, felt this way. "Some," said Isabel, "are very bitter."[38]

Religious training was stressed, and the "common branches" of school subjects were taught—in English. The question of language was not usually a point of contention for the families sending their children to the mission. They wanted their offspring to learn English in order to better deal with whites. As Gyongossy recalled, her grandfather wanted her to attend the mission in order to read and write English and learn how to "walk with the people." The price, as far as her grandfather was concerned, was not a loss of traditional life. One could learn about the white world but keep to the old ways. In their own way, intended or not, the Catholic missionaries helped support this view. Without question, education aimed at acculturation, but contradictory to that were segregationist tactics employed by mission officials who believed it was necessary to shield Indians from whites. It was little wonder that missionaries at Holy Rosary, and at other mission schools, referred to students and church parishioners as "our" Indians and saw their role as preparing youngsters to take their place within Sioux neighborhoods. Said one Holy Rosary cleric: "It has been the constant endeavor of the school authorities and all those who assisted them so to develop the head, heart and hand of the Indian child to make it a good, useful and happy member of the community in which it was destined to spend its life." It was not until the mid–twentieth century that the mission modified this position and began to take in children with the express intent of finding adoptive parents who might or might not be part of the nearby community.[39]

Certainly after Wounded Knee, orphaned children were residents and students at Holy Rosary, and the mission continued to take in orphaned and non-orphaned alike. It was not until 1893, however, that a mission school in the Dakotas was considered to be an orphanage, as well as a school. The orphan school, St. Andrew's, opened near the Sisseton Agency in South Dakota after Martin Marty, by then the bishop of Dakota Territory, traveled through the southern sections of the territory making plans for schools and churches. The Sisseton and Wahpeton Sioux accepted, even welcomed, the Catholics, and the two groups implored Marty to send a priest to them. Marty could not oblige. Priests were unavailable to the Indians because the church was building up its parishes for white settlers. Nevertheless, Bishop Marty attempted to make some gesture of good intent and to add a Catholic presence. He encouraged an Ursuline nun, Sister Aloysia Deering, to open a school at the Sisseton Agency.[40]

Sister Aloysia, referred to in one Catholic history as a "free-lance Ursuline," operated a private school in East Grand Forks, North Dakota, before being contacted by the bishop. Without any other assignments or prospects, she accepted his invitation to go to Sisseton. In 1893 she opened St. Andrew's Mission School, about two miles from the Sisseton Agency. At a time when the Bureau of Catholic Indian Missions was finding it difficult to keep what school contracts it had, there was no possibility of St. Andrew's Mission receiving a contract and federal stipends. Support for the mission school fell to Sister Aloysia, which in itself is not surprising. Missions were supposed to be largely self-supporting, and nuns were expected to accomplish this through their own creativity. To that end, Sister Aloysia persuaded Benedictine Sisters teaching in Webster to file for homesteads, prove them up, and then donate the land or money from land sales to St. Andrew's. The plan, however, did not reap the expected benefits, and no community of Sisters from a religious order joined the Ursuline nun at Sisseton. Occasionally, Sisters from Sacred Heart Convent at Yankton assisted, but for daily operations Sister Aloysia had only herself and two or three laywomen. Following the pattern of other mission schools, St. Andrew's took in both orphans and non-orphans, but at this mission orphans were by far the majority. Within one year of opening, there were twelve non-orphans and forty orphans at the mission. The number of orphans led many to refer to the mission as St. Andrew's Orphanage.[41]

The beginning of St. Andrew's is fairly well documented, but its end is obscured in generalities. One history states that the school closed in 1910 when government contracts were no longer awarded to mission schools. Since St. Andrew's never received contracts, this obviously was not the reason for closure. Another historical overview simply notes that the place was short-lived, but it fails to provide a closing date. In truth, St. Andrew's Mission School closed under a dark cloud of public accusations and complaints from local Catholic parishioners—both Indian and white. Without a stable source of financial support and without an adequate number of personnel, St. Andrew's good intentions fell short, and the place was doomed to represent the "bad" orphanage. In 1902 the *South Dakota Farmer*, a well-known regional newspaper, announced that Sister Aloysia had been arrested for inhumane treatment of children at the mission. When white authorities visited the mission, they found that the children were "ragged and dirty and their bodies were emaciated from lack of food." The few parents who paid for their children to live at the mission and to receive an education were outraged. The largest measure of rage, however, rested on the fact that the orphaned, from infants to adolescents, were under the care of a nun who violated their trust.[42]

Some credited the nun for placing a number of orphaned children with Indian families and, therefore, following a type of foster care practice that was common in other Catholic orphanages and charities such as the New York Foundling Hospital. On the other hand, placements were suspect. Had the children been placed out because the Sister believed home life was best and had benevolent feelings for the children's welfare? Or had they been placed simply to ease the burden of their upkeep at St. Andrew's? The answer was never clear, and whatever her motives, conditions at St. Andrew's could not be excused. The mission closed, and Sister Aloysia left Sisseton; if, in fact, she was arrested as the newspaper reported, she was not incarcerated. It was not until the late 1930s that another orphan home appeared at Sisseton—the Tekakwitha Orphanage.[43]

Wounded Knee orphaned children through quick, irretractable violence. The youngsters at Tekakwitha Orphanage were victims of another scourge. The years of the Great Depression, with its natural disasters and reeling national economy, left families and children destitute and starving. Not all the deprivations could be laid at the feet of drought and hard times nationwide, however. The Dawes Act and its 160-acre allotments, as well as reluctance to encourage stock raising rather than crop production, came back to take its toll. One government report accurately noted that allotment acreage was "pathetically inadequate to support a family." Neither white nor Indian could survive on such small parcels, and Indians were at a greater disadvantage because they could not afford to upgrade equipment, buy seed, or feed stock. Federal relief came primarily from distribution of food and supplies, including livestock from the federal government's cattle-purchase program that paid stock raisers, the majority of whom were white, for their cattle. Many individuals, however, had no land to fall back on for any kind of sustenance. Allotments were leased and brought little in return, and in numerous localities, including Sisseton, all land once available for allotment was gone. The Sissetons and Wahpetons would become, said the agent, impoverished "wanderers" with no land to tie or sustain them.[44]

Indians trained in vocational trades fared little better. Vocational education was touted by the Indian Bureau and education reformers, but the depression played a cruel trick on those who prepared to be mechanics, carpenters, or metalworkers. Although the government initiated the Emergency Conservation Work program, usually called the Civilian Conservation Corps–Indian Division, which employed over fourteen thousand nationally and hired Indian workers for public improvement programs on reservations, the picture of vocational employment was muddied. Thomas Biolsi's work on the New Deal's impact on the Pine Ridge and Rosebud Reservations demonstrates that although a large percentage of men were employed through CCC relief programs, available funds allowed employment for less than half of those who needed it. This left the option of seeking vocational trade work off-reservation. Away from the reservation, however, Indians encountered a situation that a member of the Prairie Band Potawatomie described straightforwardly: "If they ran out of workers, then they'd take an Indian. Usually you were the last hired and the first laid off." Even when work could be found, it did not necessarily pay a living wage. Recalled Raymond Sundown who learned barbering at Thomas Indian School: "At that time a shave was 25 cents and a haircut was 35 cents. Out of a dollar I earned 40 cents. That's what I made a living on. I decided I had to leave barbering. . . . I just could not make a living cutting hair because people didn't have the money for haircuts." In 1940, when national recovery was making progress, 33 percent of all Indian males off-reservation were unemployed. Additionally, many never left reservations, knowing what awaited them. Among the Sioux, about 40 percent of all high school graduates stayed home—unemployed.[45]

Tekakwitha at Sisseton opened to address the immediate needs of Sioux families directly affected by the Great Depression. The orphanage took its name from Kateri Tekakwitha, a Mohawk who was beatified by the Catholic Church three hundred years after her death. The decision to use this name was fitting. Kateri Tekakwitha was a devout Indian convert to Catholicism who experienced the personal loss of family at an early age. Tekakwitha's parents and siblings died in a smallpox epidemic, and Kateri was left to be raised in the household of an uncle. The orphanage bearing her name was intended for youngsters who were bereft of parents, but most who arrived at Tekakwitha Orphanage were not true orphans. They were casualties of the economic climate of the 1930s, which only worsened the already bad conditions experienced by the Sioux. Said one account of Tekakwitha: "Due to the extreme poverty of many Native Americans, parents could not afford a balanced diet, proper clothing for their children, much less a religious and secular education." Chronic poverty and illness, combined with alcoholism and an overwhelming sense of hopelessness, also produced what one writer delicately referred to as "irregular marital conditions." Without cohesive family bonds, temporary living arrangements and spousal abandonment "left many homeless waifs."[46]

The orphanage, established by Father John Pohlen, opened in 1937 in an old house moved from the town of Sisseton and placed across the road from the site of the former St. Andrew's. There were plans to construct a building that would accommodate fifty children, but until the new orphan home opened in August 1938, the old house had to do. Sisters of the Divine Savior, who were already in charge of a small hospital opened by Father Pohlen, agreed to take responsibility for the orphanage, too, but during the interim between the orphanage's opening in 1937 and completion of the new building in 1938, three Indian women were employed to look after the first children to arrive.[47]

Tekakwitha was unlike other Indian orphanages in that it did not immediately have its own school. Youngsters of school age were transported by bus to Sisseton, where they attended St. Peter's School. This proved to be a temporary arrangement. Quite simply put, the white parishioners who sent their children to St. Peter's School did

Sister Kathryn DeMarrais (Sister Irene) teaching at Tekakwitha Orphanage, Sisseton, South Dakota, 1955. SDS-W Archives, Milwaukee.

not want white and Indian children in the same classrooms. Mingling "retarded" Caucasian children. To keep the white parishioners happy and to school the Indian children, Father Pohlen found another old building, in this case a country schoolhouse, and moved it to the grounds of Tekakwitha. When the school opened in 1941, only first and second graders attended, under the direction of Sister Irene De-Marrais, an enrolled member of the Sisseton-Wahpeton Sioux on the Lake Traverse Reservation. The next year, 1942, Indian attendance at St. Peter's ended, and in 1943 a new school building was completed at Tekakwitha. During the 1940s and 1950s, new additions made the orphanage "a completely self-contained unit" with classrooms, dormitories, a gymnasium, and chapel. Growth had been a matter of necessity, since the number of residents increased and resistance to

Indian youngsters at St. Peter's continued until the 1960s, when a shortage of teaching nuns forced the issue of accepted integration.[48]

After the school at Tekakwitha closed, the orphanage name was dropped in favor of Tekakwitha Children's Home, and for another twenty years it remained open. From its beginning, the population was a mix of orphaned and non-orphaned children. A few youngsters had parents who paid a small fee for board and education. Some residents were true orphans or half-orphans, and some were estranged from their families. Accounts of Tekakwitha state that some children were abandoned by parents or relatives. One has to wonder, however, if they were truly abandoned by irresponsible and uncaring adults or if "abandoned" meant that families placed youngsters into the care of the Sisters at Tekakwitha because there the children would have the food, shelter, and education that parents were unable to provide. For the majority of those whose lives included a stay at Tekakwitha, the most common denominator was poverty.

Another Indian orphanage to appear out of the great want of the 1930s was Father Sylvester Eisenman's St. Placid Home for Infants near Marty, South Dakota. Beginning in 1933, the St. Placid Home took in the orphaned child and the sick.

> Our family at Marty was at the supper table. My uncle Father Sylvester came over and asked: "Mary Elizabeth, can you help me for a little while?" . . . we drove northwest several miles past the town of Lake Andes. There we searched through a field of dried corn for an opening and a tiny unpainted frame dwelling. . . . Father Sylvester went inside for a few minutes and came out with a bundle of life entrusted to him. . . . Less than a year old, the little boy had survived solely on dried corn.[49]

The child's condition was not a product of parental neglect. It was an immediate result of the drought and heat that made it next to impossible to raise crops or keep livestock during the years of the Great Depression. In 1931, record-breaking temperatures in South Dakota scorched the earth, and a plague of grasshoppers devoured crops. By 1932, approximately fourteen hundred Yankton Sioux were destitute, and low market prices for crops reduced families' abilities to feed themselves or their livestock. Winters were more bitter when there was no money to buy fuel. "The extreme poverty of our Indians," wrote Father

Eisenman, "is almost unbelievable. Grasshoppers and hot winds have played havoc with the fields and gardens." The priest pleaded for more federal aid while he set up soup kitchens and attempted to find a private benefactor who would hear his cry for a hospital.[50]

Just as at Sisseton, no nearby medical facilities served the Indian community, with predictable results. Cases of tuberculosis went untreated—and undiagnosed. Minor infections and viruses became serious, complicated by poverty and malnutrition, which lowered resistance and made recovery difficult. Injuries went untreated. A local hospital was an urgent necessity. The priest and others at the mission for the Yankton Sioux underscored the need for such a facility by recording instance after instance of suffering made more horrifying by the lack of health care.

An Indian named Benjamin Franklin dies in his shack today. . . . Next to him lay the emaciated form of his stepdaughter, Sophie Standing Bear, in the advanced stage of tuberculosis. . . . Milly Ghost Bear, a full-blood Indian woman from the Rosebud country, lies sick with TB. . . . [She] asks a kind neighbor to take care of her only child, and then passes away. . . . Just came from the two-room Little Owl hut where Eunice Thunder Horse and her baby are dying from TB. Such misery, it just hurts a person down to one's stomach to witness it.[51]

Father Eisenman's hoped-for hospital did not materialize until 1937, but during the period of waiting and lobbying the priest acted to save what children he could with the St. Placid Home for Infants. It was envisioned as a place where infants and school-age children would receive medical care and where youngsters might recuperate from infectious diseases without infecting their classmates attending the mission's day school. The home opened in 1933 in a large farmhouse, but there was not enough space to accommodate the number of children who were candidates for admittance. As a result, the home first focused on treating the very young and providing a refuge for "the homeless." In 1936, for example, there were twelve children in the home, all under the age of five. Cribs and clothing were donated by charities and individuals, and an experienced nurse was persuaded to head a small staff of helpers recruited by Father Eisenman. As one of those helpers recalled, "I had just graduated from Mount Mary Academy, Yankton. . . . 'Could you

Helpers hold two of their charges at the St. Placid Home for Infants, South Dakota, ca. 1940. Marquette University Archives.

come help at St. Placid till I find a girl?' Father asked. I went back with them that same night. I remember next day a tiny bundle brought in. . . . We loved those babies."[52]

Some children were true orphans, but most came from impoverished families or had only one living parent. Among the latter was the three-year-old great-great-granddaughter of Struck by the Ree, who in the mid-1800s sought a Catholic mission for the Yankton Sioux. The girl came to the home when her mother was taken to a tuberculosis sanitarium. For Father Eisenman, there was symbolic symmetry in the girl's arrival. Her great-great-grandfather's insistence on a Catholic presence among his people proved a saving force for this child relative. Also arriving at the home was the infant son of John Two Sticks, who placed the boy into Eisenman's hands when he was unable to care for the child alone. Making the eight-day trip from "the Pine Ridge country," and sometimes caught in blizzard conditions, the father visited his son as often as possible. The grueling trips were worth it, said the priest, "when you see his affection for his little Joseph . . . [who] nestles contentedly on his daddy's lap."[53]

Before St. Placid was founded, youngsters in Father Eisenman's mission area were placed in Catholic orphanages that were not just for Indians. When, for example, a woman died leaving seven children, the baby boy went to a Catholic orphanage in Sioux City, where he died soon after. "The poor little one was not able to survive the loss of its mother." Of the remaining children, two went to St. Theresa's orphanage in Turton, South Dakota, and four made the mission school at Marty their home.[54]

Tekakwitha and St. Placid, which closed in 1947, were responses to localized effects of the Great Depression. Nationally, the problems of child care were so significant that by 1939 an estimated eight million children of all backgrounds were part of families receiving some kind of economic aid. During the course of the depression, the number may have varied up or down by several million. Single parents and families in crisis who relied on the long tradition of placing their children in orphanages during hard times more often than not found this option closed. As a result, a glaring minority of orphanage residents, estimated at only about 10 percent, were true orphans. Overwhelmed by the numbers seeking admittance, orphan asylums simply refused to take more children. As a last resort, parents and local communities committed children to state industrial schools or juvenile reformatories— not because the youngsters were delinquent but because this shifted the cost of maintenance to the state. Indian families sought out boarding schools, but during the 1930s the commissioner of Indian affairs, John Collier, closed many of these. When boarding schools became unavailable, Indian families and relatives followed white practice and placed their youngsters in state facilities. It was a custom that continued long after the depression ended. Said a report based on figures from the 1950s: "The unduly high proportion of Indian youngsters in the state training schools may be due partly to the fact that they provide better shelter, food and education than can the average Indian home."[55]

Given the circumstances that surrounded child protection during the 1930s, the appearance of new Catholic orphanages is rather astounding. The Catholics increased rather than reduced the number of child care institutions. For the Sioux, there was not a church or diocese mandate to build orphanages. In fact, the Catholic diocese in South Dakota was still working to establish a Catholic Charities program and a Family Service Agency in the 1950s. The orphanages created for Sioux children appeared only through the work of individual priests, nuns, or religious orders. They came into being because immediate circumstances cried out for help that neither federal nor state authorities could, or would, provide.[56]

Orphanages among the Sioux contradicted national trends for insti-tution building. When orphanages proliferated nationally during the last decades of the 1800s, they were almost nonexistent among the Sioux. Then, during the 1930s, when orphanages either closed their doors or refused to expand in the face of demand, new orphan homes opened on Sioux reservations. These did, however, reflect one general aspect of all types of orphanages. Most orphan asylums housed small numbers, with the median at eighty or fewer residents, rather than large populations of two hundred or more. For the Sioux orphanages, or for that matter St. Benedict's on the White Earth Reservation, it is doubtful that administrators intentionally restricted the population out of a sense of current social welfare policies. Presumably the insti-tutions would have reached out to more youngsters if economics and too few staff had not hindered efforts. They fit Sister Blandina Segale's description of the mission work in Santa Fe: "poorest of the poor, and working among the poor."

EPILOGUE: FINAL TRANSITION

My mother died of tuberculosis when I was a baby about five or six
months old. My grandmother brought us up until I was old enough to
go down to the Thomas Indian School.[1]

By the early twentieth century, Indian orphanages were established,
and accepted, institutions within tribal communities. So, too, was the
word "orphan," in both its legal definition of a parentless child and its
vernacular implications of a child whose circumstances were so impoverished that he or she was to all intents and purposes no different
from an orphan. Orphanages attended to the basic needs of youngsters
and provided an education to those placed into institutional care.
More often than not, native groups most familiar with these orphan
homes regarded them primarily as places of learning, and relatives
often sought out orphan homes for dependent children, believing that
they offered shelter and education unavailable to a child who remained in the larger community.

Generally, white culture regarded all orphan asylums as an acceptable way for society to deal with orphaned and/or destitute children.
Food, shelter, and an education were provided to the "luckless" child.
Orphanages were a mainstay of child rescue in America for over a century, and popular culture's image of the orphan was often more sentimental than authentic. In the real world of orphanages, some were
inclusive, taking in children of all ethnic, religious, and racial backgrounds. There were also orphanages for specific groups within the
population—Jewish children, Catholic children, German-speaking
children, those of African ancestry. In both inclusive and restricted institutions, Indian children sometimes could be found. From time to
time, the New England Home for Little Wanderers and New York's
Graham Home counted Indian youngsters among their charges, and
the first orphan to enter the St. Vincent Orphanage in Santa Fe was a
Navajo, not part of the Hispanic community the orphanage intended

to serve. Despite the presence of Indian orphans in non-Indian orphanages, the larger orphaned and destitute populations were housed in orphanages designed to care for Indians only. If the dominant culture noticed Indian orphanages at all, it did not question their presence. Within the larger scheme of things, Indian orphanages simply limited their services to an identifiable group. These orphanages were just one type of institution on the charitable, social welfare landscape.

Nevertheless, orphanages for Indian children and teenagers were visual reminders of Euro-America's attempt to eradicate Indian culture, if not the Indian. These orphanages came at a heavy price. They appeared only after severe circumstances altered traditional values and kinship systems to the point that the orphan asylum became a viable mechanism for providing child nurture and education. The American Civil War, the reservation system and allotment, direct military conflict, and the Great Depression all contributed to the American Indian's "discovery of the asylum." These were the large events that altered native culture and diminished traditional patterns of child care. Far more difficult to identify were the precise points in time that a native society was overwhelmed by the cumulative effects of war, disease, starvation, relocation, removal, ill-conceived federal policies, and missionary influence. The Senecas, for example, were already struggling with drastically altered lifestyles demanded by the reservation system when the American Civil War dealt another blow, and the Sioux were in dire straits long before the Great Depression. The weight of successive strikes to traditional beliefs and customs and gender-specific roles and responsibilities debilitated rather than exterminated.

Although orphanages were a product of Euro-American culture and emerged from events that placed native culture under siege, both the Indian communities in which these orphanages operated and many of the orphan homes' non-Indian administrators viewed the institutions as a shield against total encroachment by white society, a last bastion. Many non-Indian orphan homes were regarded in the same way by their administrators and financial contributors: the homes protected residents from the larger world. Still, Indian orphanages were expected to perform the task of preparing youngsters to live in a culture that was dominated by white values and beliefs. Each Indian orphanage dealt with this duality of protection and acculturation in its own way. Some were more focused on assimilation and acculturation than others, and changes in administration and economic fortunes determined the extent, and arguably the impact, of programs.

Indian orphanages exhibited many of the same traits identified with non-Indian orphanages, and they were often comparable to Indian boarding schools. Although the Indian boarding school was categorized as an institution of learning and the Indian orphanage as one of charity, they shared certain characteristics that most often hinged on the expected outcome of programs that intended to instill belief systems of the white dominant culture. A parting of the ways was evident, however, in those orphanages that were not taken over by the Indian Bureau and operated as if they were nothing more, or less, than another Indian boarding school. Those outside the purview of the federal government did not always have the funds to do more than provide basic common school education. On the other hand, some non-bureau-run orphanages had enough funds and staff to allow them to borrow, if they wished, from progressive movements such as the recreation and kindergarten programs and cottage housing. Schools operated by the Indian Bureau enacted changes only when directed to do so by bureau officials in Washington, D.C., and generally lagged behind when adopting new ideas or education models.

If the Indian Bureau, as well as past and present-day historians of Indian education, regarded orphanages and boarding schools as one and the same, it was because basic educational programs were so similar. Lines between the two also blurred when a small portion of youngsters moved from one to the other because family circumstances made it necessary, because the Indian Bureau entered the picture, or because some residents of Indian orphanages "graduated" to Indian boarding schools. Since they demonstrated similarities and sometimes shared populations, there was often very little that separated the boarding school from the orphanage in operational procedures.

Indian orphanages were not static, nor were they immune to changes in social welfare philosophy. They were as subject to the winds of change as orphanages that served other groups. When nationally accepted social welfare and charity policies began to alter in the early twentieth century, orphanages as an American institution came to face their own transitional moment. They began to fall out of favor with social work professionals, experts in child development, educators, and a growing cross section of the American population. Over a period of time, orphanages were assigned a negative label, and their numbers declined. For Indian groups, the demise of orphanages directly corresponded to the rise in placement of Indian children in foster care and adoptive homes. Thus, the stage was set for Indian rebellion against a system that engaged in wholesale removal of children from their tribal communities. It was this moment that led to demands for passage of the Indian Child Welfare Act, and the 1950s provided the backdrop for this transition, which can best be characterized as a period that witnessed a decided shift away from orphanages.

Few Indian orphanages still operated in the 1950s, and all but Murrow Indian Orphanage, Goodland Presbyterian Children's Home, the Oklahoma state-run home, and Tekakwitha Indian Mission disappeared by 1959. Holy Rosary Mission, for example, became Red Cloud Indian School, and Wheelock survived until 1955, when the federal government was in the process of divesting itself of Indian programs. Decline in the number of Indian orphanages was not a peculiar set of circumstances. It reflected a national trend. Orphanages, once hailed as the enlightened approach to child rescue, were no longer considered the best option by the mid-1900s. There were general rumblings as early as the 1920s, when some social work professionals aggressively questioned the role of orphanages and their place in the modern world. Dr. Rex Rudolph Reeder, a well-known leader in child welfare and superintendent of the Orphan Asylum Society of New York, was convinced that only a minority of children truly required institutional care. Other social work professionals took the point further by suggesting that incarcerating minors for some crimes was counterproductive to rehabilitation. A growing number of charitable institutions' directors agreed that institutions were outmoded, and services gradually began to reflect this outlook. The New England Home for Little Wanderers, for example, began as a charity that served youngsters with every imaginable problem, but by the mid-1900s its focus narrowed to the child and adolescent with emotional problems and learning disabilities. Among the Indian institutions, Tekakwitha altered its approach late in the twentieth century when it reopened in 1988 as the Tekakwitha Adolescent Treatment Facility for youngsters with problems of drug and/or alcohol dependency.[2]

Many of the most visible and articulate progressive reformers of the early 1900s, such as Grace Abbott and Homer Folks, believed that concern for children was purely humanitarian. When children needed help, they got it. People like Abbott and Folks failed to see or acknowledge that social welfare policies were dictated by urban-based, white middle-class professionals—like themselves—who defined what was in a child's "best interest." Of course, Reeder and those who shared his views were among this same group, and they found the work of orphanages lacking. They laid the groundwork for reconfiguring orphanages that remained operational and for the ultimate move away from institutional care. In the growing clamor to abandon the orphanage as a form of child rescue, numerous institutions and their administrators were distressed to find themselves faced with the prospect of being considered out-of-date and uninformed if they persisted in supporting orphanages. The Hebrew Orphan Asylum, as illustration, met the problem by taking small steps toward dismantling the institution. The asylum compromised by first removing some of its charges from the orphanage and boarding them out in urban homes. Other institutions, particularly those for specifically defined ethnic or racial groups, demonstrated equal reluctance to totally abandon the idea of the orphanage. Directors argued that their institutions were the children's only hope.[3] The Hebrew Orphan Asylum's dilemma was indicative of the slow shift in social welfare thought that was helped along by the Great Depression, when orphan homes could not support the number who sought admittance or when these homes closed for lack of financial support.

Even as these discussions and changes took place, child populations in orphanages continued to grow, but the trend began to reverse by the mid-1900s. Slowly, institutionalization was replaced by a social welfare policy that made "home" its rallying cry. At first glance, it would seem that this move to home care was the result of aid-to-mothers programs, early-twentieth-century mandates to work with and rehabilitate families, and the Aid to Dependent Children program that came out of the Social Security Act of 1935. Too often this was not the case. Home most often meant somewhere other than a child's family home. For many who fell into the network of social welfare programs, foster care and, less often, adoption became the progressive response to creating a home life for children, no matter their ethnic or racial backgrounds.

In the 1940s and 1950s, foster care for all children replaced orphanage placements at a steady pace. Much of this change could be laid at the feet of new concerns among social work professionals, who questioned institutional care and its long-term effects on the emotional and social development of children. Reeder, echoing the concerns expressed by a minority of child rescue workers of the nineteenth century, including Charles Loring Brace, was adamant that no orphan asylum was "a real childhood home." This remained an argument for moving away from the orphanage in favor of home placement. The argument for home was, in fact, a component of the Meriam Report's discussion on Indian education in boarding schools. "Education and social work lays stress on upbringing in the natural setting of home and family life," wrote W. Carson Ryan Jr., the educator responsible for the report's education section. Should not, asked the report, Indian education be community centered, with youngsters allowed to live at home for their schooling? As this portion of the Meriam Report suggested, the push for home reached into multiple permutations of institutional life, not just orphanage versus foster care.[4]

Indian communities that once included an orphanage had little voice when closures came. They were forced to accept foster care, as well as adoption, when home care began to dominate the social service policy. Foster care was an idea whose time fully arrived by the late 1950s, and a number of factors prompted a dramatic rise during the 1960s and 1970s. One was a public awakening to child abuse. In the early 1900s, reformers and federal agencies such as the U.S. Children's Bureau worked to correct abuse of child laborers in terms of the long hours demanded, the dangerous work, and no promises of schooling. At the same time, a few bold reformers tackled the taboo subject of sexual abuse, although studies were limited to the lower classes and immigrants (primarily in urban settings), and findings went unnoticed by the general public. It was not until the early 1960s that the subject of child abuse, specifically physical abuse, received significant attention from the American public. The catalyst was a medical journal article entitled "The Battered-Child Syndrome." The response was a loud outcry that failed to differentiate abuse from neglect, which, in itself, was difficult to define because poverty was too often a mitigating factor. Nevertheless, charges of abuse and neglect brought more social workers into domestic settings, and the inclination to use foster care rather than orphanages was substantially supported when the federal government increased funding for foster care. Correspondingly, institutional care dropped. In 1951, institutionalization accounted for 43 percent of the children and teenagers outside the homes of family or relatives; by 1962, just over ten years later, the number was at 31 percent.[5] Orphanages declined as social welfare strategies adopted a belief in home care as the most acceptable form of child protection, responded to the newfound social ill of abuse, and accepted federal moneys that paid for one form of child care but not another.

In the years after World War II, reduced numbers of orphanages and changes in social welfare policies made it more probable that orphaned and/or destitute Indian children would be placed in foster care or adopted by non-Indian families. The possibility, if not probability, increased when the federal government chose to play a role. During the twentieth century, the federal government continued to argue that it was, in effect, the guardian of native peoples. Nevertheless, in a number of ways it abrogated guardianship of orphaned and destitute children long before termination policies severed Indian-federal relationships in the 1950s. With the exception of the two Oklahoma orphanages turned into federal boarding schools, the Bureau of Indian Affairs recognized, and accepted, that the State of New York maintained a facility for Indian children under its state welfare department and that Indian orphanages operated by religious groups interacted with state welfare agencies. Although these were not large-scale arrangements, except in New York, welfare workers in the first half of the twentieth century identified Indian children and teenagers who were candidates for an orphan home and placed them accordingly.

Events in Indian-federal relations during the 1950s served to heighten the involvement of social agencies in Indian lives. The federal government's termination policy influenced the future of child protection and rescue on and off reservations. Termination shifted the balance of services to the states, and state welfare agencies were allowed to take a broader step toward dispensing social services and deciding when children should be removed from their biological families and placed under state guardianship. Wrote historian Francis Paul Prucha: "The involuntary separation of children from their parents that had marked the old boarding school experience was being continued now by child custody proceedings." The Bureau of Indian Affairs also played a role by participating in the Indian Adoption Project of the 1950s and seeking to increase the number of its own bureau-employed social workers with summer internships for prospective social workers and with the Government Training Act of 1958, which encouraged professional training for bureau staff. The door opened even wider when termination was coupled with the federal relocation plan that lured American Indians, including the Sioux, to urban centers with the prospect of employment. Since the government never adequately evaluated the success of this program, it is impossible to know how many of the relocated failed and became names and numbers on case files overseen by social workers. It is impossible to know how many children were removed from urban families because of poverty.[6]

Indian orphanages, by their location on reservations, offered a way for youngsters to maintain contact with their tribal groups. Orphanages provided a point of identity for both residents and the larger Indian community. As Indian orphanages closed, however, there were fewer options that promised to keep children among their own people. Whether or not it was understood, these orphanages came to serve a purpose that went beyond children surviving the terrors of an uncertain childhood or learning a skill for their future livelihood. Indian orphanages were born out of circumstances that had all the makings of cultural genocide, but orphanages, unlike off-reservation boarding schools and non-Indian orphanages, also provided a way to keep youngsters near their home areas, no matter how much those may have changed in the face of outside influences. Termination and the decline in national interest to support orphanages were the last transitional changes on the tortuous road that began with orphanages as a response to cultural disintegration and ended with creation of the Indian Child Welfare Act as a way for a people to reclaim their children.

NOTES

INTRODUCTION: ROOTS OF PROTEST

1. "Minutes of the Meeting of the New Mexico Commission on Indian Affairs, May 11, 1959," 23, box 222, New Mexico—Welfare no. 2, White House Conference on Children and Youth: Records, 1930–70, Dwight D. Eisenhower Presidential Library, Abilene, Kans. (hereinafter cited as White House Conference, DDE Library).

2. Michael Paul Rogin, *Fathers and Children: Andrew Jackson and the Subjugation of the American Indian* (New York: Alfred A. Knopf, 1975), 189; Peggy Eaton, *The Autobiography of Peggy Eaton* (New York: Charles Scribner's Sons, 1932), 167; Renee Sansom Flood, *Lost Bird of Wounded Knee: Spirit of the Lakota* (New York: Scribner, 1995; reprint, New York: Da Capo Press, 1998), 70.

3. Frank Dekker Watson, *The Charity Organization Movement in the United States: A Study in American Philanthropy* (New York: Macmillan, 1922), 174, 416–17; Walter I. Trattner, *From Poor Law to Welfare State: A History of Social Welfare in America* (New York: Free Press, 1974), 180–81; Percy G. Kammerer, "The Relation of the Church to Social Work," *The Family* 8 (June 1927): 120–22; Richard C. Cabot, "The Inter-relation of Social Work and Spiritual Life," *The Family* 8 (November 1927): 211–17; Dr. B. S. Winchester, "Spiritual Factors in Family Life," *The Family* 8 (December 1927): 279–81; Marilyn Irvin Holt, *The Orphan Trains: Placing Out in America* (Lincoln: University of Nebraska Press, 1992), 169, 175–76.

4. Elizabeth Pleck, *Domestic Tyranny: The Making of Social Policy Against Family Violence from Colonial Times to the Present* (New York: Oxford University Press, 1987), 79, 131; Sanford N. Katz, *When Parents Fail: The Law's Response to Family Breakdown* (Boston: Beacon Press, 1971), 52–53, 57, 62.

5. William Byler, "The Destruction of American Indian Families," in *The Destruction of American Indian Families,* ed. Steven Unger (New York: Association on American Indian Affairs, 1977), 1–2; Evelyn Lance Blanchard and Russell Lawrence Barsh, "What Is Best for Tribal Children? A Response to Fischler," *Social Work* 25 (1980): 354; Marc Mannes, "Factors and Events Leading to the Passage of the Indian Child Welfare Act," *Child Welfare* 74 (1995): 265, 267; Marc Mannes, "Seeking the Balance Between Child Protection and Family Preservation in Indian Child Welfare," *Child Welfare* 72 (1993): 141–42, 44; Sharon O'Brien, *American Indian Tribal Governments* (Norman: Uni-

versity of Oklahoma Press, 1989), 89; "South Dakota Report to 1960 White House Conference on Children and Youth," 13, pamphlet, box 106, South Dakota—State Reports file, White House Conference, DDE Library. Social Service Case Files, Sisseton Indian Agency, Record Group 75, National Archives and Records Administration—Central Plains Region (hereinafter cited as Sisseton, NA, Central Plains) are restricted, but case files do reflect monitoring on and off the reservation.

6. Patricia M. Collmeyer, "From 'Operation Brown Baby' to 'Opportunity': The Placement of Children of Color at the Boys and Girls Aid Society of Oregon (1944–1977)," *Child Welfare* 74 (1995): 242, 255; Ronald S. Fischler, "Protecting American Indian Children," *Social Work* 25 (September 1980): 341.

7. Stephanie Coontz, *The Way We Never Were: American Families and the Nostalgia Trap* (New York: Basic Books, 1992), 38–39; Clark E. Vincent, "Unwed Mothers and the Adoption Market: Part 1—Psychological and Familial Factors," 2–3, typescript, box 197, Individual Authors file, White House Conference, DDE Library.

8. Mario Gonzalez and Elizabeth Cook-Lynn, *The Politics of Hallowed Ground: Wounded Knee and the Struggle for Indian Sovereignty* (Urbana: University of Illinois Press, 1999), xiii, 379; Heinrich Kreiger, "Principles of the Indian Law and the Act of June 18, 1934," *George Washington Law Review* 3 (March 1935): 289, 304; Richard O. Clemmer, "Hopis, Western Shoshones, and Southern Utes: Three Different Responses to the Indian Reorganization Act of 1934," *American Indian Culture and Research Journal* 10, no. 2 (1986): 15; Paula Mitchell Marks, *In a Barren Land: American Indian Dispossession and Survival* (New York: William Morrow, 1998), 272–73, 280–81.

9. "Indians—Criminal Offenses and Civil Causes—State Jurisdiction, Chapter 505—Public Law 280 [H.R. 1063]," in *United States Code, 83rd Congress—First Session, 1953*, vol. 1 (St. Paul, Minn.: West Publishing, 1953), 663–65; "Indians—Criminal Offenses and Civil Causes—State Jurisdiction, Senate Report No. 699," in *United States Code, 83rd Congress—First Session, 1953*, vol. 2 (St. Paul, Minn.: West Publishing, 1953), 2409–14; "Just Bad Indians: State Jurisdiction over Indian Affairs," *New Republic* 148 (March 30, 1963): 8; Carole E. Goldberg, "Public Law 280: The Limits of State Jurisdiction over Indians," *U.C.L.A. Law Review* 22 (1975): 537, 549–50, 594; Vine Deloria Jr. and Clifford M. Lytle, *American Indians, American Justice* (Austin: University of Texas Press, 1983), 19, 176–77.

10. Blanchard and Barsh, "What Is Best for Tribal Children?" 356; Marks, *In a Barren Land*, 280; Sandra L. Cadawalader and Vine Deloria Jr., eds., *The Aggressions of Civilizations: Federal Indian Policy Since the 1880s* (Philadelphia: Temple University Press, 1984), 79. For termination examples, see "Termination of Federal Supervision over Menominee Indians, Title 25, Nos. 891, 893, 900," in *United States Code, 1958 Edition*, vol. 5 (Washington, D.C.: Government Printing Office, 1959), 4256, 4258; and "Termination of Federal Supervision over Ottawa Indians, Title 25, Nos. 841, 844," in *United States Code, 1958 Edition*, vol. 5, 4253–54.

11. William A. Brophy and Sophie D. Aberle, comps., *The Indian: America's Unfinished Business* (Norman: University of Oklahoma Press, 1966), 56; O'Brien, *American Indian Tribal Governments*, 89.

12. Mannes, "Factors and Events," 267; Francis Paul Prucha, *The Great Father: The United States Government and the American Indians*, abridged ed. (Lincoln: University of Nebraska Press, 1986), 378; David Fanshel, *Far from the Reservation: The Transracial Adoption of American Indian Chil-*

dren (Metuchen, N.J.: Scarecrow Press, 1972), ix, 24, 33–34; Alison R. Bernstein, *American Indians and World War II: Toward a New Era in Indian Affairs* (Norman: University of Oklahoma Press, 1991), 168; "Statement by the Bureau of Indian Affairs, for the 1965 Report to the Nation Being Made by the National Committee on Children and Youth," 2–3, typescript, box 288, folder 14, White House Conference, DDE Library.

13. "P.L. 95-608 [S. 1214]; Nov. 8, 1978, Indian Child Welfare Act of 1978," in *United States Code, 95th Congress—Second Session, 1978,* vol. 2 (St. Paul, Minn.: West Publishing, 1979), Sec. 2 (4) and (5), Sec. 3 (4) and (8), p. 92, Stat. 3069–77; Blanchard and Barsh, "What Is Best for Tribal Children?" 354; Deloria and Lytle, *American Indians, American Justice,* 213; Fergus M. Bordewich, *Killing the White Man's Indian: Reinventing Native Americans at the End of the Twentieth Century* (New York: Doubleday, 1996), 84; O'Brien, *American Indian Tribal Governments,* 90, 212, 238; Craig J. Dorsay, *Social Work Practice and the Indian Child Welfare Act* (Salt Lake City: University of Utah, Utah Child Welfare Training Project, 1986), 1–3. Some argue that the money has never been adequate, particularly when Indian tribes have to compete for grant moneys to support on-reservation programs. See the video *History of the Indian Child Welfare Act* (Portland, Ore.: National Indian Child Welfare Association, 1991).

14. Blanchard and Barsh, "What Is Best for Tribal Children?" 351; Mannes, "Factors and Events," 142–44; Terry L. Cross, "Drawing on Cultural Tradition in Indian Child Welfare Practice," *Social Casework* 67 (1986): 284.

15. Blanchard and Barsh, "What Is Best for Tribal Children?" 356; John G. Red Horse, "Family Structure and Value Orientation in American Indians," *Social Casework* 61 (October 1980): 462–64; John G. Red Horse, "American Indian Elders: Unifiers of Indian Families," *Social Casework* 61 (October 1980): 490–91.

16. Bernard W. Sheehan, "Indian-White Relations in Early America: A Review Essay," in *Native Americans Today: Sociological Perspectives,* ed. Howard M. Bahr, Bruce A. Chadwick, and Robert C. Day (New York: Harper and Row, 1972), 8, 14; Kevin Abing, "A Holy Battleground: Methodist, Baptist, and Quaker Missionaries Among Shawnee Indians, 1830–1844," *Kansas History* 21 (summer 1998): 126, quoting John G. Pratt to Lucius Bolles, October 5, 1838, American Indian Correspondence, American Baptist Foreign Mission Society, American Baptist Historical Society, Valley Forge, Pa.

17. Fischler, "Protecting American Indian Children," 342–46; Wendell H. Oswalt, *Other Peoples, Other Customs: World Ethnography and Its History* (New York: Holt, Rinehart and Winston, 1972), 32–33, 37–39.

18. "Rewrite Indian Adoption Law, Advocates Say," *Topeka* (Kans.) *Capital-Journal,* May 14, 1995; Collmeyer, "From 'Operation Brown Baby,'" 254–55; Fanshel, *Far from the Reservation,* 25.

19. *History of the Indian Child Welfare Act* (video).

20. Ibid.; Gerald Vizenor, *The People Named the Chippewa: Narrative Histories* (Minneapolis: University of Minnesota Press, 1984), 105; Karl Menninger to Morris Udall, Chairman, House Committee on Interior and Insular Affairs, March 3, 1978, and Karl Menninger to President Jimmy Carter, November 3, 1978, box 2, Indians, Congressional Bills, Karl A. Menninger Collection, Menninger Foundation Archives, Topeka, Kans.

21. Fischler, "Protecting American Indian Children," 342; John H. Oberly, "Annual Report of the Commissioner of Indian Affairs," in *Report of the Secretary of the Interior,* vol. 2, Doc. 1, pt. 5, 50th Cong., 2d sess. (Washington, D.C.: Government Printing Office, 1888), lxxxix.

22. Charles Loring Brace, *The Dangerous Classes of New York and Twenty Years Work Among Them* (New York: Wynkoop and Hollenbeck, 1872), 235–36; James C. Baccus, "'Your Gift Is Their Tomorrow': A History of North Dakota's Children's Home Society," *North Dakota History* 32 (January 1965): 154.

23. Lewis Meriam, "The Effects of Boarding Schools on Indian Family Life: 1928," in *Destruction of American Indian Families*, 14–17.

24. Fischler, "Protecting American Indian Children," 342; Sherman Alexie, *The Lone Ranger and Tonto Fistfight in Heaven* (New York: Atlantic Monthly Press, 1993; reprint, New York: HarperCollins, 1994), 34.

25. Clarice Snoddy, "The Social Adjustment of the American Indian" (1928), 16–17, Snoddy Papers, Manuscripts, Kansas State Historical Society, Topeka, Kans. (hereinafter cited as KSHS); Prucha, *The Great Father*, 378.

26. Sherman Alexie, *Indian Killer* (New York: Warner Books, 1996), 44; Barbara Kingsolver, *Pigs in Heaven* (New York: HarperCollins, 1993).

27. Charles Fergus, *Shadow Catcher, A Novel* (New York: Soho Press, 1991), 37; Louis L. Pfaller, *James McLaughlin: The Man with an Indian Heart* (New York: Vantage Press, 1978), 3, 193; James McLaughlin, *My Friend the Indian* (New York: Houghton Mifflin, 1910), 96; Flood, *Lost Bird of Wounded Knee*, 70.

CHAPTER 1. CRUMBLING CULTURE

1. Alfred Halfmoon, interview with author, May 3, 1999, Wichita, Kans.

2. Ibid. For an important study of grandmothers' roles, see Marjorie M. Schweitzer, ed., *American Indian Grandmothers: Traditions and Transitions* (Albuquerque: University of New Mexico Press, 1999).

3. "Woody Crumbo," typescript, 1, and Connie Kachel White, "Native Visions," *Wichita State University Alumni News*, August 1994, 15–19, Woody Crumbo vertical file, Mid-America All-Indian Center, Wichita, Kans. Woodrow Wilson "Woody" Crumbo was one of four artists to be awarded the 1998 Lifetime Achievement Award from the Southwest Association for Indian Arts. See "Recognition," *Southwest Art* 28 (June 1998): 124.

4. "Interview with Mr. C. A. Myers," vol. 37, pp. 413, 414–15, Indian-Pioneer History Project for Oklahoma, WPA, Oklahoma Historical Society, Oklahoma City, Okla. (hereinafter cited as IPH).

5. W. P. Letchworth, "Dependent and Delinquent Children: Institutions in New York in 1877," *American Journal of Education* 28 (1878): 913; "Minutes of the Meeting of the New Mexico Commission on Indian Affairs, May 11, 1959," p. 26, box 222, folder 15, White House Conference, DDE Library.

6. Michael Grossberg, "Who Gets the Child? Custody, Guardianship, and the Rise of a Judicial Patriarchy in Nineteenth-Century America," *Feminist Studies* 9 (summer 1983): 236, 240–41, 247. For an example of one woman's "private law" petition, see the case of Elizabeth Collins, Illinois General Assembly, Private Laws, *1837*, 57–58, Illinois State Archives, Springfield, Ill.

7. Gonzalez and Cook-Lynn, *Politics of Hallowed Ground*, xiii, xiv; Cadawalader and Deloria, *Aggressions of Civilizations*, 199–200; *Report of the Secretary of the Interior*, vol. 1, Ex. Doc. 5, 47th Cong., 2d sess. (Washington, D.C.: Government Printing Office, 1882), vii; Kreiger, "Principles of the Indian Law," 289, 297, 300.

8. Elinor Nims, "Experiments in Adoption Legislation," *Social Service Review* 1 (June 1927): 241–48.

9. Royal B. Hassrick, *The Sioux: Life and Customs of a Warrior Society* (Norman: University of Oklahoma Press, 1964), 110–11; Lillian Petershoare, "Tlingit Adoption Practices, Past and Present," *American Indian Culture and Research Journal* 9, no. 2 (1985): 1.

10. Hassrick, *The Sioux*, 110; Charles Alexander Eastman (Ohiyesa), *Indian Boyhood* (Boston: Little, Brown, 1902; reprint, Lincoln: University of Nebraska Press, 1991), xiii.

11. David Leeming and Jake Page, *The Mythology of Native North America* (Norman: University of Oklahoma Press, 1998), 165–66; Jesse J. Cornplanter, *Legends of the Longhouse by Jesse J. Cornplanter of the Senecas, Told to Sah-Nee-Weh, the White Sister* (Philadelphia: Lippincott, 1938), 167–81.

12. Robert H. Lowie, *The Crow Indians* (New York: Rinehart, 1935; reprint, Lincoln: University of Nebraska Press, 1983), 7, 113; Leeming and Page, *Mythology of Native North America*, xii.

13. Ruth Holmes Whitehead, *Six Micmac Stories* (Halifax, Nova Scotia, Canada: Nimbus Publisher and the Nova Scotia Museum, 1992), 7; Cornplanter, *Legends of the Longhouse*, 73–80.

14. Eastman, *Indian Boyhood*, 4.

15. Whitehead, *Six Micmac Stories*, 11–15; Cornplanter, *Legends of the Longhouse*, 167–81.

16. Vizenor, *The People Named the Chippewa*, 8–12; Dean R. Snow, *The Iroquois* (Oxford: Blackwell, 1994), 4–5. Evil Twin/Good Twin stories differ substantially from the Twins as Heroes theme; for example, the Navajo twin myth portrays both as good, bringing peace and harmony to the world by defeating evil monsters. See Leeming and Page, *Mythology of Native North America*, 154–58.

17. Cornplanter, *Legends of the Longhouse*, 80; Sylvester M. Morey and Olivia L. Gilliam, eds., *Respect for Life: The Traditional Upbringing of American Indian Children* (Garden City, N.Y.: Waldorf Press, 1974), 9.

18. Lowie, *The Crow Indians*, 237.

19. Fanny S. French, "The Beggar Child and Church," *Ladies' Repository* 18 (October 1858): 607; E. L. Doctorow, *The Waterworks* (New York: Signet Books, 1994), 99.

20. Horatio Alger Jr., *Bound to Rise; or, Harry Walton's Motto* (Philadelphia: John C. Winston, 1873), vii–viii; Leeming and Page, *Mythology of Native North America*, 165.

21. Daniel Beekman, *The Mechanical Baby: A Popular History of the Theory and Practice of Child Raising* (Westport, Conn.: Laurence Hill, 1977), 55; Black Elk, *The Sacred Pipe: Black Elk's Account of the Seven Rites of the Oglala Sioux*, recorded and edited by Joseph Epes Brown (Norman: University of Oklahoma Press, 1953; reprint, Norman: University of Oklahoma Press, 1981), 43.

22. Bernard Wishy, *The Child and the Republic: The Dawn of Modern American Child Nurture* (Philadelphia: University of Pennsylvania Press, 1968), 11–12, 23; Carl N. Degler, *At Odds: Women and Family in America from the Revolution to the Present* (New York: Oxford University Press, 1980), 67; Frances Fox Piven and Richard A. Cloward, *Regulating the Poor: The Functions of Public Welfare* (New York: Pantheon Books, 1971), 46; David J. Rothman, *Conscience and Convenience: The Asylum and Its Alternatives in Progressive America* (Boston: Little, Brown, 1980), 52; Michael B. Katz, *In the Shadow of the Poorhouse: A Social History of Welfare in America* (New York: Basic Books, 1986), 4, 6.

23. F. A. Steel, "The Cult of the Child," *Littel's Living Age* 237 (April–June 1903): 761; Wishy, *The Child and the Republic*, 81–82; Margaret Connell Szasz, "Native American Children," in *American Childhood: A Research Guide and Historical Handbook*, ed. Joseph M. Hawes and N. Ray Hiner (Westport, Conn.: Greenwood Press, 1985), 326.

24. Morey and Gilliam, *Respect for Life*, 148.

25. Cross, "Drawing on Cultural Tradition," 284, 285; Petershoare, "Tlingit Adoption Practices," 4; Jules Henry, *Culture Against Man* (New York: Random House, 1963), 332; "Ada M. Roach, Second Interview," vol. 484, p. 486, IPH; Hassrick, *The Sioux*, 316; George Bird Grinnell, *The Cheyenne Indians: Their History and Ways of Life*, vol. 1 (Lincoln: University of Nebraska Press, Bison Books, 1972), 103, 104; "Leon Shenondoah," in *Ne'Ho Niyo'De:No': That's What It Was Like*, comp. and ed. Alberta Austin (Lackawanna, N.Y.: Rebco Enterprises, 1986), 175; Anthony F. C. Wallace, *The Death and Rebirth of the Seneca* (New York: Alfred A. Knopf, 1969; reprint, New York: Vintage Books, 1972), 36–39; Angie Debo, *The Road to Disappearance: A History of the Creek Indians* (Norman: University of Oklahoma Press, 1941), 18–19; Lowie, *The Crow Indians*, 35–42; Morey and Gilliam, *Respect for Life*, 68, 69; Szasz, "Native American Children," 316, 318–20; Arrell M. Gibson, *The Chickasaws* (Norman: University of Oklahoma Press, 1971), 21; Coontz, *The Way We Never Were*, 45.

26. Wishy, *The Child and the Republic*, 45; William C. Brown, "Tendency of Punishments," *Mother's Assistant and Young Lady's Friend* 1 (April 1841): 84; F. D. Huntington, "Home Training of Children," *Monthly Religious Magazine* 10 (January 1853): 24.

27. Szasz, "Native American Children," 318–20; Michael C. Coleman, *American Indian Children at School, 1850–1930* (Jackson: University Press of Mississippi, 1993), ix; Grinnell, *The Cheyenne Indians*, 102, 108–12; "Report of C. H. Grover, Agent, Pottawatomie and Great Nemaha Agency," in *Report of the Secretary of the Interior*, vol. 2, Ex. Doc. 1, pt. 5, 50th Cong., 1st sess. (Washington, D.C.: Government Printing Office, 1887), 894; L. F. Spencer, U.S. Indian agent, Rosebud Agency, to Commissioner of Indian Affairs, in *Annual Reports of the Department of the Interior: Report of the Commissioner of Indian Affairs*, Doc. No. 5, 55th Cong., 2d sess. (Washington, D.C.: Government Printing Office, 1897), 125; Eastman, *Indian Boyhood*, 49.

28. Mentor L. Williams, "Introduction," in *Schoolcraft's Indian Legends from Algic Researches, the Myth of Hiawatha, Oneota, the Red Race in America, and Historical and Statistical Information Respecting . . . the Indian Tribes of the United States*, ed. Mentor L. Williams (East Lansing: Michigan State University Press, 1956), xii; Arthur C. Parker, "The Constitution of the Five Nations or the Iroquois Book of the Great Law," in *Parker on the Iroquois*, ed. William N. Fenton (Syracuse, N.Y.: Syracuse University Press, 1968), 11.

29. Mary Henderson Eastman, *Dahcotah; or, Life and Legends of the Sioux Around Fort Snelling* (New York: Wiley, 1849; reprint, Afton, Minn.: Afton Historical Society Press, 1995), xvi, 4, 9; Hassrick, *The Sioux*, 210–15.

30. William N. Fenton, ed., "Seneca Indians by Asher Wright (1859)," *Ethnohistory* 4 (summer 1957): 312; Wallace, *Death and Rebirth of the Seneca*, 28–30; Debo, *Road to Disappearance*, 15, 18–19, 306; Gibson, *The Chickasaws*, 21; John Ehle, *Trail of Tears: The Rise and Fall of the Cherokee Nation* (New York: Anchor Books, Doubleday, 1989), 3; J. Leitch Wright Jr., *Creeks and Seminoles: The Destruction and Regeneration of the Muscogulge People*

(Lincoln: University of Nebraska Press, 1986), 19; Petershoare, "Tlingit Adoption Practices," 2; Carol Johnston, "Burning Beds, Spinning Wheels, and Calico Dresses," *Journal of Cherokee Studies* 19 (1998): 4.

31. Lucy Thompson, *To the American Indian: Reminiscences of a Yukon Woman* (1916; reprint, Berkeley, Calif.: Heyday Books, 1991), 28, 189; Ehle, *Trail of Tears*, 3; Johnston, "Burning Beds," 11.

32. Carolyn Niethammer, *Daughters of the Earth: The Lives and Legends of American Indian Women* (New York: Collier Books, 1977), 96–98; Ehle, *Trail of Tears*, 3; A. P. Dixon, U.S. Indian Agent, "Report of Crow Creek and Lower Brule Agency," in *Report of the Secretary of the Interior*, vol. 2, Ex. Doc. 5, pt. 5, 52d Cong., 1st sess. (Washington, D.C.: Government Printing Office, 1892), 396–97; Moses N. Adams letter, August 9, 1872, cited in Will G. Robinson, comp., "Digest of the Reports of the Commissioner of Indian Affairs as Pertain to Dakota Indians—1869–1872," *South Dakota Report and Historical Collections* 28 (1956): 343; George Catlin, *Letters and Notes on the Manners, Customs and Conditions of the North American Indians*, vol. 1 (New York: Dover, 1973), 134.

33. Henry R. Schoolcraft, *The Myth of Hiawatha, and Other Oral Legends, Mythologic and Allegoric, of the North American Indians* (Philadelphia: J. B. Lippincott, 1856), xiii; McLaughlin, *My Friend the Indian*, 91; Sr. Lioba Brown to Rev. J. Stephan, May 18, 1890, and to Rev. P. L. Chapelle, June 16, 1891, Bureau of Catholic Indian Missions Records, Correspondence, Special Collections and University Archives, Marquette University, Milwaukee, Wis. (hereinafter cited as BCIMR); "Saint Catharine's Indian School," *The Indian Sentinel* (1903–04): 15.

34. James Mooney, *The Siouan Tribes of the East* (Washington, D.C.: Bureau of American Ethnology, Government Printing Office, 1894), 8.

35. "Report of the Commissioner of Indian Affairs," in *Report of the Secretary of the Interior [1892]*, 1235.

36. Orrick to John Doughtery, February 13, 1850, John Dougherty Letterbooks, State Historical Society of Missouri, Columbia, Mo.; Russell Thornton, *American Indian Holocaust and Survival: A Population History Since 1492* (Norman: University of Oklahoma Press, 1987), 51–53; Chas. A. Ruffee to Commissioner of Indian Affairs, March 2, 1868, Sisseton, NA, Central Plains; "Holy Rosary Mission School," *The Indian Sentinel* (1908): 28.

37. John Dougherty to William Clark, October 29, 1831, in *Correspondence on the Subject of Emigration of Indians*, vol. 2 (Washington, D.C.: Duff Green, 1835), 718–19; Brian W. Dippie, *The Vanishing American: White Attitudes and U.S. Indian Policy* (Lawrence: University Press of Kansas, 1982), 37–40; Thornton, *American Indian Holocaust and Survival*, 91–100; Mooney, *Siouan Tribes of the East*, 68–69, 72; William Warren Sweet, *Religion on the American Frontier, 1783–1840*, vol. 4, *The Methodists* (New York: Cooper Square Publishers, 1964), 508.

38. Peter C. Mancall, "'The Bewitching Tyranny of Custom': The Social Costs of Indian Drinking in Colonial America," *American Indian Culture and Research Journal* 17, no. 2 (1993): 29–30, 34; *Report of the Department of the Interior: Indian Affairs, Territories*, vol. 2, Doc. 1, 60th Cong., 1st sess. (Washington, D.C.: Government Printing Office, 1907), 438; William E. Unrau, *White Man's Wicked Water: The Alcohol Trade and Prohibition in Indian Country, 1802–1892* (Lawrence: University Press of Kansas, 1996), 122–24, and p. 124, quoting from Special Agent H. T. Ketcham to John Evans, April 4, 1864, Letter Received by the Office of Indian Affairs, Record Group

75, National Archives and Records Administration, Archives I, Washington, D.C. (hereinafter cited as NA). For a study that argues for non-European origin of venereal diseases, see Claude Quetel, *History of Syphilis*, trans. Judith Braddock and Brian Pike (Cambridge: Polity Press, 1990), chaps. 1 and 2.

39. David J. Rothman, *The Discovery of the Asylum: Social Order and Disorder in the New Republic* (Boston: Little, Brown, 1971; Katz, *In the Shadow of the Poorhouse*, 10–11; Dan Cantrall, "The Illinois State Board of Public Charities and the County Poorhouses, 1870–1900: Institutional Ideal vs. County Realities," *Transactions of the Illinois State Historical Society* (1988): 50.

40. "The First Orphan Asylum in This Country," *Baldwin Place Home for Little Wanderers* 7 (June 1871): 87; J. S. Holliday, "An Historian Reflects on Edgewood Children's Center," *California History* 44 (spring 1985): 122–31; Rothman, *Discovery of the Asylum*, 206–7; Robert H. Bremmer, *The Public Good: Philanthropy and Welfare in the Civil War Era* (New York: Alfred A. Knopf, 1980), 85–86.

41. *Report of the State Board of Public Charities, Illinois* (Springfield, Ill.: State Printer, 1882), 107, and *Report of the State Board of Public Charities, Illinois [1894]* (Springfield, Ill.: State Printer, 1894), 48; Grace Abbott, ed., *The Child and the State*, vol. 2 (Chicago: University of Chicago Press, 1938), 63; Homer Folks, *The Care of the Destitute, Neglected, and Delinquent Children* (Albany, N.Y.: J. B. Lynon, 1900; reprint, New York: Arno Press and the New York Times, 1971), 24, 35–36; Barbara Finkelstein, "The Reconstruction of Childhood in the United States, 1790–1870," in *American Childhood: A Research Guide and Historical Handbook*, 112.

42. Katz, *In the Shadow of the Poorhouse*, 119; Rothman, *Discovery of the Asylum*, 206; Eve P. Smith, "Bring Back the Orphanages? What Policymakers of Today Can Learn from the Past," *Child Welfare* 74 (January/February 1995): 125.

43. "An Interview with Mrs. Ida Cunnetabby, Davis, Oklahoma," vol. 21, p. 348, IPH; Hyman Bogen, *The Luckiest Orphans: A History of the Hebrew Orphan Asylum of New York* (Urbana: University of Illinois Press, 1992), 127–29; Isabel Gap Gyongossy, interview with author, April 12, 1999, Wichita, Kans.; Brenda J. Child, *Boarding School Seasons* (Lincoln: University of Nebraska Press, 1998), 15, 20–21.

44. For references to good and bad orphanages, see Bernadine Courtright Barr, "A Hive of Industry: The Curriculum of the Iowa Soldiers' Orphans' Home, 1900–1945" (paper, Stanford University School of Education); Nurith Zmora, *Orphanages Revisited: Child Care Institutions in Progressive Era Baltimore* (Philadelphia: Temple University Press, 1994); Timothy A. Hacsi, *Second Home: Orphan Asylums and Poor Families in America* (Cambridge, Mass.: Harvard University Press, 1998).

45. For two Jewish orphanage examples, see Bogen, *Luckiest Orphans*, and Gary Palster, *Inside Looking Out: The Cleveland Jewish Orphan Asylum, 1868–1924* (Kent, Ohio: Kent State University Press, 1990). Although Bogen's book title suggests that the Jewish orphanage was one of the shining "good" orphanages, the subject is balanced by the inclusion of subjects, including punishment and sexual abuse, in which the institution fell far short. The Cleveland institution was one of eleven in the city for the poor and/or orphaned; see *The World's History of Cleveland: Commemorating the City's Centennial Anniversary* (Cleveland: The World, 1896), 197. For a discussion of Protestant and Catholic conflict, see Holt, *Orphan Trains*, 106–10. For quote, A. L. interview with author, April 12, 1994, Salina, Kans.

46. "Report of the Commissioner of Education for the Year 1877," *American Journal of Education* 28 (1878): 182–208; B. R. Sulgrove, *History of Indianapolis and Marion County, Indiana* (Philadelphia: L. H. Everts, 1884), 382–83; Collmeyer, "From 'Operation Brown Baby,'" 242–63; Wilma Peebles-Wilkins, "Jane Porter Barrett and the Virginia Industrial School for Colored Girls: Community Response to the Needs of African-American Children," *Child Welfare* 74 (January/February 1995): 143–61.

47. Roberta Starr Hirshson, *"There's Always Someone There. . . .": The History of the New England Home for Little Wanderers* (Boston: the author and New England Home for Little Wanderers, 1989), 36–37; "The Objects and Plan of the Home," *New England Home for Little Wanderers Advocate and Report* 24 (January 1890): 1, 39.

48. "Fortieth Annual Report and Quarterly Advocate," *Little Wanderers' Advocate* 41 (May 1905): 48; *The Story of Graham School* (n.p.: ca. 1950), 9, 12, 14; Maurice V. Odquist, *The History of Graham* (n.p., 1960), 5.

CHAPTER 2. FIRST SOLUTION: SENECA

1. J. B. Jewell, U.S. Indian Agent, "Report of Agent in New York," in *Annual Reports of the Department of the Interior [1897]*, 206–7.

2. Charles Leslie Glenn Jr., *The Myth of the Common School* (Amherst: University of Massachusetts Press, 1988), 78–79, 80–81, 88–97, 263; *New York Times*, October 11, 1861, 5; Josiah Strong, *Our Country: Its Possible Future and Its Present Crisis*, rev. ed. (New York: Baker and Taylor, 1891; reprint, Cambridge, Mass.: Belknap Press of Harvard University Press, 1963), 56–57.

3. Irving Howe and Kenneth Libo, *World of Our Fathers* (New York: Harcourt Brace Jovanovich, 1976), 271–76. Selma Berrol, "Immigrant Children at School, 1880–1940: A Child's Eye View," in *Small Worlds: Children and Adolescents in America, 1850–1950*, ed. Elliott West and Paula Petrik (Lawrence: University Press of Kansas, 1992), 43, states that the "conventional view" that all immigrant parents avidly sought educational opportunities for their children has been challenged by studies that find "no such unanimity."

4. "Contract for Holy Rosary Mission School, Pine Ridge Reservation, South Dakota, for the Fiscal Year 1908," Holy Rosary Mission, BCIMR.

5. Fenton, "Seneca Indians by Asher Wright," 304–5; Mooney, *Siouan Tribes of the East*, 8; Snow, *The Iroquois*, 138–39; Wallace, *Death and Rebirth of the Seneca*, 322–23.

6. Snow, *The Iroquois*, 1, 157–58; Wallace, *Death and Rebirth of the Seneca*, 21, 184, 219–21; Thomas S. Abler, ed., *Chainbreaker: The Revolutionary War Memoirs of Governor Blacksnake as Told to Benjamin Williams* (Lincoln: University of Nebraska Press, 1989), 203, 207; Alvin M. Josephy Jr., *Now That the Buffalo's Gone: A Study of Today's American Indians* (New York: Alfred A. Knopf, 1982), 4; Morey and Gilliam, *Respect for Life*, xi–xii, quoting from *The Colonial Records of Pennsylvania, 1735–1745*, vol. 4, pp. 729–35. The Quaker-Seneca relationship continued into the twentieth century. For example, in 1960, Senecas on the Allegany Reservation lost approximately one-third of their land, including sacred ground, to dam and reservoir construction; the Quakers aided the Senecas in receiving over $15 million in damages. See Annette Rosenstiel, *Red and White: Indian Views of the White Man, 1492–1982* (New York: Universe Books, 1983), 54.

7. Abler, *Chainbreaker*, 207; Levinus K. Painter, *The Collins Story: A His-*

tory of the Town of Collins, Erie County, New York (Gowanda, N.Y.: Niagara Frontier Publishing, 1962), 28.

8. Coleman, *American Indian Children at School,* 43; Wallace, *Death and Rebirth,* 314–15; Robert H. Keller Jr., *American Protestantism and United States Indian Policy, 1869–82* (Lincoln: University of Nebraska Press, 1983), 68; "Contract Schools Ledger," Record of School Contracts, 1887–1911, Records of the Education Division, Bureau of Indian Affairs, box 1, RG 75, NA (hereinafter cited as Education, BIA, NA); Donald J. Berthrong, "From Buffalo Days to Classrooms: The Southern Cheyennes and Arapahos and Kansas," *Kansas History* 12 (summer 1989): 101–13; *The Halstead* (Kans.) *Independent: A Souvenir Edition,* August 12, 1937, 32. Under the heading "Mission Schools," Cheyenne and Arapaho Agency records, NA, Ft. Worth, contain information on Mennonite missions in Oklahoma and in Kansas.

9. Wallace, *Death and Rebirth,* 184.

10. Ibid., 28, 40; W. M. Beauchamp, "Iroquois Women," *Journal of American Folklore* 13 (April–June 1900): 85–86; Donald A. Grindle Jr., "Iroquois Political Theory and the Roots of American Democracy," in *Exiled in the Land of the Free: Democracy, Indian Nations, and the U.S. Constitution,* by Vine Deloria Jr. et al. (Santa Fe, N.M.: Clear Light Publishers, 1992), 273–74.

11. Wallace, *Death and Rebirth,* 28; Abler, *Chainbreaker,* 24, 158, 168; Painter, *The Collins Story,* 28; *Centennial, 1855–1955: Thomas Indian School* (Iroquois, N.Y.: Thomas Indian School, 1955), 1. For one argument that women's power stemmed from their domesticity, see Leslee M. Scott, "Indian Women as Food Providers and Tribal Counselors," *Oregon Historical Quarterly* 42 (1941): 208–19.

12. Wallace, *Death and Rebirth,* 323.

13. Bordewich, *Killing the White Man's Indian,* 257; Snow, *The Iroquois,* 164–68.

14. Wallace, *Death and Rebirth,* 221, 323; Abler, *Chainbreaker,* 220–21; Painter, *The Collins Story,* 28; Snow, *The Iroquois,* 166–67; Laurence M. Hauptman, *Between Two Fires: American Indians in the Civil War* (New York: Free Press, 1995), 163.

15. *Centennial,* 1.

16. Wallace, *Death and Rebirth,* 193–94.

17. Ibid., 94; Fenton, "Seneca Indians by Asher Wright," 320; Letchworth, "Dependent and Delinquent Children," 913, 914; *Centennial,* 1; Painter, *The Collins Story,* 28.

18. *Centennial,* 2; Painter, *The Collins Story,* 28; Letchworth, "Dependent and Delinquent Children," 914.

19. Bremmer, *The Public Good,* 85–86; Holt, *Orphan Trains,* 74–76; Katz, *In the Shadow of the Poorhouse,* 119; Edith Abbott, "The Civil War and the Crime Wave of 1865–70," *Social Service Review* 1 (June 1927): 215–16, 219.

20. Snow, *The Iroquois,* 178–79; Hauptman, *Between Two Fires,* 161–83, 188; Henry G. Waltmann, "Ely Samuel Parker, 1869–71," in *The Commissioners of Indian Affairs, 1824–1977,* ed. Robert M. Kvasnicka and Herman J. Viola (Lincoln: University of Nebraska Press, 1979), 123–24.

21. Snow, *The Iroquois,* 178–70; Fenton, "Seneca Indians by Asher Wright," 320; Hauptman, *Between Two Fires,* 170, 188.

22. *Centennial,* 2; Michael B. Katz, *Poverty and Policy in American History* (New York: Academic Press, 1983), 61.

23. Jewell, "Report of Agent in New York [1897]," 201.

24. Ibid.; Snow, *The Iroquois,* 166, 176; John H. Oberly, "Report of the

Indian School Superintendent," in *Report of the Secretary of the Interior*, vol. 2, Ex. Doc. 1, pt. 5, 49th Cong., 1st sess. (Washington, D.C.: Government Printing Office, 1885), 111.

25. Jewell, "Report of Agent in New York [1897]," 201; William Hughes, "Indians of New York: Glorious Past History and Pitiable Present Condition," *The Indian Sentinel* (1912): 10.

26. Wm. H. Ketcham to Rev. Thomas O'Gorman, December 1, 1906, Dakotas, General Correspondence, BICMR.

27. *Report of the Secretary of the Interior [1882]*, xv.

28. Oberly, "Report of the Indian School Superintendent [1885]," 109–11.

29. Jewell, "Report of Agent in New York [1897]," 201.

30. J. H. Welch, "Report of Superintendent of the Leech Lake Boarding School," in *Report of the Secretary of the Interior [1892]*, 264.

31. E. L. Trotzkey, *Institutional Care and Placing Out: The Place of Each in the Care of Dependent Children* (Chicago: Marks Nathan Jewish Orphan Home, 1930), 64–65; Rothman, *Discovery of the Asylum*, 235–36.

32. "Report of the Commissioner of Education for the Year 1877,"184; Jewell, "Report of Agent in New York [1897]," 206–7; Abbott, *The Child and the State*, 63.

33. "Virginia Snow," 192, in *Ne'Ho Niyo'De:No'*.

34. Ibid., 192–93; "Raymond Sundown," 221, in *Ne'Ho Niyo'De:No'*; Treasurer's Monthly Reports, miscellaneous, April and August 1901, box 1, folder 9; April 1903, box 1, folder 8; September and December 1903, box 1, folder 9; October 1913, box 1, folder 49; August 1914, box 2, folder 3; Supplies, March 1919, box 2, folder 21; General Administration, September 24, box 3, folder 9, Thomas Indian School Records, New York State Archives, Albany, N.Y. (hereinafter cited as Thomas, NY State Archives).

35. Coleman, *American Indian Children at School*, 82–83; Treasurer's Monthly Reports, Miscellaneous, March and April 1901, box 1, folder 1; September 1903, box 1, folder 9; October 1912, box 1, folder 46; August 1914, box 2, folder 3; January 15, box 2, folder 5; Abstract of Vouchers, June 1915, box 2, folder 6; Journal Accounts, voucher register, vol. 14, pp. 308–19, 1913, Thomas, NY State Archives. These are just a few examples that included haircuts and clothing.

36. "Arnold Doxtator," 25, "Cephus Hill," 54, "Calvin Kettle," 88, "Lena Nephew," 127, and "Florence White," 250, all in *Ne'Ho Niyo'De: No'*.

37. Treasurer's Monthly Reports, Miscellaneous, March 1901, box 1, folder 1; November 1903, box 1, folder 9; December 1904, box 1, folder 14; Voucher Register, vol. 14, p. 304, December 1912; and Supplies, November 1914, box 2, folder 4, Thomas, NY State Archives.

38. Child Commitment Contracts, 1881–1896, and Voucher Register, June and July 1903, vol. 13, pp. 72, 78, Thomas, NY State Archives.

39. Bremner, *The Public Good*, 85.

40. "Calvin Kettle," 88–89, in *Ne'Ho Niyo'De:No'*; Oberly, "Report of the Indian School Superintendent [1885]," 108.

41. Calvin Derrick, "The No-Man's Land of Childhood," in *Public Welfare in the United States: The Annals*, ed. Howard W. Odum (Philadelphia: American Academy of Political and Social Sciences, 1923), 212; Jacob A. Riis, "Christmas Reminder of the Nobelist Work in the World," *Forum* 16 (January 1894): 624; Holt, *Orphan Trains*, 17, 18, 50.

42. Treasurer's Monthly Reports, Personal and Special Services, November 1923, box 3, folder 6; April, May, and June 1924, box 3, folder 8; May and June

1932, box 4, folder 8; and Miscellaneous, July 1914, box 2, folder 3, Thomas, NY State Archives.

43. "Cherokee Orphan Training School, Annual Report, 1913," 3, Superintendent's Annual Narrative and Statistical Report, NA, Central Plains (hereinafter cited as SANSR, NA, Central Plains).

44. Miscellaneous, December 1904, box 1, folder 4, March 1915, box 2, folder 5, and General Administration, October 1919, box 2, folder 24, Thomas, NY State Archives; Sarah B. Cooper, "Kindergarten for Neglected Children," *American Journal of Education* 31 (1881): 206–8; *The Magic City: Chicago World's Columbian Exposition, 1893* (St. Louis: Historical Publishing Co., 1894), Children's Building photographs in "Lady Managers" section.

45. Journal Accounts, voucher register, June 1889, vol. 4, box 1, Thomas, NY State Archives; *Centennial*, 2.

46. Journal Accounts, voucher register, vol. 14, pp. 301, 306, November and December 1912, Thomas, NY State Archives; David Wallace Adams, *Education for Extinction: American Indians and the Boarding School Experience, 1875–1928* (Lawrence: University Press of Kansas, 1996), 229–31; Bremmer, *The Public Good*, 30; "Dastardly Attempt at Incendiarism," *The Progress*, White Earth Reservation, Minn., January 28, 1888, p. 2.

47. Journal Accounts, voucher register, April 1901, vol. 12, p. 343; June 1902, and July 1902, vol. 12, pp. 449, 457; and September 1903, vol. 13, p. 89; Treasurer's Monthly Reports, travel expenses, February 1919, box 2, folder 21, Thomas, NY State Archives.

48. Journal Accounts, voucher register, March 1901, April 1901, vol. 12, pp. 335, 343; and April 1902, vol. 12, p. 435, Thomas, NY State Archives; "Calvin Kettle," 89, in *Ne'Ho Niyo'De:No'*.

49. Journal Accounts, voucher register, March 1885, and May 1905; Treasurer's Monthly Reports, Hospital and Medical Supplies, February 1901, box 1, folder 1; Miscellaneous, June 1915, box 2, folder 6; November 1915, box 2, folder 8; General Plant Services, March 1919, box 2, folder 21; Traveling Expenses, April 1918, box 2, folder 18, Thomas, NY State Archives; "Virginia Snow," 194, "Mary Pembleton," 139, and "Florence White," 250, in *Ne'Ho Niyo'De:No'*.

50. Adams, *Education for Extinction*, 130; Samuel M. Cart to Comm. of Indian Affairs, June 8, 1891, Santa Fe Indian School, microfilm, roll 1, and Superintendent's Report, August 27, 1892, p. 10, microfilm, roll 2, Record Group 75, National Archives, Rocky Mountain Region, Denver, Colo. (hereinafter cited as Santa Fe, NA, Rocky Mt.).

51. Samuel H. Preston and Michael R. Haines, *Fatal Years: Child Mortality in Late Nineteenth-Century America* (Princeton, N.J.: Princeton University Press, 1991), 50; Holt, *Orphan Trains*, 108; *Centennial*, 4; "The Greatest Reform School in the World: A Guide to the Records of the New York House of Refuge, A Brief History, 1824–1857," 1–2, NY State Archives; Treasurer's Monthly Reports, General Supplies, April 1915, box 2, folder 6; July 1915, box 2, folder 7, Thomas, NY State Archives.

52. Preston and Haines, *Fatal Years*, 8–9; Watson, *Charity Organization Movement in the United States*, 293–95; Dippie, *Vanishing American*, 345; Transportation of Inmates, July 1915, box 2, folder 1, and October 15, box 2, folder 8, Thomas, NY State Archives.

53. *Centennial*, 2, 6; Painter, *The Collins Story*, 29.

54. Katharine P. Hewins, "Division of Responsibility Between Family and Children's Agencies," *Family* 3 (November 1922): 179; "The Conference of

Charities and Correction," *School and Society* 1 (February 20, 1915): 288; Mary F. Bogue, "Administration of Mothers' Aid in Ten Localities," in *The Family and Social Services in the 1920's: Two Documents*, ed. David J. Rothman and Sheila M. Rothman (New York: Arno Press and the New York Times, 1972), 1–3; Emma Octavia Lundberg, "Progress of Mothers' Aid Administration," *Social Service Review* 2 (September 1928): 435; Steven Mintz and Susan Kellogg, *Domestic Revolutions: A Social History of American Family Life* (New York: Free Press, 1988), chap. 4; *White House Conference on Children in a Democracy, Washington, D.C., January 18–20, 1940, Final Report*, 26, box 1, file 4, White House Conference, DDE Library.

55. Correspondence and Subject Files, 1899–1958, Thomas, NY State Archives, contains within a broad cross section of reports, minutes of meetings, and memorandums, correspondence related to enrollment of Thomas graduates at other institutions, including Carlisle, Hampton Institute, and Haskell Institute. Willard W. Beatty, *An Informal Report on the Thomas Indian School, 1946*, Central Files, New York, 1940–1952, Bureau of Indian Affairs, RG 75, NA; Painter, *The Collins Story*, 29; Laurence M. Hauptman, *The Iroquois Struggle for Survival: World War II to Red Power* (Syracuse, N.Y.: Syracuse University Press, 1986), 12–13.

56. "Martha Hughson," 58, "Lena Nephew," 126–27, "Mary Pembleton," 139, "Virginia Snow," 194–95, "Raymond Sundown," 221, in *Ne'Ho Niyo'De:No'*.

57. Michele "Midge" Dean Stock, Manager-Director, Seneca-Iroquois National Museum, to author, May 16, 2000; Painter, *Collins Story*, 29; Hauptman, *The Iroquois Struggle for Survival*, 13; Laurence M. Hauptman, *The Iroquois and the New Deal* (Syracuse, N.Y.: Syracuse University Press, 1981), 156. During the New Deal a tribal museum was established at the school and a mural depicting Iroquois life was developed, but financing never expanded beyond this project.

CHAPTER 3. ORPHANS AMONG US: CHEROKEE

1. "Interview with Arlie Reeves (Cherokee Woman)," vol. 8, p. 341, IPH.

2. Ibid., 341–42.

3. J. F. Thompson to S. Mayes, Oct. 3, 1896, Cherokee Council and Senate Documents, Orphan Asylum, 1890–1902, Record Group 75, National Archives and Records Administration—Southwest Region, Ft. Worth, Tex. (hereinafter cited as NA, Ft. Worth); "Sequoyah Orphan Training School, May 20, 1932," SANSR, NA, Central Plains; Mrs. R. L. Fite, "Historical Statement," *Journal of Cherokee Studies* 10 (spring 1985): 121, 137.

4. "W. T. Worley Interview," vol. 11, p. 575, IPH.

5. J. R. Bioinu to S. Mayes, April 20, 1897, Cherokee Orphan Asylum, NA, Ft. Worth.

6. John H. Oberly, "Report of the Indian School Superintendent [1885]," 77–79; Abraham Eleazer Knepler, "Education in the Cherokee Nation," *Chronicles of Oklahoma* 21 (December 1943): 386–87; Johnston, "Burning Beds," 9.

7. Ehle, *Trail of Tears*, 193–95.

8. Ibid., 194–95; Joan Greene, "Civilize the Indian: Government Policies, Quakers, and Cherokee Education," *Journal of Cherokee Studies* 10 (fall 1985): 192; Coleman, *American Indian Children at School*, 38–39; Knepler,

"Education in the Cherokee Nation," 393–94; Herman J. Viola, "Thomas L. McKenney," in *Commissioners of Indian Affairs*, 3.

9. Angie Debo, *And Still the Waters Run: The Betrayal of the Five Civilized Tribes* (Princeton, N.J.: Princeton University Press, 1940), 4, 8; Knepler, "Education in the Cherokee Nation," 378.

10. Ehle, *Trail of Tears*, 198–99; Rogin, *Fathers and Children*, 194–95; Wright, *Creeks and Seminoles*, 73–74, 79.

11. Johnston, "Burning Beds" 8, 9, 67.

12. Ibid., 9; Mary Young, "The Cherokee Nation: Mirror of the Republic," in *Major Problems in American Indian History*, ed. Albert L. Hurtado and Peter Iverson (Lexington, Mass.: D. C. Heath, 1994), 220; John S. D. Eisenhower, *Agent of Destiny: The Life and Times of General Winfield Scott* (New York: Free Press, 1997), 187.

13. Hauptman, *Between Two Fires*, 5–6, 17; Ronald N. Satz, "Carey Allen Harris, 1836–38," in *Commissioners of Indian Affairs*, 18–20.

14. Ehle, *Trail of Tears*, 340, 358, 390–93; Eisenhower, *Agent of Destiny*, 185; Hauptman, *Between Two Fires*, 5; Ronald N. Satz, "Thomas Hartley Crawford, 1838–45," in *Commissioners of Indian Affairs*, 24.

15. Ehle, *Trail of Tears*, 341.

16. Ibid., 358, 390–93; Eisenhower, *Agent of Destiny*, 191–92; Hauptman, *Between Two Fires*, 5.

17. Hauptman, *Between Two Fires*, 45; Fite, "Historical Statement," 119; Ehle, *Trail of Tears*, 274; "The Cherokee Orphan Asylum: History of an Old School Now Extinct, from Facts Gathered by James R. Carselowey, Field Worker," vol. 19, pp. 33–34, IPH; "Sallie Rogers McSpadden," vol. 76, p. 158, IPH; Knepler, "Education in the Cherokee Nation," 378; Young, "Cherokee Nation," 224.

18. Oberly, "Report of the Indian School Superintendent [1885]," 111.

19. Knepler, "Education in the Cherokee Nation," 380; Young, "Cherokee Nation," 224; William G. McLoughlin, *After the Trail of Tears: The Cherokees' Struggle for Sovereignty, 1839–1880* (Chapel Hill: University of North Carolina Press, 1993), 240; "Narrative, Section III—Schools, 1914," 1, SANSR, NA, Central Plains.

20. Hauptman, *Between Two Fires*, 42, 44–45, 61.

21. Ibid., 42; William H. Graves, "The Five Civilized Tribes and the Beginning of the Civil War," *Journal of Cherokee Studies* 10 (fall 1985): 205–7, 210–11; "Cantonment Is Named for Col. W. A. Phillips," *Salina* (Kans.) *Journal*, October 6, 1942, 1, 7.

22. Hauptman, *Between Two Fires*, 186; "Interview with Lottie Durham," vol. 23, p. 142, IPH; Graves, "Five Civilized Tribes," 206, 209.

23. Debo, *Road to Disappearance*, 153; Robert W. Richmond, *Kansas: A Land of Contrasts* (St. Charles, Mo.: Forum Press, 1974), 88; "The Recollections of a Cherokee Freedman Dennis Vann," vol. 11, p. 66, IPH.

24. Hauptman, *Between Two Fires*, 42; Fite, "Historical Statement," 120–21.

25. "Agreement with the Cherokee, 1835 [New Echota Treaty]," in *Treaties and Agreements of the Five Civilized Tribes* (Washington, D.C.: Institute for the Development of Indian Law, n.d.), Article 11, p. 51; McLoughlin, *After the Trail of Tears*, 241; "Santa Claus Among the Foundlings," *Frank Leslie's Illustrated Newspaper*, January 20, 1872, 295.

26. "Agreement with the Cherokee, 1835," Article 11, p. 51; Knepler, "Education in the Cherokee Nation," 398; J. F. Thompson to S. H. Mayes, October 3, 1896, Cherokee Orphan Asylum, NA, Ft. Worth; "The Cherokee Orphan

Asylum . . . from Facts Gathered by James R. Carselowey," vol. 19, p. 34, IPH; "Letter of W. A. Duncan," *Cherokee Advocate*, Tahlequah, Cherokee Nation, August 24, 1872; "First Annual Message of Honorable S. H. Mayes, Principal Chief," *Cherokee Advocate*, November 13, 1895.

27. McLoughlin, *After the Trail of Tears*, 241; "Experiences of a Pioneer Woman, Interview with Laura E. Harsha," vol. 4, pp. 438–39, IPH; "An Interview with Mrs. Mary J. Baker," vol. 99, pp. 381–82, IPH.

28. "The Cherokee Nation's First White Orphan Home—Compiled from Old Documents Left by the Late Rev. W. A. Duncan," vol. 83, pp. 457–58, IPH.

29. "Report of the Commissioner of Education for the Year 1877," 189; "Cornelia A. Chandler Interview," vol. 9, p. 7, IPH.

30. "George French Interview," vol. 3, p. 603, IPH.

31. "Names of Pupils Who Are Registered in Cherokee Orphan Asylum,"February 5, 1900, Cherokee Orphan Asylum, NA, Ft. Worth; Child, *Boarding School Seasons*, 79.

32. Theda Perdue, *Nations Remembered: An Oral History of the Chero-kees, Chickasaws, Creeks, and Seminoles in Oklahoma, 1865–1907* (Nor-man: University of Oklahoma Press, 1993), 124.

33. *Annual Reports of the Department of the Interior: Indian Affairs, Part II, Commission to the Five Civilized Tribes*, Doc. No. 5, 57th Cong., 2d sess. (Washington, D.C.: Government Printing Office, 1903), 305–6; Devon A. Mih-esuah, *Cultivating the Rosebuds: The Education of Women at the Cherokee Female Seminary, 1851–1909* (Urbana: University of Illinois Press, 1993), 120, 122, 127, 128.

34. Fite, "Historical Statement," 134; W. W. Hastings," vol. 4, p. 464, IHP; Debo, *And Still the Waters Run*, 368–69.

35. "Sallie E. [Jones] Dick Interview," vol. 3, p. 15, IPH; Holt, *Orphan Trains*, 145, 183.

36. Surveys, Orphan Asylum Reservation, Cherokee Nation, May 20, 1890, and Phoenix Insurance Company Policy, June 1903, Cherokee Orphan Asy-lum, NA, Ft. Worth.

37. "Henry Payne," vol. 76, p. 239, IPH; "Arch Nelms," vol. 76, p. 242, IPH; J. M. McClure to Samuel Mayes, January 10, 1899, and Geo. Bhule to Samuel Mayes, June 9, 1898, Cherokee Orphan Asylum, NA, Ft. Worth.

38. "Mrs. Susanna Adair Davis Interview," vol. 2, p. 460, IPH; "Florence Caleb Smith Interview," vol. 9, p. 470, IPH.

39. O. J. Stowell to D. M. Wisdom, February 11, 1897, and D. M. Wisdom to S. H. Mayes, February 13, 1897, Cherokee Orphan Asylum, NA, Ft. Worth.

40. Senate Bill Number Seven, December 1901, and Board of Education of the Cherokee Nation to J. F. Thompson, January 10, 1899, Cherokee Orphan Asylum, NA, Ft. Worth.

41. William C. Rogers to Senate Branch of the National Council, Novem-ber 1900, and untitled document, December 1900, Cherokee Orphan Asylum, NA, Ft. Worth.

42. Fite, "Historical Statement," 157; Narcissa Owen, *Memoirs of Narcissa Owen, 1831–1907* (Siloam Springs, Ark.: Simon Sager Press and Siloam Springs Museum, 1983), 88–89; Carl T. Steen, "Home for the Insane, Deaf, Dumb, and Blind of the Cherokee Nation," *Chronicles of Oklahoma* 21 (1943): 408, 409; Mihesuah, *Cultivating the Rosebuds*, 87. For ledgers, see Cherokee Orphan Asylum, NA, Ft. Worth.

43. Mihesuah, *Cultivating the Rosebuds*, 87; "George French Interview," vol. 3, p. 603, IPH.

44. Grocery list receipts, January 14 and February 8, 1902; Invoice, Hogan Mercantile Co., Salina, I.T., February 1903, Cherokee Orphan Asylum, NA, Ft. Worth.

45. Invoice, American Book Company, September 4 and September 24, 1901, March 17, 1903, Cherokee Orphan Asylum, NA, Ft. Worth; "Walter Adair Thompson Interview," vol. 10, p. 481, IPH.

46. Phoenix Insurance Company policy, June 1903, and Cherokee Board of Education to Principal Chief William C. Rogers, November 23, 1903, Cherokee Orphan Asylum, NA, Ft. Worth.

47. Cherokee Board of Education to Principal Chief William C. Rogers, November 23, 1903, and E. C. Alberty to Cherokee Board of Education, July 29, 1904, Cherokee Orphan Asylum, NA, Ft. Worth; "Susanna Adair Davis Interview," vol. 2, p. 460, IPH; *Annual Reports of the Department of the Interior: Indian Affairs, Part II, [1903]*, 246.

48. "Susanna Adair Davis Interview," vol. 2, p. 460, IPH; "The Cherokee Nation's First White Orphan Home—Compiled from Old Documents Left by the Late Rev. W. A. Duncan," vol. 83, pp. 459–60, IPH.

49. *Annual Reports of the Department of the Interior: Indian Affairs, Part II [1903]*, 246; E. C. Alberty to Cherokee Board of Education, July 29, 1904, Cherokee Orphan Asylum, NA, Ft. Worth.

50. "Mrs. Martha (Goins) Pippin," vol. 40, p. 90, IPH.

51. Phoenix Insurance Company policy, June 1903, and Senate Bill No. 14, December 5, 1903, Cherokee Orphan Asylum, NA, Ft. Worth.

52. Rothman, *Discovery of the Asylum*, 112–13.

53. Ibid., 131; Dew M. Wisdom, U.S. Indian Agent, "Report of Union Agency," in *Annual Reports of the Department of the Interior [1897]*, 39–40; Owen, *Memoirs of Narcissa Owen*, 53.

54. Wisdom, "Report of Union Agency [1897]," 39–40; Steen, "Home for the Insane, Deaf, Dumb, and Blind," 412.

55. J. M. Spadding to D. W. Bushyhead, October 1, 1885, Cherokee Council and Senate Letters and Other Documents, Cherokee Insane Asylum, 1890–1902, NA, Fort Worth; "Annual Report of the Medical Superintendent of the Cherokee Male and Female Seminaries, National Prison and Insane Asylum," *Cherokee Advocate*, Tahlequah, Cherokee Nation, October 25, 1895, 2; Senate Bill No. 12, December 3, 1903, Cherokee Orphan Asylum, NA, Ft. Worth; "Public Schools Under Contract," ledger, p. 110, Record of School Contracts, 1887–1911, box 1, Education, BIA, NA; *Report of the United States Indian Inspector for the Indian Territory to the Secretary of the Interior for the Year Ended June 30, 1905* (Washington, D.C.: Government Printing Office, 1905), 39. For one overview of the Canton asylum, see Scott Riney, "Power and Powerlessness: The People of the Canton Asylum for Insane Indians," *South Dakota History* 1 and 2 (spring/summer 1997): 39–64.

56. "Act to ratify and confirm an agreement with Cherokee Tribe, 1900," 10, Dawes Commission, NA, Ft. Worth; *Report of the U.S. Indian Inspector for the Indian Territory to the Secretary of the Interior [1905]*, 48, 55, 57; Cherokee Board of Education to W. C. Rogers, Principal Chief, July 5, 1906, and John D. Benedict to W. C. Rogers, July 1905, and Acting Commissioner to W. C. Rogers, September 18, 1909, Cherokee Orphan Asylum, NA, Ft. Worth.

57. "Narrative Section III—Schools, 1914," 1, SANSR, NA, Central Plains.

CHAPTER 4. AFTER THE WAR: CHICKASAW

1. "An Interview with Mrs. Ida Cunnetabby, Davis, Oklahoma," vol. 21, p. 348, IPH.

2. Gibson, *The Chickasaws*, 260–62, 269–70.

3. Ibid., 234–35; Grant Foreman, *Advancing the Frontier, 1830–1860* (Norman: University of Oklahoma Press, 1933), 96; Carolyn Thomas Foreman, "Education Among the Chickasaw Indians," *Chronicles of Oklahoma* 15 (June 1937): 141, 157 (latter page quoting from 1849 report of commissioner of Indian affairs).

4. John M. Brewer, *The Vocational-Guidance Movement: Its Problems and Possibilities* (New York: Macmillan, 1919), 230–33, 275. K. Tasianina Lomawaima, *They Called It Prairie Light: The Story of the Chilocco Indian School* (Lincoln: University of Nebraska Press, 1994), 65, argues that vocational education did many things but agrees that it was an upper-class movement for social control.

5. "Report of the Commissioner of Indian Affairs," in *Report of the Secretary of the Interior [1892]*, 62–63; Francis Paul Prucha, *American Indian Policy in Crisis: Christian Reformers and the Indian, 1865–1900* (Norman: University of Oklahoma Press, 1976), 293; Bremmer, *The Public Good*, 30.

6. Gibson, *The Chickasaws*, 109, 231–32; Wright, *Creeks and Seminoles*, 229–30; Foreman, "Education Among the Chickasaw Indians," 139–40, 142, 144; Sandra Faiman-Silva, *Choctaws at the Crossroads: The Political Economy of Class and Culture in the Oklahoma Timber Region* (Lincoln: University of Nebraska Press, 1997), 41; Clara Sue Kidwell, *Choctaws and Missionaries in Mississippi, 1818–1918* (Norman: University of Oklahoma Press, 1995), 101.

7. Marjorie Hall Young, "'Stars in the Dark Night': The Education of Indian Youth at Choctaw Academy," *Chronicles of Oklahoma* 75 (fall 1997): 298–99.

8. Articles of Agreement, School Superintendent, Chickasaw Nation, August 18, 1887, Chickasaw Orphan Home, NA, Ft. Worth.

9. Caroline Davis, "Education of the Chickasaws, 1856–1907," *Chronicles of Oklahoma* 15 (December 1937): 423, 429; "Biography of Mr. Overton Lavers, 1937," vol. 6, pp. 316–17, IPH.

10. Articles of Agreement, School Superintendent, Chickasaw Nation, August 18, 1887, Chickasaw Orphan Home, NA, Ft. Worth; Davis, "Education of the Chickasaws," 423.

11. Davis, "Education of the Chickasaws," 417, 421; Gibson, *The Chickasaws*, 271, 280.

12. Davis, "Education of the Chickasaws," 429; Gibson, *The Chickasaws*, 235, 236, 280; "An Interview with Mrs. Ida Cunnetabby, Davis, Oklahoma," vol. 21, p. 38, IPH.

13. "Interview with Lottie Durham," vol. 23, p. 143, IPH; Davis, "Education of the Chickasaws," 445; "Act to Establish an Academy of 40 or 60 Orphan Girls, Under Care of Presbyterian Church in United States (South)," in *General and Special Laws of the Chickasaw Nation, 1878–1884* (Muskogee: Chickasaw Nation, 1884), 242; Sammy D. Hogue, *The Goodland Indian Orphanage: A Story of Christian Missions* (Goodland, Okla.: Goodland Indian Orphanage, 1940), 71–72 (Hogue's work also is found in Goodland Presbyterian Children's Home, *Reflections of Goodland*, vol. 1 [Wolfe City, Tex.: Henington Publishing, 1992]); Natalie Morrison Denison, "Missions and Missionaries of

the Presbyterian Church, U.S., Among the Choctaws—1866–1907," *Chronicles of Oklahoma* 24 (winter 1946–47): 433. It was not possible to determine if R. S. Bell, the orphan asylum superintendent, was Robert Bell of the earlier mission school or if they were relatives, perhaps father and son. Robert Bell of the earlier school would have been in his seventies at the time the asylum was operational.

14. *Vindicator,* Atoka, I.T., July 1, 1876.

15. Ibid.

16. Ibid.; Foreman, "Education Among the Chickasaw Indians," 56–57.

17. J. B. Jeter, Superintendent, to Board of Education, August 31, 1895, Choctaw Schools, Spencer Academy, NA, Ft. Worth.

18. "Carrie E. Wilcox Interview," vol. 49, p. 356, IPH.

19. "Interview with Miss Augusta Tucker, Teaching School in the 1880's Indian Territory," vol. 47, p. 339, IPH.

20. Coleman, *American Indian Children at School,* 68.

21. Gregory C. Thompson, "John D. C. Atkins, 1885–1888," in *Commissioners of Indian Affairs, 1824–1977,* 184; "Report of E. C. Osborne, Agent, Ponca, Pawnee, and Otoe Agency, Indian Territory," in *Report of the Secretary of the Interior [1887],* 889.

22. Thompson, "John D. C. Atkins," 184; Abing, "A Holy Battleground," 124; "Communication," *The Progress,* White Earth Reservation, Minn., May 12, 1888, 2.

23. "Commissioner Atkins Will Resign!" *The Progress,* May 5, 1888, 1.

24. Superintendent's Annual Report, 1899, Chickasaw Orphan Home, NA, Ft. Worth; "An Interview with Susan Lewis Brown, Full-Blood Chickasaw Woman," vol. 51, p. 160, IPH; "An Interview with Mrs. Ida Cunnetabby, Davis, Oklahoma," vol. 21, p. 348, IPH.

25. "Carrie E. Wilcox Interview," vol. 49, p. 356, IPH; Report, Quarter ending November 1, 1904, Chickasaw Orphan Home, NA, Ft. Worth.

26. "Biography of Mr. Overton Lavers," vol. 6, p. 316, IPH; "An Interview with Susan Lewis Brown, Full-Blood Chickasaw Woman," vol. 51, p. 159, IPH; "An Interview with Mrs. Ida Cunnetabby, Davis, Oklahoma," vol. 21, p. 349, IPH.

27. "Carrie E. Wilcox Interview," vol. 49, p. 356, IPH; "Experiences of an Indian Territory Teacher, Story Given by Mrs. Minnie Rector Fitts," vol. 3, p. 502, IPH.

28. "Carrie E. Wilcox Interview," vol. 49, p. 356, IPH; Sharon Skolnick (Okee-Chee) and Manny Skolnick, *Where Courage Is Like a Wild Horse: The World of an Indian Orphanage* (Lincoln: University of Nebraska Press, 1997), 8.

29. "Elsie Jacobs," 61, in *Ne'Ho Niyo'De:No'*; Miriam Formanek-Brunell, "The Politics of Doll Play in Nineteenth-Century America," in *Small Worlds,* 108, 116, 118, 123; Treasurer's Report, Miscellaneous, January 1915, box 2, folder 5, Thomas, NY State Archives (this is only one example of Thomas expenditures); Creek Orphan Home, photo no. 1277, Archives and Manuscripts, Oklahoma Historical Society (hereinafter cited as OHS).

30. "Interview with Aaron Hamilton, Chickasaw, Oklahoma," vol. 27, pp. 223, 225, IPH.

31. "An Interview with Susan Lewis Brown, Full-Blood Chickasaw Woman," vol. 51, p. 159, IPH.

32. Ibid. In Santa Fe Indian School documents there are several letters on the subject of handcuffs. For one example, see Samuel M. Cart to Comm. of

Indian Affairs, April 30, 1891, microfilm, roll 1, Santa Fe, NA, Rocky Mt. For later superintendent's viewpoint, see A. H. Viets to Comm. of Indian Affairs, August 30, 1899, microfilm, roll 5, Santa Fe, NA, Rocky Mt.

33. "Investigative Papers of Dr. R. N. Saunders," March 23, 1881, and severance notice, March 23, 1881, Chickasaw Orphan Home, NA, Ft. Worth.

34. Samuel M. Cart to Comm. of Indian Affairs, October 21, 1891, microfilm, roll 1, Santa Fe, NA, Rocky Mt.; Albert H. Kimball to J. Q. Smith, May 11, 1877, Sisseton, NA, Central Plains.

35. Cantrall, "Illinois State Board of Public Charities and the County Poorhouses," 51–52.

36. W. S. Derrick to D. H. Johnston, Governor of the Chickasaw Nation, October 1, 1900, Chickasaw Orphan Home, NA, Ft. Worth; "Act of January 12, 1901," Chickasaw Legislative Documents, NA, Ft. Worth.

37. W. S. Derrick to D. H. Johnston, October 1, 1900, Chickasaw Orphan Home, NA, Ft. Worth; R. C. Robe to John P. Turnbull, October 1890, and Receipt of Payment to Dr. R. W. Cheatham, October 8, 1890, Wheelock, NA, Ft. Worth; "Experiences of Pioneer Teacher of Indian Territory Days, Mrs. Anna Patterson Shortall," vol. 9, pp. 314–15, IPH; "Cemeteries—Chickasaw: Chickasaw Orphans Home," vol. 57, pp. 313–15, IPH. Another sign of Wheelock deaths was the purchase of two dozen coffin handles. See Receipt of Payment to J. W. Rodgers, October 28, 1890, Wheelock, NA, Ft. Worth.

38. Bill No. 42 [1900], Choctaw Schools, Spencer Academy, NA, Ft. Worth.

39. *Annual Report of the Department of the Interior, 1900* (Washington, D.C.: Government Printing Office, 1900), 112, 688; *Annual Report of the Department of the Interior, 1901* (Washington, D.C.: Government Printing Office, 1901), 129–30; Davis, "Education of the Chickasaws," 437–38, 440; Gibson, *The Chickasaws*, 304, 308.

40. Quarter ending November 11, 1904, Chickasaw Orphan Home, NA, Ft. Worth.

41. "An Act Providing for the Continuance of the School at the Chickasaw Orphan Home," 1906, Chickasaw Orphan Home, NA, Ft. Worth.

42. "Resolution of Respect to the Memory of Mrs. Vinnie Ream Turman," 1904, Chickasaw Orphan Home, NA, Ft. Worth.

43. "C. E. Wilcox to Hon. J. D. Benedict, May 26, 1907, Ralph Rose Documents," vol. 9, pp. 455–56, IPH.

44. "Appropriation Act, 1896," Chickasaw Orphan Home, NA, Ft. Worth; "Carrie E. Wilcox Interview," vol. 49, p. 356, IPH; "Biography of Mr. Overton Lavers," vol. 6, p. 316–17, IPH.

45. W. S. Derrick to D. H. Johnston, June 1899, and October 1, 1900, Chickasaw Orphan Home, NA, Ft. Worth.

46. "C. E. Wilcox to Hon. J. D. Benedict, May 26, 1907, Ralph Rose Documents," vol. 9, p. 455, IPH; "Report of Chickasaw Orphan Home, Quarter Ending Nov. 11th, 1904," "Report of Chickasaw Orphan Home, Quarter Ending, Nov. 10, 1905," and "Report of Chickasaw Orphan Home, Quarter Ending, May 11th, 1906," Chickasaw Orphan Home, NA, Ft. Worth.

47. Henry E. Fritz, *The Movement for Indian Assimilation, 1860–1890* (Philadelphia: University of Pennsylvania Press, 1963), 67; "An Act Providing for the Payment of Board and Tuition of Chickasaw Children Who May Attend Schools Other Than Tribal Schools," Chickasaw Schools, Miscellaneous, 1901–1908, NA, Ft. Worth; Davis, "Education of the Chickasaws," 447.

48. "St. Elizabeth's Indian School," *The Indian Sentinel* (1904–5): 38; D. Felix De Grosse to J. A. Stephan, February 4, 1899, Chickasaw Reservation,

BCIMR; Acting Commissioner, Office of Indian Affairs, to D. T. Flynn, May 13, 1899, Sac and Fox Agency, BCIMR.

49. "C. E. Wilcox to Hon. J. D. Benedict, May 26, 1907, Ralph Rose Documents," vol. 9, pp. 455–56, IPH.

50. Kate Barnard, *Second Report of the Commissioner of Charities and Corrections, 1910* (Oklahoma City: Warden Publishing, 1911), 68.

51. Deputy Clerk of Circuit Court, Jasper County, Illinois, writing for the father of John B. Harris, to Agent Jones, April 11, 1896, and Office of Indian Affairs to Wm. Ucholson, and Commissioner of Indian Affairs to George S. Doane, February 13, 1895, Vital Statistics and Related Material, Quapaw Agency, NA, Ft. Worth. Materials, including the *New York Tribune* clipping, in Dawes Commission to the Five Civilized Tribes, Creek Nation, NA, Ft. Worth, confirm that the commission was well aware of roll theft and frauds.

52. "The Day That Si Met Kate in Oklahoma," *Tanana Miner*, Chena, Alaska, November 9, 1908, box 13, file 17, Oklahoma Department of Charities and Corrections, Administrative Files, 1907–1945, Oklahoma State Archives, Oklahoma City, Okla. (hereinafter cited as Charities, Okla. Archives); Debo, *And Still the Waters Run*, 184.

53. Barnard, *Second Report of the Commissioner of Charities and Corrections, 1910*, 40; Kate Barnard, *Third Report of the Commissioner of Charities and Corrections, 1911* (Oklahoma City: Oklahoma Engraving and Printing, 1912), 194; Kate Barnard, *Fourth Report of the Commissioner of Charities and Corrections, 1912* (Oklahoma City: Oklahoma Engraving and Printing, 1913), 135, 140–54.

54. Too-Qua-Stee, "The Story of Allotment," *Weekly Chieftain*, Vinita, I.T., September 3, 1903, 4.

55. *Annual Reports of the Department of the Interior: Indian Affairs, Part II [1903]*, 250.

56. Lawrence C. Kelly, "Cato Sells, 1913–1921," in *Commissioners of Indian Affairs*, 245; Debo, *And Still the Waters Run*, 111; *Department of the Interior, Annual Report for 1908*, vol. 2 (Washington, D.C.: Government Printing Office, 1908), 241, 245; Ora Eddleman Reed, "The Indian Orphan," *Sturm's Oklahoma Magazine* 5 (January 1908): 81–83.

57. Kelly, "Cato Sells, 1913–1921," 245; Debo, *And Still the Waters Run*, 327–32; David L. Johnson and Raymond Wilson, "Gertrude Simmons Bonnin, 1876–1938: 'Americanize the First Indian,'" *American Indian Quarterly* 12 (winter 1988): 35.

58. "Scandal in Oklahoma," in *Native American Testimony: A Chronicle of Indian-White Relations from Prophecy to the Present, 1492–2000*, rev. ed., ed. Peter Nabokov (New York: Penguin Books, 1999), 300–303.

59. Barnard, *Second Report of the Commissioner of Charities and Corrections, 1910*, 68–69.

CHAPTER 5. THE MISSIONARIES: CHOCTAW AND CREEK

1. "Orphan Schools, Chapter VIII," in Bill No. 65, *Acts of the Choctaw Nation*, 64, Choctaw Schools, NA, Ft. Worth.

2. Angie Debo, *The Rise and Fall of the Choctaw Republic*, 2d ed. (Norman: University of Oklahoma Press, 1961), 16–17; William Warren Sweet, *Religion on the American Frontier, 1783–1840*, vol. 2, *The Presbyterians* (New York: Cooper Square Publishers, 1964), 635; "Interview with Miss

Augusta Tucker, Teaching School in the 1880's Indian Territory," vol. 47, p. 339, IPH; Hogue, *Goodland Indian Orphanage*, 19.

3. Ruth W. Messinger, "The History, Present Program and Population of Goodland Presbyterian Children's Home in Hugo, Oklahoma" (master's thesis, University of Oklahoma, 1964), 10; Hogue, *Goodland Indian Orphanage*, 13, 16.

4. David W. Baird, "Cyrus Byington and the Presbyterian Choctaw Mission," in *Churchmen and the Western Indians, 1820–1920*, ed. Clyde A. Milner II and Floyd A. O'Neill (Norman: University of Oklahoma Press, 1985), 6–7, 10–11; Faiman-Silva, *Choctaws at the Crossroads*, 39; Kidwell, *Choctaws and Missionaries*, 30; Sweet, *Religion on the American Frontier*, 636, 637.

5. Baird, "Cyrus Byington," 8–9; Kidwell, *Choctaws and Missionaries*, 54.

6. Baird, "Cyrus Byington," 8–9; Berrol, "Immigrant Children at School, 1880–1940," 47–48; Child, *Boarding School Seasons*, 29; Kidwell, *Choctaws and Missionaries*, 55.

7. Debo, *Rise and Fall of the Choctaw Republic*, 50–56.

8. Faiman-Silva, *Choctaws at the Crossroads*, 51–53; Foreman, "Education Among the Chickasaw Indians," 146; "Section III, School Privileges," 7, SANSR, NA, Central Plains; Perdue, *Nations Remembered*, 139.

9. Debo, *Rise and Fall of the Choctaw Republic*, 60, 236, 240; Baird, "Cyrus Byington," 26; Foreman, "Education Among the Chickasaw Indians," 142, quoting from *Annual Report of the Commissioner of Indian Affairs* (Washington, D.C.: Government Printing Office, 1848), 407.

10. "Board of Education," in Bill No. 65, *Acts of the Choctaw Nation [1898]*, 53–55, NA, Ft. Worth. Choctaw Neighborhood Schools (1886–98), Choctaw Schools, NA, Ft. Worth, lists schools by county and contains monthly reports on school sites and numbers in attendance; in Atoka County, for example, there was an average of twelve schools with a student population that ranged from four to fifteen pupils per school, per month.

11. "Supplementary Articles to the Preceding Treaty [Treaty with the Choctaw, 1830]," in *Treaties and Agreements of the Five Civilized Tribes*, 119–20; "Interview with Miss Augusta Tucker, Teaching School in the 1880's Indian Territory," vol. 47, p. 342, IPH; Debo, *Rise and Fall of the Choctaw Republic*, 233.

12. Foreman, *Advancing the Frontier*, 306; Debo, *Rise and Fall of the Choctaw Republic*, 16, 232; Deloria and Lytle, *American Indians, American Justice*, 196–97.

13. Bill No. 6, October 10, 1900, Records of the Choctaw Senate, NA, Ft. Worth.

14. Debo, *Rise and Fall of the Choctaw Republic*, 82.

15. "An Interview with Mrs. Emma Jean Ross Overstreet," vol. 38, pp. 432–33, IPH; J. S. Murrow to Brethren Composing the Choctaw and Chickasaw Baptist Association, July 1874, box 1, Letters of the Choctaw-Chickasaw Baptist Association file, Rev. Joseph S. Murrow Collection, OHS. For Murrow and Indian University, see John Williams and Howard L. Meredith, *Bacone Indian University* (Oklahoma City: Western Heritage Books and Oklahoma Heritage Association, 1980), 5, 13, 17; and J. S. Murrow to Samuel Checote, Principal Chief, Creek Nation, November 10, 1881, and Receipt of Payment from Creek Nation, December 15, 1891, Creek Principal Chief Documents, NA, Ft. Worth.

16. W. S. Derrick to D. W. Johnston, 1899, Chickasaw Orphan Home, NA, Ft. Worth.

17. Debo, *Rise and Fall of the Choctaw Republic*, 68, 238–39; Acts of the Choctaw Nation, November 11, 1881, and November 2, 1883, Choctaw Nation, NA, Ft. Worth; "John M. Robe," vol. 76, p. 424, IPH.

18. Baird, "Cyrus Byington," 26–27.

19. Choctaw Nation Bill No. 27, October 22, 1883, Armstrong Academy, NA, Ft. Worth; Debo, *Rise and Fall of the Choctaw Republic*, 60, 158–59. For names, see Payment Vouchers, Armstrong Academy, NA, Ft. Worth.

20. Choctaw Nation Bill No. 27, and Students and Classes, December 20, 1899, Armstrong Academy, NA, Ft. Worth.

21. "Narrative Section" (1933) and (1935), SANSR, NA, Central Plains; "List of Nonreservation Schools and Reservations and Agencies, 1917," box 1, Office file of Hervey B. Peairs, Chief Supervisor of Education and General Superintendent, 1910–1927, RG 75, NA (hereinafter cited as Peairs, NA); "School Data—1940—Wheelock Academy, Indian School," 1, typescript, Wheelock vertical file, OHS.

22. "Narrative Section, 1933," SANSR, NA, Central Plains; "School Data—1940," 1, Wheelock vertical file, OHS; Grant Foreman, *The Five Civilized Tribes* (Norman: University of Oklahoma Press, 1934), 58–59.

23. "John M. Robe," vol. 76, p. 424, IPH; R. C. Robe to John Turnbull, October 1890, and R. C. Robe to Choctaw Superintendent of Schools, 1892, Wheelock, NA, Ft. Worth; Mrs. Thoru Wilson, "Wheelock—Through the Years," 30, Wheelock vertical file, OHS.

24. Receipt of Payment, American Book Company, November 11, 1891, and "Report of R. C. Robe to Choctaw Superintendent of Schools, 1892," Wheelock, NA, Ft. Worth; "School Data—1940," 2, and Wilson, "Wheelock—Through the Years," 29–30, Wheelock vertical file, OHS.

25. D. Willis, Sheriff of Cedar County, to J. Gardner, September 8, 1885, Spencer Academy, NA, Ft. Worth.

26. "Narrative Section, 1933," SANSR, NA, Central Plains; Armstrong Orphan School Inventory, 1889, Armstrong Academy, NA, Ft. Worth; Alfred Docking to John P. Turnbull, 1889, Spencer Academy, NA, Ft. Worth.

27. Students and Classes, December 20, 1889, and Armstrong Orphan School Inventory, 1889, Armstrong Academy, NA, Ft. Worth.

28. "Report of C. J. Ralston, Superintendent of Armstrong Orphan Home, July 31, 1890," Armstrong Academy, NA, Ft. Worth.

29. "An Interview with Alice Perry, Choctaw Freedwoman," vol. 93, p. 258, IPH; Atoka Commercial Club to Gilbert W. Dukes and Choctaw National Council, [1901], Atoka Orphan Academy, NA, Ft. Worth. One of those signing the petition was Butler S. Smiser, a white who married a Choctaw woman to gain Choctaw citizenship and who was a former superintendent of the Baptist academy. For a brief reference to Smiser, see Debo, *Rise and Fall of the Choctaw Republic*, 227.

30. "C. J. Ralston, Superintendent's Report, 1892," Armstrong Academy, NA, Ft. Worth; Debo, *Rise and Fall of the Choctaw Republic*, 238; Wilbert H. Ahern, "Assimilationist Racism: The Case of the 'Friends of the Indian,'" *Journal of Ethnic Studies* 4 (summer 1976): 28–29.

31. "Superintendent's Report, 1894," and Students and Classes, 1899, and Supervision, Students, and Classes, 1894, Armstrong Academy, NA, Ft. Worth.

32. Wayne E. Fuller, *The Old Country School: The Story of Rural Education in the Middle West* (Chicago: University of Chicago Press, 1988), 240–41; Ledger, 1894, Armstrong Academy, NA, Ft. Worth.

33. "Superintendent's Report, January 12, 1892," 13, and "Superintendent's Report, August 27, 1892," 10, microfilm, roll 2, Santa Fe, NA, Rocky Mt.; Thomas M. Jones to W. N. Hailman, March 20, 1894, microfilm, roll 3, Santa Fe, NA, Rocky Mt.; Thomas M. Jones to Comm. of Indian Affairs, May 24, 1897, microfilm, roll 4, Santa Fe, NA, Rocky Mt.

34. Beekman, *Mechanical Baby*, 109–12; Hamilton Cravens, "Child-Saving in the Age of Professionalism, 1915–1930," in *American Childhood: A Research Guide and Historical Handbook*, 416–17; L. H. Weir and Abbie Condit, "The Leisure of the Child," in "Standards of Child Welfare: A Report of the Children's Bureau Conferences, May and June, 1919," Conference Series No. 1, Children's Bureau Publication No. 60 (1919), 55; William A. McKeever, "A Modern Dictator for the Rural School," *Country Gentleman* 77 (December 7, 1912): 6; *White House Conference on Children in a Democracy*, 189, 191, White House Conference, DDE Library. Dominick J. Cavallo, *Muscles and Morals: Organized Playgrounds and Urban Reformers, 1890–1920* (Philadelphia: University of Pennsylvania Press, 1981), offers a good overview of the national playground movement, which focused on thwarting juvenile delinquency with play.

35. Treasurer's Monthly Reports for Thomas routinely included lists of recreational items purchased. For a few examples, see Miscellaneous, November 1903, box 1, folder 9, December 1904, box 1, folder 14, October 1913, box 1, folder 94, Thomas, NY State Archives. For Creek and Cherokee, see photographs nos. 520, 528, and 1580, Archives and Manuscripts, OHS. For "Outdoor Girl," see Lois Rudnick, "The New Woman," in *1915, The Cultural Moment*, ed. Adele Heller and Lois Rudnick (New Brunswick, N.J.: Rutgers University Press, 1991), 70–73; Rosalind Rosenberg, *Beyond Separate Spheres: Intellectual Roots of Modern Feminism* (New Haven, Conn.: Yale University Press, 1982), especially chap. 3, "The New Psychology and the New Woman."

36. "School Data—1940," 2, and Wilson, "Wheelock—Through the Years," 28, Wheelock vertical file, OHS; Bill No. 12, An Act Canceling the Contract of E. H. Wilson, Superintendent of Wheelock Orphan Seminary, March 23, 1899, Records of the General Council, NA, Ft. Worth.

37. Hogue, *Goodland Indian Orphanage*, 63–65; Debo, *And Still the Waters Run*, 7; Denison, "Missions and Missionaries," 438.

38. Hogue, *Goodland Indian Orphanage*, 67–69; "Goodland Orphanage, Goodland, Oklahoma," vol. 84, p. 378, IPH; "An Interview with Mrs. Serena Perkins, widow," vol. 39, pp. 459–60, IPH.

39. Hogue, *Goodland Indian Orphanage*, 71–73; "Lucy Kingsbury Hatchkin Forrest," vol. 74, p. 143, IPH.

40. Messinger, "Goodland Presbyterian Children's Home," 13; Hogue, *Goodland Indian Orphanage*, 73–75; "Goodland Orphanage, Goodland, Oklahoma," vol. 84, p. 387–88, IPH.

41. Bill No. 45 [November 8, 1897], in *Acts of the Choctaw Nation*, 35, and "An Act Relating to the Orphan Academy at Atoka Indian Territory, March 25, 1899," Records of the General Council, NA, Ft. Worth; "Interview with John Mehnker, white man—80 Years Old," vol. 6, p. 383, IPH.

42. Department of the Interior to Choctaw National Council, April 8, 1899, and April 14, 1899, Atoka Orphan Academy, NA, Ft. Worth; U.S. Indian Inspector of Indian Territory to S. J. Homes, April 20, 1899, and Atoka petition, October 8, 1901, Atoka Orphan Academy, NA, Ft. Worth.

43. "Incorporation of Murrow Indian Orphans' Home, granted in November 1902," Benevolent Associations, U.S. District Court, South McAlester, I.T.,

U.S. Court Records, NA, Ft. Worth; "From an Old Clipping found in an old record of the Baptist church of Atoka, Oklahoma," vol. 34, pp. 184–85, IPH; Clara A. McBride, "Fifty Beautiful Years," *Indian Orphan* 5 (November 1, 1907), clipping, box 1, biographical file, Murrow Collection, OHS; "An Interview with Alice Perry, Choctaw Freedwoman," vol. 93, pp. 257–58, IPH.

44. "Incorporation of Murrow Indian Orphans' Home, granted in November 1902," NA, Ft. Worth; "Interview with Mrs. Celia Brown McGahey," vol. 7, pp. 29–30, IPH.

45. Bill No. 42, November 5, 1903, and Bill No. 32, Memorial, November 24, 1905, in *Acts of the Choctaw Nation*, 50–51, Records of the General Council, NA, Ft. Worth; "Home for Indian Orphans," *Sturm's Oklahoma Magazine* 3 (November 1906): 91–92; Reed, "The Indian Orphan," 83.

46. Reed, "The Indian Orphan," 83; "From an Old Clipping found in an old record of the Baptist church of Atoka, Oklahoma," vol. 34, p. 185, IPH.

47. Samuel Checote, Principal Chief, to National Council, October 27, 1881, and J. S. Murrow to Samuel Checote, Principal Chief, November 10, 1881, and receipt, signed by A. C. Bacone, December 15, 1881, and A. C. Bacone to Principal Chief, September 26, 1887, Creek, Principal Chief Documents, NA, Ft. Worth; Williams and Meredith, *Bacone Indian University*, 5, 13, 46–47; Debo, *Road to Disappearance*, 310–11.

48. Debo, *Road to Disappearance*, 98–99, 265.

49. Resolution, Indian Mission Conference, Oct. 2–6, 1872, and *Thomas B. Ruble* v. *Creek Nation*, deposition, October 11, 1872, and Samuel Checota, Principal Chief, September 19, 1881, and Samuel Checota to U.S. Secretary of the Interior, January 17, 1882, and Resolution, Creek Nation Education Committee, November 4, 1893, Creek Schools, NA, Ft. Worth; "Interview with M. E. Harris," vol. 4, p. 374, IPH; "Interview with Mr. Sam Todd," vol. 10, p. 554, IPH; "Interview with Henry Vogel," vol. 11, pp. 92–93, IPH. Debo, *Road to Disappearance*, 352, states that the orphanage was built in 1895, but records indicate that it was at least four years earlier. The home was a two-story structure with a metal roof; see Insurance Policy, Springfield Fire & Marine Insurance Co., 1899, Creek Orphan Asylum, NA, Ft. Worth.

50. Debo, *Road to Disappearance*, 249; Act, Certified and Approved, October 24, 1881, and Monday Durant to Samuel Checote, December 27, 1881, and Pleasant Porter to Hiram Price, July 28, 1882, and Henry Reed to Council of Muskogee Nation, October 10, 1882, NA, Ft. Worth.

51. "Interview with George McIntosh," vol. 7, pp. 72, 82, IPH; Debo, *Road to Disappearance*, 99; Rogin, *Fathers and Children*, 194–95; Wright, *Creeks and Seminoles*, 307.

52. Wiley Britton, *The Civil War on the Border*, vol. 2 (New York: G. P. Putnam's Sons, 1904), 24–25; McLoughlin, *After the Trail of Tears*, 320; Kent Carter, "Choctaw-Chickasaw Enrollment, Part I," *Prologue: Quarterly of the National Archives and Records Administration* 31 (winter 1999): 231–33.

53. M. W. Barnett to Board of Education, January 26, 1895, and Joseph Howard, Superintendent, Teachers Report, 1897, and Payment Receipts, 1891–1908, and Appropriations, 1893, Creek Colored Orphan Home, NA, Ft. Worth; Land Conveyance, February 1, 1889, Salary List, 1889, Survey, 1890, Acting Commissioner for the Five Civilized Tribes to W. C. Rogers, March 13, 1911, Cherokee Schools—Colored High School, NA, Ft. Worth; Teacher's Quarterly Report, Oct. 1–Dec. 31, 1905, and Teacher's Quarterly Report, Jan. 1–Feb. 6, 1906, and H.R. Bill No. 5976, as cited in Department of the Interior, Commissioners to Sen. Moses Clapp, Jan. 18, 1906, Dawes Commission, NA,

Ft. Worth; "Report of the Commissioner of Indian Affairs," in *Report of the Secretary of the Interior, [1887]*, 91; Debo, *Road to Disappearance*, 311, 352; Tim Gammon, "The Black Freedmen of the Cherokee Nation," *Negro History Bulletin* 40 (May–June 1977): 733–35; Daniel F. Littlefield, *The Chickasaw Freedmen: A People Without a Country* (Westport, Conn.: Greenwood Press, 1980), 15–16; Gibson, *The Chickasaws*, 275–78, 293; Lomawaima, *They Called It Prairie Light*, 149; Thos. Jones to Commissioner of Indian Affairs, September 5, 1896, microfilm, roll 3, Santa Fe, NA, Rocky Mt.

54. J. P. Whitehead, resolution, October 8, 1885, Creek Schools, NA, Ft. Worth; "Henry S. Myers Interview," vol. 37, p. 419, IPH; "Siegal E. McIntosh Interview," vol. 35, p. 236, IPH.

55. P. R. Ewing to National Council, October 7, 1895, Creek Orphan Asylum, NA, Ft. Worth.

56. A. P. Rowland, American Baptist Publishing Society, to Peter Ewing, April 14, 1895, Creek Orphan Asylum, NA, Ft. Worth; Edward Everett Dale, ed., "The Journal of Alexander Lawrence Posey, January 1 to September 4, 1897," *Chronicles of Oklahoma* 46 (winter 1967–68): 395.

57. "An Interview with Lena Benson Tiger," vol. 112, pp. 230–32, IPH; "Susan H. Tiger Interview," vol. 47, pp. 124–25, IPH; "Joe M. Grayson Interview," vol. 26, pp. 351, 363, IPH; "Experiences of Pioneer Teacher of Indian Territory Days, Mrs Anna Patterson Shortall," vol. 9, p. 314, IPH. For information on clans, see Wright, *Creeks and Seminoles*, 19–20.

58. "Teachers' Report, March–May 1896," and "Report for 2nd Quarter, 1897–98," and "Superintendent's Annual Report, October 1899," Creek Orphan Asylum, NA, Ft. Worth; "Interview with Dicey Stake Adams," vol. 12, p. 77, IPH; "An Interview with Lena Benson Tiger," vol. 112, pp. 238–39, IPH; "Susan H. Tiger Interview," vol. 47, p. 125, IPH; "Softkee," in *The Multicultural Recipe Book* (Stillwater, Okla.: Title V Parent Committee for Indian Education, 1995). The coloring for blue dumplings originally came from burned bean shells or corn cobs; today, grape juice often is substituted to achieve the same color.

59. Dale, "Journal of Alexander Lawrence Posey," 402.

60. Debo, *Road to Disappearance*, 374; *Annual Reports of the Department of the Interior: Indian Affairs, Part II, [1903]*, 252; "A Pioneer Woman of the Muskogee-Creek Nation, Interview with Mrs. Minda G. Hardin," vol. 4, p. 290, IPH.

CHAPTER 6. TRIBAL DISSOLUTION: OKLAHOMA

1. "Narrative Section III—Schools, 1912," SANSR, 1912, NA, Central Plains.

2. Frederick E. Hoxie, *A Final Promise: The Campaign to Assimilate the Indians, 1880–1920* (Lincoln: University of Nebraska Press, 1984), 33; Mrs. Willie Chapman to Kate Barnard, April 23, 1908, box 17, file 17, Charities, Okla. Archives; "Sequoyah O. T. School, 1928," 3, SANSR, NA, Central Plains. Among the private orphanages were Baptist Orphan's Home of Oklahoma; Methodist Orphanage; St. Joseph's Orphanage; Francis E. Williard Orphanage; and Odd Fellow's Orphan Home.

3. Property Return, Inventory, 1906, and C. F. Larrabee to Walter Falwell, May 16, 1906, and John D. Benedict to J. Geo. Wright, November 4, 1905, Dawes Commission, NA, Ft. Worth.

4. "Report of the Dawes Commission, November 20, 1894," in *Documents of United States Indian Policy*, ed. Francis Paul Prucha (Lincoln: University of Nebraska Press, 1975), 195; "Report of the Commissioner of Indian Affairs," in *Annual Reports of the Department of the Interior: Indian Affairs, Part I*, Doc. No. 5, 57th Cong., 2d sess. (Washington, D.C.: Government Printing Office, 1903), 130; *Annual Reports of the Department of the Interior: Indian Affairs, Part II, [1903]*, 240–41, 274–75; Joe C. Jackson, "Church School Education in the Creek Nation, 1898–1907," *Chronicles of Oklahoma* 46 (autumn 1968): 320.

5. "In Oklahoma, Indian Schools Said to Be Conducted Loosely," *Wichita* (Kans.) *Daily Beacon*, February 18, 1902, 3.

6. John D. Benedict to J. Geo. Wright, November 4, 1905, Dawes Commission, NA, Ft. Worth; Jackson, "Church School Education in the Creek Nation," 316–17, 327.

7. A. H. Mike to Walter Falwell, June 28, 1905, and "Teacher's Quarterly Report, Oct. 1–Dec. 21, 1905," Creek Schools, NA, Ft. Worth. Files of the superintendent of Indian schools contain individual course of study reports from a number of schools; for example, Superintendent Hervey Peairs notified a teacher at Fort Berthold Indian School that his work was to be commended, except in one area: "You have followed the State course of study quite closely except in the first grade language and reading." Peairs then went on to outline a comparison between the teacher's program and the acceptable course. See Hervey B. Peairs to Thomas Jackson, n.d., box 1, Peairs, NA.

8. "Some Interesting Facts About Negro School at Boley—Why the Latin?" *Muskogee* (Okla.) *Times-Democrat*, September 16, 1909, 1; "Creek Supervisor of Schools, Monthly Report, March 1905," and Commissioner to Moty Tiger, November 5, 1909, Dawes Commission, NA, Ft. Worth; "Superintendent's Annual Narrative and Statistical Reports, 1912," 7, SANSR, NA, Central Plains; "Report of the Governor of Oklahoma," in *Report of the Department of the Interior: Indian Affairs, Territories [1907]*, 677.

9. Kelly, "Cato Sells," 245; Debo, *And Still the Waters Run*, 90–91; Mrs. Jessie Moree to J. P. Thompson, October 11, 1924, and J. P. Thompson to Mrs. Jessie Moree, October 13, 1924, box 5, file 6, Charities, Okla. Archives; "Cherokee Orphan Training School, 1914," 1, SANSR, NA, Central Plains.

10. "Cherokee Orphan Training School, 1912," 8, SANSR, NA, Central Plains.

11. "Superintendent's Annual Narrative and Statistical Reports" (1916), pp. 3–5, (1919), p. 1, (1920), pupils enrolled form (1921), SANSR, NA, Central Plains.

12. "Superintendent's Annual Narrative and Statistical Reports" (1912), pp. 1–3, 5, 8, (1913), pp. 1–3, (1914), pp. 1–4, SANSR, NA, Central Plains; Donal F. Lindsey, *Indians at Hampton Institute, 1877–1923* (Urbana: University of Illinois Press, 1994), 33, 125; Barnard, *Second Report of the Commissioner of Charities and Corrections, 1910*, 87.

13. Barnard, *Second Report of the Commissioner of Charities and Corrections, 1910*, 88.

14. Ibid.; "Report of the Superintendent of Indian Schools," in *Report of the Department of the Interior: Indian Affairs, Territories [1907]*, 130.

15. Memorandum, August 22, 1917, box 1, Peairs, NA.

16. "Narrative Section III—Schools" (1912), (1914), and (1929), SANSR, NA, Central Plains; A. H. Mike to W. Falwell, January 4, 1906, Dawes Commission, NA, Ft. Worth; Lawrence C. Kelly, "Charles Henry Burke, 1921–1929," in *Commissioners of Indian Affairs*, 255.

17. Mollie V. Garther, "Education for True Womanhood in Indian Schools," in *Superintendent of Indian Schools, Annual Report, 1897* (Washington, D.C.: Government Printing Office, 1897), 64; "Plan to Educate Indians," *Spokesman Review,* April 9, 1926, clipping, box 1, Peairs, NA; "Cherokee Orphan Training School, 1920," and "Sequoyah O. T. School, 1928," SANSR, NA, Central Plains.

18. "Virginia Snow," 193, in *Ne'Ho Niyo'De:No'.*

19. Jean Swift Dobbs, "Child Health Work at K.S.A.C.," *Home Economics News* 2 (December 1925): 35; Thomas F. Vance et al., "The Development of Children in the Home Management House at the Iowa State College," *Journal of Experimental Education* 2 (December 1933): 166–69; Beulah I. Coon, "Home Economics Section," *American Vocational Association News Bulletin* 2 (February 1927): 26.

20. "Sequoyah Orphan Training School" (1928), p. 4, and (1929), p. 4, SANSR, NA, Central Plains.

21. Lomawaima, *They Called It Prairie Light,* 81, 82; Mary Faulkner, "The Vocational School for Girls," *American Vocational Association News Bulletin* 1 (August 1926): 12; Brewer, *Vocational-Guidance Movement,* 23; Marilyn Irvin Holt, *Linoleum, Better Babies, and the Modern Farm Woman, 1890–1930* (Albuquerque: University of New Mexico Press, 1995), 41.

22. Steven J. Crum, "Henry Roe Cloud, a Winnebago Indian Reformer: His Quest for American Indian Higher Education," *Kansas History* 11 (autumn 1988): 171; Albert H. Leake, *The Vocational Education of Girls and Women* (New York: Macmillan, 1918), 8–9.

23. "Wheelock Female Orphan Academy, 1913," 19, and "Sequoyah Orphan Training School" (1928), p. 3, (1932), sec. 1, p. 2, SANSR, NA, Central Plains; R. W. Morrish, "Organization of Kansas Boys' and Girls' Clubs," Kansas State Agricultural College, Division of College Extension, Bulletin No. 30 (January 1922), 4–5.

24. "Wheelock Female Orphan Academy" (1913), p. 20, (1914), 10, SANSR, NA, Central Plains.

25. Adams, *Education for Extinction,* 316–17; Prucha, *Great Father,* 265.

26. Hervy B. Peairs to Mrs. Susan F. Nichols, [July] 1911, vol. 1, Peairs, NA; "Sequoyah Orphan Training School, 1933," 6–7, SANSR, NA, Central Plains.

27. "American Indian Legends," 6, 10, typescript, Office of Indian Affairs, Bulletin 17 (1922), Haskell Institute files, Library, KSHS.

28. "Haskell Celebration, October 27–30—1926," 4, 9, and "'Hiawatha' by Haskell Students," play program, 1926, Haskell Institute files, Library, KSHS; Schoolcraft, *Myth of Hiawatha,* 2, 51; Dippie, *Vanishing American,* 211–12.

29. Goodland Indian School, Photo No. 2361.A, Archives and Manuscripts Division, OHS; A. M. Gibson, "Joe Kagey: Indian Educator," *Chronicles of Oklahoma* 38 (spring 1960): 13, 14; Hogue, *Goodland Indian Orphanage,* 106.

30. "Wheelock Academy" (1932), p. 1, (1935), p. 1, and "Seqyoyah Orphan Training School, 1933," 6–7, SANSR, NA, Central Plains. For one reference to home industries, see Anne M. Evans, "Women's Rural Organizations and Their Activities," U.S. Department of Agriculture, Bulletin No. 719 (August 29, 1918): 1, 3–4, 8.

31. "Wheelock Female Orphan Academy, Report 1912," 8, SANSR, NA, Central Plains.

32. "Wheelock Academy, 1930," 7, and "Sequoyah Orphan Training School, Report 1931," 1, and "Sequoyah O. T. School, Report 1928," 1, SANSR, NA, Central Plains; Todd J. Kosmerick, "Exploring New Territory: The History of

Native Americans as Revealed Through Congressional Papers at the Carl Albert Center, Part I," *Western Historical Quarterly* 30 (summer 1999): 206–7.

33. Thornton, *American Indian Holocaust and Survival*, 103, 172–73; "Report of the Superintendent of Indian Schools [1907]," 131; "Narrative Section II—Health, 1915," 1, and "Superintendent's Annual Narrative and Statistical Reports," (1914) p. 2, (1917) p. 1, (1918) p. 1, SANSR, NA, Central Plains.

34. "Superintendent's Report, Aug. 27, 1892," 10, microfilm, roll 2, Santa Fe, NA, Rocky Mt.; "Superintendent's Annual Narrative and Statistical Reports" (1913), p. 1, (1914), pp. 1–2, (1917), p. 2, (1918), p. 2, SANSR, NA, Central Plains; Kelly, "Charles Henry Burke," 255.

35. "Sequoyah Orphan Training School" (1928), p. 2, (1932), p. 4. (1933), p. 1, SANSR, NA, Central Plains.

36. "Superintendent's Annual Narrative and Statistical Reports" (1929), p. 1, (1930), pp. 1–2, SANSR, NA, Central Plains; Quetel, *History of Syphilis*, 6–7, 183, 192, 198, 200, 249.

37. Williams and Meredith, *Bacone Indian University*, 46–47; "Report of the Murrow Indian Orphans' Home for the Year Ending September 30, 1912," in *Fourth Report of the Commissioner of Charities and Corrections, 1912*, 444–45.

38. Hogue, *Goodland Indian Orphanage*, 107; Messinger, "Goodland Presbyterian Children's Home," 13–14.

39. Hogue, *Goodland Indian Orphanage*, 85–87.

40. Debo, *And Still the Waters Run*, 325–26; Kelly, "Charles Henry Burke," 259–60.

41. "Report of the Murrow Indian Orphans' Home for the Year Ending September 30, 1912," 444–45.

42. "Report of the Oklahoma Benevolent and Orphanage Association," in *Fourth Report of the Commissioner of Charities and Corrections, 1912*, 447–49; Mabel Bassett, *Report of the Commissioner of Charities and Corrections, 1923* (Sapulpa, Okla.: Quality Print Shop, 1924), 50, 54; Mabel Bassett, *Report of the Commissioner of Charities and Corrections, 1924* (Gutherie, Okla.: Oklahoma Printing Co., 1925), 26; Skolnick and Skolnick, *Where Courage Is Like a Wild Horse*, 133–37, 139–43.

43. "Report of the Murrow Indian Orphans' Home for the Year Ending September 30, 1912," 446–47; Holt, *Linoleum, Better Babies, and the Modern Farm Woman*, 23–24; Gregory C. Thompson, "John D. C. Atkins, 1885–88," in *Commissioners of Indian Affairs*, 182, 184. A childhood memory of the author's husband, Daniel D. Holt, is of his Baptist church, where the donation of clothing was called "Bundles for Bacone"—a play on "Bundles for Britain."

44. Kellee Green, "The Fourteenth Numbering of the People: The 1920 Federal Census," *Prologue: Quarterly of the National Archives* 23 (summer 1991): 138–39; Reuben Hill, "The American Family Today," 6, typescript, box 120, Workgroups 39–42 file, White House Conference (1960), DDE Library.

45. Hogue, *Goodland Indian Orphanage*, 87, 104; Messinger, "Goodland Presbyterian Children's Home," 15–17; Barr, "A Hive of Industry," 18.

46. Messinger, "Goodland Presbyterian Children's Home," 16, 29.

47. Walter Angelo Bennett, "Life and Letters of Oscar Gardner" (graduate thesis, Presbyterian Theological Seminary, 1961), 109.

48. *Annual Report of the Department of the Interior: Indian Affairs, Part II, [1903]*, 246; W. T. Whitaker to Kate Barnard, December 6, 1907, and W. T.

Whitaker to Kate Barnard, October 1908, box 17, file 17, Charities, Okla. Archives.

49. "Truth About Orphan Home," *Muskogee* (Okla.) *Times-Democrat,* November 12, 1909, 1; Barnard, *Third Report of the Commissioner of Charities and Corrections, 1911,* 274–75.

50. Barnard, *Second Report of the Commissioner of Charities and Corrections, 1910,* 38, 40, 49; Barnard, *Fourth Report of the Commissioner of Charities and Corrections, 1912,* 267.

51. Barnard, *Fourth Report of the Commissioner of Charities and Corrections, 1912,* 135; Kate Barnard to Charles Brady, July 21, 1908, box 17, file 17, Charities, Okla. Archives.

52. Barnard, *Fourth Report of the Commissioner of Charities and Corrections, 1912,* 407–17.

53. Skolnick, *Where Courage Is Like a Wild Horse,* 5, 53.

54. Messinger, "Goodland Presbyterian Children's Home," 19, 29.

55. "Forum IV—Work-Groups 39 through 42," 4, typescript, box 120, Work-groups 39–42 file, White House Conference (1960), DDE Library; *Standards of Child Health, Education, and Social Welfare, Based on Recommendations of the 1940 White House Conference on Children in a Democracy and Conclusion of Discussion Groups,* U.S. Children's Bureau, Publication 287, ca. 1942, box 1, file 10, White House Conference, DDE Library.

CHAPTER 7. CATHOLIC OUTPOSTS: OJIBWAY AND SIOUX

1. Sister Blandina Segale, *At the End of the Santa Fe Trail* (Columbus, Ohio: Columbian Press, 1932; reprint, Albuquerque: University of New Mexico Press, 1999), 98.

2. Ibid., 107–8; Nancy Hanks, "Lamy's Legacy: Catholic Institutions of New Mexico Territory," in *Seeds of Struggle/Harvest of Faith: The Papers of the Archdiocese of Santa Fe Catholic Church Cuarto Centennial Conference on the History of the Catholic Church in New Mexico,* ed. Thomas J. Steele, S.J., Paul Rhetts, and Barbe Awalt (Albuquerque, N.M.: LPD Press and the Archdiocese of Santa Fe, 1998), 389, 410 n. 19; *New Mexico Department of Public Welfare, Annual Report, Fiscal Year Ending June 30, 1951* (Santa Fe: New Mexico Department of Public Welfare, 1952), 41; "Orphanage for Girls Stirs Many Memories," *Journal North,* Santa Fe, N.M., September 15, 1984, 6–7, clipping files, New Mexico State Library, Santa Fe, N.M. The industrial school is not to be confused with St. Catharine's Industrial School, which opened in 1887 to train boys and then closed; it reopened as a girls' school in 1894. See J. B. Salpointe, *Soldiers of the Cross: Notes on the Ecclesiastical History of New Mexico, Arizona, and Colorado* (Banning, Calif.: St. Boniface's Industrial School, 1898), 273–74; and "Saint Catharine's Indian School," 12–19.

3. James H. Carleton to Chief of the Agricultural Bureau, Washington, D.C., November 1, 1864, in *Condition of the Indian Tribes: Report of the Joint Special Committee Appointed Under Joint Resolution of March 3, 1865* (Washington, D.C.: Government Printing Office, 1867), 209; Ben C. Cutler, Assist. Adj. Gen., in General Orders No. 4, Hdq. Dept. of New Mexico, February 18, 1865, reprinted in *Condition of the Indian Tribes,* 258–66.

4. Flood, *Lost Bird of Wounded Knee,* 60; Dee Brown, *Bury My Heart at Wounded Knee: An Indian History of the American West* (New York: Holt, Rinehart and Winston, 1971), 417–18.

5. Charles Alexander Eastman (Ohiyesa), *From the Deep Woods to Civilization: Chapters in the Autobiography of an Indian* (Boston: Little, Brown, 1916), 234–35.

6. Philip S. Hall, *To Have This Land: The Nature of Indian/White Relations, South Dakota, 1888–1891* (Vermillion: University of South Dakota Press, 1991), 90–98; John Jutz to Fr. Stephan, December 16, 1890, Holy Rosary Mission, BCIMR.

7. Examination of John P. Williamson, Yankton Agency, September 9, 1865, in *Condition of the Indian Tribes*, 413.

8. Dr. Charles Alexander Eastman, "The Story of the Little Big Horn," 353–58, pamphlet file, Sioux, Library, KSHS; Michael L. Tate, *The Frontier Army in the Settlement of the West* (Norman: University of Oklahoma Press, 1999), 251.

9. Unrau, *White Man's Wicked Water*, 20, 76; Benj. Thompson to N. G. Taylor, January 5, 1868, and Charles Crisser to Comm. of Indian Affairs, October 13, 1880, Sisseton, NA, Central Plains; "Local," *Roberts County Banner*, Sisseton, S.D., May 28, 1903, 4, and September 10, 1903, 2. Goodwill Mission was a government contract school under the Presbyterian Board of Home Missions. See Contract Schools Ledger, Record of School Contracts, 1887–1911, box 1, Education, BIA, NA.

10. Keller, *American Protestantism*, 186; P. Flor. Digmann to Rev. W. H. Ketcham, October 16, 1902, BCIMR; Monsignor Augustin Ravoux, V.G., *Reminiscences, Memoirs and Lectures* (St. Paul, Minn.: Brown, Treacy and Co., 1890), 47; Hassrick, *The Sioux*, 287–88.

11. J. G. Hamilton to J. Smith, January 18, 1877, Sisseton, NA, Central Plains.

12. J. A. Stephan to Rev. John Jutz, February 9, 1891, Holy Rosary Mission, BCIMR.

13. Vizenor, *The People Named the Chippewa*, 78–90; Melissa L. Meyer, *The White Earth Tragedy: Ethnicity and Dispossession at a Minnesota Anishinaabe Reservation, 1889–1920* (Lincoln: University of Nebraska Press, 1994), 10–11; *The Progress*, White Earth Reservation, March 25, 1886, October 22, October 29, 1887. For examples of published reminiscences, see "The Ojibwas, Their Customs and Traditions," *The Progress*, December 24, 1887, January 28, 1888.

14. P. Flor. Digmann to Rev. W. H. Ketcham, October 16, 1902, St. Francis Mission, Rosebud Agency, BCIMR; Loring Benson Priest, *Uncle Sam's Stepchildren: The Reformation of United States Indian Policy, 1865–1887* (New York: Octagon Books, 1972), 136.

15. "History of OMI/CUSP Ministry Among Native Americans in the Midwest," 3, typescript, Archives, Catholic Diocese of Sioux Falls, SD (hereinafter cited as Archives, Sioux Falls); Ethel Nurge, "Dakota Diet: Traditional and Contemporary," in *The Modern Sioux: Social Systems and Reservation Culture*, ed. Ethel Nurge (Lincoln: University of Nebraska Press, 1970), 58; Angie Debo, *A History of the Indians of the United States* (Norman: University of Oklahoma Press, 1970), 256, 282; David A. Nichols, "The Other Civil War: Lincoln and the Indians," *Minnesota History* 44 (spring 1974): 3–15; H. B. Whipple to E. S. Parker, Commissioner of Indian Affairs, October 5, 1869, Sisseton, NA, Central Plains.

16. H. B. Whipple to E. S. Parker, October 5, 1869, Benjamin Thompson to N. G. Taylor, December 30, 1867, C. H. Mix to N. G. Taylor, Benjamin Thompson to O. H. Browning, Secretary of the Interior, April 7, 1868, Daniel

Renville to Benjamin Thompson, April 12, 1869, and J. G. Hamilton to J. Smith, January 18, 1877, Sisseton, NA, Central Plains; Robinson, "Digest of the Reports of the Commissioner of Indian Affairs," 313. For one overview of 1880s drought, see Sam S. Kepfield, "'They Were in Far Too Great Want': Federal Drought Relief to the Great Plains, 1887–1895," *South Dakota History* 28 (winter 1998): 244–70.

17. "Report of the Commissioner of Indian Affairs," in *Report of the Secretary of the Interior [1892],* 4; P. Flor. Digmann to Rev. J. A. Stephan, August 16, 1892, St. Francis Mission, Rosebud Agency, BCIMR.

18. P. Flor. Digmann to Rev. W. H. Ketcham, October 16, 1902, St. Francis Mission, Rosebud Agency, BCIMR.

19. Fergus, *Shadow Catcher,* 19–22; "Joseph Kossuth Dixon," in *Indian Life: Transforming an American Myth,* ed. William W. Savage Jr. (Norman: University of Oklahoma Press, 1977), 284, quoting from Joseph K. Dixon, *The Vanishing Race: The Last Great Indian Council* (Garden City, N.Y.: Doubleday, Page, 1914), 3–36.

20. Charles R. Kutzleb, "Educating the Dakota Sioux, 1876–1890," *North Dakota History* 32 (October 1965): 197–98, 204, 211; Johnson and Wilson, "Gertrude Simmons Bonnin," 3–17; Adams, *Education for Extinction,* 47–48, 97, 55; "The Sioux Commission," *The Progress,* White Earth Reservation, August 11, 1888, 1.

21. William Wilson Manross, *A History of the American Episcopal Church* (New York: Morehouse Publishing, 1935), 338–39.

22. N. G. Lee to Comm. of Indian Affairs, March 5, 1880, and Charles Crisser to R. E. Trowbridge, July 19, 1880, Sisseton, NA, Central Plains.

23. Contract Schools Ledger, box 1, Record of School Contracts, 1887–1911, Education, BIA, NA; T. J. Morgan to Rev. Father Chapelle, Bureau of Catholic Indian Missions, in *Report of the Secretary of the Interior [1892],* 163; [Pratt] to Rev. John Jutz, April 27, 1891, Holy Rosary Mission, BICMR; "Editorial," *The Indian Sentinel* (1903–4): 28; Prucha, *American Indian Policy in Crisis,* 306–8; Francis Paul Prucha, "Thomas Jefferson Morgan," in *Commissioners of Indian Affairs,* 199, 201.

24. Waltmann, "Ely Samuel Parker," in *Commissioners of Indian Affairs,* 125–26; Bishop H. B. Whipple to N. G. Taylor, December 10, 1868, Sisseton, NA, Central Plains; "An Appeal in Behalf of Catholic Indian Missions," *The Indian Sentinel* (1902–3): 29. For listings of contracts awarded, see the ledgers "Public Schools Under Contract," Record of School Contracts, 1887–1911, box 1, Education, BIA, NA. For a biographical overview of Bishop Whipple, see Martin N. Zanger, "'Straight Tongue's Heathen Wards': Bishop Whipple and the Episcopal Mission to the Chippewas," in *Churchmen and the Western Indians,* 177–214.

25. "Their Wondrous Works and Ways," in *Native American Testimony,* 21; Sr. Mary Ione Hilger, O.S.B., *The First Sioux Nun: Sister Marie-Josephine Nebraska, S.G.M.* (Milwaukee, Wis.: Bruce Publishing, 1963), 70, 74–76, 109.

26. Sr. Lioba Brown to Rev. J. W. Stephan, May 18, 1890, White Earth Agency, BCIMR. The sister's surname was Braun, but she often anglicized the name to Brown.

27. Carol J. Berg, O.S.B., "Agents of Cultural Change: The Benedictines at White Earth," *Minnesota History* 48 (winter 1982): 163, 168; P. Aloysius Hermanutz, "St. Benedict's Mission and School," *The Indian Sentinel* (1911): 28.

28. Vizenor, *The People Named the Chippewa,* 13, 16, 18, 31; Meyer, *The White Earth Tragedy,* 42.

29. Berg, "Agents of Cultural Change," 162–63, 165; *The Progress*, White Earth Reservation, January 14, 1888, p. 2; Vizenor, *The People Named the Chippewa*, 87; "Treaty with the Chippewa of the Mississippi and the Pillager and Lake Winnibigoshish Bands, 1863," in *Treaties and Agreements of the Chippewa Indians* (Washington, D.C.: Institute for the Development of Indian Law, n.d.), Article 13, p. 102.

30. Katharine Drexel was canonized on October 1, 2000. Berg, "Agents of Cultural Change," 166–67; "For the New Mission School," *The Progress*, White Earth Reservation, March 9, 1889, 2; Sr. Lioba Brown to Rev. P. L. Chapelle, June 6, 1891, White Earth Agency, BCIMR; T. J. Sheehan, "Report of Agent in Minnesota; Report of White Earth Agency," in *Report of the Secretary of Interior [1888]*, 148; B. P. Schuler, "Report of Agent in Minnesota," in *Report of the Secretary of Interior*, vol. 2, Ex. Doc. 1, pt. 5, 51st Cong., 2d sess. (Washington, D.C.: Government Printing Office, 1890), 411; George Steel, "Report of the White Earth Agency," in *Report of the Secretary of Interior [1892]*, 261; Simon Michelet, "Report of Agent for White Earth Agency," in *Annual Reports of the Department of the Interior: Indian Affairs, Part I [1903]*, 225; "Statistics as to Indian Schools," in *Annual Reports of the Department of the Interior: Indian Affairs, Part I [1903]*, 681.

31. Theo. H. Beaulieu to Fr. J. Stephan, February 12, 1890, and Sr. Lioba Brown to Rev. P. L. Chapelle, June 6, 1891, White Earth Agency, BCIMR; "Editorial," *The Indian Sentinel* (1906): 27; Berg, "Agents of Cultural Change," 169.

32. Child, *Boarding School Seasons*, 13–14, 17–18; J. A. Stephan to Rev. Aloysius Hermanutz, February 7, 1890, and Sisters of St. Benedict to Father William H. Ketcham, September 24, 1910, White Earth Agency, BCIMR.

33. Simon Lampee, O.S.B., "Twenty-one Years Among the Chippews of Minnesota," *The Indian Sentinel* (1910): 38–39; Hermanutz, "St. Benedict's Mission," 30.

34. Child, *Boarding School Seasons*, 10, 13; Lampee, "Twenty-one Years Among the Chippews of Minnesota," 38; Fr. Aloysious Hermanutz to Director, Catholic Indian Bureau, March 31, 1901, White Earth Agency, BCIM Records; Michelet, "Report of Agent for White Earth Agency," 224.

35. Berg, "Agents of Cultural Change," 167; Edward MacGaffey, "A Pattern for Progress: The Minnesota Children's Code," *Minnesota History* 41 (spring 1969): 230, 235.

36. Susan Carol Peterson and Courtney Ann Vaughn-Roberson, *Women with Vision: The Presentation Sisters of South Dakota, 1880–1985* (Urbana: University of Illinois Press, 1988), 46–47; Robert W. Galler Jr., "A Triad of Alliances: The Roots of Holy Rosary Indian Mission," *South Dakota History* 28 (fall 1998): 149–51, 157; Theo. Henry, S.J., "Holy Rosary Mission," *The Indian Sentinel* 1 (1919): 15.

37. Francis Paul Prucha, *The Churches and the Indian Schools, 1888–1912* (Lincoln: University of Nebraska Press, 1979), 58–59; "Holy Rosary Mission School," 29–30.

38. John Jutz to Rev. J. Stephan, March 26, May 9, May 10, 1890, BCIMR; Isabel Gap Gyongossy interview, 1999.

39. Isabel Gap Gyongossy interview, 1999; Galler, "A Triad of Alliances," 160; "Holy Rosary Mission School," 30.

40. Kutzleb, "Educating the Dakotah Sioux," 200; "Tekakwitha Indian Mission," Tekakwitha Orphanage files, and "History of OMI/CUSP Ministry Among Native Americans in the Midwest," 3, Archives, Sioux Falls. Here, the

words "nun" and "sister" are used interchangeably, but the Catholic Church distinguishes "nun" and "sister": nuns lived a cloistered life and took solemn vows; sisters were involved in an active ministry and took simple vows.

41. "History of OMI/CUSP Ministry Among Native Americans in the Midwest," 1, Archives, Sioux Falls.

42. Ibid.; "Tekakwitha Indian Mission," Archives, Sioux Falls; *South Dakota Farmer*, November 7, 1902, 4. St. Andrew's does not appear in any of the ledger files for federal contract schools, and there is no reference in the records of the Bureau of Catholic Indian Missions, which was the intermediary in awarding contracts.

43. *South Dakota Farmer*, November 7, 1902, 4.

44. Bernstein, *American Indians and World War II*, 13–15; R. Douglas Hurt, *Indian Agriculture in America: Prehistory to the Present* (Lawrence: University Press of Kansas, 1987), 177, 183–84.

45. Bernstein, *American Indians and World War II*, 16–17; Hurt, *Indian Agriculture in America*, 176; Thomas Biolsi, *Organizing the Lakota: The Political Economy of the New Deal on the Pine Ridge and Rosebud Reservations* (Tucson: University of Arizona Press, 1992), 112–16; "Members of the Prairie Band: Lorenzo Mattwaoshshe and James Wabaunsee Interview [1930]," in *Model Ts, Pep Chapels, and a Wolf at the Door: Kansas Teenagers, 1900–1941*, ed. Marilyn Irvin Holt (Lawrence: University of Kansas, Division of Continuing Education, 1994), 177; "Raymond Sundown," 222, in *Ne'Ho Niyo'De:No'*.

46. "Tekakwitha Indian Mission," Archives, Sioux Falls; "Our Little Sister Kateri Tekakwitha, Lily of the Mohawks," *The Indian Sentinel* (1908): 9; Snow, *The Iroquois*, 122.

47. "Tekakwitha Indian Mission," and "History of OMI/CUSP Ministry Among Native Americans in the Midwest," 4, Archives, Sioux Falls.

48. Ibid. Sister Irene DeMarrais was once Sister Kathryn DeMarrais; photos of her at Tekakwitha identify her with the latter name. S. Aquin Gilles, provincial archivist, Sisters of the Divine Savior, to the author, September 1, 2000.

49. Mary Eisenman Carson, *Blackrobe for the Yankton Sioux: Fr. Sylvester Eisenman, O.S.B. (1891–1948)* (Chamberlain, S.D.: Tipi Press, 1989), 235.

50. Ibid., 228–30; Timothy Sexton, "St. Paul's Mission," p. 3, typescript, Archives, St. Paul's Indian Mission, Marty, S.D. (hereinafter cited as St. Paul's Mission).

51. Carson, *Blackrobe for the Yankton Sioux*, 222, 230, 232.

52. Ibid., 235–36; "St. Paul's Mission and School," p. 46, typescript, St. Paul's Mission.

53. Carson, *Blackrobe for the Yankton Sioux*, 236–37.

54. Ibid., 223.

55. *White House Conference on Children in a Democracy, 1940, Final Report*, 256, 258, 260, and "Minnesota Report to the 1960 White House Conference on Children and Youth, March 27–April 2, 1960," 3, typescript, box 78, Minnesota Reports and Publications file, White House Conference, DDE Library; Kenneth R. Philp, "John Collier, 1933–45," in *Commissioners of Indian Affairs*, 276; Smith, "Bring Back the Orphanages?" 125.

56. South Dakota Governor's Committee on Children and Youth, "South Dakota Report to 1960 White House Conference on Children and Youth," 13, box 106, South Dakota—State Report file, White House Conference, DDE Library.

EPILOGUE: FINAL TRANSITION

1. "Lena Nephew," 126, in *Ne'Ho Niyo'De:No'*.
2. "Wheelock Academy, School's Hectic History at End, No. 75 in a series of profiles on sites. . . ," *Sunday Oklahoman*, Oklahoma City, Okla., October 22, 1972, 12; R. R. Reeder, "Our Orphaned Asylums," *Survey* 54 (June 1925): 285; Marshall E. St. Edward Jones, "Foster-Home Care of Delinquent Children," *Social Service Review* 10 (September 1936): 450–63; "The New England Home for Little Wanderers," informational letter, 1989, New England Home for Little Wanderers; "Tekakwitha Indian Mission," Archives, Sioux Falls.

3. Bogen, *Luckiest Orphans*, 163–64. Among those who argued that both orphanages and home care had a place in child rescue was E. L. Trotzkey, whose publication title, *Institutional Care and Placing Out: The Place of Each in the Care of Dependent Children*, from 1930 made the position clear. For a good overview of progressive reformers and social policy, see Susan Tiffin, *In Whose Best Interest? Child Welfare Reform in the Progressive Era* (Westport, Conn.: Greenwood Press, 1982).

4. Reeder, "Our Orphaned Asylums," 285; Coleman, *American Indian Children at School*, 50–51.

5. Smith, "Bring Back the Orphanages?" 134–35; Holt, *Linoleum, Better Babies, and the Modern Farm Woman*, 186–88; Tim Hacsi, "From Indenture to Family Foster Care: A Brief History of Child Placing," *Child Welfare* 74 (January/February 1995): 174–75.

6. "Statement by the Bureau of Indian Affairs, for the 1965 Report to the Nation Being Made by the National Committee on Children and Youth," 2, typescript, box 288, folder 14, White House Conference, DDE Library; Patrick K. Ourada, "Glenn L. Emmons (1953–61)," in *Commissioners of Indian Affairs*, 305–8; Prucha, *Great Father*, 378.

BIBLIOGRAPHY

FEDERAL ARCHIVES

National Archives and Records Administration, Archives I, Washington, D.C.
Bureau of Indian Affairs, Record Group 75
    Central Files, New York, 1940–52
    Office Files of Hervey B. Peairs
    Records of the Education Division
National Archives and Records Administration—Central Plains Region,
    Kansas City, Mo.
Bureau of Indian Affairs, Record Group 75
    Superintendents Annual Narrative and Statistical Reports
    Sisseton Indian Agency
National Archives and Records Administration—Southwest Region, Fort
    Worth, Tex.
Bureau of Indian Affairs, Record Group 75
    Cherokee National Records
    Cheyenne and Arapaho Agency
    Chickasaw National Records
    Choctaw National Records
    Creek National Records
    Dawes Commission
    Quapaw Agency
    U.S. Court Records
National Archives and Records Administration, Rocky Mountain Region,
    Denver, Colo.
Bureau of Indian Affairs, Record Group 75
    Santa Fe Indian School
National Archives and Records Administration, Dwight D. Eisenhower
    Presidential Library, Abilene, Kans.
    White House Conference on Children and Youth: Records, 1930–70
    Central Files, General File

OTHER ARCHIVES

Catholic Community Center, Sisseton, S.D.
    Tekakwitha Orphanage files

Catholic Diocese of Sioux Falls, Sioux Falls, S.D.
    Tekakwitha Orphanage files
Illinois State Archives, Springfield, Ill.
    Illinois General Assembly, Private Laws, 1837
Kansas State Historical Society, Topeka, Kans.
    Haskell Institute files
    Sioux, pamphlet file
    Snoddy Papers
Marquette University, Special Collections and University Archives,
    Milwaukee, Wis.
    Bureau of Catholic Indian Missions Records
Menninger Foundation Archives, Topeka, Kans.
    Karl A. Menninger Collection
Mid-America All Indian Center, Wichita, Kans.
    Woody Crumbo, vertical file
New Mexico State Library, Santa Fe, N.M.
    St. Vincent Orphanage for Girls, vertical file
New York State Archives, Albany, N.Y.
    Thomas Indian School Records
Oklahoma Historical Society, Oklahoma City, Okla.
    Indian-Pioneer History Project for Oklahoma, WPA
    Joseph S. Murrow Collection
    Wheelock, vertical file
Oklahoma State Archives, Oklahoma City, Okla.
    Oklahoma Department of Charities and Corrections, Administration
    Files, 1907–45
Sacred Heart Monastery, Richardson, N.D.
    Katharine Drexel files
St. Paul's Indian Mission, Marty, S.D.
    St. Placid Home for Infants files
State Historical Society of Missouri, Columbia, Mo.
    John Dougherty Letterbooks

FEDERAL GOVERNMENT PUBLICATIONS

Annual Report of the Commissioner of Indian Affairs. Washington, D.C.:
    Government Printing Office, 1848.
Annual Report of the Department of the Interior, 1900. Washington, D.C.:
    Government Printing Office, 1900.
Annual Report of the Department of the Interior, 1901. Washington, D.C.:
    Government Printing Office, 1901.
Annual Reports of the Department of the Interior: Indian Affairs, Part I. Doc.
    No. 5, 57th Cong., 2d sess. Washington, D.C.: Government Printing Office,
    1903.
*Annual Reports of the Department of the Interior: Indian Affairs, Part II,
    Commission to the Five Civilized Tribes*. Doc. No. 5, 57th Cong., 2d sess.
    Washington, D.C.: Government Printing Office, 1903.
*Annual Reports of the Department of the Interior: Report of the Commis-
    sioner of Indian Affairs*. Doc. No. 5, 55th Cong., 2d sess. Washington, D.C.:
    Government Printing Office, 1897.

Condition of the Indian Tribes: Report of the Joint Special Committee, Appointed Under Joint Resolution of March 3, 1865. Washington, D.C.: Government Printing Office, 1867.

Correspondence on the Subject of Emigration of Indians. Vol. 2. Washington, D.C.: Duff Green, 1835.

Department of the Interior, Annual Report for 1908. Washington, D.C.: Government Printing Office, 1908.

Evans, Anne M. *Women's Rural Organizations and Their Activities.* U.S. Department of Agriculture, Bulletin No. 719. August 29, 1918.

Fenton, William N. "Iroquois Suicide: A Study in the Stability of a Culture Pattern." *Bureau of American Ethnology, Bulletin* 128 (1941): 80–137.

Mooney, James. *The Siouan Tribes of the East.* Washington, D.C.: Bureau of American Ethnology, Government Printing Office, 1894.

Report of the Department of the Interior: Interior Affairs, Territories. Vol. 2, Doc. 1, 60th Cong., 1st sess. Washington, D.C.: Government Printing Office, 1907.

Report of the Secretary of the Interior. Vol. 1, Ex. Doc. 5, 47th Cong., 2d sess. Washington, D.C.: Government Printing Office, 1882.

Report of the Secretary of the Interior. Vol. 2, Ex. Doc. 1, pt. 5, 49th Cong., 1st sess. Washington, D.C.: Government Printing Office, 1885.

Report of the Secretary of the Interior. Vol. 2, Ex. Doc. 1, pt. 5, 50th Cong., 1st sess. Washington, D.C.: Government Printing Office, 1887.

Report of the Secretary of the Interior. Vol. 2, Doc. 1, pt. 5, 50th Cong., 2d sess. Washington, D.C.: Government Printing Office, 1888.

Report of the Secretary of the Interior. Vol. 2, Ex. Doc. 1, pt. 5, 51st Cong., 2d sess. Washington, D.C.: Government Printing Office, 1890.

Report of the Secretary of the Interior. Vol. 2, Ex. Doc. 5, pt. 5, 52d Cong., 1st sess. Washington, D.C.: Government Printing Office, 1892.

Report of the United States Indian Inspector for the Indian Territory to the Secretary of the Interior for the Year Ended June 30, 1905. Washington, D.C.: Government Printing Office, 1905.

Superintendent of Indian Schools, Annual Report, 1897. Washington, D.C.: Government Printing Office, 1897.

United States Code, 83rd Congress—First Session, 1953. Vols. 1 and 2. St. Paul, Minn.: West Publishing, 1953.

United States Code, 1958 Edition. Vol. 5. Washington, D.C.: Government Printing Office, 1959.

United States Code, 95th Congress—Second Session, 1978. Vol. 2. St. Paul, Minn.: West Publishing, 1979.

U.S. Department of the Interior. Children's Bureau. *Standards of Child Welfare: A Report of the Children's Bureau Conferences, May and June 1919.* Conference Series No. 1, Children's Bureau Publication No. 60. Washington, D.C.: Government Printing Office, 1919.

U.S. Office of Indian Affairs. *Rules for the Indian School Service, 1898.* Washington, D.C.: Government Printing Office, 1898.

INDIAN NATION DOCUMENTS

General and Special Laws of the Chickasaw Nation, 1878–1884. Muskogee: Chickasaw Nation, 1884.

STATE DOCUMENTS AND PUBLICATIONS

Barnard, Kate. *Second Report of the Commissioner of Charities and Corrections, 1910.* Oklahoma City: Warden Publishing, 1911.

——. *Third Report of the Commissioner of Charities and Corrections, 1911.* Oklahoma City: Oklahoma Engraving and Printing, 1912.

——. *Fourth Report of the Commissioner of Charities and Corrections, 1912.* Oklahoma City: Oklahoma Engraving and Printing, 1913.

Bassett, Mabel. *Report of the Commissioner of Charities and Corrections, 1924.* Gutherie, Okla.: Oklahoma Printing Co., 1925.

Morrish, R. W. *Organization of Kansas Boys' and Girls' Clubs.* Kansas State Agricultural College, Division of College Extension, Bulletin No. 30. January 1922.

New Mexico Department of Public Welfare, Annual Report, Fiscal Year Ending June 30, 1951. Santa Fe: New Mexico Department of Public Welfare, 1952.

Report of the State Board of Public Charities, Illinois. Springfield, Ill.: State Printer, 1882.

Report of the State Board of Public Charities, Illinois. Springfield, Ill.: State Printer, 1894.

UNPUBLISHED

Barr, Bernadine Courtright. "A Hive of Industry: The Curriculum of the Iowa Soldier's Orphans' Home, 1900–1945." Paper, Stanford University School of Education, 1994.

Bennett, Walter Angelo. "Life and Letters of Oscar Gardner." Graduate thesis, Presbyterian Theological Seminary, 1961.

Messinger, Ruth W. "The History, Present Program and Population of Goodland Presbyterian Children's Home in Hugo, Oklahoma." Master's thesis, University of Oklahoma, 1964.

BOOKS

Abbott, Grace, ed. *The Child and the State.* Vol. 2. Chicago: University of Chicago Press, 1938.

Abler, Thomas S., ed. *Chainbreaker: The Revolutionary War Memoirs of Governor Blacksnake as Told to Benjamin Williams.* Lincoln: University of Nebraska Press, 1989.

Adair, James. *The History of the American Indians.* New York: Johnson Reprint, 1925.

Adams, David Wallace. *Education for Extinction: American Indians and the Boarding School Experience, 1875–1928.* Lawrence: University Press of Kansas, 1996.

Alexie, Sherman. *Indian Killer.* New York: Warner Books, 1996.

——. *The Lone Ranger and Tonto Fistfight in Heaven.* New York: Atlantic Monthly Press, 1993. Reprint, New York: HarperCollins, 1994.

Alger, Horatio, Jr. *Bound to Rise; or, Harry Walton's Motto.* Philadelphia: John C. Winston, 1873.

Austin, Alberta, comp. and ed. *Ne'Ho Niyo'De:No': That's What It Was Like.* Lakawanna, N.Y.: Rebco Enterprises, 1986.

Ayer, Edward E. *Report on Menominee Indian Reservation.* N.p., 1914.

Bahr, Howard M., Bruce A. Chadwick, and Robert C. Day, eds. *Native Americans Today: Sociological Perspectives.* New York: Harper and Row, 1972.

Bataille, Gretchen M., and Kathleen Mullen Sands. *American Indian Women: Telling Their Lives.* Lincoln: University of Nebraska Press, 1984.

Beekman, Daniel. *The Mechanical Baby: A Popular History of the Theory and Practice of Child Raising.* Westport, Conn.: Laurence Hill and Co., 1977.

Berkhofer, Robert F., Jr. *The White Man's Indian: Images of the American Indian from Columbus to the Present.* New York: Alfred A. Knopf, 1978.

Bernstein, Alison R. *American Indians and World War II: Toward a New Era in Indian Affairs.* Norman: University of Oklahoma Press, 1991.

Beuf, Ann H. *Red Children in White America.* Pittsburgh: University of Pennsylvania Press, 1977.

Biolsi, Thomas. *Organizing the Lakota: The Political Economy of the New Deal on the Pine Ridge and Rosebud Reservations.* Tucson: University of Arizona Press, 1992.

Black Elk. *The Sacred Pipe: Black Elk's Account of Seven Rites of the Oglala Sioux.* Recorded and edited by Joseph Epes Brown. Norman: University of Oklahoma Press, 1953. Reprint, Norman: University of Oklahoma Press, 1981.

Bogen, Hyman. *The Luckiest Orphans: A History of the Hebrew Orphan Asylum of New York.* Urbana: University of Illinois Press, 1992.

Bordewich, Fergus M. *Killing the White Man's Indian: Reinventing Native Americans at the End of the Twentieth Century.* New York: Doubleday, 1996.

Brace, Charles Loring. *The Dangerous Classes of New York and Twenty Years Work Among Them.* New York: Wynkoop and Hallenbeck, 1872.

Bremmer, Robert H. *The Public Good: Philanthropy and Welfare in the Civil War Era.* New York: Alfred A. Knopf, 1980.

Brewer, John M. *The Vocational-Guidance Movement: Its Problems and Possibilities.* New York: Macmillian, 1919.

Britton, Wiley. *The Civil War on the Border.* Vol. 2. New York: G. P. Putnam's Sons, 1904.

Brophy, William A., and Sophie D. Aberle, comps. *The Indian: America's Unfinished Business.* Norman: University of Oklahoma Press, 1966.

Brown, Dee. *Bury My Heart at Wounded Knee: An Indian History of the American West.* New York: Holt, Rinehart and Winston, 1971.

Cadawalader, Sandra L., and Vine Deloria Jr., eds. *The Aggressions of Civilizations: Federal Indian Policy Since the 1880s.* Philadelphia: Temple University Press, 1984.

Carson, Mary Eisenman. *Blackrobe for the Yankton Sioux: Fr. Sylvester Eisenman, O.S.B. (1891–1948).* Chamberlain, S.D.: Tipi Press, 1989.

Catlin, George. *Letters and Notes on the Manners, Customs and Conditions of the North American Indians.* Vol 1. New York: Dover, 1973.

Cavallo, Dominick J. *Muscles and Morals: Organized Playgrounds and Urban Reformers, 1890–1920.* Philadelphia: University of Pennsylvania Press, 1981.

Centennial, 1855–1955: Thomas Indian School. Iroquois, N.Y.: Thomas Indian School, 1955.

Child, Brenda J. *Boarding School Seasons.* Lincoln: University of Nebraska Press, 1998.

Clements, William M., ed. *Native American Folklore in Nineteenth-Century*

Periodicals. Athens, Ohio: Swallow Press/Ohio State University Press, 1986.

Cohen, Sol. *Progressive and Urban School Reform: The Public Education Association of New York City, 1895–1954.* New York: Teachers College Press, 1964.

Coleman, Michael C. *American Indian Children at School, 1850–1930.* Jackson: University Press of Mississippi, 1993.

Conference of Western Attorneys General. *The American Indian Law Deskbook.* 2d ed. Niwot: University Press of Colorado, 1998.

Coontz, Stephanie. *The Social Origins of Private Life: A History of American Families, 1600–1900.* New York: Verso, 1988.

———. *The Way We Never Were: American Families and the Nostalgia Trap.* New York: Basic Books, 1992.

Cornplanter, Jesse J. *Legends of the Longhouse by Jesse J. Cornplanter of the Senecas: Told to Sah-Nee-Weh the White Sister.* Introduction by Carl Carmer. New York: Lippincott, 1938.

Cowger, Thomas W. *The National Congress of American Indians.* Lincoln: University of Nebraska Press, 1999.

Debo, Angie. *And Still the Waters Run: The Betrayal of the Five Civilized Tribes.* Princeton, N.J.: Princeton University Press, 1940.

———. *A History of the Indians of the United States.* Norman: University of Oklahoma Press, 1970.

———. *The Rise and Fall of the Choctaw Republic.* 2d ed. Norman: University of Oklahoma Press, 1961.

———. *The Road to Disappearance: A History of the Creek Indians.* Norman: University of Oklahoma Press, 1941.

Degler, Carl N. *At Odds: Women and Family in America from the Revolution to the Present.* New York: Oxford University Press, 1980.

Deloria, Vine, Jr. *We Talk, You Listen.* New York: Macmillan, 1970.

———, ed. *American Indian Policy in the Twentieth Century.* Norman: University of Oklahoma Press, 1985.

Deloria, Vine, Jr., and Clifford M. Lytle. *American Indians, American Justice.* Austin: University of Texas Press, 1983.

Deloria, Vine, Jr., et al. *Exiled in the Land of the Free: Democracy, Indian Nations, and the U.S. Constitution.* Santa Fe, N.M.: Clear Light Publishers, 1992.

Devens, Carol. *Countering Colonization: Native American Women in the Great Lakes Missions, 1630–1900.* Berkeley: University of California Press, 1992.

Dippie, Brian W. *The Vanishing American: White Attitudes and U.S. Indian Policy.* Lawrence: University Press of Kansas, 1982.

Doctorow, E. L. *The Waterworks.* New York: Signet Books, 1994.

Dorsay, Craig J. *Social Work Practice and the Indian Child Welfare Act.* Salt Lake City: University of Utah, Utah Child Welfare Training Project, 1986.

Eastman, Charles Alexander (Ohiyesa). *From the Deep Woods to Civilization: Chapters in the Autobiography of an Indian.* Boston: Little, Brown, 1916.

———. *Indian Boyhood.* Boston: Little, Brown, 1902. Reprint, Lincoln: University of Nebraska Press, 1991.

Eastman, Elaine Goodale. *Pratt: The Red Man's Moses.* Norman: University of Oklahoma Press, 1935.

Eastman, Mary Henderson. *Dahcotah: or, Life and Legends of the Sioux Around Fort Snelling.* New York: Wiley, 1849. Reprint, Afton, Minn.: Afton Historical Society Press, 1995.

Eaton, Peggy. *The Autobiography of Peggy Eaton.* New York: Charles Scribner's Sons, 1932.

Ehle, John. *Trail of Tears: The Rise and Fall of the Cherokee Nation.* New York: Anchor Books, Doubleday, 1989.

Eisenhower, John S. D. *Agent of Destiny: The Life and Times of General Winfield Scott.* New York: Free Press, 1997.

Faiman-Silva, Sandra. *Choctaws at the Crossroads: The Political Economy of Class and Culture in the Oklahoma Timber Region.* Lincoln: University of Nebraska Press, 1997.

Fanshel, David. *Far from the Reservation: The Transracial Adoption of American Indian Children.* Metuchen, N.J.: Scarecrow Press, 1972.

Fass, Paula. *Outside In: Minorities and the Transformation of American Education.* New York: Oxford University Press, 1989.

Fenton, William N., ed. *Parker on the Iroquois.* Syracuse, N.Y.: Syracuse University Press, 1968.

Fergus, Charles. *Shadow Catcher, A Novel.* New York: Soho Press, 1991.

Finkelstein, Barbara. *Governing the Young: Teacher Behavior in Popular Primary Schools in the Nineteenth-Century United States.* New York: Falmer Press, 1989.

Flood, Renee Sansom. *Lost Bird of Wounded Knee: Spirit of the Lakota.* New York: Da Capo Press, 1998.

Folks, Homer. *The Care of the Destitute, Neglected, and Delinquent Children.* Albany, N.Y.: J. B. Lynon, 1900. Reprint, New York: Arno Press and the New York Times, 1971.

Foreman, Grant. *Advancing the Frontier, 1830–1860.* Norman: University of Oklahoma Press, 1933.

———. *The Five Civilized Tribes.* Norman: University of Oklahoma Press, 1934.

Frazier, Ian. *On the Rez.* New York: Farrar, Straus and Giroux, 2000.

Fritz, Henry E. *The Movement for Indian Assimilation, 1860–1890.* Philadelphia: University of Pennsylvania Press, 1963.

Fuller, Wayne E. *The Old Country School: The Story of Rural Education in the Middle West.* Chicago: University of Chicago Press, 1988.

Garraghan, Gilbert J. *Chapters in Frontier History: Research Studies in the Making of the West.* Milwaukee, Wis.: Bruce Publishing, 1934.

Gibson, Arrell M. *The Chickasaws.* Norman: University of Oklahoma Press, 1971.

Gieven, Philip. *The Protestant Temperament: Patterns of Child-Rearing: Religious Experience and the Self in Early America.* New York: New American Library, 1977.

Glenn, Charles Leslie, Jr. *The Myth of the Common School.* Amherst: University of Massachusetts Press, 1988.

Goffman, Erving. *Essays on the Social Situation of Mental Patients and Other Inmates.* Chicago: Aldine, 1961.

Gonzalez, Mario and Elizabeth Cook-Lynn. *The Politics of Hallowed Ground: Wounded Knee and the Struggle for Indian Sovereignty.* Urbana: University of Illinois Press, 1999.

Goodland Presbyterian Children's Home. *Reflections of Goodland.* Vol. 1. Wolfe City, Tex.: Henington Publishing, 1992.

Gordon, Milton. *Assimilation in American Life.* New York: Oxford University Press, 1964.

Guilliford, Andrew. *America's Country Schools.* 3d ed. Niwot: University Press of Colorado, 1996.

Hacsi, Timothy A. *Second Home: Orphan Asylums and Poor Families in America.* Cambridge, Mass.: Harvard University Press, 1998.

Hall, Philip S. *To Have This Land: The Nature of Indian/White Relations, South Dakota, 1888–1891.* Vermillion: University of South Dakota Press, 1991.

Handy, Robert T. *A Christian America: Protestant Hopes and Christian Realities.* New York: Oxford University Press, 1971.

Hassrick, Royal B. *The Sioux: Life and Customs of a Warrior Society.* Norman: University of Oklahoma Press, 1964.

Hauptman, Laurence M. *Between Two Fires: American Indians in the Civil War.* New York: Free Press, 1995.

——. *The Iroquois and the New Deal.* Syracuse, N.Y.: Syracuse University Press, 1981.

——. *The Iroquois Struggle for Survival: World War II to Red Power.* Syracuse, N.Y.: Syracuse University Press, 1986.

Havighurst, Robert J., and Bernice L. Neugarten. *American Indian Children and White Children: A Sociopychological Investigation.* Chicago: University of Chicago Press, 1995.

Hawes, Joseph M., and N. Ray Hiner, eds. *American Childhood: A Research Guide and Historical Handbook.* Westport, Conn.: Greenwood Press, 1985.

Heller, Adele, and Lois Rudnick, eds. *1915, The Cultural Moment.* New Brunswick, N.J.: Rutgers University Press, 1991.

Henry, Jules. *Culture Against Man.* New York: Random House, 1963.

Hilger, Sr. Mary Ione, O.S.B. *The First Sioux Nun: Sister Marie-Josephine Nebraska, S.G.M.* Milwaukee, Wis.: Bruce Publishing, 1963.

Hinsley, Curtis M., Jr. *Savages and Scientists: The Smithsonian Institution and the Development of American Anthropology.* Washington, D.C.: Smithsonian Institution Press, 1981.

Hirshson, Roberta Starr. *"There's Always Someone There. . . .": The History of the New England Home for Little Wanderers.* Boston: The author and New England Home for Little Wanderers, 1989.

Hogue, Sammy D. *The Goodland Indian Orphanage: A Story of Christian Missions.* Goodland, Okla.: Goodland Indian Orphanage, 1940.

Holt, Marilyn Irvin. *Linoleum, Better Babies, and the Modern Farm Woman, 1890–1930.* Albuquerque: University of New Mexico Press, 1995.

——. *The Orphan Trains: Placing Out in America.* Lincoln: University of Nebraska Press, 1992.

——. ed. *Model Ts, Pep Chapels, and a Wolf at the Door: Kansas Teenagers, 1900–1941.* Lawrence: University of Kansas, Division of Continuing Education, 1994.

Horn, Margo. *Before It's Too Late: The Child Guidance Movement in the United States, 1922–45.* Philadelphia: Temple University Press, 1989.

Howe, Irving, and Kenneth Libo, eds. *How We Lived: A Documentary History of Immigrant Jews in America, 1880–1930.* New York: Richard Marck, 1979.

——. *World of Our Fathers.* New York: Harcourt Brace Jovanovich, 1976.

Hoxie, Frederick E. *A Final Promise: The Campaign to Assimilate the Indians, 1880–1920.* Lincoln: University of Nebraska Press, 1984.

Hurt, R. Douglas. *Indian Agriculture in America: Prehistory to the Present.* Lawrence: University Press of Kansas, 1987.

Hurtado, Albert L., and Peter Iverson, eds. *Modern Problems in American Indian History.* Lexington, Mass.: D. C. Heath, 1994.

Josephy, Alvin M., Jr. *Now That the Buffalo's Gone: A Study of Today's American Indians.* New York: Alfred A. Knopf, 1982.

Katz, Michael B. *In the Shadow of the Poorhouse: A Social History of Welfare in America.* New York: Basic Books, 1986.

———. *Poverty and Policy in American History.* New York: Academic Press, 1983.

———. *Reconstructing American Education.* Cambridge, Mass.: Harvard University Press, 1987.

Katz, Sanford N. *When Parents Fail: The Law's Response to Family Breakdown.* Boston: Beacon Press, 1971.

Keller, Morton. *Regulating a New Society: Public Policy and Social Change in America, 1900–1933.* Cambridge, Mass.: Harvard University Press, 1994.

Keller, Robert H., Jr. *American Protestantism and United States Indian Policy, 1869–82.* Lincoln: University of Nebraska Press, 1983.

Kidwell, Clara Sue. *Choctaws and Missionaries in Mississippi, 1818–1918.* Norman: University of Oklahoma Press, 1995.

King, Irving. *The Psychology of Child Development.* Chicago: University of Chicago Press, 1903.

Kingsolver, Barbara. *Pigs in Heaven.* New York: HarperCollins, 1993.

Koreker, Marvin E. *Comanches and Mennonites on the Oklahoma Plains.* Hillsboro, Kans.: Kindred Productions, 1997.

Kvasnicka, Robert M., and Herman J. Viola, eds. *The Commissioners of Indian Affairs, 1824–1977.* Lincoln: University of Nebraska Press, 1979.

Leake, Albert H. *The Vocational Education of Girls and Women.* New York: Macmillan, 1918.

Leeming, David, and Jake Page. *The Mythology of Native North America.* Norman: University of Oklahoma Press, 1998.

Lindsey, Donal F. *Indians at Hampton Institute, 1877–1923.* Urbana: University of Illinois Press, 1994.

Littlefield, Daniel F. *The Chickasaw Freedmen: A People Without a Country.* Westport, Conn.: Greenwood Press, 1980.

Lomawaima, K. Tsianina. *They Called It Prairie Light: The Story of the Chilocco Indian School.* Lincoln: University of Nebraska Press, 1994.

Lowie, Robert H. *The Crow Indians.* New York: Rinehart, 1935. Reprint, Lincoln: University of Nebraska Press, 1983.

The Magic City: Chicago World's Columbian Exposition, 1893. St. Louis: Historical Publishing Co., 1894.

Manross, William Wilson. *A History of the American Episcopal Church.* New York: Morehouse Publishing, 1935.

Mardock, Robert Winston. *The Reformers and the American Indian.* Columbia: University of Missouri Press, 1971.

Marks, Paula Mitchell. *In a Barren Land: American Indian Dispossession and Survival.* New York: William Morrow, 1998.

McBeth, Sally J. *Ethnic Identity and the Boarding School Experience of West-Central Oklahoma American Indians.* New York: University Press of America, 1984.

McBride, Bunny. *Women of the Dawn.* Lincoln: University of Nebraska Press, 1999.

McLaughlin, James. *My Friend the Indian.* New York: Houghton Mifflin, 1910.

McLoughlin, William G. *After the Trail of Tears: The Cherokees' Struggle for Sovereignty, 1839–1880.* Chapel Hill: University of North Carolina Press, 1993.

——. *The Cherokees and Christianity, 1794–1870: Essays on Acculturation and Cultural Persistence.* Athens: University of Georgia Press, 1994.

McReynolds, Edwin C. *The Seminoles.* Norman: University of Oklahoma Press, 1957.

Meyer, Melissa L. *The White Earth Tragedy: Ethnicity and Dispossession at a Minnesota Anishinaabe Reservation, 1889–1920.* Lincoln: University of Nebraska Press, 1999.

Mihesuah, Devon A. *Cultivating the Rosebuds: The Education of Women at the Cherokee Female Seminary, 1851–1909.* Urbana: University of Illinois Press, 1993.

Milner, Clyde A., II, and Floyd A. O'Neil, eds. *Churchmen and the Western Indians, 1820–1920.* Norman: University of Oklahoma Press, 1985.

Morey, Sylvester M., and Olivia L. Gilliam, eds. *Respect for Life: The Traditional Upbringing of American Indian Children.* Garden City, N.Y.: Waldorf Press, 1974.

The Multicultural Recipe Book. Stillwater, Okla.: Title V Parent Committee for Indian Education, 1995.

Nabokov, Peter, ed. *Native American Testimony: A Chronicle of Indian-White Relations from Prophecy to the Present, 1492–2000.* Rev. ed. New York: Penguin Books, 1999.

Niethammer, Carolyn. *Daughters of the Earth: The Lives and Legends of American Indian Women.* New York: Collier Books, 1977.

Nurge, Ethel, ed. *The Modern Sioux: Social Systems and Reservation Culture.* Lincoln: University of Nebraska Press, 1970.

O'Brien, Sharon. *American Indian Tribal Governments.* Norman: University of Oklahoma Press, 1989.

Odquist, Maurice V. *The Story of Graham.* N.p., 1960.

Odum, Howard W., ed. *Public Welfare in the United States: The Annals.* Philadelphia: American Academy of Political and Social Sciences, 1923.

Olson, James S., and Raymond Wilson. *Native Americans in the Twentieth Century.* Urbana: University of Illinois Press, 1986.

O'Neill, William L. *Divorce in the Progressive Era.* New Haven, Conn.: Yale University Press, 1976.

Oswalt, Wendell H. *Other Peoples, Other Customs: World Ethnography and Its History.* New York: Holt, Rinehart and Winston, 1972.

Owen, Narcissa. *Memoirs of Narcissa Owen, 1831–1907.* Siloam Springs, Ark.: Simon Sager Press and Siloam Springs Museum, 1983.

Painter, Levinus K. *The Collins Story: A History of the Town of Collins, Erie County, New York.* Gowanda, N.Y.: Niagara Frontier Publishing, 1962.

Palster, Gary. *Inside Looking Out: The Cleveland Jewish Orphan Asylum, 1868–1924.* Kent, Ohio: Kent State University Press, 1990.

Pascoe, Peggy. *Relations of Rescue: The Search for Female Moral Authority in the American West, 1874–1939.* New York: Oxford University Press, 1990.

Pearce, Roy H. *The Savages of America: A Study of the Indian and the Idea of Civilization.* Baltimore: Johns Hopkins University Press, 1953.

Perdue, Theda. *Nations Remembered: An Oral History of the Cherokees, Chickasaws, Choctaws, Creeks, and Seminoles in Oklahoma, 1865–1907.* Norman: University of Oklahoma Press, 1993.

Peterson, Susan Carol, and Courtney Ann Vaughn-Roberson. *Women with Vision: The Presentation Sisters of South Dakota, 1880–1985.* Urbana: University of Illinois Press, 1988.

Pfaller, Louis L. *James McLaughlin: The Man with an Indian Heart.* New York: Vantage Press, 1978.

Piven, Frances Fox, and Richard A. Cloward. *Regulating the Poor: The Functions of Public Welfare.* New York: Pantheon Books, 1971.

Platt, Anthony. *The Child Savers: The Invention of Delinquency.* Chicago: University of Chicago Press, 1969.

Pleck, Elizabeth. *Domestic Tyranny: The Making of Social Policy Against Family Violence from Colonial Times to the Present.* New York: Oxford University Press, 1987.

Preston, Samuel H., and Michael R. Haines. *Fatal Years: Child Mortality in Late Nineteenth-Century America.* Princeton, N.J.: Princeton University Press, 1991.

Priest, Loring Benson. *Uncle Sam's Stepchildren: The Reformation of United States Indian Policy, 1865–1887.* New York: Octagon Books, 1972.

The Problem of Indian Administration. Baltimore: Johns Hopkins University Press, 1928.

Proceedings of the Seventh Annual Meeting of the Lake Mohonk Conference of the Friends of the Indian. Boston: Lake Mohonk Conference, 1889.

Prucha, Francis Paul. *American Indian Policy in Crisis: Christian Reformers and the Indian, 1865–1900.* Norman: University of Oklahoma Press, 1976.

———. *The Churches and the Indian Schools, 1888–1912.* Lincoln: University of Nebraska Press, 1979.

———. *The Great Father: The United States Government and the American Indians.* Abridged ed. Lincoln: University of Nebraska Press, 1986.

———, ed. *Americanizing the American Indians: Writings by the "Friends of the Indian," 1880–1900.* Cambridge, Mass.: Harvard University Press, 1973.

———. *Documents of United States Indian Policy.* Lincoln: University of Nebraska Press, 1975.

———. *Documents of United States Indian Policy.* 2d ed., expanded. Lincoln: University of Nebraska Press, 1990.

Quetel, Claude. *History of Syphilis.* Translated by Judith Braddock and Brian Pike. Cambridge: Polity Press, 1990.

Ravoux, Monsignor Augustin, V.G. *Reminiscences, Memoirs and Lectures.* St. Paul, Minn.: Brown, Treacy and Co., 1890.

Richmond, Robert W. *Kansas, a Land of Contrasts.* St. Charles, Mo.: Forum Press, 1974.

Rogin, Michael Paul. *Fathers and Children: Andrew Jackson and the Subjugation of the American Indian.* New York: Alfred A. Knopf, 1975.

Rosenberg, Rosalind. *Beyond Separate Spheres: Intellectual Roots of Modern Feminism.* New Haven, Conn.: Yale University Press, 1982.

Rosenstiel, Annette. *Red and White: Indian Views of the White Man, 1492–1982.* New York: Universe Books, 1983.

Rothman, David J. *Conscience and Convenience: The Asylum and Its Alternatives in Progressive America.* Boston: Little, Brown, 1980.

———. *The Discovery of the Asylum: Social Order and Disorder in the New Republic.* Boston: Little, Brown, 1971.

Rothman, David J., and Sheila M. Rothman, eds. *The Family and Social Services in the 1920's: Two Documents.* New York: Arno Press and the New York Times, 1972.

Salpointe, J. B. *Soldiers of the Cross: Notes on the Ecclesiastical History of New Mexico, Arizona, and Colorado.* Banning, Calif.: St. Boniface's Industrial School, 1898.

Sanderson, Dwight. *The Farmer and His Community.* New York: Harcourt, Brace, 1922.

Savage, William W., Jr., ed. *Indian Life: Transforming an American Myth.* Norman: University of Oklahoma Press, 1977.

Schoolcraft, Henry R. *The Myth of Hiawatha, and Other Oral Legends, Mythologic and Allegoric, of the North American Indians.* Philadelphia: J. B. Lippincott, 1856.

———. *Notes on the Iroquois: or, Contributions to the Statistics, Aboriginal History, Antiquities, and General Ethnology of Western New York.* Albany, N.Y.: Erastus H. Pease, 1847.

Schweitzer, Marjorie M., ed. *American Indian Grandmothers: Traditions and Transitions.* Albuquerque: University of New Mexico Press, 1999.

Seaver, J. E. *Narrative of the Life of Mrs. Mary Jemison.* Norman: University of Oklahoma Press, 1992.

Segale, Sr. Blandina. *At the End of the Santa Fe Trail.* Columbus, Ohio: Columbian Press, 1932. Reprint, Albuquerque: University of New Mexico Press, 1999.

Shoemaker, Nancy, ed. *Negotiations of Change: Historical Perspectives on Native American Women.* New York: Routledge, 1995.

Skolnik, Sharon (Okee-Chee), and Manny Skolnik. *Where Courage Is Like a Wild Horse: The World of an Indian Orphanage.* Lincoln: University of Nebraska Press, 1997.

Snow, Dean R. *The Iroquois.* Oxford: Blackwell, 1994.

Steele, Thomas J., S.J., Paul Rhetts, and Barbe Awalt, eds. *Seeds of Struggle/Harvest of Faith: The Papers of the Archdiocese of Santa Fe Catholic Cuarto Centennial Conference on the History of the Catholic Church in New Mexico.* Albuquerque, N.M.: LPD Press and the Archdiocese of Santa Fe, 1998.

Stocking, George W. *Race, Culture, and Education: Essays in the History of Anthropology.* New York: Free Press, 1968.

The Story of Graham School. N.p., ca. 1950.

Strong, Josiah. *Our Country: Its Possible Future and Its Present Crisis.* Revised ed. New York: Baker and Taylor, 1891. Reprint, Cambridge, Mass.: Belknap Press of Harvard University Press, 1963.

Sulgrove, B. R. *History of Indianapolis and Marion County, Indiana.* Philadelphia: L. H. Everts, 1884.

Sweet, William Warren. *Religion on the American Frontier, 1783–1840.* Vol. 2, *The Presbyterians.* New York: Cooper Square Publishers, 1964.

———. *Religion on the American Frontier, 1783–1840.* Vol. 4, *The Methodists.* New York: Cooper Square Publishers, 1964.

Szasz, Margaret Connell. *Education and the American Indian: The Road to Self-Determination, 1928–1973.* Albuquerque: University of New Mexico Press, 1974.

———, ed. *Between Indian and White Worlds: The Cultural Broker.* Norman: University of Oklahoma Press, 1994.

Tate, Michael L. *The Frontier Army in the Settlement of the West.* Norman: University of Oklahoma Press, 1999.

Thompson, Lucy. *To the American Indian: Reminiscences of a Yukon Woman.* 1916. Reprint, Berkeley, Calif.: Heyday Books, 1991.

Thornton, Russell. *American Indian Holocaust and Survival: A Population History Since 1492.* Norman: University of Oklahoma Press, 1987.

Tiffin, Susan. *In Whose Best Interest? Child Welfare Reform in the Progressive Era.* Westport, Conn.: Greenwood Press, 1982.

Trattner, Walter I. *From Poor Law to Welfare State: A History of Social Welfare in America.* New York: Free Press, 1974.

Treaties and Agreements of the Chippewa Indians. Washington, D.C.: Institute for the Development of Indian Law, n.d.

Treaties and Agreements of the Five Civilized Tribes. Washington, D.C.: Institute for the Development of Indian Law, n.d.

Trennert, Robert A., Jr. *The Phoenix Indian School: Forced Assimilation in Arizona, 1891–1935.* Norman: University of Oklahoma Press, 1988.

Trotzkey, E. L. *Institutional Care and Placing Out: The Place of Each in the Care of Dependent Children.* Chicago: Marks Nathan Jewish Orphan Home, 1930.

Unger, Steven, ed. *The Destruction of American Indian Families.* New York: Association on American Indian Affairs, 1977.

Unrau, William E. *White Man's Wicked Water: The Alcohol Trade and Prohibition in Indian Country, 1802–1892.* Lawrence: University Press of Kansas, 1996.

Vizenor, Gerald. *The People Named the Chippewa: Narrative Histories.* Minneapolis: University of Minnesota Press, 1984.

———, ed. *Escorts to White Earth, 1868–1968: 100 Year Reservation.* Minneapolis: University of Minnesota Press, 1968.

Wagner, Roy. *The Invention of Culture.* Englewood Cliffs, N.J.: Prentice-Hall, 1975.

Wallace, Anthony F. C. *The Death and Rebirth of the Seneca.* New York: Alfred A. Knopf, 1969. Reprint, New York: Vintage Books, 1972.

Watson, Frank Dekker. *The Charity Organization Movement in the United States: A Study in American Philanthropy.* New York: Macmillan, 1922.

West, Elliott, and Paula Petrik, eds. *Small Worlds: Children and Adolescents in America, 1850–1950.* Lawrence: University Press of Kansas, 1992.

White, Richard. *The Roots of Dependency: Subsistence Environment and Social Change Among the Choctaws, Pawnees, and Navajos.* Lincoln: University of Nebraska Press, 1983.

Whitehead, Ruth Holmes. *Six Micmac Stories.* Halifax, Nova Scotia, Canada: Nimbus Publisher and the Nova Scotia Museum, 1992.

Williams, John, and Howard L. Meredith. *Bacone Indian University.* Oklahoma City: Western Heritage Books and Oklahoma Heritage Association, 1980.

Williams, Mentor L., ed. *Schoolcraft's Indian Legends from Algic Researches, the Myth of Hiawatha, Oneota, the Red Race in America, and Historical and Statistical Information Respecting . . . the Indian Tribes of the United States.* East Lansing: Michigan State University Press, 1956.

Wilson, Edmund. *Apologies to the Iroquois.* New York: Farrar, Straus, and Cudahy, 1960.

Wilson, Raymond. *Ohiyesa: Charles Eastman, Santee Sioux.* Urbana: University of Illinois Press, 1983.

Wishy, Bernard. *The Child and the Republic: The Dawn of Modern American Child Nurture.* Philadelphia: University of Pennsylvania Press, 1968.

The World's History of Cleveland: Commemorating the City's Centennial Anniversary. Cleveland, Ohio: The World, 1896.

Wright, J. Leitch, Jr. *Creeks and Seminoles: The Destruction and Regeneration of the Muscogulge People.* Lincoln: University of Nebraska Press, 1986.

Zmora, Nurith. *Orphanages Reconsidered: Child Care Institutions in Progressive Era Baltimore.* Philadelphia: Temple University Press, 1994.

ARTICLES

Abbott, Edith. "The Civil War and the Crime Wave of 1865–70." *Social Service Review* 1 (June 1927): 212–34.

Abing, Kevin. "A Holy Battleground: Methodist, Baptist, and Quaker Missionaries Among Shawnee Indians, 1830–1844." *Kansas History* 21 (summer 1998): 118–37.

Adams, David Wallace. "Education in Hues: Red and Black at Hampton Institute, 1878–1893." *South Atlantic Quarterly* 76 (spring 1977): 159–76.

Ahern, Wilbert H. "Assimilationist Racism: The Case of the 'Friends of the Indian.'" *Journal of Ethnic Studies* 4 (summer 1976): 23–32.

"An Appeal in Behalf of Catholic Indian Missions." *Indian Sentinel* (1902–3): 29–30.

Anderson, Paul Gerard. "The Origin, Emergence, and Professional Recognition of Child Protection." *Social Service Review* 61 (June 1989): 222–44.

Baccus, James C. "'Your Gift Is Their Tomorrow': A History of North Dakota's Children's Home Society." *North Dakota History* 32 (January 1965): 139–84.

Bachtold, L. M. "Hopi Indians: Historical Perspective, Adaptation." *Child Today* 7 (November 1978): 23–26.

Bannan, Helen M. "The Idea of Civilization and American Indian Reformers in the 1880s." *Journal of American Culture* 1 (winter 1978): 787–99.

Barrett, James R. "Americanization from the Bottom Up: Immigration and the Remaking of the Working Class in the United States, 1880–1930." *Journal of American History* 79 (December 1992): 996–1020.

Beauchamp, W. M. "Iroquois Women." *Journal of American Folklore* 13 (April–June 1900): 81–91.

Berg, Carol J., O.S.B. "Agents of Cultural Change: The Benedictines at White Earth." *Minnesota History* 48 (winter 1982): 158–70.

Berthrong, Donald J. "From Buffalo Days to Classrooms: The Southern Cheyennes and Arapahos and Kansas." *Kansas History* 12 (summer 1989): 101–13.

Bigglestone, William E. "Oberlin College and the Beginning of the Red Lake Mission." *Minnesota History* 45 (spring 1976): 21–31.

Billington, Monroe. "Black Slavery in Indian Territory: The Ex-Slave Narratives." *Chronicles of Oklahoma* 60 (spring 1982): 56–65.

Blanchard, Evelyn Lance, and Russell Lawrence Barsh. "What Is Best for Tribal Children? A Response to Fischler." *Social Work* 25 (1980): 350–57.

Bonnin, Gertrude (Zitkala-Sa). "Impressions of an Indian Childhood." *Atlantic Monthly* 85 (January 1900): 37–47.

———. "The School Days of an Indian Girl." *Atlantic Monthly* 85 (February 1900): 381–86.

Brown, Helen Williston. "The Deforming Influences of the Home." *Journal of Abnormal Psychology* 12 (April 1917): 49–57.

Brown, Judith K. "Economic Organization and the Powers of Women Among the Iroquois." *Ethnohistory* 17 (Summer–Fall 1970): 151–67.

Brown, Loren. "The Establishment of the Dawes Commission for Indian Territory." *Chronicles of Oklahoma* 18 (1940): 171–81.

Brown, William C. "The Tendency of Punishments." *Mother's Assistant and Young Lady's Friend* 1 (April 1841): 84.

Cabot, Richard C. "The Inter-relation of Social Work and Spiritual Life." *The Family* 8 (November 1927): 211–17.

Cantrall, Dan. "The Illinois State Board of Public Charities and the County Poorhouses, 1870–1900: Institutional Ideal vs. County Realities." *Transactions of the Illinois State Historical Society* (1988): 49–57.

Carter, Kent. "Choctaw-Chickasaw Enrollment, Part 1." *Prologue: Quarterly of the National Archives and Records Administration* 31 (winter 1999): 231–45.

"Catholic Indian Schools." *The Indian Sentinel* (1916): 12–15.

Clemmer, Richard O. "Hopis, Western Shoshones, and Southern Utes: Three Different Responses to the Indian Reorganization Act of 1934." *American Indian Culture and Research Journal* 10, no. 2 (1986): 15–40.

Coleman, Louis. "Cyrus Byington: Missionary to the Choctaws." *Chronicles of Oklahoma* 62 (Winter 1984–85): 360–87.

Coleman, Michael C. "The Responses of American Indian Children to Presbyterian Schooling in the Nineteenth Century: An Analysis Through Missionary Sources." *History of Education Quarterly* 27 (winter 1987): 473–97.

Collmeyer, Patricia M. "From 'Operation Brown Baby' to 'Opportunity': The Placement of Children of Color at the Boys and Girls Aid Society of Oregon (1944–1977)." *Child Welfare* 74 (1995): 242–63.

"The Conference of Charities and Correction." *School and Society* 1 (February 20, 1915): 287–89.

Coon, Beulah I. "Home Economics Section." *American Vocational Association News Bulletin* 2 (February 1927): 26–32.

Cooper, Sarah B. "Kindergarten for Neglected Children." *American Journal of Education* 31 (1881): 206–8.

Cross, Terry L. "Drawing on Cultural Tradition in Indian Child Welfare Practice." *Social Casework* 67 (1986): 283–89.

Crum, Steven J. "Henry Roe Cloud, a Winnebago Indian Reformer: His Quest for American Indian Higher Education." *Kansas History* 11 (autumn 1988): 171–84.

Dale, Edward Everett, ed. "The Journal of Alexander Lawrence Posey, January 1 to September 4, 1897." *Chronicles of Oklahoma* 46 (winter 1967–68): 393–432.

Davis, Caroline, "Education of the Chickasaws, 1856–1907." *Chronicles of Oklahoma* 15 (December 1937): 415–48.

Denison, Natalie Morrison, "Missions and Missionaries of the Presbyterian Church, U.S., Among the Choctaws—1866–1907." *Chronicles of Oklahoma* 24 (winter 1946–47): 426–48.

Dlugokinski, Eric, and Lyn Kramer. "A System of Neglect: Indian Boarding Schools." *American Journal of Psychiatry* 131 (June 1974): 670–73.

Dobbs, Jean Swift. "Child Health Work at K.S.A.C." *Home Economics News* 2 (December 1925): 35–36.

DuBois, Cora. "The Dominant Value Profile of American Culture." *American Anthropologist* 57 (1955): 1232–39.

Dyck, Stanley P. "The Halstead Indian Industrial School." *Mennonite Life* 43 (June 1987): 4–10.

"Editorial." *The Indian Sentinel* (1903–4): 28.

"Editorial." *The Indian Sentinel* (1906): 27.

Faulkner, Mary. "The Vocational School for Girls." *American Vocational Association News Bulletin* 1 (August 1926): 26.

Fenton, William N., ed. "Seneca Indians by Asher Wright (1859)." *Ethnohistory* 4 (summer 1957): 302–21.

"The First Orphan Asylum in This Country." *Baldwin Place Home for Little Wanderers* 7 (June 1871): 87.

Fischler, Ronald S. "Protecting American Indian Children." *Social Work* 25 (September 1980): 341–49.

Fite, Mrs. R. L. "Historical Statement." *Journal of Cherokee Studies* 10 (spring 1985): 117–85.

Foreman, Carolyn Thomas. "Education Among the Chickasaw Indians." *Chronicles of Oklahoma* 15 (June 1937): 139–65.

———. "Two Notable Women of the Creek Nation." *Chronicles of Oklahoma* 35 (autumn 1957): 315–37.

"Fortieth Annual Report and Quarterly Advocate." *Little Wanderers' Advocate* 41 (May 1905): 1–52.

French, Fanny S. "The Beggar Child and Church." *Ladies' Repository* 18 (October 1858): 607.

Fritz, Henry. "The Last Hurrah of Christian Humanitarian Reform: The Board of Indian Commissioners, 1909–1918." *Western Historical Quarterly* 16 (April 1985): 147–62.

Galler, Robert W., Jr. "A Triad of Alliances: The Roots of Holy Rosary Indian Mission." *South Dakota History* 28 (fall 1998): 144–60.

Gammon, Tim. "The Black Freedmen of the Cherokee Nation." *Negro History Bulletin* 40 (May–June 1977): 732–35.

Gibson, A. M. "Joe Kagey: Indian Educator." *Chronicles of Oklahoma* 38 (spring 1960): 12–19.

Goldberg, Carole E. "Public Law 280: The Limits of State Jurisdiction over Indians." *U.C.L.A. Law Review* 22 (1975): 535–99.

Goldenweiser, A. A. "Functions of Women in Iroquois Society." *American Anthropologist* 17 (1915): 376–77.

Graves, William H. "The Five Civilized Tribes and the Beginning of the Civil War." *Journal of Cherokee Studies* 10 (fall 1985): 205–14.

Green, Kellee. "The Fourteenth Numbering of the People: The 1920 Census." *Prologue: Quarterly of the National Archives* 23 (summer 1991): 137–44.

Greene, Joan. "Civilize the Indian: Government Policies, Quakers, and Cherokee Education." *Journal of Cherokee Studies* 10 (fall 1985): 192–204.

Grossberg, Michael. "Who Gets the Child? Custody, Guardianship, and the Rise of a Judicial Patriarchy in Nineteenth-Century America." *Feminist Studies* 9 (summer 1983): 235–60.

Hacsi, Tim. "From Indenture to Family Foster Care: A Brief History of Child Placing." *Child Welfare* 74 (January/February 1995): 162–80.

Hareven, Tamara. "The History of the Family and the Complexity of Social Change." *American Historical Review* 96 (February 1991): 95–124.

Hawes, Dorothy. "The First Good Years of Indian Education: 1894 to 1898." *American Indian Culture and Research Journal* 5 (1981): 63–82.

Henry, Theo., S.J. "Holy Rosary Mission." *The Indian Sentinel* 1 (1919): 15–17.

Hermanutz, P. Aloysius. "St. Benedict's Mission and School." *The Indian Sentinel* (1911): 26–34.

Hilliard, Asa G., III. "Respecting the Child's Culture." *Children Today* 8 (January–February 1979): 21.

Holliday, J. S. "An Historian Reflects on Edgewood Children's Center." *California History* 44 (spring 1985): 122–31.

"Holy Rosary Mission School." *The Indian Sentinel* (1908): 23–34.

"Home for Indian Orphans." *Sturm's Oklahoma Magazine* 3 (November 1906): 91–92.

Hoxie, Frederick E. "Exploring a Cultural Borderland: Native American Journeys of Discovery in the Early Twentieth Century." *Journal of American History* 79 (December 1992): 969–95.

Hughes, William. "Indians of New York: Glorious Past History and Pitiable Present Condition." *The Indian Sentinel* (1912): 9–12.

Huntington, F. D. "Home Training of Children." *Monthly Religious Magazine* 10 (January 1853): 24.

Jackson, Joe C. "Church School Education in the Creek Nation, 1898 to 1907." *Chronicles of Oklahoma* 46 (autumn 1968): 312–30.

Johnson, David L., and Raymond Wilson. "Gertrude Simmons Bonnin, 1876–1938: 'Americanize the First Indian.'" *American Indian Quarterly* 12 (winter 1988): 27–40.

Johnston, Carol. "Burning Beds, Spinning Wheels, and Calico Dresses." *Journal of Cherokee Studies* 19 (1998): 3–17.

Jones, Marshall E. St. Edward. "Foster-Home Care of Delinquent Children." *Social Service Review* 10 (September 1936): 450–63.

"Just Bad Indians: State Jurisdiction over Indian Affairs." *New Republic* 148 (March 30, 1963): 8–9.

Kammerer, Percy G. "The Relation of the Church to Social Work." *The Family* 8 (June 1927): 120–22.

Kepfield, Sam S. "'They Were in Far Too Great Want': Federal Drought Relief to the Great Plains, 1887–1895." *South Dakota History* 28 (winter 1998): 244–70.

King, Wilma. "Multicultural Education at Hampton Institute—The Shawnees: A Case Study, 1900–1923." *Journal of Negro Education* 57 (1988): 524–35.

Knepler, Arbaham Eleazer. "Education in the Cherokee Nation." *Chronicles of Oklahoma* 21 (December 1943): 378–410.

Kosmerick, Todd J. "Exploring New Territory: The History of Native Americans as Revealed Through Congressional Papers at the Carl Albert Center, Part I." *Western Historical Quarterly* 30 (summer 1999): 203–11.

Kreiger, Heinrich. "Principles of the Indian Law and the Act of June 18, 1934." *George Washington Law Review* 3 (March 1935): 279–308.

Kutzleb, Charles R. "Educating the Dakota Sioux, 1876–1890." *North Dakota History* 32 (October 1965): 197–211.

Lampee, Simon, O.S.B. "Twenty-one Years Among the Chippewas of Minnesota." *The Indian Sentinel* (1910): 37–43.

Letchworth, W. P. "Dependent and Delinquent Children: Institutions in New York in 1877." *American Journal of Education* 28 (1878): 913–20.

Lindsey, Lilah Denton. "Memories of the Indian Territory Mission Field." *Chronicles of Oklahoma* 36 (1958): 181–98.

Lundberg, Emma Octavia. "Progress of Mothers' Aid Administration." *Social Service Review* 2 (September 1928): 435–36.

MacGaffey, Edward. "A Pattern for Progress: The Minnesota Children's Code." *Minnesota History* 41 (spring 1969): 229–36.

Mancall, Peter C. "'The Bewitching Tyranny of Custom': The Social Costs of Indian Drinking in Colonial America." *American Indian Culture and Research Journal* 17, no. 2 (1993): 15–42.

Mannes, Marc. "Factors and Events Leading to the Passage of the Indian Child Welfare Act." *Child Welfare* 74 (1995): 264–82.

———. "Seeking the Balance Between Child Protection and Family Preservation in Indian Child Welfare." *Child Welfare* 72 (1993): 141–50.

Mathes, Valerie Sherer. "American Indian Women and the Catholic Church." *North Dakota History* 47 (fall 1980): 20–25.

———. "A New Look at the Role of Women in Indian Society." *American Indian Quarterly* 2 (summer 1975): 131–39.

———. "Nineteenth Century Women and Reform: The Women's National Indian Association." *American Indian Quarterly* 14 (winter 1990): 11.

McKeever, William A. "A Modern Dictator for the Rural School." *Country Gentleman* 77 (December 7, 1912): 6.

Monroe, Will S. "Children's Ambitions." *Journal of Education* 43 (June 18, 1896): 414.

———. "Play Interests of Children." *National Education Association Proceedings* 43 (1899): 1088.

Nichols, David A. "The Other Civil War: Lincoln and the Indians." *Minnesota History* 44 (spring 1974): 3–15.

Nims, Elinor. "Experiment in Adoption Legislation." *Social Service Review* 1 (June 1927): 241–48.

Norton, Mary Aquinas. "Catholic Missions and Missionaries Among the Indians of Dakota." *North Dakota Historical Quarterly* 5 (April 1931): 149–65.

"The Objects and Plan of the Home." *New England Home for Little Wanderers Advocate and Report* 24 (January 1890): 1–40.

"Our Little Sister Kateri Tekakwitha, Lily of the Mohawks." *The Indian Sentinel* (1908): 9.

Peebles-Wilkins, Wilma. "Jane Porter Barrett and the Virginia Industrial School for Colored Girls: Community Response to the Needs of African-American Children." *Child Welfare* 74 (January/February 1995): 143–61.

Petershoare, Lillian. "Tlingit Adoption Practices, Past and Present." *American Indian Culture and Research Journal* 9, no. 2 (1985): 1–32.

"Recognition." *Southwest Art* 28 (June 1998): 124.

Red Horse, John G. "American Indian Elders: Unifiers of Indian Families." *Social Casework* 61 (October 1980): 490–93.

———. "Family Structure and Value Orientation in American Indians." *Social Casework* 61 (October 1980): 462–67.

Reed, Ora Eddleman. "The Indian Orphan." *Sturm's Oklahoma Magazine* 5 (January 1908): 81–83.

Reeder, R. R. "Our Orphaned Asylums." *Survey* 54 (June 1925): 285.

"Report of the Commissioner of Education for the Year 1877." *American Journal of Education* 28 (1878): 182–208.

Riis, Jacob A. "Christmas Reminder of the Nobelist Work in the World." *Forum* 16 (January 1894): 624.

Riney, Scott. "Power and Powerlessness: The People of the Canton Asylum for Insane Indians." *South Dakota History* 1 and 2 (spring/summer 1997): 39–64.

Robinson, Will G., comp. "Digest of the Reports of the Commissioner of Indian Affairs as Pertain to Dakota Indians—1869–1872." *South Dakota Report and Historical Collections* 28 (1956): 313–49.

"Saint Catharine's Indian School." *The Indian Sentinel* (1903–4): 12–19.

"St. Elizabeth's Indian School." *The Indian Sentinel* (1904–5): 38.

"Santa Claus Among the Foundlings." *Frank Leslie's Illustrated Newspaper* 33 (January 20, 1872): 295.

Schusky, Ernest L. "Reader's Response: American Indians on Their Own." *Christian Century* 94 (March 30, 1977): 303–6.

Scott, Leslee M. "Indian Women as Food Providers and Tribal Counselors." *Oregon Historical Quarterly* 42 (1941): 208–19.

Smith, Eve P. "Bring Back the Orphanages? What Policymakers of Today Can Learn from the Past." *Child Welfare* 74 (January/February 1995): 115–42.

Spindler, George. "Male and Female Adaptations in Cultural Change." *American Anthropologist* 60 (April 1958): 229–31.

Starkloff, C. F. "The Church Between Cultures: Missions on Indian Reservations." *Christian Century* 93 (November 3, 1976): 955–59.

Steel, F. A. "The Cult of the Child." *Littel's Living Age* 237 (April–June 1903): 761.

Steen, Carl T. "The Home for the Insane, Deaf, Dumb, and Blind of the Cherokee Nation." *Chronicles of Oklahoma* 21 (1943): 402–17.

Tessendorf, K. C. "Red Death on the Missouri: American Indian Epidemic of Smallpox." *American West* 14 (January 1977): 48–53.

Trennert, Robert A. "Corporal Punishment and the Politics of Indian Reform." *History of Education Quarterly* 29 (winter 1989): 595–617.

———. "Educating Indian Girls at Non-reservation Boarding Schools, 1878–1920." *Western Historical Quarterly* 13 (July 1982): 271–90.

"Tribute to St. Benedict's Mission School." *The Indian Sentinel* 1 (1919): 18.

Vance, Thomas F., et al. "The Development of Children in the Home Management House at Iowa State College." *Journal of Experimental Education* 2 (December 1933): 166–69.

Winchester, Dr. B. S. "Spiritual Factors in Family Life." *The Family* 8 (December 1927): 279–81.

Young, Marjorie Hall. "'Stars in the Night': The Education of Indian Youth at Choctaw Academy." *Chronicles of Oklahoma* 75 (fall 1997): 280–305.

NEWSPAPERS

Cherokee Advocate, Tahlequah, Cherokee Nation, 1872, 1895.

Halstead Independent: A Souvenir Edition, Halstead, Kansas. August 12, 1937.

Muskogee Times-Democrat, Muskogee, Oklahoma, 1909.

New York Times, New York, New York, 1861.

The Progress, White Earth Reservation, Minnesota, 1886–89.

Roberts County Banner, Sisseton, South Dakota, 1903.

Salina Journal, Salina, Kansas, 1942.

South Dakota Farmer, Sioux Falls, South Dakota, 1902.

Sunday Oklahoman, Oklahoma City, Oklahoma, 1972.

Topeka Capital-Journal, Topeka, Kansas, 1995.

Vindicator, Atoka, Indian Territory, 1876.

Weekly Chieftain, Vinita, Indian Territory, 1903.

Wichita Daily Beacon, Wichita, Kansas, 1902.

VIDEO

History of the Indian Child Welfare Act. Portland, Oreg.: National Indian Child Welfare Association, 1991.

INDEX

Children
  Indian culture and, 24–33, 148, 151,
    154–55
  institutionalization and, 3–4
  nature of debated, 29–31
  in nineteenth-century literature, 28–31
Children's Law (1875), 60
Child Welfare League of America, 9
Chilocco Indian School (I.T.), 16, 19, 110,
  175, 189, 194
Chippewa Indians. *See* Ojibway Indians
Choctaw Academy (Ky.), 119–20
Choctaw and Chickasaw Baptist Association, 170
Choctaw Board of Education, 162, 206
Choctaw Indians
  acculturation and, 19, 151
  adoption practices of, 148
  agriculture and, 150, 152, 153
  allotment and, 170
  boarding schools and, 120, 123, 157–58
  childrearing practices of, 151, 154–55
  Civil War and, 148, 150, 155, 159
  Creek Wars and, 199
  dissolution and, 136, 146, 167, 170
  1852 Marriage Law of, 155
  English and, 125, 150
  family status in, 153, 154–55
  freedmen and, 170–71
  missionaries and, 141, 148–52, 163,
    166, 167, 168, 170
  mortality among, 135, 154
  orphanages for, 43, 64, 115, 116, 120,
    135, 156–72, 177, 189, 213
  Orphan Fund of, 148, 149, 157
  removal of, 91, 116, 152
  school system of, 125, 136, 148, 149,
    153–54, 159, 184
  slavery and, 150, 152, 153
  women's roles and, 154–55
Choctaw Nation, 116, 149, 154, 156, 159,
  172
Choctaw National Council, 157, 158,
  163, 164, 168, 169, 206
Cholera, 41, 152
Civic Service House (Mass.), 194
Civilian Conservation Corps–Indian
  Division, 243
Civil War
  Cherokees and, 86, 94–97, 115, 156
  Chickasaws and, 115, 122
  children and, 30, 86
  Choctaws and, 148, 150, 155, 159
  Creeks and, 95, 115, 156, 172, 175
  Euro-American women and, 60–61
  orphanages and, 41, 97, 120
  Seminoles and, 175

Senecas and, 60–61, 252
Sioux and, 222
social services and, 2
Colbert, Holmes, 124
Colbert, Pitman, 119
Colbert Institute (I.T.), 122
Colby, Brig. Gen. Leonard W., 17, 217
Cole, Lottie, 160
Collier, John, 249
Colorado, 9
Colored Orphan Asylum (Ind.), 45
Columbus (Miss.), 150
Comanche Indians, 39, 95, 214
Commissioners of Indian Affairs. *See*
  specific names
Committee on the Prevention of Tuber-
  culosis, 80
Common school agenda, 49–50, 51, 52,
  69, 74
Congregational missionaries, 98, 150,
  230, 233
Conjunctivitis, 203, 207
Continental Congress, 87
Contract schools
  agreements, 52
  Catholic, 141, 229, 230, 234, 236, 241
  Cherokee, 63
  controversies, 141
  Ponca, 127
  Presbyterian, 230
  Quaker, 63, 230
  types, 64
Cook, Hattie, 234
Cook, Rev. Charles, 217
Corlett, William W., 229
Cornish Orphan's Home (Okla.), 208
Cornplanter (Seneca leader), 53
Cornplanter, Jesse, 27
Cotton Gin Port (Miss.), 119
Cowen, Philip, 82
Coweta Mission School (I.T.), 173
Coweta National Boarding School (I.T.),
  173
Crawford, Rev. C. R., 221
Creek Board of Education, 176
Creek Colored Orphan Home (I.T.), 166,
  173, 174, 176–77, 181, 185, 186, 191
Creek Indians, 2, 19
  acculturation and, 130, 178
  allotment and, 142, 183
  Bacone University and, 172
  boarding schools and, 120
  childrearing practices of, 32
  Civil War and, 95, 115, 156, 172,
    174–75
  dissolution and, 136, 180, 183, 185,
    186